Manuscripts of the Wycliffite Bible
in the Bodleian and Oxford College Libraries

EXETER MEDIEVAL TEXTS AND STUDIES

Series Editors: Vincent Gillespie and Richard Dance

Founded by M.J. Swanton and later co-edited by Marion Glasscoe

Manuscripts of the Wycliffite Bible in the Bodleian and Oxford College Libraries

Elizabeth Solopova

LIVERPOOL UNIVERSITY PRESS

First published 2016 by
Liverpool University Press
4 Cambridge Street
Liverpool
L69 7ZU

This paperback edition first published 2021

British Library Cataloguing-in-Publication data
A British Library CIP record is available

ISBN 978-1-78138-298-1 cased
ISBN 978-1-80034-922-3 paperback

Typeset by Carnegie Book Production, Lancaster

Contents

Acknowledgements

The current investigation was made possible by a grant awarded by the Leverhulme Trust to Anne Hudson and myself to undertake a study of the manuscripts of the Wycliffite Bible in Oxford Libraries (2011–15). I am enormously grateful to the Trust for their generosity and to Anne Hudson for her continuing support of my research, as well as for discussing with me on numerous occasions all aspects of the present catalogue and commenting on its drafts. The publication of this catalogue was made possible by generous grants from the Neil Ker Memorial Fund and the Marc Fitch Fund. I am immensely grateful for their invaluable support.

I am indebted to all Oxford holders of the manuscripts of the Wycliffite Bible. The largest number of manuscripts described in the catalogue are in the Bodleian Library and I am grateful to its staff for their patience and indispensable help. I am particularly grateful to Bruce Barker-Benfield for advising me on many occasions on various aspects of manuscript descriptions. I am also grateful to the following bodies for granting access to manuscripts of the Bible in their holdings: the Principal and Fellows of Brasenose College, Oxford; the Dean and Fellows of Christ Church, Oxford; the President and Fellows of Corpus Christi College, Oxford; the Rector and Fellows of Lincoln College, Oxford; the Warden and Fellows of New College, Oxford; the Provost and Fellows of Oriel College, Oxford; the Provost, Fellows and Scholars of the Queen's College, Oxford; the President and Fellows of St John's College, Oxford; the President and Fellows of Trinity College, Oxford; the Master and Fellows of University College, Oxford; and the Provost and Fellows of Worcester College, Oxford. I am particularly grateful to the librarians of the collections listed above for their generous help during my visits.

I am indebted to the members of the advisory group of the Leverhulme-funded study for discussing with me various aspects of this work: Mishtooni

Bose, Kantik Ghosh, Ralph Hanna, Linne Mooney, Christina von Nolcken, Michael Sargent and Jocelyn Wogan-Browne. I am also grateful to the contributors of my forthcoming edited collection *The Wycliffite Bible: Origin, History and Interpretation* (Brill). My work with them stimulated further research on the manuscripts and enlightened many of the descriptions in the present catalogue.

I am enormously grateful to the Faculty of English Language and Literature at Oxford University and Brasenose College, Oxford, for their hospitality during my work on this project and their support of this research.

Abbreviations

Coxe (1852) Coxe, H. O., *Catalogus codicum mss. qui in collegiis aulisque Oxoniensibus hodie adservantur*, 2 vols (Oxford: Oxford University Press, 1852)

Coxe (1973) Coxe, H. O., *Catalogi codicum manuscriptorum Bibliothecae Bodleianae pars secunda codices Latinos et Miscellaneos Laudianos complectens* (Oxford, 1885), reprinted with corrections, additions and an introduction by R. W. Hunt (Oxford: Bodleian Library, 1973)

Deanesly (1920) Deanesly, M., *The Lollard Bible and other medieval biblical versions* (Cambridge: Cambridge University Press, 1920)

DIMEV Mooney, L. R., Mosser, D. W. and Solopova, E., with Radcliffe, D. H., *The Index of Middle English Verse, based on the Index of Middle English Verse (1943), its Supplement (1965) and archival research* (http://www.dimev.net/)

Dove (2007) Dove, M., *The first English Bible: the text and context of the Wycliffite versions* (Cambridge: Cambridge University Press, 2007)

Dove (2010) Dove, M., *The earliest advocates of the English Bible: the texts of the medieval debate* (Exeter: University of Exeter Press, 2010)

EV the Earlier Version of the Wycliffite Bible

Forshall and Madden (1850) Forshall, J. and Madden, F. (eds), *The Holy Bible…in the earliest English versions made from the Latin Vulgate by John Wycliffe and his followers*, 4 vols (Oxford: Oxford University Press, 1850)

Foster (1887–88) Foster, J., *Alumni Oxonienses: the members of the University of Oxford, 1715–1886*, 4 vols (London: Joseph Foster; Oxford: Parker and Co., 1887–88)

Foster (1891–92) Foster, J., *Alumni Oxonienses: the members of the University of Oxford, 1500–1714*, 4 vols (London: Joseph Foster; Oxford: Parker and Co., 1891–92)

Fristedt (1953–73) Fristedt, S. L., *The Wycliffe Bible*, 3 vols (Stockholm: Almqvist & Wiksells, 1953–73)

Jolliffe (1974) Jolliffe, P. S., *A check-list of Middle English prose writings of spiritual guidance* (Toronto: Pontifical Institute of Mediaeval Studies, 1974)

de Hamel (2001) de Hamel, C., *The book: a history of the Bible* (London: Phaidon, 2001)

Hanna (2005) Hanna, R., *London literature, 1300–1380* (Cambridge: Cambridge University Press, 2005)

Harper (1991) Harper, J., *The forms and orders of Western liturgy from the tenth to the eighteenth century: a historical introduction and guide for students and musicians* (Oxford: Clarendon Press, 1991)

Hennig (1955) Hennig, J., 'Versus de mensibus', *Traditio* 11 (1955), pp. 65–90

Hudson (1978) Hudson, A., *Selections from English Wycliffite writings* (Cambridge: Cambridge University Press, 1978)

Hudson (1985) Hudson, A., *Lollards and their books* (London: Hambledon Press, 1985)

Hudson (1988) Hudson, A., *The premature reformation: Wycliffite texts and Lollard history* (Oxford: Clarendon Press, 1988)

Hudson (1989) Hudson, A., 'Lollard book production', in Griffiths, J. and Pearsall, D. A. (eds), *Book production and publishing in Britain 1375–1475* (Cambridge: Cambridge University Press, 1989), pp. 125–42

Hudson (2006) Hudson, A., 'The Carthusians and a Wycliffite Bible', in Kras, P. *et al.* (eds), *Ecclesia, cultura, potestas: studia z dziejów kultury i społeczenstwa* (Krakow: Societas Vistulana, 2006), pp. 731–42

Hudson and Gradon (1983–96) Hudson, A. and Gradon, P., *English Wycliffite sermons*, 5 vols (Oxford: Clarendon Press, 1983–96)

IMEP *Index of Middle English prose*, 18 vols (Cambridge, 1984–)

IMEV Brown, C. and Robbins, R. H., *The index of Middle English verse* (New York: Printed for the Index Society by Columbia University Press, 1943)

IMEV Supplement Brown, C., Robbins, R. H., Cutler, J. L.,

Supplement to the index of Middle English verse (Lexington: University of Kentucky Press, 1965)

IPMEP Lewis, R. E., Blake, N. F. and Edwards, A. S. G., *Index of printed Middle English prose* (New York and London: Garland, 1985–)

Ker (1964) Ker, N. R., *Medieval libraries of Great Britain, a list of surviving books*, 2nd edn (London, 1964); *Supplement to the second edition*, ed. A. G. Watson (London: Offices of the Royal Historical Society, 1987)

Ker (1969–2002) Ker, N. R., Piper, A. J., Watson, A. G. and Cunningham, I. C., *Medieval manuscripts in British libraries*, 5 vols (Oxford: Clarendon Press, 1969–2002)

Lindberg (1959–97) Lindberg, C. (ed.), *The earlier version of the Wycliffite Bible,* 8 vols (Stockholm: Almqvist & Wiksell, 1959–97)

Lindberg (1989) Lindberg, C. (ed.), *The Middle English Bible, The Book of Judges* (Oslo: Norwegian University Press, 1989)

Lindberg (1999–2004) Lindberg, C. (ed.), *King Henry's Bible, MS Bodley 277: the revised version of the Wyclif Bible*, 4 vols (Stockholm: Almqvist & Wiksell, 1999–2004)

LV the Later Version of the Wycliffite Bible

Macray (1878) William D. Macray, *Catalogi codicum manuscriptorum Bibliothecæ Bodleianæ partis quintæ fasciculus secundus, viri munificentissimi Ricardi Rawlinson, J.C.D., codicum classem tertiam, in qua libri theologici atque miscellanei, complectens; accedit in uniuscujusque classis codicum contenta index locupletissimus* (Oxford, 1878)

Morey (2000) Morey, J. H., *Book and verse: a guide to Middle English biblical literature* (Urbana: University of Illinois Press, 2000)

NIMEV Boffey, J. and Edwards, A. S. G., *A new index of Middle English verse* (London: British Library, 2005)

NT New Testament

ODNB *Oxford Dictionary of National Biography* (http://www.oxforddnb.com/)

ONT Old and New Testaments

OT Old Testament

Pächt and Alexander (1966–73) Pächt, O. and Alexander, J. J. G., *Illuminated manuscripts in the Bodleian Library, Oxford*, 3 vols (Oxford, 1966–73)

Peikola (2003) Peikola, M., 'The Wycliffite Bible and "Central Midland Standard": assessing the manuscript evidence', *Nordic Journal of English Studies* 2 (2003), pp. 29–51

Pfaff (2009) Pfaff, R. W., *The liturgy in medieval England: a history* (Cambridge: Cambridge University Press, 2009)

Proctor and Wordsworth (1886) Proctor, F. and Wordsworth, C., *Breviarium ad usum insignis ecclesie Sarum*, 3 vols (London: Cambridge University Press, C. J. Clay and Sons, 1886)

Samuels (1969) Samuels, M. L., 'The dialects of MS Bodley 959' [1969], reprinted in McIntosh, A., Samuels, M. L. and Laing, M. (eds), *Middle English dialectology: essays on some principles and problems* (Aberdeen: Aberdeen University Press, 1989), pp. 136–49

Scott (1996) Scott, K. L., *Later Gothic manuscripts, 1390–1490*, Survey of manuscripts illuminated in the British Isles (HMMSBI 6), 2 vols (London: Harvey Miller, 1996)

Scott (2000–02) Scott, K. L. (gen. ed.), *An index of images in English manuscripts from the time of Chaucer to Henry VIII,* c.*1380*–c.*1509: the Bodleian Library, Oxford*, 3 vols (Turnhout: Harvey Miller Publishers, 2000–02)

Scott (2002) Scott, K. L., *Dated and datable English manuscript borders,* c.*1395–1499* (London: British Library, 2002)

Severs, Hartung, Beidler (1967–) Severs, J. B., Hartung, A. E., Beidler, P. G., *A manual of the writings in Middle English, 1050–1500*, 11 vols (New Haven: Connecticut Academy of Arts and Sciences, 1967–)

Solopova (2013) Solopova, E., 'Manuscript Evidence for the Patronage, Ownership and Use of the Wycliffite Bible', in Poleg, E. and Light, L. (eds), *Form and Function in the Late Medieval Bible* (Leiden: Brill, 2013), pp. 333–49

Stegmüller (1950–80) Stegmüller, F., *Repertorium Biblicum Medii Aevi*, 11 vols (Madrid: Consejo Superior, 1950–80)

Summary catalogue, vol. 1 Hunt, R. W., *Summary catalogue of western manuscripts in the Bodleian Library at Oxford*, vol. 1, *Historical introduction and conspectus of shelf-marks* (Oxford: Clarendon Press, 1953; reprinted with corrections, 1980)

Summary catalogue, vol. 2, part I Madan, F. and Craster, H. H. E., *Summary catalogue of western manuscripts in the Bodleian Library at Oxford*, vol. 2, part I *(collections received before 1660 and miscellaneous*

MSS acquired during the first half of the 17th century), nos. 1–3490 (Oxford: Clarendon Press, 1922)

Summary catalogue, vol. 2, part II Craster, H. H. E. and Denholm-Young, N., *Summary catalogue of western manuscripts in the Bodleian Library at Oxford*, vol. 2, part II *(collections and miscellaneous MSS acquired during the second half of the 17th century), nos. 3491–8716* (Oxford: Clarendon Press, 1937)

Summary catalogue, vol. 3 Madan, F., *Summary catalogue of western manuscripts in the Bodleian Library at Oxford*, vol. 3 *(collections received during the 18th century), nos. 8717–16669* (Oxford: Clarendon Press, 1895)

Summary catalogue, vol. 4 Madan, F., *Summary catalogue of western manuscripts in the Bodleian Library at Oxford*, vol. 4 *(collections received during the first half of the 19th century) nos. 16670–24330* (Oxford: Clarendon Press, 1897)

Summary catalogue, vol. 5 Madan, F., *Summary catalogue of western manuscripts in the Bodleian Library at Oxford*, vol. 5 *(collections received during the second half of the 19th century and miscellaneous MSS acquired between 1695 and 1890) nos. 24331–31000* (Oxford: Clarendon Press, 1905)

Summary catalogue, vol. 6 Madan, F. and Craster, H. H. E., *Summary catalogue of western manuscripts in the Bodleian Library at Oxford*, vol. 6 *(accessions, 1890–1915) nos. 31001–37299* (Oxford: Clarendon Press, 1924)

Wells (1916) Wells, J. E., *A manual of the writings in Middle English, 1050–1400* (New Haven, Conn.: Yale University Press, 1916), with nine supplements, 1919–50

List of manuscripts

The list includes shelfmarks of manuscripts in an alphabetical order, a brief description of contents and sigla assigned to manuscripts in Forshall and Madden (1850) and, if different, in Dove (2007).

Bodleian Library

Oxford College libraries

List of plates

(between pages 76 and 77)

Images of all manuscripts described in this catalogue are available in *The Wycliffite Bible: Image Archive* (http://wycliffite.bodleian.ox.ac.uk/)

1

Introduction

The Wycliffite Bible (WB) is the first complete translation of the Bible in English produced at the end of the 14th century by the followers of the Oxford theologian John Wyclif. The identity of the translators remains uncertain, but the scale and scholarly nature of the project suggest the involvement of many academic translators, probably based in Oxford. Though accurate, learned and orthodox, the translation was condemned and banned within twenty-five years of its appearance. The legislation promulgated early in the 15th century by the Archbishop of Canterbury Thomas Arundel prohibited the making of new versions and the use of any recent translations without episcopal approval of both the text and owner. In spite of this WB became the most widely disseminated medieval English text: it survives in around 250 complete or partial copies, most professionally produced to a high standard. Several manuscripts, such as MS Bodl. 277, are large format, richly decorated and known to have been owned by the members of the royalty and aristocracy.

The translation survives in two versions: the Earlier Version (EV), a literal rendering of the Latin text, and the Later Version (LV), its more idiomatic revision. The manuscripts of LV considerably outnumber those of EV, and out of 64 copies described in the present catalogue only twelve contain the EV text and a further seven combine EV and LV, mostly through the inclusion of EV prologues (such manuscripts are listed in Appendix III).

Scholarly investigation in the past fifty years has concentrated on the translation's origin and revisions, drawing mostly on a limited number of extant copies.[1] The majority of the manuscripts, particularly those

1 Important recent studies include books and articles by Dove (2007) and Peikola (2003; 'Aspects of mise-en-page in manuscripts of the Wycliffite Bible', in Caie, G.

seen as late, modest, 'run-of-the-mill' or textually less important, remain virtually entirely unexplored. Most conspicuously there are no catalogues of the manuscripts of WB. A list of manuscripts in Forshall and Madden's edition (1850, vol. 1, pp. xxxix–lxiv) covers only a selection of the surviving copies and provides brief descriptions that are only one or two paragraphs long. Dove (2007) offers more detailed descriptions of a small selection of important manuscripts, including nine from Oxford, and a list of all known surviving copies. This list, though undeniably a very useful point of reference, has errors in manuscript shelfmarks, the identification of the text as EV or LV, and in the description of the contents of manuscripts. The descriptions of contents are also particularly brief and provide information about biblical books included, and the presence of the tables of lections and Old Testament lectionaries (albeit both inconsistently), but not about the presence of other para-biblical materials, such as calendars and *capitula*-lists, or non-biblical texts found in many manuscripts. The present catalogue makes a step towards addressing the need for a comprehensive study of all surviving manuscripts by offering detailed descriptions and analysis of the manuscripts in Oxford collections, just over a quarter of the surviving total.

The catalogue covers manuscripts listed under 'Oxford' in Dove (2007, pp. 298–303), excluding the manuscripts of the *Glossed Gospels* (described in A. Hudson, *Doctors in English: a study of the Wycliffite gospel commentaries* (Liverpool: Exeter University Press, 2015)) and a modern transcript (MS Rawl. C. 155). These 64 complete or partial copies and fragments constitute an arbitrary selection that gives a representative view of the whole corpus: none can be shown to have belonged to the colleges, or the university library, in the medieval period, all came to their present location by post-medieval gift or purchase.

The catalogue is part of a wider study focused on the production, circulation and use of WB, the best evidenced, but least explored of European translations of the Vulgate. It is currently largely unknown where its manuscripts were made, how they reached their owners, how and by whom they were used or how their exceptionally wide production and dissemination were at all possible under the conditions of censorship. The

---

and Renevey, D. (eds), *Medieval texts in context* (London: Routledge, 2008), pp. 28–67; 'Tables of lections in manuscripts of the Wycliffite Bible', in Poleg, E. and Light, L. (eds), *Form and function in the late medieval Bible* (Leiden and Boston: Brill, 2013), pp. 351–78; 'The sanctorale, Thomas of Woodstock's English Bible, and the orthodox appropriation of Wycliffite tables of lessons', in Bose, M. and Hornbeck, J. P. (eds), *Wycliffite controversies* (Turnhout: Brepols, 2011), pp. 153–74), and editions of manuscript versions of the translation by Lindberg (1959–97; 1989; 1999–2004).

catalogue offers evidence relevant to answering these and other questions. A full discussion of the findings emerging from this work is a subject of a forthcoming monograph, but a brief account of important features of the manuscripts, designed to facilitate the use of the current catalogue, is offered below.

Contents

Complete and part-Bibles

A great majority of the manuscripts of WB do not include the full biblical text. Of around 250 known copies only just over twenty contain or are presumed to have contained the whole Bible.[2] Eight manuscripts in Oxford collections, listed in Appendix III, currently contain, sometimes through medieval augmentation, or may have originally contained the full biblical text. The current study confirms a previously made observation that the New Testament (NT) was the most widely circulated part of the translation: as can be seen from the 'List of manuscripts', twenty-one (about one-third) of copies in Oxford collections are NTs. The current catalogue also confirms that other parts of the Bible were circulated separately, including the Old Testament (OT) (four copies), gospels (nine copies), epistles (four copies), psalms (two copies) and Tobit (one copy).[3] Two manuscripts, MS Laud misc. 182 and MS Bodl. 771, contain a selection of chapters and extracts from the Bible and are probably personal collections for reading, preaching or study.

The presentation of the biblical text tends to be similar in complete and partial copies, suggesting that they are part of a single tradition. Even in lectionaries and collections of extracts, such as MS Laud misc. 182, we see the features associated with the Wycliffite biblical text as a whole, such as the use of running titles, rubrics, chapter numbers, marginal glosses and the practice of underlining added material within the text (see below).

In many copies the biblical text is accompanied by liturgical aids and other para-biblical materials, such as the *capitula*-lists or the lists of biblical books. Manuscripts containing such materials are listed in Appendix III and different types of liturgical aids are discussed in a separate section below. In several manuscripts the Wycliffite translation is combined with other Middle English texts, most commonly non-Wycliffite translations and adaptations of biblical books, but also occasionally with biblical

2 Dove (2007), p. 17.

3 The figures can be only approximate because in some cases it is impossible to be certain that a manuscript is not originally a part of a complete Testament or the Bible.

commentaries and catechetical materials. The purpose of compilations combining biblical translations of various origin seems to have been to produce what can be described as an approximation of the Bible or part-Bible from the available materials. Several scholars have commented on this practice, though primarily in relation to non-Wycliffite, Middle English adaptations of biblical books. James Morey in his *Guide to Middle English biblical literature* (2000, p. 348) points out that manuscripts containing biblical paraphrase show a tendency 'to accumulate material over time and to assume a comprehensiveness extending to both Testaments'. Writing about Middle English *Prose Version of Epistles, Acts, and Matthew* he observes that it was preceded by a prologue that consisted of a summary of Genesis and Exodus, followed by a debate on the propriety of the translation of the Bible. Morey concludes that since the material was assembled from Genesis, Exodus and nearly the entire NT the compilation was 'intended to become some sort of "Bible"' (p. 347).

As mentioned already, parts of WB were also circulated in such compilations. A number of manuscripts in the current catalogue include the gospel harmony *Oon of Foure*.[4] In compilations containing other biblical material it takes the role of the four gospels. Thus in MS Bodl. 978 *Oon of Foure* is followed by a table of lections as well as epistles, Acts and the Apocalypse in LV. The whole collection approximates the NT. MS Bodl. 771 contains *Oon of Foure*, a table of lections based on *Oon of Foure*, and what looks like a personal collection for reading. The collection consists of extracts from NT, but there are no extracts from the gospels, which suggests that it was designed to complement *Oon of Foure*. Another compilation approximating a partial NT is MS Laud misc. 33. It contains the Wycliffite translation of Pauline (Romans to Hebrews) and Catholic (James to Jude) epistles in LV combined with a text known as the *Apocalips of Jesu Crist*.[5] The *Apocalips of Jesu Crist* is a Middle English adaptation of the Apocalypse, translated from a French version, where passages of the translated text, underlined in red, are followed by passages of commentary.

---

4 See Smith, P. M., 'An edition of parts I–V of the Wycliffite translation of Clement of Llanthony's Latin gospel harmony *Unum ex Quattuor* known *as Oon of Foure*' (PhD thesis, University of Southampton, 1985, reprinted 2 vols, London: theuniversitiespress.com, 2015). On the practice of combining *Oon of Foure* with the Wycliffite translation and other liturgical and devotional texts, see Raschko, M., '*Oon of Foure*: harmonizing Wycliffite and Pseudo-Bonaventuran approaches to the Life of Christ', in Johnson, I. and Westphall, A. F. (eds), *The Pseudo-Bonaventuran Lives of Christ: exploring the Middle English tradition* (Turnhout: Brepols, 2013), pp. 341–73.

5 Morey (2000), pp. 351–3; Fridner, E. (ed.), *An English fourteenth century apocalypse version with a prose commentary* (Lund: C. W. K. Gleerup, 1961).

In MS Laud misc. 33 it is accompanied by a prologue to the Apocalypse from the Wycliffite translation (LV).

Another compilation, MS Hatton 111, combines the Middle English OT and NT materials. It starts with *Jerome's Abbreviated Psalter*, a translation of a Latin version that was included in English Books of Hours and recommended to those who could not recite the entire psalter due to business or illness.[6] In some manuscripts of the *Abbreviated Psalter* English verses alternate with Latin verses, but MS Hatton 111 includes only the English text. The *Abbreviated Psalter* is followed by a text known as the *Old Testament Sentences*,[7] consisting of extracts illustrating Christian teaching. Hatton 111 also includes a table of lections, as well as the gospels, Catholic epistles and the Apocalypse in EV, and a *capitula*-list. Interestingly, the table of lections that precedes the Wycliffite material in this volume contains only the readings from the NT books that are included in Hatton 111, but not from the Acts or Pauline epistles.

Hatton 111 is less professionally produced than many WBs but it is not a carelessly made copy. The fact that the table of lections was edited to reflect the selection of NT books in this manuscript suggests planning, as well as the skill and motivation to customise the text that could have been reproduced mechanically. The collection as a whole approximates the order of books in the Bible and can be interpreted as yet another attempt to assemble something like the Bible from available materials.

As mentioned already, a number of compilations reflect a desire to combine the biblical text with preaching or educational material. MS Holkham misc. 40 includes a Middle English non-Wycliffite translation of the General and Pauline epistles[8] and the Wycliffite translation of the gospels in EV. This is preceded by the prose *Mirror*, a collection of sermons with a prologue translated from Robert of Gretham's Anglo-Norman verse *Mirror*.[9]

---

6 Version A (Morey (2000), pp. 186–89; Wells (1916), vol. 8, p. 18; Severs, Hartung, Beidler (1967–), vol. 2, p. 387, no. 15.

7 Version 2 (Morey (2000), pp. 130–2).

8 Paues, A. C., *A fourteenth century English Biblical version* (Cambridge: Cambridge University Press, 1904), pp. 18–122; Morey (2000), pp. 346–50.

9 Paues (1904), pp. xiv–xv; Blumreich, K. M. (ed.), *The Middle English 'Mirror': an edition based on Bodleian Library, MS Holkham misc. 40* (Arizona: Centre for Medieval and Renaissance Studies, 2002); Duncan, T. G. and Connolly, M. (eds), *The Middle English 'Mirror': sermons from Advent to Sexagesima* (Heidelberg: Universitätsverlag Winter, 2003); O'Mara, V. and Paul, S. (eds), *A repertorium of Middle English prose sermons* (Turnhout: Brepols, 2007), pp. 2047–165.

Liturgical materials

Of all non-biblical texts that were circulated in WB manuscripts by far the most common were various liturgical aids. These are of four kinds: the calendar (found in four Oxford manuscripts all listed in Appendix III), the calendar-lectionary (three manuscripts), the table of lections (27 manuscripts) and the OT lectionary (six manuscripts).

The table of lections considerably outnumbers all other liturgical texts found not only in Oxford manuscripts but in the WB manuscripts in general.[10] The tables are normally, though not always, codicologically separate from other items, and are sometimes written in a more formal script than the biblical text, or by a scribe different from the scribe of the biblical text.[11] The tables fall into two groups that will be referred to below and in the descriptions of manuscripts as Type I and Type II.

The tables of Type I are found in manuscripts with LV text, though also in Christ Church MS 145, dated to the end of the 14th century, that has an EV text. In Christ Church MS 145, however, the table is a somewhat later addition. The tables of Type I typically include three sections introduced by rubrics: the temporal, starting on the first Sunday in Advent, the sanctoral and votive Masses termed 'commemorations' in rubrics that introduce them. The sanctoral of the tables of Type I includes only the proper with readings for the feasts of individual saints and no common with readings for categories of saints, such as confessors or martyrs. It is, however, typically introduced by a rubric that states that the readings are for both the proper and common, i.e., '*þe sanctorum comyn & propir to gidir*'. The inventory of feasts in the tables of Type I was very stable and transmitted with virtually no variation. Some feasts are given larger or more elaborately decorated initials, and an exact choice of such feasts varies from manuscript to manuscript, but these tend to be widely celebrated, rather than institutional or local feasts, such as the feasts of Christ, the Virgin Mary, apostles or some commonly venerated saints. The entries for feasts typically consist

---

10 The tables of lections occur in about 40 per cent of the surviving manuscripts of WB, usually at the beginning of the volume, though sometimes also in the middle or at the end (Peikola, 2013, p. 351). The table of lections is edited by Forshall and Madden (1850), vol. 4, pp. 683–97, but the text they provide is a conflation of two different versions of the table based on comparison of only eight manuscripts out of almost one hundred (Peikola (2013), pp. 354–5).

11 As with calendars, it is often difficult to be certain whether the scribe of the table is the same as the scribe of the biblical text because the tables were not copied continuously and are sometimes in a larger script than the biblical text. In MS Ashmole 1517 the OT lectionary and the table of lections are written by a scribe different from the scribe of NT.

of the name of a liturgical occasion in red, abbreviated reference to a book and chapter of the Bible, an indexing letter in red, the opening words of a reading, '*ende*' in red, the closing words of a reading and double strokes in red. The tables of Type I are written on pages specially ruled with separate columns for each component of the entries, so that all incipits, indexing letters, etc. appear in a predictable place.

The table of lections of Type II is found in a much smaller number of manuscripts many, though not all, with an EV text.[12] It consists of the temporal, commemorations and the sanctoral, subdivided, unlike in the tables of Type I, into a short proper and detailed common. Unlike in the tables of Type I, the exact selection of feasts in both the proper and common varies, though the proper normally contains biblical saints and a few widely venerated saints without local or institutional significance, such as Lawrence, George, Denis, Stephen, Martin, Thomas Becket and others. The common has entries for different categories of saints, such as martyrs, virgins, confessors, bishops and abbots.

The entries in the tables of Type II consist of the same components as in the tables of Type I, including incipits, explicits and indexing letters, but their layout and presentation are often different. The tables in MS Gough Eccl. Top. 5 and MS Hatton 111, for example, are written on pages without a special ruling. In MS Gough Eccl. Top. 5 the readings are all in black, apart from the names of some liturgical occasions, where red is used for important feasts as in liturgical calendars. In MS Hatton 111 the entries are all in black, but the names of the liturgical occasions and indexing letters are highlighted in yellow wash. Considering its variability and association with the EV text, the table of Type II is likely to represent an earlier stage in the development of the Wycliffite table of lections.

The tables of Type I are preceded by a rubric that seems to have been traditional and copied by scribes with no or little change. Such rubrics, transcribed in the descriptions of manuscripts in the catalogue, declare that the lections are for the use of Salisbury and explain the structure of the table and the use of indexing letters, for example:

> *Here bigynneþ a rule þat telliþ in whiche placis of þis book ȝe schulen fynde þe lessouns pistlis & gospels þat ben rad in þe chirche aftir þe vse of Salisbury markid wiþ lettris of þe abc þe bigynnyngis & þe eendyngis with twei strikis first is sett þe sonedaies & ferials & after þe sanctorum comoun & propre writen a clause of þe bigynnyng þerof & a clause of þe eending also.* (MS Bodl. 183)

---

12 See Peikola (2013), pp. 372–7, where such tables are given a label 'DPCV'.

The rubrics that accompany the tables of Type II tend to be simpler and do not describe the structure of the tables. The table in MS Gough Eccl. Top. 5, for example, is preceded by a rubric '*þe pistlis & þe gospels of þe newe testament vn to seint andrewes euyn*'. A somewhat longer rubric that includes a reference to the use of Salisbury but not a description of the table's structure or the use of indexing letters occurs in Brasenose College MS 10: '*Here bigynneþ a rule þat telliþ in whiche chapitris of þe bible ȝe [m]oun fynde þe lessons pistlis & gospels þat ben rad bi al þe ȝeer a[.]oute in holi chirche aftir þe vss of Salisbiry*'. Finally, the tables of Type II in Christ Church College MS 4, MS Bodl. 978 and MS Hatton 111 begin without a rubric.

The tables admit a number of variations to their structure and contents. One concerns the order of their sections. In the tables of Type II the order tends to be the same: the temporal, proper followed by the common of saints, and commemorations. In the tables of Type I commemorations can appear either at the end, or after the temporal and preceding the sanctoral.[13] The tables of both types have a similar set of commemorations but their exact wording and order may differ. Commemorations are therefore always described in the entries in the catalogue.

One of the most interesting reasons for variation in the contents of the tables of lections is a widely attested practice of editing them to reflect the range of biblical books included in individual manuscripts.[14] In spite of the rubrics invariably claiming that the tables contain the gospels and epistles read in the church throughout the year according to the use of Salisbury, many manuscripts do not contain the full version of the Sarum lectionary. Such edited tables are based on the standard inventory of feasts, but omit references to readings from books other than those included in a manuscript. Considering that most WBs are part-Bibles, examples of this are very common. As mentioned already, the table of Type II in MS Hatton 111, dating from the first quarter of the 15th century, contains the readings only from those NT books that are included in this manuscript, namely the gospels and James–Apocalypse. MS Douce 265, a NT probably written around the middle of the 15th century, contains a table of lections with readings only from NT.

The tables of lections accompany not only WB but also *Oon of Foure*. The tables found in the manuscripts containing *Oon of Foure* are not an

13 See Peikola (2013), pp. 372–7, for examples of both orders.

14 See Dove (2007), p. 60 and Solopova, E., 'Manuscript evidence for the patronage, ownership and use of the Wycliffite Bible', in Poleg and Light (2013), pp. 333–49 at pp. 338–40.

independent creation but an adaptation of the Wycliffite tables, and have the same inventory of feasts. It seems that the tables of both types were adapted for use with *Oon of Foure*. In MS Bodl. 978 *Oon of Foure* is followed by a table of Type II which has references to both biblical books and *Oon of Foure* (fols. 170r–181v). The table consists of the temporal, proper, common and commemorations, and is written without a special ruling. The readings from the gospels include references to the part, chapter and indexing letter of *Oon of Foure*. The tables in other manuscripts containing *Oon of Foure*, similarly to the tables of Type I, consist of the temporal, a single sanctoral and commemorations. Such a table is found, for example, in MS Bodl. 771 that contains *Oon of Foure* and extracts from NT in EV.

Incipits and explicits in the tables of all types, including those that accompany *Oon of Foure*, derive most commonly from LV as suggested by selective checking, though a certainty that this is true for all readings in such tables is impossible without an edition. A small number of tables, such as the one in MS Hatton 111, have incipits from EV. Incipits in some tables, such as the one that accompanies *Oon of Foure* in MS Bodl. 978, do not correspond to either WB or *Oon of Foure*, and may have been translated independently.

Perhaps the most difficult question raised by the tables of lections is that of their origin and underlying models.[15] Many surviving Latin tables differ from the Wycliffite tables in both content and presentation, though some close parallels can be found as well. A number of Latin tables, including those found in the manuscripts of WB, do not contain explicits or indexing letters, and are laid out differently and without the use of colour characteristic of the tables of Type I. A Latin table that accompanies NT in EV in New College MS 67, for example, consists of the temporal and sanctoral and is imperfect at the end. It is laid out in two columns with the names of the liturgical occasions written in the outer margins and underlined in red. The entries consist of the opening words of readings followed by a reference to a book and chapter of the Bible, all in black, and do not include the indexing letters or explicits.

A much closer, though not an exact analogy to the Wycliffite tables in terms of both content and layout is a Latin table of lections added in the late 14th or early 15th centuries to a 13th-century English Bible, London, British Library, Royal MS 1 B X (fols. 34r–39v).[16] It consists of the temporal, proper, common and commemorations and is laid out in five columns with different elements of the entries contained in each column. The entries

15 See a discussion of the origin of the tables in Peikola (2013).

16 Peikola (2013), pp. 356–7.

consist of the name of the liturgical occasion, a description of the reading as '*evangelum*' or '*epistola*', a reference to a book and chapter of the Bible, an indexing letter, and the opening and closing words of each reading. The colour is not used in the same way as in the tables of Type I and instead of '*ende*' the columns with the opening and closing words have the headings '*Principia*' and '*ffines*'.[17]

The method of indexing using letters pre-dates WB by about a century and a half. According to several studies by R. H. Rouse and M. A. Rouse, an interest in indexing in the Middle Ages grew with the establishment of standard chapter divisions in the Bible traditionally attributed to Stephen Langton and in existence by 1203.[18] The first verbal concordance to the Latin Bible was produced by the Dominicans at St Jacques under the direction of Hugh of St Cher. It consisted of the alphabetical listing of thousands of words accompanied by references to the book, chapter and section of the Bible. The creators of the concordance could not use page references for indexing because in manuscript copies the same material never appeared on the same page. Instead the St Jacques Dominicans devised a system of dividing chapters into sevenths, each designated by the first seven letters of the alphabet, A–G. This system was used in the third concordance, likely to have been a 'corporate project of the St Jacques Dominicans', that was best known in the Middle Ages and survives in at least eighty manuscripts, the majority of which were written in Paris between *c.*1280 and 1330.[19] The third concordance retained A–G notation for indicating the division of lengthier chapters but also introduced the subdivision of shorter chapters into four parts labelled A–D. According to Rouse and Rouse, one of the effects of the concordance was the widespread adoption of the Dominican reference system of the citing of a

17 Such layout is found in some Wycliffite tables of lections as well. The table in Cambridge, Emmanuel College MS 21 starts with a column containing the names of liturgical occasions followed by a column with references to the books and chapters of the Bible in red. These are followed by two more columns, one with the heading '*biginningis*' and another with the heading '*eendingis*' containing the opening and closing words of each reading in black.

18 Rouse, R. H. and Rouse, M. A., 'The verbal concordance to the scriptures', *Archivum Fratrum Praedicatorum* 44 (1974), pp. 5–30; Rouse, R. H. and Rouse, M. A., 'Development of research tools in the thirteenth century', in *Authentic witnesses: approaches to medieval texts and manuscripts* (Notre Dame, Ind.: University of Notre Dame Press, 1991), pp. 221–55; Rouse, R. H. and Rouse, M. A., 'La naissance des index', in Martin, H.-J. and Chartier, R. (eds), *Histoire de l'édition française*, vol. 1, *Le livre conquérant* (Paris: Promodis, 1983), pp. 77–85.

19 Rouse and Rouse (1974), pp. 17, 20–1.

letter A–G along with a chapter number. By the last quarter of the 13th century this was a common method of citing the Bible.[20]

In spite of its relative popularity, the method of reference using indexing letters seems to have been little known in England outside academia and possibly outside the friars. The WB may have been the first English text where this system was employed. Some manuscripts of WB attest to a traditional seven-letter sequence, A–G, but in most an eleven-letter sequence, A–L, is used, presumably a modification of the A–G system to make references to longer chapters more precise. As shown by Peikola, most tables using a shorter system, A–G, are found in the manuscripts with EV text.[21]

The indexing letters appear not only in the tables of lections and lectionaries (see below), but also in the margins of biblical text. In almost all surviving copies of WB and *Oon of Foure*, however, they are not applied consistently to mark subdivisions of the chapters but appear only at the beginnings of lections. The only exception in the present catalogue is MS Hatton 111 that contains an EV text laid out in one column with the indexing letters entered in the margins in a medieval hand but probably not by the main scribe. The letters consistently subdivide chapters into sevenths instead of just marking the beginnings of lections that are highlighted with yellow wash. The use of the indexing letters to mark the beginnings of lections rather than subdivisions of chapters is probably a Wycliffite innovation, but it is not entirely without a precedent. Latin Bibles containing the tables of lections with indexing letters do not always have letters in the biblical text.[22] It appears that subdivisions into sevenths were often expected to be mental rather than physical.[23]

An interesting modification of the Dominican system, perhaps reflecting its insufficient understanding by some makers of the Bibles, is found in MS Bodl. 771. It contains a table of lections based on *Oon of Foure* where the entries for readings consist of the name of the liturgical occasion and a

---

20 Rouse and Rouse (1974), p. 22

21 Peikola (2013), p. 359.

22 The indexing letters A–G (probably added) appear written in the inner margin consistently throughout the entire text of a 13th-century Latin bible, MS Laud lat. 13; another Latin bible, MS Rawl. G. 5, also dating from the 13th century, contains an original table of lections with indexing letters but no letters in the biblical text.

23 MS Auct. D. 5. 9 is a 13th-century Latin bible that was made for a Dominican, probably in France, and owned in England. It includes a table of lections with indexing letters, but there are no indexing letters in the biblical text. Instead every chapter throughout the entire bible is subdivided with absolute consistency into seven sections by points in the inner margin.

reference to a part and chapter of *Oon of Foure* followed not by an indexing letter but by the first letter of a reading. The first letters of readings are also written out in red in the margins of the text.[24]

The NT in the manuscripts of WB is often combined not with the complete OT, but with OT Mass readings, presumably in order to avoid the expense of copying the entire OT and due to the importance of liturgical readings to the Bible's audience. There were two ways of presenting the OT readings: full OT readings were sometimes included in the tables of lections, but much more often they were compiled into separate OT lectionaries. Two manuscripts in the present catalogue, listed in Appendix III, contain the tables of lections with usual short references for NT readings and the OT readings written out in full. The catalogue also includes the descriptions of six manuscripts containing a separate OT lectionary (listed in Appendix III). As pointed out already, unlike the tables of lections, OT lectionaries contain not just the references but the full text of readings from OT books. Such lectionaries accompany the Wycliffite NTs and occur, according to Dove, in twenty-five manuscripts.[25]

Similar to the tables of lections, the lectionaries fall into two groups, referred to below and in the descriptions of manuscripts as Type I and Type II. A lectionary of Type I is found in MS Laud misc. 388 in the present catalogue. It consists of four parts: the temporal starting in Advent, a detailed sanctoral, commemorations, and what is termed in a rubric 'non-Sarum' readings, but is essentially a very short common. This common includes only five readings.[26] MS Laud misc. 388 is imperfect at the end and contains only the first and the beginning of the second of these readings, but all five are preserved in other manuscripts containing lectionaries of this type, including London, British Library, Egerton MS 1171 and London, British Library, Harley MS 6333. These readings are introduced by rubrics such as '*In þe birþe of manye martris a pistle*' (MS Laud Misc. 388, fol. 297v) and include those for the feasts of many martyrs (Wisdom 10); a confessor and doctor (Wisdom 7); a confessor and abbot (Ecclesiasticus 2);[27] and a virgin and martyr (Ecclesiasticus 24 and Isaiah 61–62).[28]

---

[24] See also a discussion of the practice of marking lections with their incipits or opening and closing letters in the margins of the biblical text at the end of this section.

[25] Dove (2007), p. 61.

[26] These readings are listed under the '*Common Sanctorum*' in Forshall and Madden (1850), vol. 4, pp. 696–7.

[27] '*In þe feeste of o confessor & abbot apistil*' according to the rubric in Egerton MS 1171, but listed under the feast of many martyrs in Forshall and Madden (1850), vol. 4, p. 697.

[28] '*Anoþer of þe same of o virgyn & martir Isaie lxi & lxij capitulo*' according to the

The lectionary of Type II consists of somewhat different parts and in a different order. It is found, for example, in closely related MSS Ashmole 1517 and Selden Supra 51, possibly of London origin, in MS Rawl. C. 259, MS Bodl. 665 and MS Christ Church 146. It includes the temporal, commemorations and the sanctoral subdivided, as in the tables of lections of Type II, into a short proper and a detailed common. Similar to the tables of lections of Type II, the proper in lectionaries of Type II includes mostly biblical and a small number of widely venerated saints, and an exact inventory of such feasts varies from manuscript to manuscript. The common in all manuscripts contains the readings for the categories of saints, namely the vigil of one apostle, the feasts of an evangelist, a single martyr, many martyrs, a confessor and bishop, a confessor and doctor, a confessor and abbot, a virgin and martyr, a virgin non-martyr, and many virgins.[29]

The exact nature of the text of the readings in OT lectionaries remains unclear in the absence of an edition. The majority of readings in the manuscripts discussed above, independently of the type of the lectionary, derive from LV though some come from EV and there is no clear pattern explaining such variation. Their close connection with WB is evident in the fact that in all manuscripts added material within the text (see a discussion of the added material below) is underlined in red just as in the continuous biblical text in the Wycliffite translation.

The OT lectionary, independently of the type, is a unified text and not just a collection of extracts from WB. Lectionaries of Type I are presented with running titles indicating liturgical seasons in the temporal and months in the sanctoral. In all lectionaries the readings are preceded by rubrics stating the liturgical occasion and giving book and chapter references. In all lectionaries the readings also commonly begin with introductory statements that are not in the biblical text but a translation of statements which accompany them in the text of the Mass, such as '*The lord seiþ þese þingis*'.[30] These additions are underlined in red in all manuscripts to indicate that they are not part of the biblical text. This practice is explained in a rubric at the end of the table of lections in MS Ashmole 1517 that points

rubric in Egerton MS 1171, but listed under the feast of a 'virgin, not martyr' in Forshall and Madden (1850), vol. 4, p. 697.

29 The temporal in MS Ashmole 1517, MS Selden Supra 51 and MS Bodl. 665 contains the same inventory of feasts as in the lectionaries of Type I, whereas the temporal in MS Rawl. C. 259 contains in addition to this a reading for two feasts of Edmund Rich (fol. 203r).

30 '*The lord seiþ þese þinges*' corresponds to '*Hec dicit dominus*' in the Sarum Missal; see Legg, J. Wickham (ed.), *The Sarum Missal* (Oxford, 1916).

out that introductory statements underlined in red in the lectionary are not in the biblical text and therefore should not be sought in the table of lections: '*þe lokeris in þis kalender be riȝt wel war: for he shal not fynde alle þe bigynnyngis of þe lessuns of þe olde lawe acorde wiþ þe kalender for bi ordyaunce of þe chirche: þer is sett to þe bigynnyngis of many lessuns more & oþer wyse þan it is in þe bible & þat is drawun vndir wiþ a stryk of reed ynke & it is not in þe kalender. for it is not so in þe text & also it is in þe same maner of manye of þe endingis of þo lessuns*' (fol. 5v).

All lectionaries include a troped lesson for the first Mass at Christmas that does not derive from WB and must have been translated independently.[31] It is a translation of *Laudes Deo* and a lesson from *Missa in gallicantu* according to the Sarum rite, based on the Vetus Latina, rather than the Vulgate text of Isaiah 9. It is accompanied by a lengthy rubric explaining that during the service it is performed by two voices. In all manuscripts in the present catalogue the parts of the two voices are distinguished with one underlined in red.

In all lectionaries the readings used for more than one occasion are not repeated but are replaced by cross-references. In most manuscripts such cross-references refer to liturgical occasions declared in the rubrics at the start of each reading. In MS Laud misc. 388, however, cross-references refer to numbered leaves and only occasionally to feasts or months, usually also accompanied by a leaf number. Such references take advantage of the original foliation which occurs only in the part of the manuscript containing the OT readings. The method of reference is explained in a rubric on fol. 282r: '*þis lessoun ȝe schulen fynde writen al out to fore in þe. xxv. leef of þese leefes þat ben markid. In whiche leefes ben conteyned alle þe lessons & pistlis of þe oolde lawe. and þei ben markid wiþ lettris of noumbrari as is i. ij. & iij. on þe riȝtside of þe leef. in þe hiȝer part of þe margyn*'.

Most lectionaries use indexing letters and double strokes to link OT readings to the tables of lections. The indexing letters appear in the margins at the beginnings of readings and double strokes at their ends in all manuscripts apart from MS Selden Supra 51. In two closely related copies with lectionaries of Type II, Ashmole 1517 and Selden Supra 51, the lectionary is subdivided into five parts, marked with the letters A–E which appear at the beginning of each lection in MS Selden Supra 51 and as running titles in MS Ashmole 1517.[32] In addition, each reading is given a number, that is a1,

[31] See Solopova (2013), pp. 334–6.

[32] MS Selden Supra 51 was also intended to have running titles; the letters A–E are entered as guide letters in the top margin of each leaf, but were never overwritten in red by the rubricator.

a2, a3, etc. in MS Selden Supra 51 and 1, 2, 3, etc. in MS Ashmole 1517. The same letters and numbers are used as part of references to OT readings in the calendar-lectionary and the table of lections in MS Selden Supra 51, and in the table of lections in MS Ashmole 1517. As a result, the entries for OT readings in the tables of lections in these manuscripts include in addition to usual components (indexing letters, incipits, etc.) identifiers of these readings consisting of the letters and numbers described above.[33]

The table of lections and indexing letters were not the only means of locating Mass readings in WBs. Following a practice found in Latin Bibles, the lections in some EV manuscripts are marked with liturgical rubrics within the biblical text. MS Holkham misc. 40, for example, contains the four gospels in EV. The text is complete, but includes rubrics identifying lections for the temporal, sanctoral and commemorations. The beginning of each lection is signalled by a rubric in red, specifying the liturgical occasion, whereas the end of each lection is marked with the word '*ende*' in red. Considering that liturgical rubrics are found only in the manuscripts of EV, it seems likely that they represent an early stage in the development of the liturgical apparatus of WB, later abandoned in favour of the tables of lections and indexing letters.

Yet another way of identifying lections within the biblical text was the inclusion of Latin incipits in the margins. This practice is found in MS Laud misc. 33, that does not have the indexing letters but contains Latin incipits written at the start of lections in the margins. In Corpus Christi College MS 4 the Latin incipits are occasionally written out in the margins in the original or contemporary hand, e.g., '*ab initio & ante secula*' (fol. 222v) at the start of the reading for the Eve of the Assumption and commemorations of Our Lady (Ecclesiasticus 24). In MS Douce 369 the lections are occasionally marked with a red bracket in the margin and sometimes with their opening and final letters written out in red in the margins. Such markings are probably a later addition. In many manuscripts the lections are also highlighted within the text with red or yellow wash and with red or blue paraphs. All these ways of marking the lections within the text are of lesser importance in the manuscripts of WB than the indexing letters and double strokes, and are more characteristic of EV than LV manuscripts.

The calendars found in four manuscripts in the present catalogue are similar in content and appearance to other late medieval liturgical calendars, though unlike the calendars in Latin liturgical books their decoration tends to be modest. The colours used for the text are red and black (with initials occasionally in blue), and only very rarely gold (as in MS Fairfax 11). The

33 The same system is used in Cambridge, Trinity College MS B.10.20.

only decoration is penwork on 'KL' monograms, large initials for '*Kalendae*' that appear at the beginnings of months. The calendars are usually codicologically separate from other texts and, like most Latin calendars, are laid out one month per page. Some calendars are probably written by scribes different from the scribes of the biblical text, suggesting specialisation, though it is always difficult to be certain because the script of the calendars tends to be more formal and sometimes larger than the script of the biblical text. Both Latin and English calendars are attested. The calendars in Latin are found in MS Fairfax 11 and MS Rawl. C. 259, whereas the calendars in English are found in MS Rawl. C. 237 and MS Selden Supra 49. The calendars are in no way 'Lollard' and contain all features found in other late medieval liturgical calendars, including the golden numbers and the dominical letters, verses on the 'Egyptian' days[34] (e.g., MS Fairfax 11, MS Rawl. C. 237), notes on the number of days in months (MS Rawl. C. 237), notes on the number of hours in day and night (MS Fairfax 11) and commemorations of historical events (MS Rawl. C. 259). The calendars are all for the use of Sarum, though regional or institutional features are also occasionally present (see 'The place of production', below). The calendars are on the whole carefully produced, and seem to have been intended for practical use, though only one calendar in the present catalogue, of MS Fairfax 11, is graded (for secular use).[35]

The calendar-lectionaries are all in English and have a layout similar to liturgical calendars, but in addition to the usual information include references for Sarum readings consisting, as for the tables of lections, of an indication of the biblical source, an indexing letter in red, the opening words of each reading, '*ende*' in red and the closing words of each reading (without the opening or closing words in MS Fairfax 2). Normally calendar-lectionaries include only the readings for the sanctoral and therefore occur in manuscripts that also contains the tables of lections. It appears that the makers of the manuscripts felt that the tables of lections adequately represented the temporal, but not the sanctoral, presumably because they did not contain calendar dates. The calendars and calendar-lectionaries were included to supply this information. This is suggested by the fact that in

---

[34] The verses on the 'Egyptian' days are described, with a selection edited, in Hennig (1955).

[35] Graded calendars include an indication of the number of lessons appointed to be read at Mass at a particular feast. The highest number of readings in monastic use, assigned to particularly important feasts, is twelve and in secular use is nine. In the manuscripts of the Wycliffite Bible, not only in Oxford but generally, the grading is found only in Latin calendars and is always for secular use.

Cambridge, Emmanuel College MS 34, Cambridge, Gonville and Caius College MS 343/539 and Cambridge, Trinity College MS B. 10. 20 the sanctoral is entirely omitted in the tables of lections and its role is taken over by the calendar-lectionary. The tables of lections in these manuscripts include only the temporal followed by commemorations. This does not happen in all manuscripts containing the calendar-lectionaries: the tables in MS Laud misc. 388 and MS Selden Supra 51 in the present catalogue include all three sections, the temporal, sanctoral and commemorations. MS Ashmole 1517 may have originally included a calendar-lectionary: it is imperfect at the beginning and contains a table of lections that consists of only the temporal and commemorations.

The calendar-lectionaries have cross-references to the tables of lections, suggesting that they were expected to be used together. The calendar-lectionary in Cambridge, Emmanuel College, MS 34, for example, includes a note, '*Twelfþe day pistil & gospel is in þe temporal*', referring to the table of lections that lists the readings for the temporal. In MS Fairfax 2 the calendar-lectionary is the only liturgical aid that accompanies a complete Bible. It is unique in that unlike other calendar-lectionaries it attempts to represent not only the sanctoral, but also the temporal and commemorations. The readings for the dominicals and ferials are listed at the end of each month and commemorations appear in the lower part of the leaves for October, November and December.

Presentation of the biblical text

The presentation of the biblical text tends to be relatively variable in the manuscripts of EV, but shows signs of standardisation in professionally produced manuscripts of LV. The biblical text is accompanied by running titles and subdivided into chapters numbered in red Roman or Arabic numerals, or numerals spelt out as words in Latin or English. Many manuscripts also include rubrics, glosses, specially marked non-biblical material within the text, and are copied on parchment in double columns in textura and carefully corrected in the original or contemporary hands. These features are briefly discussed below.

Rubrics

Rubrics typically appear at the beginnings of biblical books and prologues. In EV manuscripts their wording and presentation are variable and they are sometimes absent altogether. In MS Hatton 111, for example, Mark is preceded by '*Here endiþ mathew ewangelist in his gospels*' and '*Marke*', whereas John by '*Here endiþ luke in þe gospels. Here bigynneþ þe gospel aftir þe writyng of Ioon*'. MS Rawl. C. 258 has short rubrics such as '*Heer bigynneþ mark*' (fol. 26v), whereas in MS Holkham misc. 40 only some of the prologues, but not the gospels are preceded by rubrics. Christ Church MS 145 has no rubrics, though spaces appear to have been left for them at the beginnings of some books and prologues.

The rubrics are much more standardised in LV manuscripts. They tend to have similar wording as can be seen in the collation of rubrics to the gospels and their prologues in nine manuscripts in Appendix VII. Typically, a rubric at the beginning of a prologue declares: '*Here eendiþ þe gospel of Mark & bigynneþ þe prolog on luk*' and a rubric at the beginning of a book '*Ierom in his prolog on luk seiþ playnli þis sentence...*' (MS Fairfax 11). The exact wording may vary slightly and the scribes did not seem to have copied the rubrics word for word, but maintained an overall form including references to Jerome in the rubrics that follow prologues. Such references are characteristic primarily of LV manuscripts and, as the collation shows, are absent in MS Douce 369 and MS Bodl. 277, the last heavily revised by someone with access to both LV and EV texts.[36] References to Jerome occurs occasionally in EV manuscripts, such as Queen's College MS 369, but are absent in most.

References to Jerome probably reflect a desire to declare the authorship of the prologues and to distinguish them from the biblical text. The attribution appears at the end rather than the beginning of the prologues and this is paralleled by the attributions typically found in glosses that occur in the margins of the manuscripts of WB, such as '*lire here*', '*austin here*' always at the end rather than the beginning of a gloss (see MS Bodl. 554). It is also worth noting that a wording similar to the rubrics in LV manuscripts is used repeatedly in references to Jerome in the General Prologue:

> '*Ierom seiþ al þis sentence in þe prologe on þe firste book of Kyngis*' (ll. 24–5)
>
> '*Ierom seiþ þis pleynli in þe prologe on Prouerbis*' (l. 53)
>
> '*Ierom seiþ in þe prologe on Esdre*' (l. 59)
>
> '*Ierom seiþ þis in þe ij. book on Amos, and in þe iiij. c° [of Amos]*' (ll. 2554–5).[37]

This suggests a close connection between the General Prologue and the apparatus that accompanies the biblical text in the manuscripts of LV.

---

36 Dove (2007), p. 152.

37 Quotations are from Dove (2010).

Corrections

A great majority of copies, even the most modest, are corrected in the original or contemporary hands, often very extensively. In luxury copies, such as MS Bodl. 277, this seems to have been a planned stage in the production process. The text was corrected and omissions added in the margins before the manuscript was passed to the illuminators. Several pages of MS Bodl. 277 have illuminated borders that curl around the text in the margins, such as corrections and glosses (e.g., fols. 97r, 167r, 179v). The same is found in MS Bodl. 183 (e.g., fols. 82v, 173v, 192v, 212v) and in a large-format, richly illuminated manuscript of EV, London, British Library, Egerton MS 617/618, dated before 1397 and made for Thomas of Woodstock, duke of Gloucester, the youngest son of Edward III. In all these and several other manuscripts the artists, who added the borders, had to work around corrections and made an effort not to obscure them.

Corrections in WB tend to be not only numerous, but conspicuous, clearly visible even in luxurious presentation copies where the appearance of the page was evidently very important. As mentioned already, corrections often occur in the margins, rather than over erasures within the text. The erroneous text is also usually crossed out rather than underdotted, frequently in red ink (e.g., MS Laud misc. 182, MS Laud misc. 361, MS Rawl. C. 259, MS Rawl. C. 883, MS Selden Supra 51, etc.). Corrections in the margins are sometimes enclosed in frames that may be in red and even flourished (e.g., MS Ashmole 1517, MS Bodl. 277, MS Gough Eccl. Top. 5, Queen's College MS 388). It seems that the patrons expected the text to be corrected and the presence of corrections was a selling point rather than evidence of a poorly produced copy. It also seems that the scribes' work was supervised and efforts were made to achieve textual accuracy. Some manuscripts, particularly those in EV, contain stylistic and linguistic corrections (MS Bodl. 959, MS Douce 369, New College MS 67, MS Fairfax 21).

Added material

In many manuscripts non-biblical material interpolated into the biblical text is underlined in red or black ink to make evident its non-Scriptural status. Such material includes:

(1) intertextual glosses, usually short explanations of words or concepts (e.g., '*ȝiue he to hir a lybel þat is a litel book of forsakinge*', MS Rawl. G. 258, fol. 4r)

(2) alternative translations, usually synonyms or synonymic expressions recorded as alternative renderings of Latin words and phrases (e.g., '*gesse or deeme*', '*vndo or destrie*', MS Rawl. G. 258, fol. 3v)

(3) words absent in Latin, but added by the translators for clarity or to meet the requirements of grammar in the English text (e.g., '*forsoþe þes þinges ben þe lawe*' (MS Rawl. G. 258, fol. 5v).

Interestingly, all these types of added material are found and appear underlined not only in WB but also in *Oon of Foure*. In MS Bodl. 771 such underlined additions include, for example, '*day of iewis stenofegie þat is a feste of tabernaclis*' (fol. 43r); '*defame or gretely publishe*' (fol. 26r); '*it shal be more sufferable eiþer esier*' (fol. 27r), and '*þe mayden was marye*' (fol. 9r). Textual and liturgical apparatus that accompanies *Oon of Foure* is very similar to that of WB and attests to a close relationship between the two texts.[38] It seems that *Oon of Foure* was treated in the same way as the biblical text and probably seen as equivalent to it by many makers and users of manuscripts.

Sometimes the underlinings appear only in a part of the biblical text but not throughout. In MS Ashmole 1517, for example, they are found in epistles, but not in gospels; in MS Bodl. 183 in OT but not in NT; in MS Bodl. 665, MS Laud misc. 388 and MS Christ Church 146 in OT lectionary but not in NT; and in MS Dugdale 46 in 2 Corinthians, but only very occasionally in other epistles.

The underlinings are present in EV manuscripts but they seem to be characteristic of the text that follows the production break at Baruch 3:20 that occurs in some early manuscripts and probably indicates a change in the authorship of the translation in EV.[39] The underlinings are absent in MS Bodl. 959 (Genesis–Baruch 3:20) and MS Douce 370 (Genesis–2 Chronicles). In the first part of MS Douce 369 (Numbers 20:2–Baruch 3:20) added material is only occasionally underlined faintly in brown ink and in Christ Church MS 145 very occasionally in red. In Corpus Christi College MS 4 added material is consistently underlined in red or black ink starting with Baruch 3 and until the end of NT, but before Baruch 3 it is underlined only very rarely. And, on the contrary, the added material is underlined in red consistently in the text of EV copies that follows Baruch 3, including the second part of MS Douce 369 (Isaiah–Acts 28:15), MS Rawl. C. 258 (NT) and New College MS 67 (NT). New College MS 67 even preserves the evidence of how the scribe worked: points in black ink usually occur in the margins against lines containing such underlined text. The material is also underlined in brown ink in MS Hatton 111 (gospels and James–Apocalypse) and MS Holkham misc. 40 (gospels), and in red

38 See also Raschko (2013).

39 See Dove (2007), pp. 71–2.

or black in Queen's College MS 369 (Matthew–1 Timothy). As can be seen from this, there is a difference in the treatment of added material in EV text before and after Baruch 3:20: it tends to be underlined in the biblical books that follow Baruch, including NT.

Underlinings in red or black are present in many high-quality illuminated manuscripts of LV, including complete Bibles MS Bodl. 277 (underlined in black throughout), MS Fairfax 2 (occasionally underlined in red), Lincoln College MS Lat. 119 (underlined in red or black), St John's College Oxford MS 7 (underlined in red consistently throughout) and Queen's College MS 388 (underlined in black). And, on the contrary, the manuscripts in which the underlinings are absent tend to be complete or partial NTs in LV, including the following:

MS Bodl. 665 (NT), MS Douce 240 (NT), MS Douce 258 (General epistles), MS Douce 265 (NT), MS Gough Eccl. Top. 5 (NT), MS Laud misc. 25 (gospels), MS Laud misc. 207 (Matthew–Mark in LV), MS Laud misc. 361 (NT), MS Laud misc. 388 (NT), MS Lyell 27 (epistles), MS Rawl. C. 237/MS Rawl. C. 238 (NT), MS Christ Church 146 (NT), St John's College MS 79 (Matthew–John 13:4).

The underlinings seem to be an early feature associated primarily with the EV text after the break at Baruch 3:20 and with the entire text of LV as attested in carefully produced complete Bibles, rather than in commercially produced NTs.[40] The manuscript tradition seems to suggest that this feature originated with EV translators responsible for the text after Baruch 3:20, was then adopted by LV translators but diluted and partially abandoned during the commercial production of WB in the first and second quarters of the 15th century.

Glosses

Extensive marginal commentary appears only in the manuscripts of LV, but short marginal glosses are occasionally found in EV manuscripts, including Christ Church MS 145 that has a few glosses in OT. The only exception is heavily glossed New College MS 67, a NT in EV containing, according to Lindberg (1959–97, vol. 7 (1994), p. 24), a revised text strongly influenced by LV. In addition to New College MS 67 the only other Oxford manuscript

---

40 The absence of underlinings does not mean that the intertextual glosses were not used in EV translation before Baruch 3:20. Dove (2007, pp. 154–5) cites glosses shared by all EV manuscrips in OT, but observes that they become much more common after Baruch 3:20. She also observes that variant translations are characteristic of EV manuscripts only after Baruch 3:20.

containing extensive marginal commentary is MS Bodl. 554. This very modest copy, less professionally produced than many WBs, preserves the Wycliffite psalter glosses better than any other known manuscript.[41] Short marginal glosses appear in most complete Bibles in LV, described in the present catalogue, including MS Bodl. 277, MS Fairfax 2, Lincoln College MS Lat. 119, St John's College MS 7 (very occasionally), whereas Queen's College MS 388 includes a few of the series of glosses in the Pentateuch written within the text.[42] The manuscripts that have no glosses, in addition to a very late psalter, New College MS 320, and MS Douce 36, containing only the Book of Tobit, are all complete or partial NTs:

MS Bodl. 531 (NT), MS Bodl. 665 (NT), MS Douce 240 (NT), MS Douce 258 (epistles), MS Douce 265 (NT), MS Fairfax 21 (Romans–Apocalypse), MS Gough Eccl. Top. 5 (NT), MS Junius 29 (NT), MS Laud misc. 24 (Matthew–Mark), MS Laud misc. 25 (gospels), MS Laud misc. 33 (epistles), MS Laud misc. 207 (Matthew–Mark), MS Laud misc. 361 (NT), MS Laud misc. 388 (NT), MS Lyell 26 (NT), MS Lyell 27 (epistles), MS e Mus. 110 (NT), MS Rawl. C. 237/MS Rawl. C. 238 (NT), MS Rawl. C. 257 (NT), MS Rawl. C. 259 (NT), Brasenose College MS 10 (NT), MS Christ Church 146 (NT), MS Christ Church 147 (epistles).

The glosses seem to occur more frequently in OT than in NT, and are found in partial OTs, such as MS Bodl. 296 (Genesis–Psalms), MS Bodl. 554 (psalms), Corpus Christi College MS 20 (1 Ezra–2 Maccabees) and New College MS 66 (Genesis–Psalms). They seem to be an early feature associated with carefully produced complete Bibles in LV, rather than EV manuscripts or NTs in LV. Within the NT the glosses are almost entirely absent in the gospels.

Codicological boundaries

All liturgical materials tend to be codicologically separate from the biblical text, presumably because they were copied and disseminated independently and were seen as optional add-ons appropriate for certain patrons. Calendars and the tables of lections are usually codicologically separate from the biblical text, though there are exceptions.[43] They are, however, not always separate from one another and appear in the same quires in MS Fairfax 11, MS Laud misc. 388 and MS Selden Supra 51, which suggests

[41] Dove (2007), p. 156.

[42] Dove (2007), p. 264.

[43] The table of lections is not separate from other texts in MS Bodl. 531, MS Gough Eccl. Top. 5, MS Hatton 111 and New College MS 67.

that they were designed to be used together and their joint inclusion in manuscripts was planned and intentional. The OT lectionary is codicologically separate in four out of six manuscripts that include it (MS Ashmole 1517, MS Laud misc. 388, MS Rawl. C. 259 and MS Selden Supra 51). The *capitula*-list is separate in two out of five manuscripts (MS e Mus. 110 and MS Selden Supra 51).

Biblical books, on the contrary, seem to have been copied continuously and there is little evidence of codicological boundaries suggesting their separate production. OT and NT are codicologically separate in three complete Bibles, MS Bodl. 277, Corpus Christi College MS 4, Queen's College MS 388, and in MS Bodl. 183 that starts with NT and includes a selection of OT books at the end.

Psalms occasionally start on a new quire. This happens in MS Bodl. 296 where they have no prologue and in MS Douce 369, MS Bodl. 959 and New College MS 66 where their prologues are in the preceding quires. St John's College MS 7 has a production break after Job that ends on a shorter than normal quire; the psalms are not included and Proverbs start on a new quire.[44] St John's gospel starts on a new quire in MS Bodl. 665 and MS Laud misc. 388. There are a few other examples of codicological boundaries at the start of biblical books, but they are rare and do not follow any obvious pattern.[45]

The production break at Baruch 3:20 is found in MS Douce 369 and MS Bodl. 959. In MS Bodl. 959 most books start on a new leaf, probably reflecting its unique textual history. Most unusually, in MS Douce 369 the books are numbered in the upper right corners of leaves in a contemporary hand throughout both parts. The prologues are not numbered separately, but have the same number as either the preceding or following book (see the description).

When parts of WB are combined with other texts they are sometimes, though not always, codicologically separate.[46] In MS Bodl. 978 *Oon of Foure* and the epistles are separate from other texts; in MS Douce 258

44 This copy also ends with a shorter than normal quire, but a rubric implies that more material was expected to be added, possibly the NT.

45 In MS Dugdale 46 Galatians, in MS Rawl. C. 258 the Acts, in MS Christ Church 147 Hebrews, in MS Rawl. C. 257 Romans and in MS Douce 370 4 Kings start on a new quire. In MS Rawl. C. 752 the gospels are separate from the Apocalypse and Jude, and the two parts are written by different scribes and flourished by different artists. In MS Rawl. C. 259 Mark, John, the prologue to Romans, and Philippians start on new pages.

46 Non-biblical texts appear on the same quires as the biblical texts in MS Holkham misc. 40 and MS Laud misc. 33.

the 'Commendation of the Souls' and the Wycliffite commentary on the Athanasian Creed are in a different hand and separate from the gospel readings and epistles; in New College MS 67 the tracts are separate from NT. In MS Hatton 111 *Jerome's Abbreviated Psalter* is separate from the *Old Testament Sentences* and the table of lections, that are in turn separate from the NT. As mentioned already, however, the table of lections includes the readings only from those NT books that are included in Hatton 111 which suggests that the parts were expected to be together.

Layout

In the majority of manuscripts, the biblical text is laid out in two columns. A single column layout is found in predominantly small and often informal part-Bibles in EV and LV:

MS Bodl. 554, psalms in LV, *c.*231 × 165 mm

MS Bodl. 978, *Oon of Foure*, Catholic epistles, Acts and the Apocalypse in LV, *c.*128 × 95 mm

MS Douce 258, 'Commendation of the Souls', the Wycliffite commentary on the Athanasian Creed, gospel readings for Christmas in LV, General epistles in LV, *c.*181 × 125 mm

MS Hatton 111, *Jerome's Abbreviated Psalter*, gospels and James–Apocalypse in EV, *c.*122 × 90 mm

MS Laud misc. 36, gospels in LV, *c.*164 × 113 mm

MS Laud misc. 182, chapters and extracts from OT and NT in LV, *c.*166 × 114 mm

MS Laud misc. 207, Matthew–Mark in LV, *c.*198 × 105 mm

MS Christ Church 147, Galatians–Hebrews in LV, *c.*195 × 130 mm

New College MS 67, NT in EV, *c.*195 × 144 mm

Trinity College MS 93, summary of the Bible, *c.*206 × 138 mm

University College MS 96, General Prologue, chapters from the gospels in LV, *c.*175 × 140 mm.

As can be seen from the above list, the majority of manuscripts in single columns range in length from *c.*122 mm to *c.*198 mm, with the main exception being MS Bodl. 554 that is *c.*231 mm long. MS Bodl. 554 and New College MS 67, both in single columns, are also the only two extensively glossed copies in Oxford collections. It seems that a single-column layout was chosen for practical reasons: to fit the text in the written space of smaller manuscripts and to accommodate extensive marginal apparatus.

Manuscripts that contain exclusively or predominantly non-biblical text, such as Trinity College MS 93 and University College MS 96, are also in single columns. In MS Holkham misc. 40 the layout changes from one to two columns with the two-column layout reserved for the biblical text. As mentioned already, MS Holkham misc. 40 contains the prose *Mirror*, a non-Wycliffite Middle English translation of the General and Pauline epistles, as well as the gospels in EV. Whereas the *Mirror* is laid out in a single column, the epistles and the gospels are laid out in two columns. A switch from a single- to double-column layout happens discretely on the verso of the leaf containing the end of the *Mirror*.

Script

A great majority of the manuscripts are in a rather informal approximation of textura. Manuscripts in Anglicana include two early EV copies, Worcester College MS E. 10. 7 and parts of MS Bodl. 959, as well as MS Laud misc. 36 containing the gospels in LV and University College MS 96 containing the General Prologue and extracts from the gospels in LV. The script in Corpus Christi College MS 20, containing 1 Ezra–2 Maccabees in LV, switches midway from Anglicana to textura. The first 50 folios containing the biblical text are in Anglicana. Psalms start on a new leaf of the quire containing the end of Job and are in textura which is also used in the rest of the book. Textura was clearly seen as an appropriate script for the biblical text, but it may have been felt to be particularly appropriate for psalms: 15th-century Latin psalters were written exclusively in textura and on parchment in England.[47] Admittedly though the only manuscript written in Secretary and on paper in the present catalogue is New College MS 320, containing psalms, though it is also by far the latest in date (*c.*1500).

Patronage and ownership

The place of production

Very little is known about the medieval ownership, let alone original patronage of the manuscripts of WB. Only in a few cases do we know the owners' names from medieval inscriptions, whereas any information about the place of production or patronage is even rarer. Since so few manuscripts contain names, other sources of information about patronage need to be

47 See Solopova, E., *Latin liturgical psalters in the Bodleian Library: a select catalogue* (Oxford: Bodleian Library, 2013).

considered, such as liturgical evidence. The study of the calendars included in the manuscripts of WBs has produced some interesting results. The calendars are liturgically more diverse than the tables of lections. As mentioned earlier, the inventory of saints in the tables of Type I, that have an extensive sanctoral, was very stable and did not reflect local liturgical uses, whereas the sanctoral in the tables of Type II was short, included biblical and a few widely venerated saints, and also did not have regional features. In spite of the dominance of the use of Sarum in 15th-century England, the calendars found in WBs occasionally include local or institutional saints. MS Fairfax 11, for example, contains a calendar with non-Sarum features, suggesting that it may have been made for a patron connected to Hereford Cathedral.[48] It probably, however, was not made in Hereford, but in a London workshop where it was written by the same scribe and illuminated by the same artist as MS Bodl. 183 (see the description).

In several cases calendars suggest that the manuscripts were made for patrons in London. The calendar of MS Laud misc. 388 includes Erkenwald, bishop of London, a non-Sarum and characteristically London saint, whereas the calendar of MS Rawl. C. 259 includes notes in the original hand commemorating the arrival of the Black Death in London and the 'Grote Mandrenke' storm of 1362 that devastated southern and eastern England. Medieval and early modern additions in MS Laud misc. 388 suggest ownership in London. Added notes on a flyleaf draw attention to a passage describing the conversion of St Paul, whereas liturgical notes in Latin on fol. 210v mention the feasts of St Paul. In the 16th century the manuscript belonged to William Charke, a protestant scholar, preacher and writer who spent much of his career in London. The London origin of several illuminated WB, including MS Bodl. 277 in the present catalogue, is also suggested by art historical evidence.

Clerical owners

Earlier scholarship almost unanimously assumed that the audience of WB was primarily lay and that clerical ownership was an exception. This assumption was made on the basis of language, and perhaps also on the basis of polemical statements in the Wycliffite texts, such as the General Prologue to WB. The Prologue presents the translation as addressed to lay believers as evident in several contentious passages, such a much-cited assertion that '*þe [lewid] peple crie after holy writte to kunne it and kepe it wiþ greet cost and perel of her liyf*' (ll. 2797–9).[49] Idealisation of the

48 See Solopova (2013).

49 Dove (2010), p. 80.

poor, '*lewid*' and 'simple' is, however, generally characteristic of Lollard discourse and may be at least partly politically and ideologically motivated. In addition, the translators' original intentions, even if they were known, must be distinguished from the actual use of the translation in the late 14th and 15th centuries. The study of the manuscripts suggests that many Bibles were in clerical hands and many were probably made for clerical patrons. Medieval additions and modifications in the manuscripts point to the frequency of clerical ownership of WB. A luxurious complete Bible, MS Bodl. 277, for example, has an inscription asserting that it belonged to King Henry VI and was given by him to the London charterhouse. As demonstrated by Anne Hudson, numerous 15th-century additions suggest that the manuscript was used while in the possession of the charterhouse.[50] Some additions show that the text was compared to a Latin Bible, but the majority relate to Carthusian liturgy. Lections for various offices during the year are marked with notes stating the liturgical occasion when they were due to be read and similar notes are found in other Carthusian books.

MS Bodl. 531 is a Wycliffite NT, written in the first half of the 15th century. On its final page there is an elaborate legal note in English, written in a late 15th-century hand and signed '*By me Ryc(ardus) merton chanon*'. In this note a priest Richard Merton denies a charge against him for what is described as 'multiplying words' concerning the burning of a house of a certain Thomas Donsturfyld.[51] Two other manuscripts in Oxford collections have ownership inscriptions of members of religious orders (MS Bodl. 771 and MS Rawl. C. 258), and MS Bodl. 771 was probably made for a member of a religious community (see the description).

Two manuscripts in the present catalogue include extracts from Latin theological works. MS Bodl. 554, a psalter written early in the 15th century, contains at its end an added extract in Latin from a widely circulated treatise on liturgy by a 13th-century theologian John Beleth. An added Latin extract also occurs in MS Douce 265, a NT in LV, written in the second quarter of the 15th century. An originally blank leaf at the end of the book contains an extract from Heinrich Suso's *Horologium Sapientiae* in a 15th-century hand.

Perhaps the most common type of medieval additions in the manuscripts of WB not only in Oxford but generally, which suggests clerical ownership, are Latin liturgical annotations. They can be compared to Carthusian annotations in MS Bodl. 277 though in most manuscripts they are less

---

50 Hudson (2006).

51 See also Solopova (2013), pp. 345–6.

extensive and less systematic. In MS Gough Eccl. Top. 5 Mass readings are accompanied by added notes in Latin in a 15th-century hand, specifying a liturgical occasion. An originally blank flyleaf at the start of MS Laud misc. 25 contains the beginning of a table of lections in Latin added in a 15th-century hand. The table was designed to be used with this particular book because it contains only the readings from the gospels and omits the readings from other NT and OT books.

MS Rawl. C. 237/MS Rawl. C. 238 contains at the beginning an added, but probably near contemporary, liturgical calendar in English. The calendar was presumably unfinished: some months have very few feasts. The missing Sarum feasts, however, are supplied in a 15th-century hand that also provides references for lections. The added feasts include the Visitation (promulgated in 1481), Transfiguration (promulgated in 1457), and the deposition of St Osmund, bishop of Salisbury who was canonised in 1456. All this, together with the appearance of the script, suggests that the book was used and the calendar was updated fairly late in the 15th century. Mass lections in the text of the gospels in MS Rawl. C. 237/MS Rawl. C. 238 are occasionally accompanied by added notes specifying the liturgical occasion apparently in the same late 15th-century hand that updated the calendar. And finally a parchment flyleaf at the end of the manuscript contains a table of lections in English for a part of the temporal added almost certainly by the same late 15th-century owner.

Clerical patronage is also suggested by the high quality and complexity of liturgical materials circulated with WB and described above, some in Latin, and all requiring the knowledge of liturgy, biblical text and familiarity with academic practices of structuring and searching information. It is difficult not to conclude that such liturgical aids were designed for professional use and would have been superfluous even to educated laity.

Lollard owners

Several scholars have pointed out that the manuscripts of WB are overwhelmingly orthodox and only very rarely contain anything that can be described as Lollard. Many manuscripts, however, include annotations in the margins in medieval hands, that suggest an interest in Lollardy, or at least awareness of contemporary religious controversy. MS Laud misc. 388, for example, contains fragmentary theological or preacher's notes on a flyleaf (transcribed in the description). The notes list topics discussed in gospels and epistles with references to books and chapters of NT and were probably compiled using MS Laud misc. 388. About one-third down the list is a mention of twelve vices and virtues as occurring in chapter 5 of Galatians 'at d'. A passage listing the vices and virtues (Galatians 5:19–23) occurs on fol. 161r and is indeed marked with the indexing letter 'd'. The notes also draw attention to passages containing *Pater Noster*, and a version of 'Our Father' in Luke 11 has a gloss '*pater noster*' in the margin, almost certainly in the hand responsible for the notes.

Some notes suggest an interest in Lollard ideas. They draw attention to passages against beggars and the 'idle men that live of other men's labour'. At the end there is a reference to a passage starting '*Woe unto you, scribes and Pharisees, hypocrites!*' in Matthew 23. This passage was widely used in Lollard discourse and is, for example, the subject matter of a Lollard tract *Vae Octuplex*.[52]

MS Lyell 27 contains an added piece on the duties of a woman signed by Awstyn Fyschmonger and dated 1457. This inscription is well known and cited in several publications.[53] What has so far remained unnoticed, however, is that the manuscript contains added '*nota*' and short annotations in the margins, almost certainly in the same hand as the piece on the duties of a woman. Such marginal annotations draw attention to passages on chastity, drunkenness, temptation, women and marriage, but also mark passages of possibly Lollard interest on persecutions, Eucharist and ministry, including '*þe more schulde serue þe lasse*', '*I schal distrie þe wisdom of wise men*' and on Christ as the head of the church. The owner, presumably Awstyn Fishmonger, may have been also interested in the debate about the translation of the Bible. There are two notes marking passages on the teaching of faith in different languages and the use of languages in worship in 1 Corinthians 14. One of the passages reads:

> (15) I will pray with my spirit, but I will also pray with my understanding; I will sing with my spirit, but I will also sing with my understanding. (16) Otherwise when you are praising God in the Spirit, how can someone else, who is now put in the position of an inquirer, say 'Amen' to your thanksgiving, since they do not know what you are saying? (New International Version)

These two verses are cited in full in *First seiþ Bois* (ll. 55–8), a Lollard tract on the translation of the Bible, as well as in its source, Richard Ullerston's

52 Hudson and Gradon (1983–96), vol. 2, pp. 366–78.

53 Meale, C. M. and Boffey, J., 'Gentlewomen's reading', in Hellinga, L. and Trapp, J. B. (eds), *The Cambridge history of the book in Britain*, vol. 3, *1400–1557* (Cambridge: Cambridge University Press, 1999), p. 526 and n. 1; De la Mare, A. C., *Catalogue of the collection of medieval manuscripts bequeathed to the Bodleian Library, Oxford by James P. R. Lyell* (Oxford: Clarendon Press, 1971), p. 58.

university *determinacio*.[54] The same interest in language is suggested by '*nota*' at 2 Corinthians 3:6 ('...*god which also maad vs able mynistris of þe new testament not bi lettre but be spirit*').

A 15th-century owner of MS Rawl. C. 237/MS Rawl. C. 238, almost certainly a clergyman, who updated its calendar (discussed above), is probably also responsible for marking a passage on Pharisees on fol. 100r: '*But wo to ȝou farisees þat tiþen mynte and ruwe & eche erbe & leuen doom & þe charite of god*' (Luke 11:42–3). Corpus Christi College MS 4 has multiple glosses '*of images*' and '*of idols*' added in a medieval hand and drawing attention to passages throughout the OT.

Such annotations, sometimes nothing more than pointing hands, marking passages on the poor, priesthood, Pharisees, Eucharist, corruption in the church, the use of images in worship, the use of languages in preaching, women and preaching and other, some made famous through their use by late 14th- and 15th-century writers within the context of political and religious debate, are extremely common in manuscripts of WB and deserve further study.

Conclusions

The manuscripts of WB vary in size and include portable copies as well as large-format volumes that may have been intended for use on a lectern, perhaps in private chapels. Most, though not all, are professionally and sometimes luxuriously executed, and do not look like 'illegal' productions. Several are known to have belonged to kings and members of the nobility, and many, as demonstrated by the present investigation, were used by the clergy. All this suggests that in spite of censorship in the late 14th and 15th centuries there was a scope for the legitimate production of vernacular biblical texts by the mainstream book trade in London and elsewhere, and for their sophisticated use not only by the laity, but also and perhaps predominantly by the clergy and within the religious institutions.

This investigation also suggests that not only the biblical text itself but also many features of its manuscript presentation may go back to the original translators. This is likely to include its liturgical apparatus, highly innovative, omnipresent and found already in the earliest manuscripts, but also the practice of underlining added material within the biblical text, rubrics whose wording has parallels in the General Prologue, the practices of correction and possibly other features. The manuscript tradition of WB emerges as clearly defined in ways similar to other late medieval

---

54 Dove (2010), pp. 145, 215.

religious and secular 'best-sellers'. Its identity is not confined to its text but embraces the many aspects of its execution in the manuscripts which the patrons presumably expected and the makers felt compelled to maintain. Standardisation, particularly characteristic of the manuscripts of LV, is evident in their liturgical and scholarly apparatus, decoration, language, the use of parchment, layout and script.

2

The form of entries

The manuscripts are listed by repository and shelfmark. The opening part of each entry consists of the shelfmark; sigla assigned to the manuscripts in Forshall and Madden (1850) and, if different, in Dove (2007); the *Summary catalogue* number for manuscripts in the Bodleian Library; and the identification of the place of origin and date. The body of the catalogue entries is divided into seven main sections: Text, Decoration, Dialect, Physical description, Binding, Provenance and Bibliography, each briefly explained below.

Text

The textual contents of each volume are presented as a numbered list. In the descriptions of the biblical text only deviations are recorded from the standard inventory and order of books and prologues in the Earlier and Later versions, given in Appendix I. Several descriptions include a transcription of all rubrics that appear at the beginnings of biblical books and prologues to illustrate this feature. The descriptions of the biblical text always note the presence and form of the chapter numbers, rubrics, running titles, marginal glosses and added material within the text, corrections and original or added notes in the margins. The indexing letters and double strokes in the margins, as well as any other indications of the beginning and end of Mass lections, such as rubrics or the use of red and yellow wash, are also described.

Quotations from manuscripts preserve the original spelling and capitalisation, except that a majuscule letter after a large initial is rendered as minuscule. The word division is normalised, except for inscriptions on the bindings and ownership inscriptions. Most abbreviations are expanded silently, though some are expanded within round brackets, if a more diplomatic transcription is desirable. A double vertical bar '||' indicates line breaks in lettering on bindings. In transcription of Middle English texts, special characters are used to represent thorn (þ) and yogh (ʒ). In psalms the Vulgate numbering is used throughout. Verse numbers in the biblical text correspond to those in Forshall and Madden's edition (1850) and not necessarily to the variable verse division in manuscripts.

Where textual boundaries correspond to physical divisions between the quires, this is noted in square brackets on a separate line. The descriptions of composite manuscripts follow the same pattern as elsewhere, but textual contents, decoration, dialect, script, ruling and other features of composite parts are described separately within each section.

Decoration

The illumination is described hierarchically, starting with larger initials and borders at the beginnings of texts and biblical books, and proceeding to minor initials at the beginnings of prologues, chapters and verses.

Dialect

This section describes the dialect of continuous biblical text, but not of other texts, such as para-biblical or non-biblical materials. When *Oon of Foure* takes the role of the biblical text and no other continuous biblical text is present, the dialect of *Oon of Foure* is described. An attempt is always made to describe the language within a stint of a single scribe, though it should be noted that textura, the script used in most copies, has few individual features and it can be very difficult to determine where the stint of one scribe ends and of another begins. The dialect is described by means of a questionnaire that aims to record the spellings of ten occurrences of the following words and grammatical forms:

> any, each, fire, given, life, like, much, saw (the past tense of 'see' with singular and plural forms listed separately), self, such, though, through;
>
> present indicative 3rd person singular, present indicative plural, present participle, 3rd person singular feminine pronoun in the nominative (she), 3rd person plural pronoun in the nominative (they), 3rd person plural pronoun in the oblique (them), 3rd person plural possessive (their).

The words and forms were chosen to test M. L. Samuels' hypothesis that the language of WB is a result of standardisation that took place in Middle

English in the 15th century.[55] Samuels termed this language the Central Midland Standard and wrote that it is found in 'the majority of Wycliffite manuscripts' though not limited to them and present in other religious, medical and scientific works.[56] Samuels believed that the 'commonest variety' of this language is attested in 'practically all copies of the later version of the Lollard Bible, and most copies of the earlier version'.[57] He linked its wide dissemination with the Lollard movement and wrote that the Lollards adopted it and were, 'a powerful influence in spreading it, in their bibles, sermons and tracts'.[58] Samules singled out seven forms that in his view were usual for the Central Midland Standard: sich ('such'), mych ('much'), ony ('any'), silf ('self'), stide ('stead'), ȝouun ('given') and siȝ ('saw). In a later article on the language of MS Bodl. 959 (Samuels (1969)) he added the doubling of vowels (ij) as another diagnostic feature, e.g. lijf ('life'), lijc ('like'), fijr ('fire'), as well as such spellings as þoru/þorou(ȝ) ('through'). These forms were used as diagnostic by other scholars who studied the language of the Wycliffite texts. In an article, 'The Wycliffite Bible and "Central Midland Standard": assessing the manuscript evidence', Matti Peikola presented the results of an examination of orthography in 68 scribal hands found in manuscripts containing Matthew's gospel in LV.[59] He surveyed the spelling of words chosen by Samuels in predetermined locations in the gospel. Anne Hudson, in a discussion of three widely circulated works, WB, the English Wycliffite Sermon Cycle and the first two Wycliffite revisions of Richard Rolle's *English Psalter Commentary*, examined the occurrences of Samuels' seven original diagnostic words, as well as a further five words (liif, liik, ech, þouȝ and þrouȝ), in the manuscripts of the Sermon Cycle and *Psalter Commentary*.[60] The words chosen for linguistic profiles in the present catalogue include most of those used by Samuels and these scholars. Grammatical forms of verbs and pronouns are those particularly variable in Middle English texts and recognised as valuable for a broad identification of the texts' dialect affiliations and the place of origin.[61] The analysis of

[55] Samuels, M. L., 'Some applications of Middle English dialectology', *English Studies* 44 (1963), pp. 81–94, reprinted in McIntosh, A., Samuels, M. L. and Laing, M. (eds), *Middle English dialectology: essays on some principles and problems* (Aberdeen, 1989), pp. 64–80.

[56] Samuels (1963), p. 67.

[57] Samuels (1963), p. 79 n. 5.

[58] Samuels (1963), p. 67.

[59] Peikola (2003).

[60] Anne Hudson, 'Observations on the "Wycliffite Orthography"' (forthcoming).

[61] See, for example, Fulk, R. D., *An introduction to Middle English* (Peterborough, Ont. and London: Broadview Press, 2012), pp. 120–8.

the profiles is outside the scope of this catalogue and will be presented in my article on the dialect of WB in *The Wycliffite Bible: Origin, History and Interpretation*, ed. E. Solopova (forthcoming).

When the words and forms were recorded, abbreviation for the final -n (a macron above a vowel) was silently expanded and not distinguished from -n fully written out. The number of occurrences of each spelling is indicated in brackets. In some cases, it was not possible to find ten examples of all words, because the biblical text is incomplete or subdivided into short scribal stints. Normally only one profile per manuscript is provided, but the descriptions of several early or important manuscripts include profiles for each scribe or textual part.

Physical description

The physical description is arranged under subheadings in the following order:

1. Material: parchment of unexceptional quality and weight, unless otherwise stated; parchment or paper flyleaves; materials used to repair leaves and gatherings.

2. Dimensions of leaves given in millimetres, height before width, sometimes in the form of a range (e.g., 350–355 × 200 mm).

3. Total number of leaves or pages.

4. Foliation: the actual numbering of leaves or pages in the manuscript, with an indication of medium and date. If more than one foliation or pagination is present, all are described.

5. Collation expressed as a formula where folio or page numbers of a quire are given first in round brackets. This is followed by the quire number in Roman numerals and, in round brackets, by the number of leaves in a quire and an indication of the number of leaves added (+) or removed (-). This may be further followed by relevant comments, including a statement of the position of added or excised leaves in a quire. Vertical bars indicate a change in the structure of quires. The presence of catchwords, and quire and leaf signatures is also recorded in this section.

6. Ruling: the ruling pattern; the number of written lines per page; the dimensions of the written space; the presence of prickings.

7. Script: brief characterisation of the style of writing and the colour of ink. If the original text, rather than additions, is the work of more than one scribe, this is noted in this section.

8. Rubrication: the presence of headings in a colour or script different from the main text.

9. 'Sec. Fol.' is used as an abbreviation for *secundo folio*, or the opening words on the second leaf of the manuscript, recorded to assist the identification of manuscripts described in medieval and early modern catalogues and inventories. If a manuscript begins with a table of lections, 'Sec. Fol.' records the words at the beginning of the second leaf of the table of lections as well as at the beginning of the second leaf of the following text. The quotation is always followed by a folio number and, if more than one *secundo folio* is cited, an identification of the text where the words occur.

Binding

This section describes the material of the boards, their covering material, decoration, flyleaves and any labels and lettering on the spine or the covers. The date and origin of the binding are identified whenever possible.

Provenance

The first numbered paragraph of this section includes the information relevant to the date, place and original patronage of each manuscript. The paragraphs which follow provide the information in chronological order about all known ownership and use of the manuscript.

Bibliography

Select bibliography is presented in chronological order. Where there is more than one work published in the same year, the entries are arranged in alphabetical order of authors' surnames. Full details of frequently cited works can be found in 'Abbreviations'.

3

The catalogue

1 MS Ashmole 1517

Origin: England

Date: 15th century, first quarter

Paper leaves containing a list of passages missing from the lectionary, gospels and epistles (see below) and their transcripts from some other manuscript in Elias Ashmole's hand. The leaves are pasted to the second paper flyleaf at the beginning and paginated 1–23 in the original hand and 1–27 in a modern hand.

Text

[item 1 occupies quire I]

1. (fols. 1r–5v) Table of lections, imperfect at the beginning because of the loss of one leaf, starting at Wednesday of the second week after the octave of Epiphany. Includes the temporal and commemorations only, which suggests that the table may have been originally preceded by a calendar-lectionary (see MS Selden Supra 51 and 'Liturgical materials' in the Introduction). The entries consist of the name of the liturgical occasion in red, abbreviated reference to a book and chapter of the Bible, an indexing letter in red, the opening words of a reading, '*ende*' in red, the closing words of a reading and double strokes in red. The entries for OT readings are also accompanied by letters and numbers in the margins in red, used to identify the readings in the OT lectionary (see below). Larger initials with penwork at Ash Wednesday and Ascension. Commemorations are in the following order: Our Lady, Trinity, Holy Ghost, cross, angels, *salus populi*, brothers and sisters, peace, clear weather, rain, in time of battles, '*a priest for hym silf*', pestilence of beasts, pilgrims, sinners, sick, dead and weddings. At the

end: '*þe lokeris in þis kalender be riȝt wel war: for he shal not fynde alle þe bigynnyngis of þe lessuns of þe olde lawe acorde wiþ þe kalender for bi ordyaunce of þe chirche: þer is sett to þe bigynnyngis of many lessuns more & oþer wyse þan it is in þe bible & þat is drawun vndir wiþ a stryk of reed ynke & it is not in þe kalender. for it is not so in þe text & also it is in þe same maner of manye of þe endingis of þo lessuns*'.

[item 2 occupies quires II–XXI]
2. (fols. 6r–165v) Matthew 2:5–Jude 2:23 in LV. Imperfect at the beginning and end because of the loss of leaves. Also missing are the end of Matthew (after 27:62) and the beginning of Mark (before 1:11); the end of Mark (after 16:9) and the beginning of Luke (before 1:30); the end of Luke (after 24:51) and the beginning of John (before 1:19); the beginning of Romans (before 2:13). The leaves at the start of books were undoubtedly removed because of the illumination they contained: at the beginning of Mark and Luke there are fragments of leaves with illuminated borders, and there are offsets of illumination on fol. 27r (the beginning of Mark) and fol. 64r (the beginning of John) which used to face the missing leaves. All prologues to the gospels are missing, otherwise usual prologues. Running titles in black preceded by blue paraphs on both rectos and versos, consisting of abbreviated titles of biblical books. Usual rubrics in red; chapter numbers as red Roman numerals or words. Blue paraphs at the start of sections within the text. Indexing letters in the margins entered at the start of lections, rather than consistently; double strokes at the ends of lections. Many drawings of hands pointing at the text in the margins, including some marking passages of possibly Lollard interest, such as Matthew 23:14. Corrections in the original or contemporary hands; longer omitted passages are added in the margins often enclosed in decorative frames embellished with penwork. Alternative translations (e.g., fols. 24r, 52v, 64v, etc.) are occasionally written out in the margins. Added material within the text is underlined in red in the epistles.

[item 3 occupies quires XXII–XXV]
3. (fols. 166r–192r) OT lectionary of Type II (**Plate 1**) imperfect at the beginning because of the loss of one leaf. Includes readings for the temporal, commemorations, proper and common. Only the first four readings for commemorations and the last three readings for the proper are preserved, because of a missing quire after fol. 187. The readings are preceded by rubrics in red, introductory statements (e.g., '*The lord seiþ þes þingis*', fol. 166r) underlined in red, and numbers. The lectionary is subdivided into five sections marked with letters A, B, C, D, E in the upper margin. References for OT readings in the table of lections (fols. 1r–5v) are accompanied by

letters and numbers, e.g., a1, a2, a3, etc., identifying the section where each reading occurs and its number within the section (a similar system is used in the calendar-lectionary and OT lectionary of MS Selden Supra 51). Added material within the text is underlined in red.

Decoration

The gospels and the Epistle to the Romans originally had illuminated borders at the beginnings, now all missing (see Text).

4- to 6-line red and blue 'puzzle' initials with red and purple penwork at the beginnings of 1 Corinthians–Jude.

3-line blue initials with red penwork at the beginnings of chapters and prologues.

Dialect

any(10), eche(6)/ech(4), fyre(10), gouun(10), lif(10), like(5)/lyk(2)/lyke(2)/lik(1), myche(1)/miche(9), saw(8) (sg.), sawen(6) (pl.), self(10), sich(2)/siche(7), þouȝ(8), þorow(7)/þorou(3)

-iþ(9)/-eþ(1) (pres.ind.3sg.), -en(10) (pres.ind.pl.), -inge(2)/-ing(1)/-ynge(7) (pres.part.), she(10) (3sg.fem.pronoun, nom.), þei(10) (3pl.pronoun, nom.), hem(10) (3pl.pronoun, oblique), her(10) (3pl.pronoun, possessive)

Physical description

MATERIAL: parchment; paper flyleaves

DIMENSIONS: *c.*280 × 205 mm

NUMBER OF LEAVES: 193

FOLIATION: modern in pencil: 1–40 + 40* + 41–192; 17 unnumbered paper flyleaves at the beginning and 9 at the end

COLLATION: 17 unnumbered paper flyleaves; 14 paper leaves, containing a transcript, pasted to the second flyleaf | (fols. 1–5) I (6–1) missing 1, only a stub remains with fragments of text | (fols. 6–12) II (8–1) missing 1 | (fols. 13–20) III (8) | (fols. 21–27) IV (8–1) missing 7 | (fols. 28–35) V (8) | (fols. 36–42) VI (8) 6 is fragmentary | (fols. 43–58) VII–VIII (8) | (fols. 59–65) IX (8–1) missing 6 | (fols. 66–73) X (8) | (fols. 74–80) XI (8–1) missing 8 | (fols. 81–160) XII–XXI (8) | (fols. 161–165) XXII (8–3) missing 6–8, and possibly originally followed by quires that contained the Apocalypse, now missing | (fols. 166–172) XXIII (8–1) missing 1 | (fols. 173–188) XXIV–XXV (8) | missing quire | (fols. 189–192) XXVI (4)

Catchwords survive; quire signatures survive and run consecutively a–x on fols. 6–165. A new series, less well preserved, starts on fol. 166, at the beginning of OT lectionary.

RULING: ruled for two columns with single vertical and single horizontal (on most leaves visible only at the top of the page) bounding lines extending the full height and width of page; 39 lines per page; written space: *c.*139 × 197 mm

SCRIPT: at least two different scribes, one responsible for NT, writing large, even, upright, highly professional textura; the second responsible for the table of lections and OT lectionary, writing a more informal textura; black and brown ink

RUBRICATION: rubrics in red; blue paraphs at the start of sections within the text

SEC. FOL.: '*mondai gospel*' (fol. 2r, table of lections); '*hym all þese*' (fol. 7r, gospel)

Binding

Light brown leather over pasteboard, late 17th or early 18th century. Double blind fillet lines round the outer edge and *c.*35 mm away from the spine on both covers. Geometric design on the edges of covers. Rebacked in the Bodleian: 'W 5 – 12 – 59' written in pencil on the lower pastedown. Five raised bands edged by double blind fillet lines on spine. Gilt lettering on spine: 'Ash. || 1517'. Laid paper flyleaves with watermarks, perhaps contemporary with the binding.

Provenance

1. Originally the manuscript may have contained a calendar-lectionary at the beginning and a complete NT. The OT lectionary is similar to that in MS Selden Supra 51.

2. '*john m(?)[…]th*' (fol. 64r), possibly a reference to a missing beginning of St John's gospel, 16th century (?).

3. '*Edmu[n]d peyson*', 16th century (fol. 143r).

4. Flourished 'I' with the letters T, H, R, A, V written inside it, 16th century (fol. 192r).

5. Pen trials and names in several 16th-century hands, including: '*Hary Danyell of sancte martyns farmar vnto John Gylbard of London*'; '*wyllym storky, dunston chaypman*', '*william breges*' (fol. 192v).

6. Elias Ashmole (1617–1692), see *ODNB*: transcript of missing passages (see Text); autograph on fol. 1r.

7. Ashmolean Museum, Oxford: donated by Ashmole to Oxford University in 1677.

8. Bodleian Library: transferred from the Ashmolean Museum in 1860.

Bibliography

Black, W. H., *A descriptive, analytical, and critical catalogue of the manuscripts bequeathed unto the University of Oxford by Elias Ashmole, Esq., M.D., F.R.S., Windsor Herald, also of some additional MSS. contributed by Kingsley, Lhuyd, Borlase, and others* (Oxford, 1845), no. 1517.
Forshall and Madden (1850), vol. 1, p. li.
Ogilvie-Thomson, S. J., *IMEP*, Handlist VIII (1991), p. 15.
Eldredge, L. M., *IMEP*, Handlist IX (1992), p. 108.
Scott (2000–02), vol. 1, p. 44, no. 83.
Dove (2007), p. 299.

2 MS Bodl. 183

Sigla: a – Tobit to Ecclesiasticus; *L* – prologues from Tobit to Wisdom

Origin: England

Date: 15th century, first quarter

Text

Fols. i–v are blank paper and parchment flyleaves.

[item 1 occupies quire II]
1. (fols. vi recto-xv verso) Table of lections of Type I preceded by a rubric: '*Here bigynneþ a rule þat telliþ in whiche placis of þis book ȝe schulen fynde þe lessouns pistlis & gospels þat ben rad in þe chirche aftir þe vse of Salisbury markid wiþ lettris of þe abc þe bigynnyngis & þe eendyngis with twei strikis first is sett þe sonedaies & ferials & after þe sanctorum comoun & propre writen a clause of þe bigynnyng þerof & a clause of þe eending also*'. Includes the temporal, commemorations and the sanctoral, both the proper and common according to the rubric, but only the proper is present. The entries consist of the name of a liturgical occasion in red, abbreviated reference to a book and chapter of the Bible, an indexing letter in red, the opening words of a reading, '*ende*' in red, the closing words of a reading and double

strokes. Larger initials with penwork at Christmas, Easter, Pentecost, Trinity and Candlemas. The table was apparently produced from an exemplar that had a full set of OT and NT readings, but OT readings were removed from the temporal, and only those from books included in MS Bodl. 183 were retained in the commemorations and the sanctoral. '*Osee*', erroneously entered at Friday, 17th week after Trinity (fol. x recto), suggests that the exemplar had not only NT but also OT readings (see Solopova (2013), pp. 338–40). Includes all feasts characteristic of the LV apart from Giles (1 September) (Forshall and Madden (1850), vol. 4, pp. 683, 690–6). Commemorations are in the following order: the Virgin Mary, Trinity, Holy Ghost, Cross, angels, '*ffor briþeren & sistren & salus populi*', peace, clear weather, reyn, '*In time of batels*', '*A man for him silf*', '*ffor pestilence of bestis*', pilgrims, weddings, sinners, sick, '*Pistils for dede*', '*Gospels for dede*'. At the end: '*Thus eendiþ þe kalender of lessouns pistlis & gospels*'.

2. (fols. 1r–284r) NT and part of OT (**Plate 2**), three biographies and sapiential books, in LV; OT books, except Tobit, have prologues in EV (slightly revised) (Dove (2007), p. 298). Chapter numbers in red as words in English or as Roman numerals, usually in the form '*þe i c°*', preceding each chapter. Running titles on both rectos and versos consisting of an abbreviated title of a biblical book in red preceded by a blue paraph and a chapter number on pages containing the beginnings of chapters. Indexing letters and double strokes in the margins inside the bounding lines framing each page. The indexing letters are entered at the beginnings of lections only rather than consistently; the beginnings and ends of lections are also highlighted with yellow wash. Added material within the text is underlined in red in the OT only. Contains corrections throughout presumably made in the original workshop. On fols. 82v, 173v, 192v and 212v the artist, who added the border, worked around corrections and glosses in the margins. Notes '*fro þis*' and '*hidirto*' in a medieval hand in the margins, marking passages in the Song of Song (fols. 237v–239r) and Ecclesiastes (fol. 260v), apparently added in the original workshop (the sign used to indicate the start and end of passages is also used to link glosses to the text on fol. 212v).

[NT occupies quires III–XXIII]
(fol. 1r) Prologue to Matthew ('*Matheu þat was of iude…*'). Rubric: '*Here bigynneþ þe prolog of matheu*'.

(fol. 1r) Matthew. Rubric: '*Ierom on hise two prologis on Matheu seiþ þis plainly þe firste c°*'.

(fol. 23v) Prologue to Mark ('*Mark þe gospeller was þe chosen seruaunt…*'). Rubric: '*Here eendiþ þe gospel on matheu & bigynneþ þe prolog on Mark*'.

(fol. 24r) Mark. Rubric: '*þis seiþ Ierom in his prolog on mark And here bigynneþ þe i c°*'.

(fol. 39r) Prologue to Luke ('*Luk was a man of sirie…*'). Rubric: '*Here eendiþ þe gospel of Mark & Here bigynneþ þe prolog on Luyk*'.

(fol. 39r) Luke. Rubric: '*Ierom in his prolog on luk seiþ plainli þis sentence þe firste c°*'.

(fol. 64r) Prologue to John ('*This is Joon euangelist…*'). Rubric: '*Here eendiþ þe gospel of luk & bigynneþ þe prolog on Ioon*'.

(fol. 64v) John. Rubric: '*Ierom in his prolog on Iohn seiþ al þis sentence And here bigynneþ þe gospel of Ioon þis þe firste chapitre*'. At the end '*Here endiþ þe gospel of Ioon*'.

(fol. 82v) Prologue to Romans ('*Romayns ben in þe cuntre…*'). Rubric: '*Here bigynneþ þe prolog to fore þe pistil to romayns*'.

(fol. 82v) Romans. Rubric: '*Ierom seiþ þis in his prolog to Romayns þe firste chapitre*'. Chapters 11–16 are imperfect because the lower part of fols. 89–92 is cut off.

(fol. 92v) Prologue to 1 Corinthians ('*Corynthies ben…*'). Rubric: '*Here eendiþ þe pistil of romayns & bigynneþ þe prolog to þe firste Corenthies*'.

(fol. 92v) 1 Corinthians. Rubric: '*…in his prolog on þe firste pistil to Corinthies the firste chapitre*'. The beginning of the rubric and parts of the text of the prologue and chapters 1–3 are missing because the lower part of fols. 92–93 is cut off.

(fol. 102r) Prologue to 2 Corinthians ('*Afftir penaunce…*'). Rubric: '*Here eendiþ þe firste pistil to Corinthies & here bigynneþ þe prolog on þe secunde piste* [sic] *to Corinthies*'.

(fol. 102v) 2 Corinthians. Rubric: '*Ierom in his prolog on þis epistil seiþ þis þe firste chapitre*'.

(fol. 108v) Prologue to Galatians ('*Galathies ben grekis…*'). Rubric: '*Here eendiþ þe secunde pistil to Corinthies & biginneþ þe prolog to Galathies*'.

(fol. 108v) Galatians. Rubric: '*Ierom in his prolog to galathies writiþ þus þe firste c°*'.

(fol. 111v) Prologue to Ephesians ('*Effesians ben of asie…*'). Rubric: '*Here eendiþ þe pistil to galaþies & biginneþ þe prolog on þe pistil to effeses*'.

(fol. 111v) Ephesians. Rubric: '*Ierom in his prolog on þis pistil seiþ þis þe i c°*'.

(fol. 115r) Prologue to Philippians (‘*Filipencis ben of macedonye…*’). Rubric: ‘*Here eendiþ þe pistil to effecies & bigynneþ þe prolog to þe pistlil of filipencis*’.

(fol. 115r) Philippians. Rubric: ‘*Ierom in his prolog on þis pistil seiþ al þis The firste chapitre*’.

(fol. 117v) Prologue to Colossians (‘*Colosencis ben also laodisencis…*’). Rubric: ‘*Here eendiþ þe pistil to filipensis & bigynneþ þe prolog on þe pistil to colosences*’.

(fol. 117v) Colossians. Rubric: ‘*Ierom in his prolog on þis pistil seiþ þis þe firste c^o*’.

(fol. 119v) Prologue to 1 Thessalonians (‘*Tessalonicensis ben Macedonies…*’). Rubric: ‘*Here eendiþ þe pistil to Colocensis & bigynneþ þe prolog on þe firste pistil to Tessalonycensis*’.

(fol. 119v) 1 Thessalonians. Rubric: ‘*Ierom in his prolog on þis pistil seiþ þis And here bigynneþ þe firste c^o*’.

(fol. 122r) Prologue to 2 Thessalonians (‘*The apostil wrytiþ…*’). Rubric: ‘*Here endiþ þe firste pistil to tessalonisencis and bigynneþ þe prolog to þe secunde pistil to tessalonysencis*’.

(fol. 122r) 2 Thessalonians. Rubric: ‘*Ierom in his prolog on þis pistil seiþ þis þe i c^o*’.

(fol. 123r) Prologue to 1 Timothy (‘*He enfoormeþ and techiþ …*’). Rubric: ‘*Here eendiþ þe secunde pistil to tessalonysencis & bigynneþ þe prolog on þe firste pistil to tymoþe*’.

(fol. 123r) 1 Timothy. Rubric: ‘*Ierom in his prolog on þis pistil seiþ þis The firste chapitre*’.

(fol. 126r) Prologue to 2 Timothy (‘*He writith also…*’). Rubric: ‘*Here eendiþ þe firste pistil to Tymoþe & bigynneþ þe prolog on þe secunde pistil to Timoþe*’.

(fol. 126r) 2 Timothy. Rubric: ‘*Ierom in his prolog on þis pistil seiþ þis þe firste c^o*’.

(fol. 128r) Prologue to Titus (‘*He warneþ tite…*’). Rubric: ‘*Here eendiþ þe secunde pistil to tymoþe & bigynneþ þe prolog on þe pistil to Tite*’.

(fol. 128r) Titus. Rubric: ‘*Ierom in his prolog on þis pistil seiþ þis Here bigynneþ þe firste chapitre*’.

(fol. 129r) Prologue to Philemon (‘*He makiþ famyliar…*’). Rubric: ‘*Here eendiþ þe pistil to tyte & here bygynneþ the prolog on þe pistil to ffilemon*’.

(fol. 129r) Philemon. Rubric: '*Ierom in his prolog on þis pistil seiþ þis þe firste chapitre*'.

(fol. 129v) Prologue to Hebrews ('*First it is to seie…*'). Rubric: '*Here eendiþ the pistil to filemon & bigynneþ þe prolog on þe pistil to Ebrews*'.

(fol. 130r) Hebrews. Rubric: '*Ierom in his prolog on þis pistil seiþ þis Here bigynneþ þe firste chapitre*'.

(fol. 137r) Prologue to Acts ('*Luk of antioche…*'). Rubric: '*Here eendiþ þe pistil to Ebrews And bigynneþ þe prolog on þe dedis of apostlis*'.

(fol. 137v) Acts. Rubric: '*Ierom in his prolog seiþ þis þe firste chapitre*'.

(fol. 162r) The Catholic epistles. Prologue to James ('*The ordre of þe seuene epistlis…*'). Rubric: '*Here eendiþ þe deedis of apostlis And here bigynneþ þe prolog on þe pistlis of cristen feiþ þat ben seuene in ordre*'.

(fol. 162r) James. Rubric: '*Ierom in his prolog on þis pistil seiþ al þis Here bigynneþ þe pistil of Iames þe firste chapitre*'. The text of chapters 4–5 is slightly imperfect because the lower part of fol. 164 is cut off.

(fol. 164v) 1 Peter. Rubric: '*Here eendiþ þe pistil of Iames And here bigynneþ þe firste pistil of petir þe firste c^o^*'. Slightly imperfect because the lower part of fols. 164–166 is cut off.

(fol. 167r) 2 Peter. Rubric: '*Here endiþ þe firste pistil of petir & here bigynneþ þe secunde þe i c^o^*'.

(fol. 169r) 1 John. Rubric: '*Here eendiþ þe secunde epistil of petir & here bigynneþ þe firste pistil of Ioon þe firste c^o^*'.

(fol. 171r) 2 John. Rubric: '*Here eendiþ þe firste pistil of Ioon & bigyngynneþ* [sic] *þe secunde þe firste c^o^*'.

(fol. 171v) 3 John. Rubric: '*Here eendiþ þe secunde pistil of Ioon & here bigynne þe þridde þe firste chapitre*'.

(fol. 172r) Jude. Rubric: '*Here eendiþ þe iii pistil of Ioon & here bigynneþ þe pistil of iudas þe i c^o^*'.

(fol. 172v) Prologue to Apocalypse ('*Alle men þat wole …*'). Rubric: '*Here eendiþ þe pistil of Iudas & here bigynneþ a prolog on apocalips*'.

(fol. 173v) Apocalypse. Rubric: '*Here endiþ þe prolog on þe apocalips þe firste chapitre*'. At the end: '*Here eendiþ þe apocalips of Ioon*'. Fol. 184 is ruled but blank.

[OT occupies quires XXIV–XXXVI]
(fol. 185r) Tobit. Rubric: '*Here bigynneþ tobie þe firste c^o*'.

(fol. 192r) Prologue to Judith ('*Anentis þe ebrews…*'). Rubric: '*Here eendiþ tobie And here bigynneþ þe prolog on iudith*'.

(fol. 192v) Judith. Rubric: '*Here eendiþ þe prolog of iudith & bigynneþ þe book of hir þe firste c^o*'.

(fol. 201v) Prologue to Esther '*Here endiþ þe book of iudith Here bigynneþ þe prolog on þe book of hester*'.

(fol. 202r) Esther. Rubric: '*Here eendiþ þe prolog of hester & bigynneþ &* [sic] *i c^o*'. Usual notes on the differences between the Hebrew and Latin texts in red in chapters X–XV.

(fol. 212r) Prologue to Proverbs ('*Ierom sendiþ greetinge to Cromacie…*'). Rubric: '*Here endiþ þe book of hester Here bigynneth þe prolog on þe parablis of salamon*'.

(fol. 212v) Proverbs. Rubric: '*Here eendiþ þe prolog & bigynneþ þe firste c^o*'. Glosses in the original hand on fols. 212v–213r.

(fol. 230v) Prologue to Ecclesiastes ('*Þis almoost þe fifþe…*'). Rubric: '*Here eendiþ þe parablis & bigynneþ þe prolog on ecclesiates*'.

(fol. 231r) Ecclesiastes. Rubric: '*Here eendiþ þe prolog & bigynneþ þe firste chapitre*'.

(fol. 236v) Song of Songs. Rubric: '*Her eendiþ ecclesiates & biginneþ song of songis þe i c^o*'.

(fol. 239v) Prologue to Wisdom. Rubric: '*Here eendiþ cantica canticorum & biginneþ þe prolog on sapiens*'.

(fol. 239v) Wisdom. Rubric: '*Here eendiþ þe prolog & bigynneþ sapiens i chap^o*'.

(fol. 252r) Ecclesiasticus. Rubric: '*Here eendiþ þe book of wisdom & here biginneþ þe book of ecclesiastici & biginneþ þe firste c^o*'. At the end: '*Here endiþ ecclesiasticus*'. Fol. 284v is ruled but blank.

3. (fols. 285r–286v) Fol. 285r–v is blank. Fol. 286r contains an added list of contents of the manuscript in Latin, in a late 15th-century hand, including the table of lections, NT (omitting Philemon) and OT books. At the beginning: '*In isto libro continentur omnia subscripta*'.

Decoration

Possibly decorated by the same artist as MS Fairfax 11 (de Hamel (2001), p. 178).

5- to 8-line initials on gold background and full or three-quarters borders made of pink, blue and gold bars decorated with floral designs, interlace and gold disks at the beginnings of books.

3-line gold initials on pink and blue background at the beginnings of prologues.

2- to 3-line red or blue initials with contrasting blue or red penwork at the beginnings of chapters.

Catchwords are decorated with drawings of animals, grotesques and human heads in black and red ink and yellow wash, including Christ's head (fols. 8v, 48v), crowned head (fol. 256v) and a head in a triple tiara (fol. 272v). Running titles are also occasionally decorated with similar designs.

Dialect

ony(10), ech(10), fier(10), ȝouen(10), lijf(10), lijk(10), myche(10), say(6)/sai(3) (sg.), saien(5)/siȝen(1) (pl.), silf(10), siche(6)/sich(2)/suche(2), þouȝ(8), þoru(9)/þoruȝ(1)

-iþ(9)/-eþ(1) (pres.ind.3sg.), -en(10) (pres.ind.pl.), -ynge(5)/-inge(5) (pres. part.), sche(10) (3sg.fem.pronoun, nom.), þei(10) (3pl.pronoun, nom.), hem(10) (3pl.pronoun, oblique), her(10) (3pl.pronoun, possessive)

Physical description

MATERIAL: parchment, paper flyleaves; the lower part of leaves cut off in quires XII (fols. 89–96) and XX (fols. 161–168), and damaged in quires XIV–XV (fols. 105–120)

DIMENSIONS: *c.*292 × 194 mm, originally possibly identical to Fairfax 11; leaves were trimmed in rebinding, occasionally causing the loss of decoration in the margins

NUMBER OF LEAVES: 302

FOLIATION: modern in pencil (flyleaves and the table of lections) and ink (the rest): i–xv + 1–287

COLLATION: (fol. i) paper flyleaf conjoint with the upper pastedown | (fols. ii–v) I (4) | (fols. vi–xv) II (10) | (fols. 1–280) I–XXXV (8) | (fols. 281–284) XXXVI (4) | (fols. 285–286) XXXVII (2) | (fol. 287) paper flyleaf conjoint with the lower pastedown

Quire I (table of lections) has a signature 'a'; quires containing NT (fols. 1–184) have signatures 'a–z'; and quires containing OT (fols. 185–284) have signatures 'a–n'. The last empty page of NT has an offset of decoration not found on the page it currently faces (the first page of Tobit). Catchwords survive (see Decoration); the one on fol. 216 is cut off.

RULING: ruled in ink for two columns with single vertical and double horizontal bounding lines extending the full height and width of page, and a further set of double bounding lines in all margins; prickings survive; 31–5 lines per page; written space: *c.*125 × 185 mm; nearly identical to MS Fairfax 11

SCRIPT: textura, the same hand as in MS Fairfax 11; black ink

RUBRICATION: rubrics in red; blue paraphs

SEC. FOL.: '*Gospel Matheu*' (fol. vii recto, table of lections); '*when crist schulde*' (fol. 2r, gospel)

Binding

Brown leather over thick pasteboard, 17th century. Blind fillet-line border with floral corner-pieces round the outer edge of both covers; floral blind-roll rectangular figure with floral corner-pieces at the centre and blind-roll strips with the same designs next to the spine on both covers. Re-backed in the Bodleian with the original spine relaid. Five raised bands framed by blind fillet lines on spine. Floral decoration on the edges of covers. '183' written in white paint on spine. Laid paper pastedowns and flyleaves. Fols. ii–iii and 286 have fragments of glue and red pigment and were pastedowns of an earlier binding.

Provenance

1. Written by the same scribe as MS Fairfax 11, and possibly illuminated by the same artist; MS Bodl. 665 may be also the work of this scribe (de Hamel (2001)) though this is questioned by Peikola (2003). Consists of three codicologically separate parts: the table of lections, NT and a selection of OT books. The parts were put together by a team that may have had access to several exemplars (NT and OT may have been copied from different exemplars; OT books have EV prologues). The table of lections, though described as being for the use of Sarum, was modified to reflect the selection of OT texts in this manuscript. The sanctoral contains OT readings only from Ecclesiastes, Wisdom, Proverbs, the Song of Song and Ecclesiasticus. The readings that are omitted (Malachi for Candlemas; Isaiah for Annunciation; Jeremiah and Isaiah for the eve, day and octave of John the Baptist; Ezekiel for Matthew and Luke) are all from books

that are not included in MS Bodl. 183. Commemorations omit most OT readings, apart from the ones from Ecclesiastes and Esther, both included in MS Bodl. 183. The table of lections, as is consistent with its standard form (Forshall and Madden (1850), vol. 4, pp. 683–96), does not contain any readings from Tobit or Judith, but both books are included in MS Bodl. 183.

There may have been originally another text or texts at the beginning of the OT section, as suggested by an offset of decoration on fol. 184v (see Collation). The parts were in their present order in the late 15th century as witnessed by the list of contents on fol. 286r.

2. Late 15th-century clerical (?) owner who listed the contents in Latin.

3. Robert Barker (*c.*1568–1646), king's printer, see *ODNB* entry 'Authorized Version of the Bible, translators of the'.

4. Bodleian Library: presented by Robert Barker in 1604. Earlier shelfmarks: 'Th E 5 5', 'NE. C. 4.1.' (fol. v recto).

Bibliography

Summary catalogue, vol. 2, part I, no. 2084.
Forshall and Madden (1850), vol. 1, pp. xxxv, xlvii.
Fristedt (1953–73), vol. 1, p. 15.
Ker (1969–2002), vol. 4, p. 752.
Hudson (1989), pp. 44, 140 n. 29.
The Bodleian Library and its treasures: September 17–October 14, 1990, Tokyo, Fuji Art Museum (Tokyo: Fuji Art Museum, 1990), no. 23.
Scott (1996), vol. 1, p. 78 n. 57; vol. 2, p. 79.
Lindberg (1999–2004), vol. 3, p. 5.
Scott (2000–02), vol. 1, p. 54, no. 160.
Peikola (2003), pp. 39–40.
Dove (2007), pp. 59, 94, 96, 98, 100, 141, 156, 202, 203, 298.
Scott, K. L., 'The remains of a missal: Chetham's Library MS 6713', in Smith, K. A. and Krinsky, C. H. (eds), *Tributes to Lucy Freeman Sandler: studies in manuscript illumination* (London: Harvey Miller, 2007), p. 301 n. 14.

3 MS Bodl. 277

Sigla: I; *a* – prologue to Romans; γ – General Prologue

SC no. 2124

Origin: England, London (?)

Date: 1415–1425 (?)

Text

Blank paper flyleaf at the beginning.

1. (fols. 1r–375v) ONT in LV in an apparently unique further revision preceded by chapter 1 of the General Prologue. Includes 3 Ezra, found otherwise only in EV MSS, in a lightly revised form. Prologues to Isaiah and Baruch and to the books of the NT. In addition to the LV Prologue to Romans, the EV prologue is included, possibly as an afterthought (see Collation).

Chapter numbers as red Roman numerals with blue paraphs in OT and as alternating red and blue Roman numerals in NT. Running titles in red with blue paraphs on both rectos and versos in OT, and in alternating red and blue capitals written across the opening in NT. Added material within the text is underlined in black throughout. Omissions added in the margins, often decorated with red penwork; some are in a cursive script with Secretary influence (e.g., fol. 87r–v). Occasionally an addition, originally written in the margin, is erased and entered within the text over an erasure in a contemporary hand (e.g., fol. 93v). There are two glosses in red in the margins in the hand of the original rubricator: '*Pater noster*' at Matthew 15 (fol. 303v) and '*Note þis decree*' at 1 Ezra 7:25–26 (fol. 137r), marking a passage on the observance of the law of God and the law of the king. Other marginal glosses by the original scribe, linked by sigla to the text. Very few glosses in NT. Added (?) note '*of ymages*', fol. 200r, Wisdom 15. Parchment tabs at the beginning of books throughout, apart from some short prophetic books and NT epistles. The tabs have short titles of books (e.g., '*Iudicum*') or the opening letters of such titles written on the recto in the hand responsible for most Carthusian additions (see below).

Fifteenth-century additions similar to those found in Latin bibles owned by the Carthusians (Doyle (1998); Hudson (2006)). Lections during the week for the year are marked in the margins throughout; their opening words are also often marked within the text. Such notation is absent in psalms and much of the four gospels, presumably because other copies of these texts with instructions existed (Hudson (2006), p. 737). The markings include marginal letters in red P, S and T (*Prima*, *Secunda* and *Tertia lectio*); the first of these is often followed by an indication of day (e.g., *Feria ii, Feria iij, Sabbato*) and season (e.g., *Dominica in sexagesima*, fol. 17v; *On passyon Sunday*, fol. 229r).

A different set of readings is marked '*In Refectorio*', followed by the number of leaves to be read. Occasionally these are accompanied by further comments in plummet indicating that these longer passages to be read *in refectorio* were compared with the text in another book, presumably a Latin bible (de Hamel (2001), pp. 184–5; Hudson (2006), p. 738; Dove (2007), p. 65):

In Refectorio iiij ff
in alio libro xiiij et d(imidium) (fol. 1v)

In Refectorio iij ff
in alio libro x ff et di(midium) (fol. 18r)

In Refectorio iiij fol
in alio libro xiij ff (fol. 31r)

In Refectorio xix ffoliis et di(midium) (fol. 116r)

In Refectorio xij folia (fol. 135v)

In refectorio iij fol of þis boke (right margin)
and [or *et*] *ix fol of þe latyn B…* (lower margin; the rest is cut off; fol. 159r)

In Refectorio v ff (fol. 229v)

In Refectorio iiij fol et di(midium) (fol. 239v)

In Refectorio vi et di(midium) fol (fol. 265v)

In Refectorio (fols. 332r and 332v)

Dominica in Refectorio ii folia (fol. 371r).

The notes suggest that the Latin book was much smaller than MS Bodl. 277, presumably a portable 'Parisian' bible: four leaves in MS Bodl. 277 correspond once to 14½ leaves in 'another book' and to 13 leaves on the second occasion. Several notes suggest that the text was indeed compared to a Bible, e.g., a note about omitted names of towns in Joshua 15:33 (fol. 66v); '*þe prologe wantyth*' at the beginning of Jeremiah (fol. 229r) and '*prologus car*'' at the beginning of Ezekiel (fol. 249v). Other notes include '*Cantatur in Choro*' at the beginning of the psalter (fol. 167r); '*turne to þe boke Ieremie & leve & leve* [sic] *þe boke of kynges for þat is next after ebre vse*' at the beginning of 1 Kings (fol. 78v; see Hudson (2006), p. 737); '*id est canonicum*' added to a rubric introducing Canonical epistles (fol. 365v), and '*Odyr wyse callyd Epistole Canonicales*' (fol. 366r).

Marginal divisions A–H, found in other Carthusian bibles combined with *primo*, *secundo* and *tertio*, appear in many parts of the text (Saenger (2005), p. 92 n. 71). Unlike the indexing letters they run across chapters and again suggest that the text was compared with a Latin bible. They often (though not always) start at the beginnings of books, and if a prologue is present, A is used to mark the prologue, whereas B corresponds to the beginning of the first chapter in a book (e.g., Canonical epistles, fol. 365v). If a prologue is not included, A is missing and B appears at the beginning of the first chapter (e.g., Genesis, Joshua, I Kings, Tobit, Judith, Esther, Job). At the beginning of Ezechiel (fol. 249v) a note about a missing prologue is accompanied by A, whereas B corresponds to the beginning of the first chapter. In books that do not have a prologue A tends to appear at the start of the book (e.g., Exodus, Leviticus, Deuteronomy, Judges, 2 Kings, 3 Kings). Occasionally the subdivisions are accompanied by comments which suggest comparison to another manuscript, such as '*capitulum vij*' (fol. 194v) at subdivision 'G' marking '*What nede is it to a man…*' which appears at the beginning of Ecclesiastes 7 in EV, but belongs to the end of chapter 6 in LV. On fol. 294v the subdivision 'E' is accompanied by a note '*ii col(umna)*'; on fol. 195v 'G' is accompanied by '*vi*' and on fol. 198r another 'G' is marked '*c(apitulum) viij*'.

[quires I–XXV]
(fol. 1r) Chapter 1 of the General Prologue ('*Fyue & twenty bookis…*'). Rubric: '*Prolog*'. At the end: '*Heere endiþ prolog on þe book of Genesis*'.

(fol. 1v) Genesis. Rubric: '*Here biginniþ þe book of Genesis*'.

(fol. 17v) Exodus. Rubric: '*Heere endiþ Genesis and bigynniþ Exodus*'.

(fol. 30v) Leviticus. Rubric: '*Heere endiþ Exodus and biginniþ leuyticus*'. At the end: '*Heere endiþ leuyticus*'.

(fol. 39r) Numbers. Rubric: '*Here bigynniþ þe book of Numery*'.

(fol. 51r) Deuteronomy. Rubric: '*Heere endiþ Numery and bigynniþ Deutronomye*'.

(fol. 62r) Joshua. Rubric: '*Heere endiþ þe book of Deutronomie and bigynniþ þe book of Iosie*'. At the end: '*Heere endiþ þe book of Iosue*'.

(fol. 69v) Judges. Rubric: '*Here bigynniþ þe book of Iudicum*'.

(fol. 77r) Ruth. Rubric: '*Heere endiþ þe book of Iudicum and bigynneþ þe book of Ruth*'.

(fol. 78v) 1 Kings. Rubric: '*Heere endiþ þe book of Ruth and bigynniþ þe firste book of kyngis*'. At the end: '*Heere endiþ þe firste book of kyngis*'.

(fol. 89r) 2 Kings. Rubric: '*Heere bigynniþ þe ii book of kyngis*'.

(fol. 97r) 3 Kings. Rubric: '*Hee* [sic] *endiþ þe secounde book of kyngis and bigynneþ þe þridde*'. Imperfect at the end because of the loss of a leaf after fol. 106, ends at 22:11.

(fol. 107r) 4 Kings. Begins imperfectly at 2:16.

(fol. 116r) 1 Chronicles. Rubric: '*Heere endiþ þe fourþe book of kyngis and bigynniþ þe firste book of Paralipomynon þat is of wordis of daies*'. At the end: '*Heere endiþ þe firste book of Paralipomynon*'.

(fol. 124v) 2 Chronicles. Rubric: '*Heere biginniþ þe secounde book of Paralipomynon*'. Prayer of Manasseh (fol. 135r) without a rubric. At the end: '*Heere endiþ þe seconde book of Paralipomynon*'.

(fol. 135v) 1 Ezra. Rubric: '*Heere biginniþ þe firste book of Esdre*'.

(fol. 138r) 2 Ezra. Rubric: '*Heere eendiþ þe firste book of Esdre and þe secounde biginniþ*'.

(fol. 142v) 3 Ezra. Rubric: '*Heere endiþ þe secounde book of Esdre and heere biginnyþ þe þridde book of Esdre*'.

(fol. 147v) Tobit. Rubric: '*Heere endiþ þe þridde book of Esdre and bigynniþ Thobie*'.

(fol. 150v) Judith. Rubric: '*Here endiþ Thobie and bigynniþ Iudith*'.

(fol. 154v) Esther. Rubric: '*Heere endiþ þe book of Iudith and bigynniþ Ester*'.

Usual notes on the differences between the Hebrew and Latin texts in red in chapters X–XV. At the end: '*Heere endiþ hester*'.

(fol. 159r) Job. Rubric: '*Heere bignniþ Iob*'. '*Iob was a very man in kynde…*' at the end of the second column on fol. 158v in red, by the original rubricator, with a rubric '*a glose*'.

(fol. 167r) Psalms (**Plate 3**). Rubric: '*Heere endiþ Iob And bigynniþ þe Sauter*'. At the end: '*Heere endiþ þe sauter of Dauid þe prophete*'. Laid out as prose, with alternating red and blue capitals at the beginning of verses. Psalm numbers in the margins as red Roman numerals, and occasionally also as Arabic numerals (e.g., fol. 184r). Most psalms have titles in English, underlined in red. Latin incipits in the margins. Glosses in the original hand in the margins, starting at psalm 92, commenting on the interpretation of psalms, particularly those that have 'no title in Hebrew or Jerome'. Textual divisions marked with larger initials and borders at psalms 26, 38, 52, 68, 97, 109.

(fol. 186v) Proverbs. Rubric: '*Heere bigynnip þe book of prouerbis*'.

(fol. 193r) Ecclesiastes. Rubric: '*Heere endiþ þe book of prouerbis and bigynniþ Ecclesiastes*'.

(fol. 195v) Song of Songs. Rubric: '*Heere endiþ Ecclesiastes and bigynniþ Song of songis*'.

(fol. 196v) Wisdom. Rubric: '*Heere endiþ þe book of songis and biginniþ þe book of wisdom*'.

(fol. 201v) Ecclesiasticus. Rubric: '*Heere endiþ þe book of wisdom and bigynniþ þe book of Ecclesiasticus*'.

(fol. 214r) Prologue to Isaiah ('*As seynt Ierom seiþ…*'). Rubric: '*Heere endeþ Ecclesiasticus and biginniþ a prologe on ysaie & oopere prophetis*'.

(fol. 214v) Isaiah. Rubric: '*Heere eendiþ þe prologe and biginniþ ysaie þe prophete*'. Rubric '*þe scripture of Ezechie kyng of Iuda*' at chapter 38 that starts with a small gold initial.

(fol. 229r) Jeremiah. Rubric: '*Heere endiþ ysaie and biginniþ Ieremye*'.

(fol. 246r) Lamentations of Jeremiah. Rubric: '*Heere biginnen þe lamentacions of Ieremye*'.

(fol. 247r) Prayer of Jeremiah. Rubric: '*Heere enden þe lamentacions and here biginniþ þe preier of Ieremye þe prophet*'.

(fol. 247v) Prologue to Baruch ('*Þis book whiche is titlid…*'). Rubric: '*Heere biginniþ þe prolog of Baruk*'.

(fol. 247v) Baruch. Rubric: '*Heere endiþ þe prologe and biginniþ Baruk*'. Chapter 6 with a gold initial and rubric '*Heere biginniþ þe saumple…*'.

(fol. 249v) Ezekiel. Rubric: '*Heere endiþ Baruk and biginniþ Ezechiel*'.

(fol. 265v) Daniel. Rubric: '*Heere endiþ Ezechiel and here biginniþ Daniel*'. Notes in red on the passages not found in Hebrew in chapters 3, 12.

(fol. 272r) Hosea. Rubric: '*Heere endiþ Daniel and biginniþ Osee*'.

(fol. 274r) Joel. Rubric: *'Heere endiþ Osee and biginniþ Ioel'*.

(fol. 275r) Amos. Rubric: *'Heere endiþ Ioel and biginniþ Amos'*.

(fol. 276v) Obadiah. Rubric: *'Heere endiþ amos and biginniþ Abdias'*.

(fol. 277r) Jonah. Rubric: *'Heere endiþ Abdias and biginniþ Ionas'*.

(fol. 277v) Micah. Rubric: *'Heere endiþ Ionas and biginniþ Micheas'*.

(fol. 278v) Nahum. Rubric: *'Heere endiþ Michee and biginniþ Naum'*.

(fol. 279r) Habakkuk. Rubric: *'Heere endiþ Naum and biginniþ Abacuk'*. Chapter 3 with a rubric *'þe preier of abakuc…'*.

(fol. 280r) Zephaniah. Rubric: *'Heere endiþ abakuc and biginniþ Sophonie'*.

(fol. 280v) Haggai. Rubric: *'Heere endiþ Sophonye and biginniþ Aggey'*.

(fol. 281r) Zechariah. Rubric: *'Heere endiþ Aggey and biginniþ Zacharie'*.

(fol. 283v) Malachi. Rubric: *'Heere endiþ Zacharie and biginniþ Malachie'*.

(fol. 284v) 1 Maccabees. Rubric: *'Heere endiþ Malachie and biginniþ þe firste book of Machabeis'*.

(fol. 294r) 2 Maccabees. Rubric: *'Heere endiþ þe firste book of Machabeis and biginniþ þe seconde'*. At the end: *'Heere endiþ þe secounde book of Machabeis þe whiche is þe ende of þe olde testament'*. Most of the last leaf is blank.

[quires XXVI–XXXI]
(fol. 302r) Prologue to Matthew (*'Matheu þat was of Iudee…'*). Rubric: *'Heere bigynniþ þe prologe of ierom on þe gospel of Matheu'*. At the end *'Heere endiþ þe prologe'*. 19 lines of the first column, containing the prologue, are left blank and are framed with a square border. The box may have contained pasted decoration, possibly including an indication of ownership; the edges of the box are smudged and rough as if the decoration was 'lifted off' (see Hudson (2006), p. 732).

(fol. 302r) Matthew. Rubric: *'Here bigynniþ þe gospel of Matheu'*.

(fol. 311v) Prologue to Mark (*'Mark þe gospeller was þe chosen seruaunt…'*). Rubric: *'Heere endiþ þe gospel of Matheu and biginniþ þe prologe on þe gospel of Mark'*.

(fol. 311v) Mark. Rubric: *'Heere endiþ þe prologe & bigynniþ þe gospel of Mark'*.

(fol. 317v) Prologue to Luke (*'Luye was a man of sirie…'*). Rubric: *'Heere endiþ þe gospel of Mark and biginniþ þe prologe on Luyk*'. At the end: '*Heere endiþ þe prologe*'.

(fol. 318r) Luke. Rubric: '*Here biginniþ þe gospel of luyk*'.

(fol. 327v) Prologue to John ('*This is ioon euangelist…*'). Rubric: '*Heere endiþ þe gospel of Luyk and biginniþ þe prologe of Ierom on þe gospel of Ioon*'.

(fol. 327v) John. Rubric: '*Heere endiþ þe prologe and heere biginniþ þe gospel of Ioon*'.

(fol. 334v) EV Prologue to Romans ('*First us bihoueþ vndirstonde…*'). Rubric: '*Heere endiþ þe gospel of Ioon and biginniþ þe firste prologe on þe pistle to Romayns*'. At the end: '*Heere endiþ þe firste prolog on þe pistil to Romayns*'.

(fol. 335r) LV Prologue to Romans ('*Romayns ben in þe cuntrey…*'). Rubric: '*Heere biginniþ þe ii. prologe on þe pistle to Romains*'.

(fol. 335r) Romans. Rubric: '*Heere endiþ þe prologe and here biginniþ þe pistle*'.

(fol. 338v) Prologue to 1 Corinthians ('*Corynthis ben…*'). Rubric: '*Here endiþ þe pistle to Romayns And bigynneþ þe prolog on þe firste pistle to Corinthies*'. At the end: '*þis seiþ Ierom in his prolog on þe firste pistle to corynthies*' (written in black, underlined in red).

(fol. 338v) 1 Corinthians.

(fol. 342r) Prologue to 2 Corinthians ('*Aftir penaunce…*'). Rubric: '*Heere endiþ þe firste pistle to Corinthies and biginiþ þe prologe on þe ii pistle to Corinth*'.

(fol. 342r) 2 Corinthians. Rubric: '*Heere endiþ þe prologe & biginiþ þe pistle*'.

(fol. 344v) Prologue to Galatians ('*Galathies ben grekis…*'). Rubric: '*Heere endiþ þe secounde pistle to Corynthies and biginiþ þe prologe on þe pistle to Galathies*'.

(fol. 355r) Galatians. Rubric: '*Heere endiþ þe prologe & biginniþ þe pistle*'.

(fol. 346r) Prologue to Ephesians ('*Ephecians ben of asye…*'). Rubric: '*Heere endiþ þe pistle to Galathies & biginniþ þe prologe on þe epistle to Ephesians*'.

(fol. 346r) Ephesians.

(fol. 347r) Prologue to Philippians ('*Filipencis ben of macedonye…*'). Rubric: '*Heere endiþ þe pistle to Effesians and bigynniþ þe prologe on þe pistle to Philippencis*'. At the end: '*Here endiþ þe prologe*'.

(fol. 347r) Philippians.

(fol. 348r) Prologue to Colossians ('*Colocencis ben also laodicencis...*'). Rubric: '*Heere endeþ þe pistle to Philipencis and biginiþ þe prologe on þe pistle to Colocencis*'.

(fol. 348r) Colossians. Rubric: '*Here biginniþ þe pistle*'.

(fol. 349r) Prologue to 1 Thessalonians ('*Tessalonycensis ben macedonies...*'). Rubric: '*Heere endiþ þe pistle to Colocencis and biginniþ þe prologe on þe i pistle to Thess*''.

(fol. 349r) 1 Thessalonians. Rubric: '*Here biginniþ þe pistle*'.

(fol. 349v) Prologue to 2 Thessalonians ('*Þe postle writeþ...*'). Rubric: '*Heere endiþ þe firste pistle to Tessalonicencis and biginniþ þe prologe on þe ii pistle to Thessalonycencis*'

(fol. 349v) 2 Thessalonians.

(fol. 350r) Prologue to 1 Timothy ('*He enformiþ and techiþ ...*'). Rubric: '*Heere endiþ þe ii epistle to thessalonicensis and biginniþ þe prologe of þe i epistle to Thymothe*'.

(fol. 350r) 1 Timothy. Rubric: '*Heere biginniþ þe pistle*'.

(fol. 351r) Prologue to 2 Timothy ('*He writiþ also...*'). Rubric: '*Heere endiþ þen i pistle to Thymothe & biginniþ þe prologe on þe ii*'.

(fol. 351r) 2 Timothy.

(fol. 351v) Prologue to Titus ('*He warniþ tyte...*'). Rubric: '*Heere endiþ þe ii pistle to Thymothe and biginniþ þe prologe of þe pistle to Tite*'.

(fol. 351v) Titus.

(fol. 352r) Prologue to Philemon ('*He makeþ familiar...*'). Rubric: '*Heere endiþ þe pistle to tyte & biginniþ þe prologe on þe pistle to Philemon*'.

(fol. 352r) Philemon.

(fol. 352v) Prologue to Hebrews ('*First it is to sey...*'). Rubric: '*Heere endiþ the pistle to Philemon and biginniþ þe prologe on þe pistle to Ebrewis*'.

(fol. 352v) Hebrews.

(fol. 355v) Prologue to Acts ('*Luyk of antioche...*'). Rubric: '*Heere endiþ þe pistle to Ebrewis and biginniþ þe prologe on þe dedis of apostlis*'. At the end: '*Heere endiþ þe prologe*'.

(fol. 355v) Acts.

(fol. 365v) The Catholic epistles. Prologue to James ('*Þe ordre of þe seuene epistlis…*'). Rubric: '*Heere enden þe dedis of apostlis and heere biginniþ a prologe on þe pistlis of cristen feiþ þat ben seuene in ordre*'.

(fol. 365v) James. Rubric: '*Heere endiþ þe prologe and bigynniþ þe epistle*'.

(fol. 366v) 1 Peter. Rubric: '*Heere endiþ þe epistle of iames and bigynniþ þe firste epistle of Petir*'.

(fol. 367v) 2 Peter. Rubric: '*Heere biginniþ þe ii of petre*'.

(fol. 368r) 1 John. Rubric: '*Heere endiþ þe ii epistle of petre & bigynniþ þe i epistle of Ion*'.

(fol. 369r) 2 John. Rubric: '*Heere endiþ þe i epistle of Ioon and biginniþ þe ii*'.

(fol. 369v) 3 John. Rubric: '*Heere endeþ þe ii epistle of Ioon and biginniþ þe iii*'.

(fol. 369v) Jude. Rubric: '*Heere endiþ þe þridde epistle of Ioon and biginniþ þe epistle of Iudas*'.

(fol. 370r) Prologue to the Apocalypse ('*Alle men þat wolen …*'). Rubric: '*Heere endiþ þe epistle of iudas and heere bigynniþ a prologe of þe apocalips þat is þe reuelacioun of seint Ioon*'.

(fol. 370r) Apocalypse. Rubric: '*Heer endiþ þe prologe and bigynniþ þe apocalips*'. At the end: '*Heere endiþ þe apocalips þat Ioon wroot in þe Ile of Pathmos þe whiche is þe ende of þe newe testament*'.

Fols. 375v–377v are mostly blank; a woodcut is pasted to fol. 376v. A note about the countries where the four gospels were written in a contemporary hand on fol. 377r: '*Matthew in iudee. Mark in ytalie. luyk in aca[ye?] Ioon in asy[ae?]*'.

Dialect

ony(10), ech(8)/eche(2), fijr(5)/fire(4)/fuir(1), ȝoue(7)/ȝouen(2)/ȝiuen(1), lijf(10), lijk(10), myche(10), sawȝe(2)/siȝ(3)/siȝe(1)/sayȝ(1) (sg.), saien(4)/siȝen(2)/sauȝen(1) (pl.), self(5)/silf(5), sich(2)/siche(8), þouȝ(8), þorouȝ(10)

-iþ(8)/-eþ(2) (pres.ind.3sg.), -en(10) (pres.ind.pl.), -ynge(10) (pres.part.), sche(10) (3sg.fem.pronoun, nom.), þei(10) (3pl.pronoun, nom.), hem(10) (3pl.pronoun, oblique), her(10) (3pl.pronoun, possessive)

Decoration

Full borders made of gold, pink and blue bars, decorated with foliage, flowers, gold disks, human figures and grotesques, at the beginning of Genesis, 1 Kings, 1 Chronicles, 1 Ezra, Psalms, Proverbs, Isaiah, gospels, Romans and the Apocalypse (particularly sumptuous at Genesis, Psalms, Mathew, Romans and the Apocalypse).

4- to 9-line gold initials and three-quarters borders made of gold, pink and blue bars, decorated with foliage, flowers and gold disks, at the beginning of the chapter from the General Prologue and most books. Some books do not have borders, and start with initials decorated with sprays of foliage extending into margins (e.g., minor prophets and some epistles).

3- to 7-line initials, gold or on gold background, at the beginnings of prologues.

3-line blue initials with red penwork at the beginnings of chapters.

As in other Wycliffite bibles the borders are painted avoiding the text in the margins, including corrections, psalm numbers and glosses, suggesting that such text was added before the manuscript was passed to the illuminator. Pächt and Alexander (1973) suggest with a query that the decoration could be of London origin.

Physical description

MATERIAL: parchment, paper flyleaves

DIMENSIONS: *c.*415 × 260 mm

NUMBER OF LEAVES: 377

FOLIATION: modern in pencil, 1–377

COLLATION: unnumbered paper flyleaf | (fols. 1–96) I–VIII (12) | (fols. 97–107) IX (12–1) missing 11 | 108–287) X–XXIV (12) | (fols. 288–301) XXV (14) | (fols. 302–361) XXVI–XXX (12) | (fols. 362–369) XXXI (8) | (fols. 370–375) (6) | (fols. 376–377) parchment and paper flyleaves. A leaf, corresponding in width to a single column is added in the middle of quire XXVII, after fol. 326, to finish the prologue to Romans. Catchwords survive; leaf signatures occasionally survive.

RULING: ruled in plummet for two columns with double vertical and horizontal bounding lines extending the full height and width of page; a further set of bounding lines comprising double lines in the lower and outer margins and single lines in the upper margin; 64 lines per page; written space: *c.*290 × 180 mm. Fol. 1r, containing chapter 1 of the General Prologue, has further 8 lines of text in the lower margin in both columns in order to start Genesis at the head of fol. 1v

SCRIPT: textura, black ink

RUBRICATION: rubrics in red ink

SEC. FOL.: '*& settide hym*' (fol. 2r)

Binding

Brown leather over boards. Blind fillet-line border and rectangular blind roll floral decoration with floral corner-pieces on both covers. Raised bands on spine. Gold lettering 'BIBLE || WICKLIFFE' and a fragment of a paper label with hand-written 'Bodl 277' on spine. Marbled paper pastedowns, turn-ins with circular stamps containing 'IHS' monogram. Fragments of a large woodcut (Hodnett, no. 2514) pasted to fol. 376v, depicting a group of English martyrs kneeling before a king (Henry VI); includes an antelope, his badge (animal with two horns and tusks) and the coat of arms of England (three lions passant quartered with three fleurs de lis). Fol. 377 was a pastedown of an earlier binding and contains on the verso staining from a red (leather?) binding. The red is similar to that of parchment tabs which mark the beginning of most books (see Hudson (2006), p. 734). Since the tabs have book titles in a hand responsible for most Carthusian additions, both the red leather binding and the tabs must date from the time when the manuscript was in the possession of the London charterhouse.

Provenance

1. OT and NT are codicologically separate and there are differences in their execution. Decoration of London origin (Pächt and Alexander (1973)).

2. May have originally contained a coat of arms or another indication of ownership on fol. 302r (see Text).

3. King Henry VI: two inscriptions in different, probably early 16th-century hands on fol. 375r, one crossed out, the second reading '*Hic liber erat quondam henrici sexti qui postea donabatur domui Cartusiensium quæ Londino contigua est*'. Hudson (2006, p. 736) argues against a possibility that the book belonged to Henry V, but not against a suggestion that this may be the English bible known to have been owned by Henry IV (Summerson (1997); Meale (1989)).

4. Charterhouse, London: 15th-century Carthusian additions; text compared with a portable Latin bible.

5. Sir George More (1553–1632), see *ODNB*.

6. Bodleian Library: presented by More in 1604. Earlier shelfmarks: 'Th. B. 24. 9', 'NE. C. 7. 1 (2124)' (upper pastedown).

Bibliography

Forshall and Madden (1850), vol. 1, p. xlvii; collated throughout; base text for revised 3 Ezra for which this is the only known text.

Deanesly (1920), pp. 252, 261, 382.

Summary catalogue, vol. 2, part I, no. 2124.

Thompson, E. M., *The Carthusian order in England* (London and New York: Society for Promoting Christian Knowledge/Macmillan, 1930), p. 324.

Hodnett, E., *English Woodcuts, 1480–1535*, 1st edn 1935 (Oxford: University Press, 1973).

Dodgson, C., *English woodcuts of the fifteenth century* (Strasbourg: J. H. E. Heitz, 1936), pp. 35–6.

Fristedt (1953–73), vol. 1, pp. 17, 29 and *passim*.

Lindberg (1959–97), vol. 8 (1997), p. 43, siglum 'I'.

Pächt and Alexander (1966–73), vol. 3 (1973), no. 880.

Spenser, B., 'King Henry of Windsor and the London pilgrim', in Bird. J., Chapman, H. and Clark, J. (eds), *Collectanea Londiniensia: studies in London archaeology and history presented to Ralph Merrifield* (London: London and Middlesex Archaeological Society, 1978), pp. 235–64 at p. 242.

Alexander J. J. G., 'Painting and manuscript illumination for royal patrons in the later Middle Ages', in Scattergood, V. J. and Sherborne, J. W. (eds), *English court culture in the later Middle Ages* (London: Duckworth, 1983), pp. 141–62 at p. 151.

Catto, J., Gradon P. and Hudson, A. (eds), *Wyclif and his followers: an exhibition to mark the 600th anniversary of the death of John Wyclif, December 1984 to April 1985* (Oxford: Bodleian Library, 1984), pp. 47–8.

Hudson (1989), pp. 125–42 at p. 131.

Lindberg (1989), siglum I and pp. 65, 70.

Meale, C. M., 'Patrons, buyers and owners: book production and social status' in Griffiths, J. and Pearsall, D. (eds), *Book production and publishing in Britain 1375–1475* (Cambridge: Cambridge University Press, 1989), pp. 201–38 at p. 223 n. 14.

Scott (1996), vol. 1, p. 70 n. 13.

Summerson, H., 'An English Bible and other books belonging to Henry IV', *Bulletin of the John Rylands Library* 79 (1997), pp. 109–15.

Doyle, A. I., 'English Carthusian books not yet linked with a charterhouse', in Barnard, T., Ó Cróinín, D. and Simms, K. (eds), *A miracle of learning: studies in manuscripts and Irish learning; essays in honour of William O'Sullivan* (Aldershot: Ashgate, 1998), pp. 122–36 at p. 132 n. 32.

Scott (2000–02), vol. 1, p. 58, no. 183.

de Hamel (2001), pp. 183–4, figs. 130–1.

Hanna, R., *A descriptive catalogue of the western medieval manuscripts of St John's College, Oxford* (Oxford: Oxford University Press, 2002), p. 9.

Craig, L. A., 'Royalty, virtue, and adversity: the cult of king Henry VI', *Albion* 35.2 (2003), pp. 187–209.

Hanna, R., 'English biblical texts before Lollardy and their fate', in Somerset, F., Havens, J. C. and Pitard, D. G. (eds), *Lollards and their influence in late medieval England* (Woodbridge: Boydell, 2003), pp 141–53 at p. 153 and n. 38.

Marks, R., 'Images of Henry VI', in Stratford, J. (ed.), *The Lancastrian court: proceedings of the 2001 Harlaxton Symposium* (Donington: Shaun Tyas, 2003), pp. 111–24 at p. 117.

Hanna (2005), p. 312.

Saenger, P., 'The British Isles and the origin of the modern mode of biblical citation', *Syntagma* 1 (2005), pp. 77–123.

Hudson (2006).

Brantley, J., *Reading in the wilderness: private devotion and public performance in late medieval England* (Chicago and London: University of Chicago Press, 2007), p. 353 n. 190.

Dove (2007), pp. 253–5 and *passim*.

Cole, A., *Literature and heresy in the age of Chaucer* (Cambridge: Cambridge University Press, 2008), p. 222 n. 24.

Luxford, J. M., 'Precept and practice: the decoration of English Carthusian books', in Luxford, J. M. (ed.), *Studies in Carthusian monasticism in the late Middle Ages* (Turnhout: Brepols, 2008), pp. 225–67 at pp. 232, 264–5.

4 MS Bodl. 296

Siglum: L

SC no. 2467

Origin: England

Date: 14th century, end-15th century, early

Text

Fols. 1–2 are paper flyleaves.

[quires I–XXII]

1. (fols. 1r–197r) Genesis–Psalms in LV without prologues. Running titles on the rectos consisting of an abbreviated title of the book and a folio number in red (see Foliation). Chapter numbers in red, usually in the form '*Ca*^{m} *I*'. Instructions to the rubricator often survive as part of rubrics (fol. 21v), running titles, capitals at the beginning of chapters and chapter numbers. Glosses very occasionally appear in the margins, explaining individual words and phrases, and sometimes the meaning of

passages (e.g., fols. 38r, 45v, attributed to Lyra). Added material within the text is occasionally underlined in black. Cross-references to biblical books occasionally in the margins (e.g., fols. 92r, 123r). Corrections in the original or contemporary hands. Notes in later medieval hands, e.g., '*Nota bene hoc quomodo dauyd stetit in conspectu saul et perciebat cithara et bene serenabat*' (fol. 89v).

(fol. 1r) Genesis. Rubric: '*Here biginneþ genesis*'.

(fol. 21r) Exodus. Rubric: '*Here biginnyþ exodi*'.

(fol. 33v) Leviticus. Rubric: '*Here bigynneþ þe bok of leuitici*'.

(fol. 41v) Numbers. Rubric: '*Here bigynneþ numeri*'.

(fol. 53v) Deuteronomy. Rubric: '*Here bigynneþ deutronomy*'.

(fol. 65v) Joshua. Rubric: '*Iosue*'.

(fol. 73v) Judges. Rubric: '*Here bigynneþ Iudicum*'.

(fol. 82r) Ruth. Rubric: '*Here bigynneþ þe book of Ruth*'.

(fol. 83v) 1 Kings. Rubric: '*Here bigynneþ þe bok of kinges*'.

(fol. 96r) 2 Kings. Rubric: '*þe secounde of kinges*'.

(fol. 106r) 3 Kings. Rubric: '*þe þridde of kinges*'.

(fol. 117v) 4 Kings. Rubric: '*þe iiij of kinges*'.

(fol. 128r) 1 Chronicles. Rubric: '*Here bigynneþ þe firste book of parolipominon þat is of wordes of daies*'.

(fol. 137v) 2 Chronicles. Rubric: '*The secounde book of parolypomynon*'.

(fol. 149v) 1 Ezra. Rubric: '*þe firste book of Esdras*'.

(fol. 152v) 2 Ezra. Rubric: '*Here bigynneþ þe ii book of esdras þat is clepid neemie*'.

(fol. 157r) Tobit. Rubric: '*The book of tobie*'.

(fol. 160r) Judith. Rubric: '*Here bigynneþ þe book of Iudith*'.

(fol. 164v) Esther. Rubric: '*Here bigynneþ Hester*'. Rubrics in chapters X–XV.

(fol. 168v) Job. Rubric: '*Here bigynniþ þe bok of Ioob*'. Gloss '*Iob was a very mon in kind. & his book is a very þinge oon in dede…*' added in the lower margin by the main scribe.

[quires XXIII–XXV]
(fol. 177r) Psalms with a rubric: '*(H)Ere bigynneþ þe sauter which is red comynly in chirchis þe firste salm*', ending imperfectly at 148:8. The last leaf (fol. 197) is fragmentary with the second column and the lower part of the first column cut off. Written as prose with each verse starting with a red 1-line initial. Larger initials are at the beginning of psalms 1, 26, 38, 52, 68, 80, 97 and 109. Titles in red in English, psalm numbers as part of titles; incipits in red in Latin in the margins. 'Title' glosses at the beginning of some psalms.

Decoration

Simple red and blue penwork border at the beginning of Genesis (fol. 1r).

2- to 5-line blue initials with red penwork at the beginning of books; 2- to 3-line similar initials at the beginning of chapters. Initials in a different style (plain red or blue) on fols. 49r–72v (quires VII–IX).

Dialect

oni(10), ech(2)/eche(8), fyr(10), ȝoue(4)/ȝouen(6), lif(9)/lyf(1), lik(3)/like(7), muche(5)/meche(3)/miche(2), siȝ(7) (sg.), sien(2)/siȝen(4)/seien(1) (pl.), self(10), such(9)/suche(1), þouȝ(9)/þuȝ(1), þoruȝ(1)/þorouȝ(6)/þoroȝ(1)/þorou(2)

-eþ(10) (pres.ind.3sg.), -en(10) (pres.ind.pl.), -ynge(2)/-inge(5)/-ing(3) (pres. part.), she(8)/sche(2) (3sg.fem.pronoun, nom.), þei(10) (3pl.pronoun, nom.), hem(10) (3pl.pronoun, oblique), her(1)/hir(6)/hire(3) (3pl.pronoun, possessive)

Physical description

MATERIAL: parchment, paper flyleaves

DIMENSIONS: *c.*470 × 270 mm

NUMBER OF LEAVES: i–vi + 1–199

FOLIATION: Medieval in red Roman numerals by the original (?) rubricator, in quires I–XXII (preceding psalms), in the upper margin on the recto of each leaf, and usually also in the lower margin on the rectos in black ink, I–CLXXV. This foliation continues in psalms in the lower margin on the rectos (fols. 177–180). Modern foliation in pencil throughout: i–iii + 1–201.

COLLATION: (fols. i–vi) paper flyleaves and parchment stubs | (fols. 1–192) I–XXIV (8) | (fols. 193–197) XXV (8–3) missing 6–8; fol. 197 is followed by three stubs

Catchwords survive. Quire signatures run consecutively a–y in quires I–XXII (preceding psalms) and a–c in quires VII–IX (psalms).

RULING: ruled in plummet for two columns with single vertical and horizontal bounding lines extending the full height and width of page; 52–4 lines per page on fols. 1r–17r; 57 lines per page on fol. 17v; 59–63 lines per page afterwards; written space: *c.*190 × 370 mm

SCRIPT: Anglicana; smaller script is used from fol. 15r onwards; black and brown ink

RUBRICATION: rubrics in red

SEC. FOL.: '*seide I herde*' (fol. 2r)

Binding

Brown leather over wood boards, 18th century. Blind floral roll and fillet-line border round the outer edge of both covers. Six raised bands on spine. Gold lettering on spine: '296'. Modern paper pastedowns; modern and laid paper flyleaves. A fragment from a 15th-century noted breviary of English origin at fol. vi. Fol. 198 was a pastedown of an earlier binding.

Provenance

1. Possibly vol. 1 of a two-volume bible. Shares many readings with London, British Library, Arundel MS 104 and some with Emmanuel College, Cambridge, MS 21 and Trinity College, Dublin, MS 67 (Dove (2007), p. 298).

2. '*Fulford iesus maria ffuit homo missus a deo cui nomen erat Ioannes*', 15th century (fol. 198r).

3. Thomas Herbert, first baronet (1606–1682), traveller and government official; see *ODNB*: 'T. Herbert' (fol. 1r).

4. Bodleian Library: given by Herbert on 15 June 1666. Earlier shelfmark: 'NE F. 10'.

Bibliography

Forshall and Madden (1850), vol. 1, p. xlvii.
Summary catalogue, vol. 2, part I, no. 2467.
Dove (2007), pp. 18, 96, 156, 226, 237–8, 246.

5 MS Bodl. 531

Origin: England

Date: 15th century, first quarter

Text

Fol. i is a paper flyleaf blank apart from modern notes.

1. (fols. 1r–37v) Table of lections of Type I starting with a rubric: '*Here bigynneþ a reule þat telliþ in whiche placis of þe byble ȝe may fynde þe gospels. pistlis & lessouns þat ben rad in þe chirche at masse aftir þe vss of salisbury / þe lessouns & pistlis þat ben in þe olde testament ben writun alout as þei ben rad in ordir & cootid & þe gospels & pistlis þat ben in þe newe testament ben markid in what book & capytle þei ben wiþ lettris as þei stonden in þe abc & þis rule bigynneþ at þe firste sonedai in aduent*'. OT readings are written out in full, many preceded by introductory statements, such as '*Þe lord god seiþ þes þingis*'. Entries for NT readings consist of the name of the liturgical occasion in red, abbreviated reference to a book and chapter of the NT, an indexing letter in red, the opening words of a reading, '*ende*' in red, the closing words of a reading and double strokes in red. Includes feasts characteristic of the LV (Forshall and Madden (1850), vol. 4, pp. 683, 690–6), apart from Giles (1 September). Some OT readings derive from EV (e.g., Ecclesiasticus 24, Genesis 24), whereas other from LV (e.g., Jeremiah 14, Jeremiah 23, Ecclesiasticus 44) (see MS Douce 265-a).

Includes the temporal, followed by commemorations and the sanctoral. The temporal is imperfect because of the loss of leaves after fol. 2: missing readings from Saturday of the third week in Advent to Friday of the fourth week after the octave of Epiphany. Commemorations are in the following order: the Virgin Mary, Trinity, Holy Ghost, Cross, Angels, '*of briþeren & sistris & salus populi*', peace, clear weather, rain, '*In time of batels*', '*A man for him silf*', '*ffor deeþ of bestis*', pilgrims, weddings, sinners, sick, '*Pistils at masse of requiem*', '*Gospels at masse of requiem*'. The sanctoral is preceded by a rubric: '*Here enden þe commemoraciouns & bigynneþ þe sancrorum boþe of þe comyne and propre to gidre*' (fol. 28r). Rubric at the end: '*Here endiþ þe kalender wiþ þe lessouns of þe olde lawe to gidere*'. Running titles in red with blue paraphs, e.g., '*þe þridde sundai in aduent*'. Corrections in a contemporary hand.

2. (fols. 37v–236r) NT in LV with usual prologues. Missing Matthew 9:33–12:39, because of the loss of leaves after fol. 44. Running titles in red preceded by blue paraphs, most consisting of an abbreviated title of the

biblical book on the verso and a chapter number on the recto. Chapter numbers in red usually in the form 'C^m' followed by a Roman numeral. Indexing letters in the margins, entered at the beginnings of readings rather than consistently; double strokes in the margins at the ends of readings. The beginnings and ends of readings are also highlighted red in the text. Added material within the text is underlined in red. No marginal glosses. Corrections in a contemporary hand.

(fol. 37v) Prologue to Matthew ('*Mathew þat was of iudee…*'). Rubric: '*Here bigynneþ þe prolog on þe gospl* [sic] *of matheu*'.

(fol. 38r) Matthew. Rubric: '*Ierom in his prolog on matheu seiþ al þis*'.

(fol. 62r) Prologue to Mark ('*Mark þe gospeller was þe chosene seruaunt…*'). Rubric: '*Here endiþ þe gospel of matheu and bigynneþ þe prolog on þe gospel of mark*'.

(fol. 62v) Mark. Rubric: '*Al þis seiþ Ierom in his prolog on þe gospel of mark & here bigynneþ þe firste capitle*'.

(fol. 79v) Prologue to Luke ('*Luyk was a man of sirie…*'). Rubric: '*Here endiþ þe gospel of mark and bigynneþ þe prolog on þe gospel of luyk*' (fol. 79r).

(fol. 79v) Luke. Rubric: '*Ierom in his prolog on þe gospel of luyk seiþ al þis þe firste capitle*'.

(fol. 107r) Prologue to John ('*This is Joon euaungelist…*'). Rubric: '*Here endiþ þe gospel of luyk & bigynneþ þe prolog on þe gospel of Iohn*'.

(fol. 107v) John. Rubric: '*Ierom in his prolog on Iohn seiþ al þis C^m p^m*'.

(fol. 127v) Prologue to Romans ('*Romayns ben in þe cuntre…*'). Rubric: '*Here endiþ þe gospel of Iohn & bigynneþ þe prolog on þe epistle to romayns*'.

(fol. 127v) Romans. Rubric: '*Ierom in his prolog on romayns seiþ þis C^m p^m*'.

(fol. 138v) Prologue to 1 Corinthians ('*Corynthis ben men of acaie…*'). Rubric: '*Here endiþ þ* [sic] *epistle of poul to romayns & bigynneþ þe prolog on þe firste epistle of poul to corinthis*'.

(fol. 138v) 1 Corinthians. Rubric: '*Ierom in his prolog on þis firste pistle to corinthis seiþ al þis C^m p^m*'.

(fol. 148v) Prologue to 2 Corinthians ('*Afftir penaunce…*'). Rubric: '*Here endiþ þe firste epistle of poul to corinthis & bigynneþ þe prolog on þe secunde*'.

(fol. 148v) 2 Corinthians. Rubric: '*Ierom in his prolog on þis pistle seiþ þis C^m p^m*'.

(fol. 155r) Prologue to Galatians (‘*Galathies ben greekes…*’). Rubric: ‘*Here endiþ þe secunde pistle to corinthis & bigynneþ þe prolog to galathies*’.

(fol. 155r) Galatians. Rubric: ‘*Ierom in his prolog seiþ þis C^{m} p^{m}*’.

(fol. 158r) Prologue to Ephesians (‘*Ephesians ben of asie…*’). Rubric: ‘*Here endiþ þe epistle to galathies & bigynneþ þe prolog to effecies*’.

(fol. 158r) Ephesians. Rubric: ‘*Ierom in his prolog seiþ þis C^{m} p^{m}*’.

(fol. 161v) Prologue to Philippians (‘*Philipensis ben of macedonye…*’). Rubric: ‘*Here endiþ þe epistle to effecies & bigynneþ þe prolog on þe epistle to philipencis*’.

(fol. 161v) Philippians. Rubric: ‘*Ierom in his prolog on þis epistle seiþ al þis C^{m} p^{m}*’.

(fol. 164r) Prologue to Colossians (‘*Colocensis ben laodicencis also…*’). Rubric: ‘*Here endiþ þe epistle to ffilipencis & bigynneþ þe prolog to colocencis*’.

(fol. 164r) Colossians. Rubric: ‘*Ie* [sic] *in his prolog on þe pist* [sic] *to colocencis*’ *seiþ þis C^{m} p^{m}*’.

(fol. 166v) Prologue to 1 Thessalonians (‘*Tessalonicencis ben macedonies…*’). Rubric: ‘*Here endiþ þe firste pistle to colocensis & bigynneþ þe prolog on þe firste pistle to tessalonycensis*’.

(fol. 166v) 1 Thessalonians. Rubric: ‘*Ierom in his prolog on þis pistle seiþ þis C^{m} p^{m}*’.

(fol. 168v) Prologue to 2 Thessalonians (‘*The apostle writiþ…*’). Rubric: ‘*Here endiþ þe firste pistle to tessalonycensis and bigynneþ þe prolog on ii^{e}*’.

(fol. 168v) 2 Thessalonians. Rubric: ‘*Ierom in his prolog on þis pistle seiþ þis C^{m} p^{m}*’.

(fol. 169v) Prologue to 1 Timothy (‘*He enformeþ and techiþ…*’). Rubric: ‘*Here endiþ þe secunde pistle to tessalonicensis & bigynneþ þe prolog on þe firste to timothe*’.

(fol. 169v) 1 Timothy. Rubric: ‘*Ierom in his prolog on þis pistle seiþ al þis C^{m} p^{m}*’.

(fol. 172v) Prologue to 2 Timothy (‘*He writiþ also…*’). Rubric: ‘*Here endiþ þe firste pistle to tymothe and bigynneþ þe prolog on þe secunde pistle to hym*’.

(fol. 172v) 2 Timothy. Rubric: ‘*Ierom in his prolog on þis pistle seiþ þis C^{m} p^{m}*’.

(fol. 174v) Prologue to Titus (‘*He warneþ tite…*’). Rubric: ‘*Here endiþ þe secunde pistle to tymothe & bigynneþ þe prolog on þe pistle to tite*’.

(fol. 174v) Titus. Rubric: '*Ierom in his prolog on þis pistle to tite seiþ þis C^m p^m*'.

(fol. 175v) Prologue to Philemon ('*He makiþ famyliar…*'). Rubric: '*Here endiþ þe epistle to tyte & bygynneþ þe prolog on þe epistle to ffilomon*'.

(fol. 175v) Philemon. Rubric: '*Ierom in his prolog seiþ þis C^m p^m*'.

(fol. 176r) Prologue to Hebrews ('*First it is to seye…*'). Rubric: '*Here endiþ þe pistle to ffilomon & bigynneþ þe prolog on ebreus*'.

(fol. 176r) Hebrews. Rubric: '*Ierom in his prolog on þe epistle to Ebrewis seiþ al þis C^m p^m*'.

(fol. 184v) Prologue to Acts ('*Lvk of Antioche…*'). Rubric: '*Here endiþ þe epistle to ebrewis & bigynneþ þe prolog on þe dedis of Apostlis or actus apostolorum*' (fol. 184r).

(fol. 184v) Acts. Rubric: '*Ierom in his prolog on actus apostolorum seiþ al þis C^m p^m*'.

(fol. 211v) The Catholic epistles. Prologue to James ('*The ordre of seuene epistlis…*'). Rubric: '*Here endiþ þe dedis of apostlis & bigynneþ þe prolog on þe pistlis of cristen feiþ þat ben seuene in ordre*'.

(fol. 212r) James. Rubric: '*Ierom in his prolog on þes epistlis seiþ al þis firste Iames C^m p^m*' (fol. 211v).

(fol. 214r) 1 Peter. Rubric: '*Here endiþ þe epistle to Iames & bigynneþ þe firste pistle of petre C^m p^m*'.

(fol. 217r) 2 Peter. Rubric: '*Here endiþ þe firste pistle of petre & bigynneþ þe secunde pistle C^m p^m*'.

(fol. 218v) 1 John. Rubric: '*Here endiþ þe secunde pistle of petre & bigynneþ þe firste pistle of Ion C^m p^m*'.

(fol. 221r) 2 John. Rubric: '*Here endiþ þe firste of ion & bigynneþ þe secunde C^m p^m*'.

(fol. 221v) 3 John. Rubric: '*Here endiþ þe secunde pistle of Iohn & bigynneþ þe þridde C^m p^m*'.

(fol. 221v) Jude. Rubric: '*Here endiþ þe þridde epistle of Iohn and bigynneþ þe epistle of Iudas C^m p^m*'.

(fol. 222v) Prologue to the Apocalypse ('*Alle men þat wolen …*'). Rubric: '*Here endiþ þe pistle of Iudas & bigynneþ þe prolog of apocalips*'.

(fol. 223v) Apocalypse. Rubric: '*Ierom in his prolog on apocalips seiþ al þis* C^m *p*^{m}'.

At the end added in a different hand: '*Deus qui eximie castitatis*' (15th century, second half (?)), the opening words of a prayer to St Cuthburga, the first abbess of Wimborne (printed in Perkins (1899), p. 5).

3. (fols. 236v) Note signed '*By me Ryc(ardus) merton chanon*', late 15th century (?), denying a charge brought against him: '*where as hyt was alegyt agaynyst me by the malytyose mynde of marget mukkulton to myltiply wordys as concerninge the bronunge of thomas donsturfyld howse whyc I vtterly deny by fathe and pristehode neuer to speke to hym in the cause nor neuer to haue knolege in cause lyk that hyt sholde be soo*'. Pen trials, some by the same hand.

Decoration

5- to 6-line red and blue 'puzzle' initials and penwork borders at the beginnings of books.

2- to 4-line blue initials with red penwork at the beginnings of prologues and chapters.

Dialect

ony(6)/eny(4), eche(8)/ech(2), fier(10), ȝouun(8)/ȝouen(1)/ȝyue(1), lijf(9)/lyf(1), lijk(10), myche(8)/moche(2), siȝ(4)/sawȝ(1)/saiȝ(2)/saie(1) (sg.), saien(4)/seien(1)/seie(1) (pl.), silf(10), suche(7)/such(1)/siche(2), þouȝ(8), þourȝ(6)/þurȝ(3)/þorouȝ(1)

-iþ(7)/-eþ(3) (pres.ind.3sg.), -en(10) (pres.ind.pl.), -ynge(5)/-inge(5) (pres. part.), she(10) (3sg.fem.pronoun, nom.), þei(10) (3pl.pronoun, nom.), hem(10) (3pl.pronoun, oblique), her(10) (3pl.pronoun, possessive)

Physical description

MATERIAL: parchment, paper flyleaves

DIMENSIONS: *c.*205 × 142 mm; leaves were trimmed in rebinding, frequently causing the loss of text and decoration in the margins

NUMBER OF LEAVES: 239

FOLIATION: modern in pencil, i + 1–238

COLLATION: (fol. i) paper flyleaf conjoint with the upper pastedown | (fols. 1–4) I (8–4 (?)) missing 3–6, loss of text | (fols. 5–44) II–VI (8) | (fols. 45–49) VII (8–3) missing 1–3, loss of text | (fols. 50–233) VIII–XXX

(8) | (fols. 234–236) XXXI (8–5 (?)) missing 4–8 (?), no loss of text | (fols. 237–238) paper bifolium

Quires are numbered in Arabic numerals in the lower right corner, probably in the original workshop (see the use of blue on fols. 82r, 188r, 194r); catchwords survive; leaf signatures occasionally survive

RULING: ruled in ink for two columns with double bounding lines in the upper, left and right margins, and single bounding lines in the inner and lower margins, all extending the full height and width of page; a further set of double bounding lines in the lower margin; 36–8 lines per page; written space; *c*.103 × 148 mm

SCRIPT: textura, black ink

RUBRICATION: rubrics in red

SEC. FOL.: *þou schalt be* (fol. 2r)

Binding

Brown leather over pasteboard, *c*.1600 (?), made for Edwin Sandys (?) (see Provenance). Gilt and blind fillet-line border round the outer edge of both covers. Gilt decoration with a medallion, filled with diamond-shaped figures, at the centre of covers. Six raised bands on spine, framed by gilt fillet lines. Gilt decoration on the panels between the raised bands. '531' written in white paint on spine. Fragments of two ties on both covers. Paper pastedowns and flyleaves.

Provenance

1. Added line from a collect to St Cuthburga in Latin, 15th century, second half (?) (see Pfaff (2009), pp. 381–4).

2. Late 15th-century addition by Richard Merton, canon, mentioning Marget Mukkulton and Thomas Donsturfyld (fol. 236v).

3. '*Mary Pygott…*', 16th century (?), added before the leaves were trimmed in rebinding, partially erased (fol. 187v).

4. '*John Auncelle*'; '*T. Levrett off Chearnys*'; half-erased note '*And ther was a man god saue…*', 16th-century, lower pastedown.

5. Sir Edwin Sandys (1561–1629); see *ODNB*.

6. Bodleian Library: gift of Edwin Sandys in 1603 (*Summary catalogue*, vol. 2, part I).

Earlier shelfmarks: 'Th. T. II. I' (fol. i recto); 'NE E. I. 2' (fol. i verso); '2' written in black ink on the fore-edge of textblock.

Bibliography

Forshall and Madden (1850), vol. 1, p. xlvii.
Perkins, T., *Wimborne minster and Christchurch priory* (London, 1899).
Summary catalogue, vol. 2, part I, no. 2249.
Hudson (1989), p. 140 n. 29.
Dove (2007), pp. 59 n. 116, 298.

6 MS Bodl. 554

Siglum: B-554 (Dove)

Origin: England

Date: 15th century, early

Text

Fol. i is a parchment flyleaf, mostly blank.

1. (fols. 1r–81r) Psalms 1–150 in LV, in the biblical order, written as prose, with English titles in red and numbers as part of titles. Latin incipits are written in red in the margins or on lines containing the titles up to fol. 21v, and immediately preceding the English opening words of each psalm afterwards. Psalms 1–43, therefore, have English initials, whereas psalms 44–150 have initials of their Latin incipits. Some incipits have errors (e.g., '*D(omi)ne est t(er)ra*' for '*Domini est terra*', fol. 10v). There are textual divisions at psalms 26, 38, 52, 68, 80, 97 and 109 (see Decoration). Subdivisions within psalms are not indicated, apart from psalm 118, subdivided into twenty-two 8-verse units. The seven Penitential Psalms are marked with Roman numerals in the margins in a medieval hand. Punctuated throughout with *punctus* used to mark the ends of verses and minor pauses, and *punctus elevatus* used to mark *metrum*. Extensive glosses in English in the margins throughout, including glosses on the titles, glosses explaining difficult readings and giving spiritual, moral and literal interpretation of psalms. Some glosses comment on the differences between the Latin and Hebrew texts. The glosses (apart from the title glosses which appear in the margins at the beginning of psalms) are linked to their lemmata by special signs, placed at the beginning of the gloss and above the word on which it comments (red circles with a stroke and

similar). Most glosses derive from Nicholas of Lyra's *Postilles*, but some from Augustine's *Enarrationes in Psalmos*, Jerome and Cassiodorus, often cited through Lyra, as well as from the '*comun glos*' or *Glossa Ordinaria* (Kuczynski (1994), p. 24; Dove (2007), p. 161 n. 144). The sources of most glosses are stated at their end (e.g., '*lire here*', '*austin here*' in red ink). MS Bodl. 554 preserves the Wycliffite psalter glosses better than any other manuscript (Dove (2007), p. 161). Most LV manuscripts include title glosses (that serve as prologues of psalms) as far as psalm 72, and a few include such glosses afterwards; MS Bodl. 554 includes such glosses for all psalms (Dove (2007), p. 156).

2. (fol. 81r–v) Prayer of Manasseh, beginning '*Lord god almyȝti of oure fadris abraham ysaac & iacob & of her iust seed…*'. Rubric: '*Here bigynneþ þe preier of manasses kyng of iuda*'. Glosses in the margins.

3. (fol. 81v–86r) Weekly canticles, with references to their OT sources in the margins in the hand of the original rubricator. Each is preceded by a Latin incipit, some with errors (i.e., '*domino*' for '*domini*', '*ira*' for '*iratus*' in *Confitebor*). Glosses in the margins of *Confitebor* and *Ego dixi*, fols. 81v–82r, derived entirely from Lyra (Dove (2007), p. 161 n. 144).

(1) *Confitebor tibi domino quoniam ira; Lord i shal knouleche to þe…* (Isaiah 12) ('*ysaie 12*');

(2) *Ego dixi*; *I seide in þe myddil of my daies…* (Isaiah 38:10–21) ('*ysaie 38*');

(3) *Exultauit cor meum in domino*; *Myn herte fulli ioiede…* (1 Samuel 2:1–11) ('*p^o^ Regum p^o^*');

(4) *Cantemus domino; Synge we to þe lord…* (Exodus 15:1–20) ('*exodi 15*');

(5) *Domine audiui*; *Lord I herde þyn heryng…* (Habacuc 3) ('*abacuk 3*');

(6) *Audite celi que loquar*; *Ȝe heuenes here…* (Deuteronomy 32:1–44) ('*deutronomii 32*').

4. (fols. 86r–87v) Daily canticles with references to their sources.

(1) *Benedicite omnia opera domini domino*; *Alle werkis of þe lord…* ('*Danyel 3*');

(2) *Benedictus dominus deus israel*; *Blessid be þe lord…* ('*luce p^o^*');

(3) *Magnificat anima mea*; *Mi soule magnefieþ…* ('*luce p^o^*');

(4) *Nunc dimittis*; *Lord now þou leeuest þi seruaunt…* ('*luce 2*').

Followed by a rubric '*(t)e deum laudamus*' in red, apparently in the hand of the original rubricator, but the initial is not filled in and the rest of the page is blank.

5. (fol. 88r) An extract from John Beleth's *Summa de ecclesiasticis officiis*, added in the third quarter of the 15th century in a mixed Anglicana/ Secretary hand. The extract is partly a copy and partly a summary of chapters 122, 123 and 128 (Douteil (1976), cols. 128–130), telling stories about the introduction of *letania maior* by Gregory the Great during an epidemic in Rome, and of the institution of *letania minor* by St Mamertus, Bishop of Vienne, during the earthquakes and other disasters at the end of the fifth century (published by Solopova (2012)).

6. (fol. 88v–89r) An extract, added probably in a different 15th-century hand, from Richard Rolle's *Form of Living*, chapter 6, consisting of a list of the sins of thought, word, deed and omission (published by Kuczynski (1994)).

7. (lower pastedown) Casually written 1-line inscription in a late 15th-century hand, possibly '*Thes ben þe p(ro)fessollyng en Joh(a)n belet*' or '*Thes ben [th] e prosesses oweng cu Iohan Beket*'; more erased text above the inscription. Possibly in the hand which added the price at the bottom of the pastedown (see Provenance).

8. Medical recipe '*To provok vryne*', in English, in a hand of the first half of the 16th century.

Decoration

3- to 4-line blue initials with red penwork at liturgical divisions at psalms 26 (fol. 12r), 38 (fol. 19r), 52 (fol. 26v), 68 (fol. 34v), 80 (fol. 44r), 97 (fol. 52v) and 109 (fol. 62r).

2-line similar initials at the beginnings of psalms and canticles.

1-line plain red or occasionally blue initials at the beginnings of verses.

Dialect

ony(10), ech(10), fier(10), ȝoue(10), lijf(10), lijk(10), myche(10), siȝ(6)/siȝe(1) (sg.), sien(7)/siȝen(1) (pl.), silf(10), thouȝ(2), þorou(5)

-iþ(9)/-eþ(1) (pres.ind.3sg.), -en(10) (pres.ind.pl.), -ynge(9)/-yng(1) (pres. part.), she(1) (3sg.fem.pronoun, nom.), þei(9)/thei(1) (3pl.pronoun, nom.), hem(10) (3pl.pronoun, oblique), her(10) (3pl.pronoun, possessive)

Physical description

MATERIAL: parchment

DIMENSIONS: *c.*231 × 165 mm; the leaves were trimmed in rebinding, occasionally causing the loss of text in the margins

NUMBER OF LEAVES: 90

FOLIATION: modern in ink; i + 1–89

COLLATION: (fol. i) parchment flyleaf | (fols. 1–88) I–XI (8) | (fol. 89) parchment flyleaf conjoint with the lower pastedown

Catchwords survive. Leaf signatures run consecutively a–l.

RULING: ruled in ink for a single column with single vertical and horizontal bounding lines extending the full height and width of page, and a further set of bounding lines for the gloss; 31 line per page; written space *c.*114 × 92 mm

SCRIPT: textura (psalms) and Anglicana (glosses), black ink

RUBRICATION: rubrics in red ink

SEC. FOL.: '*hast ȝoue*'

Binding

Fifteenth-century binding, worn red leather over boards, fittings of two clasps, now lost, on both covers. Sewn on five cords. '554' written on spine in black ink. Parchment pastedowns. A chain-staple mark on the lower edge of the upper board (Watson's position 4) (Hanna (2010)).

Provenance

1. Probably unfinished (see Text). Less professionally produced than many WB manuscripts (errors in Latin; the gloss is written without ruling; red ink spills on fols. 12v, 74r–v, 77r, 78v, etc.; wrong gloss entered and crossed out on fol. 30v).

2. Fifteenth-century clerical (?) owners interested in liturgy (Latin extract from Beleth) and penitential practice (English extract from Rolle).

3. On the lower pastedown: '*p(re)c(ium) x s*', presumably 'price 10 shillings', 15th century. Inscription, possibly in the same hand, perhaps containing the name 'John Beket'.

4. Sixteenth-century owner who added a medical recipe.

5. 'A. P. 7. 13' on the upper pastedown.

6. Bodleian Library: probably a gift in 1607 of Sir Richard Wolseley described as '*Liber continens expositionem vel glossam in Psalmos Anglice. 4°.*

MS' (*Summary catalogue*, vol. 2, part I). Earlier shelfmarks: 'Th. P 914', 'NE E. 6. 7'.

Bibliography

Forshall and Madden (1850), vol. 1, p. xlviii.

Summary catalogue, vol. 2, part I, no. 2326.

Deanesly (1920), p. 381.

Hargreaves, H., 'The Latin text of Purvey's psalter', *Medium Aevum* 24 (1955), pp. 73–90 at pp. 88, 90.

Douteil, H. (ed.), *Iohannis Beleth Summa de ecclesiasticis officiis*, 2 vols, *Corpus Christianorum. Continuatio Mediaevalis*; 41–41a (Turnholti: Brepols, 1976).

Ogilvie-Thomson, S. J., *IMEP*, Handlist VIII (1991), pp. 74, 75, 94.

Kuczynski, M. P., 'A fragment of Richard Rolle's *Form of Living* in MS Bodley 554', *Bodleian Library Record* 15 (1994), pp. 20–32.

Kuczynski, M. P., *Prophetic song: the psalms as moral discourse in late Medieval England* (Philadelphia: University of Pennsylvania Press, 1995), pp. 21, 71–4 (pl. 3), 173, 180, 214, 255 n. 16.

Kuczynski, M. P., 'Rolle among the reformers: orthodoxy and heterodoxy in Wycliffite copies of Richard Rolle's English Pslater', in Pollard, W. F. and Boenig, R. (eds), *Mysticism and spirituality in medieval England* (Woodbridge: D. S. Brewer, 1997), pp. 191–5 and *passim*.

Hanna, R., *IMEP*, Handlist XII, p. 5.

Kuczynski, M. P., 'An "electric stream": the religious contents' in Fein, S. (ed.), *Studies in the Harley manuscript: the scribes, contents, and social contexts of British Library MS Harley 2253* (Kalamazoo, Mich.: Medieval Institute Publications, Western Michigan University, 2000), pp. 123–61 at pp. 148–9.

Dove (2007), pp. 156, 161, 170, 183, 210, 216, 217, 218, 219, 229, 298–9.

Hanna, R., *The English manuscripts of Richard Rolle: a descriptive catalogue* (Exeter: University of Exeter, 2010), pp. 139–40.

Solopova, E., 'A previously unidentified extract about the litany in a Wycliffite psalter (Oxford, Bodleian Library, MS Bodl. 554)', *Bodleian Library Record* 24 (2011), pp. 217–23.

7 MS Bodl. 665

Origin: England

Date: 1415–1425 (?)

Text
Fols. i–iv are flyleaves, mostly blank.

[item 1 occupies quire I]
1. (fols. 1r–12v) Table of lections of Type I staring with a rubric '*Here bigynneþ a reule þat telliþ in whiche chapitris of þe bible ȝe may fynde þe lessouns pistlis & gospelis þat ben redde in þe chirche at masse aftir þe vse of Salisbiry markide wiþ lettris of þe a.b c.at þe bigynnynge of þe chapitris toward þe middil or ende aftir þe ordre as þe lettris stonden in þe abc first ben set sundaies and feriales to gidir and aftir þe sanctorum comyn & propir to gidir of al þe ȝeer first writun a clause of þe bigynnynge þerof & of þe ending þerof also*'. The entries consist of the name of the liturgical occasion in red, abbreviated reference to a book and chapter of the Bible, an indexing letter in red, the opening words of a reading, '*ende*' in red, the closing words of a reading and double strokes in red. Includes the temporal, commemorations and the sanctoral, both the proper and common according to the rubric, but only the proper is present. Includes all feasts characteristic of LV (Forshall and Madden (1850), vol. 4, pp. 683, 690–6), apart from Giles (1 September). The entries for the following feasts start with larger capitals in blue: Andrew, Nicholas, Conception of our Lady, Candlemas, Annunciation, the Finding of the Cross, Nativity of John the Baptist, James, Assumption, Nativity of our Lady, Matthew, Michaelmas, Simon and Jude, and Halloween. Commemorations are in the following order: the Virgin Mary, Trinity, Holy Ghost, Cross, angels, '*ffor briþeren & sistren & salus populi*', peace, clear weather, rain, '*In tyme of batel*', '*A man for him silf*', '*ffor pestilens of beests*', pilgrims, weddings, sinners, sick, '*pistils ffor dede*', gospels for the dead. Calendar dates for all feasts are added in an early modern hand from fol. 8r onwards.

[items 2–3 occupy quires II–XXXII]
2. (fols. 13r–226v) NT in LV with usual prologues (**Plate 4**). Usual rubrics in red. Chapter numbers in red as words in English or Roman numerals, usually in the form '*Capitulum primum*'. Running titles on both rectos and versos in black with red or blue paraphs, consisting of abbreviated titles of books and chapter numbers. Indexing letters in the margins entered at the beginnings of readings rather than consistently; double strokes in the margins at the ends of readings. Blue or red paraphs within the text, often

at the beginnings of readings. No marginal glosses; added material within the text is not underlined (but see OT lectionary below). Notes in the margins throughout in an early modern hand summarising the contents and providing cross-references to biblical books.

(fol. 13r) Prologue to Matthew ('*Matheu þat was of Iudee…*'). Rubric: '*Here bigynneþ þe newe testament capitulum primum*').

(fol. 13v) Matthew. Rubric: '*Ierom on hise twey prologis on mathew seiþ þis*' (fol. 13r).

(fol. 39r) Prologue to Mark ('*Marke þe gospeler was þe chosen seruaunte…*'). Rubric: '*Here eendiþ þe gospel of Mathew and bigynneþ þe prolog of Mark*'.

(fol. 39v) Mark. Rubric: '*Here eendiþ þe prologe for þis seiþ Ierom in his prolog on Marke & now bigynneþ þe gospel of mark þe firste c^o^*'.

(fol. 55v) Prologue to Luke ('*Luke was a man of syrie…*'). Rubric: '*Here endiþ þe gospel of mark & bigynneþ þe prolog on þe gospel of luyk*'.

(fol. 56r) Luke. Rubric: '*Ierom in his prolog seiþ al þis and heere endiþ þe prolog of luyk and now bigynneþe þe book of luyk sentence þe firste chapitir*'.

(fol. 84r) Prologue to John ('*This is Joon euangelist…*'). Rubric: '*Here bigynneþ þe prolog on þe gospel of Ioon*'.

(fol. 84r) John. Rubric: '*Ierom in his prolog on Iohn seiþ þis & here endiþ þe prolog & bigynneþ þe first c^o^*'.

(fol. 105v) Prologue to Romans ('*Romayns ben men in þe cuntrey…*'). Rubric: '*Here enden þe gospels of Ioon & bigynneþ þe prolog on þe pistle to romayns Capitulum primum*'.

(fol. 106r) Romans. Rubric: '*Þis seiþ Ierom in his prolog on þe pistle to romayns*'.

(fol. 117r) Prologue to 1 Corinthians ('*Corinthies ben men of asaye…*'). Rubric: '*Here endiþ þe pistle to Romayns & here bigynneþ þe prolog on þe firste pistle to Corinthis*'.

(fol. 117v) 1 Corinthians. Rubric: '*þis seiþ Ierom in his prolog on þe firste pistle to corinthies Capitulum primum*'.

(fol. 128r) Prologue to 2 Corinthians ('*Afftir penaunce…*'). Rubric: '*Here endiþ þe firste pistle to corinthis & bigynneþ þe prolog on þe secunde pistle to Corinthies*'.

(fol. 128r) 2 Corinthians. Rubric: '*Ierom in his prolog on þis pistle seiþ þis Capitulum primum*'.

(fol. 135r) Prologue to Galatians ('*Galathies ben grekis…*'). Rubric: '*Here endiþ þe secunde pistle to corinthis & bigynneþ þe prolog on þe pistle to Galathies*'.

(fol. 135r) Galatians. Rubric: '*Ierom in his prolog to galathis writiþ þis & here endiþ þe prolog & bigynneþ þe firste chapitir*'.

(fol. 138v) Prologue to Ephesians ('*Effecianes ben men of asie…*'). Rubric: '*Here endiþ þe pistle to galathies & bigynneþ þe prolog on þe pistle to Effesies*'.

(fol. 138v) Ephesians. Rubric: '*Ierom in his prolog on þis pistle seiþ þis þe I chapiter*'.

(fol. 142r) Prologue to Philippians ('*Filipenses ben of macedonye…*'). Rubric: '*Here endiþ þe pistle to Effecies & bigynneþ þe prolog on þe pistlle to Philipenses*'.

(fol. 142r) Philippians. Rubric: '*Ierom in his prolog on þis pistle seiþ þis Capitulum primum*'.

(fol. 144v) Prologue to Colossians ('*Colocenses ben also loadicenses…*'). Rubric: '*Here endiþ þe pistle to ffilipences & bigynneþ þe prolog on þe pistle to colocenses*'.

(fol. 144v) Colossians. Rubric: '*Ierom in his prolog on þe pistle seiþ þis Capitulum primum*'.

(fol. 147r) Prologue to 1 Thessalonians ('*Tessalonycenses ben macedonyes…*'). Rubric: '*Here endiþ þe pistle to colocensis & bigynneþ þe prolog on þe pistle to tessalonycenses*'.

(fol. 147r) 1 Thessalonians. Rubric: '*Ierom in his prolog on þis pistle seiþ þis Capitulum primum*'.

(fol. 149r) Prologue to 2 Thessalonians ('*The apostle writiþ…*'). Rubric: '*Here endiþ þe firste pistle to tessalonycenses and bigynneþ þe prolog on þe secunde pistle to tessalonycenses*'.

(fol. 149v) 2 Thessalonians. Rubric: '*Ierom in his prolog on þis pistle seiþ þis*'.

(fol. 150v) Prologue to 1 Timothy ('*He enformyþ and techiþ …*'). Rubric: '*Here endiþ þe secunde pistle to tessalonycenses & bigynneþ þe prolog on þe first pistle to tymothe*'.

(fol. 150v) 1 Timothy. Rubric: '*Ierom in his prolog on þis pistle seiþ þis*'.

(fol. 153v) Prologue to 2 Timothy (‘*He writiþ also…*’). Rubric: ‘*Here endiþ þe firste pistle to tymothe & bigynneþ þe prolog on þe secunde pistle to timothe*’.

(fol. 153v) 2 Timothy. Rubric: ‘*Ierom in his prolog on þis pistle seiþ þis*’.

(fol. 155v) Prologue to Titus (‘*He warneþ tite…*’). Rubric: ‘*Here endiþ þe secunde pistle to tymothe and bigynneþ þe prolog on þe pistle to tite*’.

(fol. 155v) Titus. Rubric: ‘*Ierom in his prolog on þis pistle seiþ þis Capitulum primum*’.

(fol. 157r) Prologue to Philemon (‘*He makiþ famyliar…*’). Rubric: ‘*Here endiþ þe pistle to tite and bigynneþ þe prolog on þe pistle to ffilemon*’.

(fol. 157r) Philemon. Rubric: ‘*Ierom in his prolog on þis pistle seiþ þis & here bigynneþ þe pistle þe firste chapitir*’.

(fol. 157v) Prologue to Hebrews (‘*First it is to seie…*’). Rubric: ‘*Here endiþ þe pistle to ffilemon and bigynneþ þe prolog on þe pistle to þe Ebrews*’.

(fol. 158r) Hebrews. Rubric: ‘*Ierom in his prolog on þis pistle seiþ þis Capitulum primum*’.

(fol. 166v) Prologue to Acts (‘*Luyk of antyoche…*’). Rubric: ‘*Here endiþ þe pistle to Ebrews and bigynneþ þe prolog on þe dedis of apostlis*’.

(fol. 167r) Acts. Rubric: ‘*Þis seiþ Ierom in his prolog þe firste chapitir*’.

(fol. 197v) The Catholic epistles. Prologue to James (‘*The ordre of þe seuen epistlis…*’). Rubric: ‘*Here bigynneþ a prolog on þe pistlis of cristen feiþ þat ben seuen in ordre*’.

(fol. 198r) James. Rubric: ‘*Ierom on þis pistle seiþ al þis*’.

(fol. 201r) 1 Peter. Rubric: ‘*Here endiþ þe pistle of Iames & bigynneþ þe first pistil of peter*’.

(fol. 204r) 2 Peter. Rubric: ‘*Here endiþ þe firste pistil of petir and bigynneþ þe secunde*’.

(fol. 206r) 1 John. Rubric: ‘*Here endiþ þe ij pistil of peter & bigynneþ þe first of Ion*’.

(fol. 209r) 2 John. Rubric: ‘*Here endiþ þe first pistil of Ioon And here bigynneþ þe secunde þe*’.

(fol. 209v) 3 John. Rubric: ‘*Here endiþ þe secunde pistil of Ioon & bigynneþ þe þridde*’.

(fol. 210r) Jude. Rubric: '*Here endiþ þe þridde pistil of Ioon and bigynneþ þe pistil of Iudas i° c°*'.

(fol. 210v) Prologue to Apocalypse ('*Alle men þat wolen…*'). Rubric: '*Here endiþ þe pistil of Iudas & bigynneþ þe prolog on þe apocalips*'.

(fol. 212r) Apocalypse.

3. (fols. 226v–266r) OT lectionary of Type II, preceded by a rubric: '*Here endiþ þe apocalips of Ioon & also þe newe testament And here bigynnen þe lessouns and pistlis of þe olde lawe þat ben redde in þe chirche bi al ȝeere þe first friday lessoun in aduent Isaie Ii c°*'. The temporal is followed by the proper (fol. 257r), the common (fol. 261v), and commemorations (fol. 265r). Each reading is preceded by a rubric, stating the liturgical occasion, and giving the title of the biblical book and a chapter number. Indexing letters are entered in the margins at the beginning of readings.

The readings start with introductory statements that precede them at Mass (e.g., '*The lord god seiþ þese þingis*', fol. 228r) underlined in red. The readings used for more than one occasion are not repeated and instead the rubrics contain cross-references, e.g., '*Seke it on S Siluestir day*' (fol. 263r). The reading for the first Mass on Christmas morning is preceded by a rubric explaining that it is performed by two voices: '*On cristemasse morewe þe firste lessoun at þe firste masse þe whiche lesson is sungun in þe pulput þe firste vers and þe laste of two to gidre but alle þe myddil vers oon syngiþ oon and anoþer syngiþ anoþer þe firste vers of þo þat ben sungen bi hemsilf is of þe tixte of Isaye þe profete and þe answere is as it were a glose of þe tixte / and so it is bi & bi þorȝout þe lessoun of whiche þis is þe first vers þat is sungen of boþe to gidre Isaye ix°*' (fol. 230v). In a passage that follows the part of one of the voices is underlining in red. At the end: '*Here enden þe lessouns and pistlis of al þe ȝeer*'. Running titles in black with red or blue paraphs on fols. 227r–236r, containing the names of liturgical seasons, e.g., '*Advent*', '*Cristmasse*', '*ffirste woke of lente*'. Added material within the text is underlined in red; no marginal glosses. Fols. 226v–228v are ruled but originally blank.

Decoration

6- to 9-line initials on gold background and full or three-quarters borders made of pink, blue and gold bars decorated with floral designs, interlace and gold disks at the beginnings of the gospels (fols. 13v, 39v, 56r, 84r), Romans (fol. 106r), Acts (fol. 167r), Catholic epistles (fol. 198r), Apocalypse (fol. 212r), and the beginning of OT lectionary (fol. 226v). The borders are the work of at least two different artists (cf. fols. 13v and 56r).

4 to 6-line gold initials on pink and blue background at the beginnings of other books and some prologues.

3-line blue initials with red penwork at the beginnings of prologues and chapters.

Catchwords decorated with foliage and flowers in black ink, red and yellow wash.

Dialect

eny(10), eche(10), fier(2)/fyer(6)/fuyr(1)/fayre(1), ȝouen(10), lijf(10), lyke(10), myche(10), siþ(2)/saiȝ(2)/sawȝ(1)/sauȝ(1)/saw(1)/say(2) (sg.), saien(1)/sien(1)/syen(1)/saye(1)/sayen(2) (pl.), silf(10), suche(8)/siche(2), þouȝ(8), þorouȝ(10)

-iþ(9)/-eþ(1) (pres.ind.3sg.), -en(10) (pres.ind.pl.), -ynge(10) (pres.part.), sche(10) (3sg.fem.pronoun, nom.), þei(10) (3pl.pronoun, nom.), hem(10) (3pl.pronoun, oblique), her(10) (3pl.pronoun, possessive)

Physical description

MATERIAL: parchment, paper flyleaves

DIMENSIONS: *c.*176 × 118 mm; leaves were trimmed in rebinding, occasionally causing the loss of text in the margins

NUMBER OF LEAVES: 169

FOLIATION: modern in pencil: i–iv + 1–169

COLLATION: (fol. i–iv) paper and parchment flyleaves | (fols. 1–2) I (12) | (fols. 13–36) II–IV (8) | (fols. 37–43) V (8–1(?)) 1(?) cancelled, no loss of text | (fols. 44–267) VI–XXXIII (8) | (fols. 268–269) parchment singleton (?) and paper flyleaf

Catchwords survive (see Decoration); leaf signatures occasionally survive. St John's gospel starts on a new quire on fol. 84r.

RULING: ruled in ink for two columns with single vertical and double horizontal bounding lines extending the full height and width of page; prickings occasionally survive; 34 lines per page; written space: *c.*115 × 80 mm

SCRIPT: small informal textura, black and brown ink; de Hamel (2001, p. 178) tentatively suggests that the manuscript may be by the same scribe as MS Fairfax 11 and MS Bodl. 183; see, however, Peikola (2003), pp. 39–40

RUBRICATION: rubrics in red

SEC. FOL.: '*Twelfþe nyȝt*" (fol. 2r, table of lections)

Binding

Black silk and leather on wood boards, badly worn, English (?), 16th century. Sown on five cords, five raised bands on spine. Recesses in/at the edge of the upper board, the clasps now missing, with holes from their attaching pins near the centre of the lower board. Silver clasps with 'IHS' and 'MR', described by Forshall and Madden in 1850, are reported lost already in the *Summary catalogue*, vol. 2, part II, in 1922. '665' written in white paint on spine. Paper pastedowns and flyleaves. Edges of textblock dyed red.

Provenance

1. Possibly made in the same workshop as MS Fairfax 11 and MS Bodl. 183.

2. Sixteenth-century owner who added notes in the margins in English and calendar dates to the sanctoral of the table of lections.

3. Bodleian Library: presented through Thomas Bodley with MS Bodl. 959 by Springham in 1602 (*Summary catalogue*, vol. 2, part II; Wheeler (1926)). Richard Springham, Magdalen College (?), Foster (1891–92), p. 1401. Earlier shelfmarks: 'B – 50' on fol. ii recto; Arch. B. 9.

Bibliography

Forshall and Madden (1850), vol. 1, p. xlvii.
Wheeler, G. W. (ed.), *Letters of Sir Thomas Bodley to Thomas James, first Keeper of the Bodleian Library* (Oxford: Clarendon Press, 1926), pp. 86–7.
Summary catalogue, vol. 2, part II, no. 2998.
Hudson (1989), p. 140 n. 29.
Ogilvie-Thomson, S. J., *IMEP*, Handlist VIII (1991), p. 17.
Scott (2000–02), vol. 1, p. 70, no. 273.
de Hamel (2001), p. 178.
Peikola (2003), pp. 39–40.
Dove (2007), pp. 59 n. 116, 299.
Solopova (2013), pp. 334–6, 338 n. 15.

8 MS Bodl. 771

SC no. 2553

Origin: England

Date: 14th century, end or 15th century, early

Text

[item 1 occupies quire I]

1. (fols. 1r–3v) Table of lections of Type I based on *Oon of Foure*, preceded by a rubric '*Her bigynneþ a kalender of alle þe gospels þat ben rad in chirche*'. The entries for readings consist of the name of the liturgical occasion, a reference to a part (in red) and chapter (in black) of *Oon of Foure*, followed by the first letter of the reading. The opening or closing words are not included. The table consists of the temporal, sanctoral (with a rubric '*Here bigynneþ þe sanctorum*') and commemorations. The sanctoral is similar to those in the manuscripts of LV (Forshall and Madden (1850), vol. 1, pp. 683–97) and has larger red initials at Andrew's day and eve, Conception of our Lady, Candlemas, Matthew the apostle, Annunciation, Philip and Jacob, 'Hooly rode' in May (Invention of the Cross), 'Midsomer day', John and Paul, Peter and Paul, Mary Magdalene, Lawrence, Assumption, Bartholomew, Nativity of our Lady, 'Hooly rode' in September (Exaltation of the Cross), Matthew, Michaelmas, Luke, Simon and Jude, All Saints. Commemorations are in the following order: Our Lady, Trinity, Cross, Holy Ghost, angels, '*at masse for breþeren*', peace, king and queen, '*to gete þe hooli gost*', a man for himself, '*to axe þe grace of þe hooly gost*', '*ffor synnes & repentours*', '*ffor tribulacioun of herte*', the sick, rain, '*forr clerete of eyr*', '*ffor tyme of bateil*', '*ffor him þat is in boondis*'. '*Weddings*' added after '*Amen dico*' at the end.

[items 2–3 occupy quires II–XVI]

2. (fols. 4r–79v) *Oon of Foure*, starting with a Prologue with a rubric '*þe prolog on a book maad of þe four gospelers*' (ed. Smith (1985)). Includes a list of chapters in twelve parts of *Oon of Foure* with their contents briefly described (fol. 4r–8r), followed by '*Here endeþ þe table of þe chapitres And biginneþ þe firste chapitre of þe firste part*' (fol. 8r). Part and chapter numbers in red. Running titles in red containing part numbers, usually as Roman numerals. Corrections by the original scribe in the margins. References to chapters in the gospels by the original rubricator at the beginning of each chapter, and sometimes elsewhere in the text. The beginnings of readings are marked in red in the text, and the first letter of each reading is written in the margin in red. A gloss within the text is underlined in red on fol. 94v;

no marginal glosses. At the end: '*here endiþ oon of foure þat is o book of alle foure gospeleris gaderid schortli into o story bi clement of lantony blessid be þe holy trinite amen*'. A leaf is missing after fol. 55 (part 8, chapter xiii).

3. (fols. 80r–118v) A personal collection for reading (?), consisting of extracts from most epistles, followed by extracts from Deeds (fol. 96vb), one short extract from the Apocalypse (fol. 97va) and extracts from the OT (fol. 97va) in EV. Includes some very short passages (one or two lines long), as well a complete book (1 Timothy, fols. 85v–88r). The extracts from epistles follow the order of epistles in the NT, whereas the extracts from the OT have a thematic organisation. The focus of the OT extracts seems to be on the moral and religious law, covering such subjects as the ten commandments (fols. 97va–102ra), including the worship of images (fols. 97va–8ra, 104ra), the fear of God (fols. 102va–b), kingship (fols. 102vb–103va), false gods (fols. 103va–104ra), priesthood (fols. 105va–106va), offerings (fols. 106va–107rb), sins (fols. 108ra–111ra), and wealth, poverty and alms (fols. 115vb–116ra). There are no extracts from the gospels, which suggests that the collection was designed for this copy or its archetype, and was meant to complement *Oon of Foure*. Notes in Latin in a 15th-century hand in the margins, some simply saying '*nota*', others drawing attention to the content of the passage, e.g., '*nota de sepulcris*', '*de superbia*'. Fragments of parchment bookmarks throughout.

Decoration

3- to 4-line red roughly drawn initials, some with penwork, at the beginning of parts of *Oon of Foure;* 2- to 3-line similar initials at the beginning of chapters.

Dialect

Oon of Foure

any(10)/ony(1), ich(5), fyr(7), ȝouun(8)/ȝouen(2), lyf(10), lyk(10), miche(9)/myche(1), siȝ(9)/saiȝ(1) (sg.), siȝen(7)/saiȝen(1) (pl.), self(3)/silf(7), sich(1)/siche(2), þouȝ(1), houȝ(10) ('how'), nouȝ(5) ('now')

-iþ(1)/-eþ(9) (pres.ind.3sg.), -en(10) (pres.ind.pl.), -ynge(3)/-inge(7) (pres. part.), she(10) (3sg.fem. pronoun, nom.), þei(8)/þey(2) (3pl.pronoun, nom.), hem(10) (3pl.pronoun, oblique), her(10) (3pl.pronoun, possessive); -z is occasionally used to represent the plural inflection of nouns

Physical description

MATERIAL: parchment, paper flyleaves

DIMENSIONS: *c.*260 × 118 mm

NUMBER OF LEAVES: 124

FOLIATION: modern in pencil and ink, i–iii 1–121

COLLATION: paper and parchment flyleaves | (fols. iii–3) I (4) | (fols. 4–51) II–VII (8) | (fols. 52–58) VIII (8–1) missing 6 | (fols. 59–114) IX–XV (8) | (fols. 115–119) XVI (6–1?) missing 6 (?) | paper and parchment flyleaves
Catchwords and occasionally quire signatures survive.

RULING: ruled in plummet for two columns with single vertical and horizontal bounding lines extending the full height and width of page; 37 lines per page; written space: *c.*178 × 112 mm

SCRIPT: very informal textura, black and brown ink; the table of lections is by a different scribe

RUBRICATION: rubrics and paraphs in red ink

SEC. FOL.: '*bootes wiþ*' (fol. 2r)

Binding

Speckled brown leather over pasteboard, late 17th or 18th century. Blind fillet-line border round the outer edge of both covers; blind rectangular frame with floral decorations and floral corner-pieces on both covers. Five raised bands on spine. Laid paper pastedowns and flyleaves. Fols. ii and 120 were the pastedowns of a medieval binding of wood boards sewn on five double cords. '771' written in dark ink on the edge of textblock.

Provenance

1. Made for a member of a monastic community (?): commemoration '*at masse for breþeren*', instead of a more usual '*For Bretheren and Sisters, and good doers/salus populi*' (see Forshall and Madden (1850), vol. 4, p. 697). Less professional appearance than is characteristic of many other manuscripts of the Wycliffite Bible; includes what appears to be a personal collection of extracts from EV designed for this copy or its archetype.

2. Letters of the alphabet in red in a medieval hand at the top of fol. ii verso.

3. Franciscan convent in Shrewsbury (?) (Ker (1964)): '*Couintre. conuentus. Fratrum Minorum Salopie…*', 15th century (fol. iii verso). The inscription can be compared with inscriptions in two other manuscripts attributed by Ker to the Franciscan convent in Shrewsbury: '*Iste liber pertinet comunitate* [? abbreviated and modified by the original hand] *Fratrum Salopie*' (Oxford,

University College MS 41, fol. 2v) and '*de communitate fratrum minorum Salopie*' (Oxford, University College MS 77, fol. 2r). The two inscriptions are in different hands, both probably of the 15th century, neither of which is the main hand of the manuscript. '*Couintre*' may be a personal name. See also MS Rawl. C. 258.

4. Thomas Rydway (also on fol. 120r), Thomas Hawys, Wyllyam Welat, Rycardus Lyne, Wylyam Justyes, Wylyam Lyne, Maryun Leypil, Aneys Colle, early 16th century (fol. ii verso).

5. In London in the 16th century (?): '*Rygt trusty and wellbelouyd frynd I grete yow well wyt all my hert desyryng to here of yowre welfere pryyng to here of myne prayng you to send me IX s by Iakys the caryar to londvn no more to yow all thys but all myty Iesu haue yow in hys kepy*' (fol. iii recto).

6. Thomas Cardiff, 16th century (fol. 1r), who owned other MSS currently in the Bodleian (*Summary catalogue*, vol. 2, part II).

7. Bodleian Library: the MS first appears in the Bodleian lists about 1655 (*Summary catalogue*, vol. 2, part II). Earlier shelfmark: 'Sup. A. Art. 58' (fol. 1r); '58' (fols. ii verso, iii recto, 1r, 120v).

Bibliography

Forshall and Madden (1850), vol. 1, p. xlvii.
Summary catalogue, vol. 2, part II, no. 2553.
Ker (1964), p. 179.
Smith, P. M., 'An edition of parts I–V of the Wycliffite translation of Clement of Llanthony's Latin gospel harmony *Unum ex Quattuor* known *as Oon of Foure*' (PhD thesis, University of Southampton, 1985).
Ogilvie-Thomson, S. J., *IMEP*, Handlist VIII (1991), p. 18.
Scott (2000–02), vol. 1, p. 73, no. 297.
Dove (2007), pp. 52 n. 78, 54, 299.
Raschko, M., '*Oon of Foure*: harmonizing Wycliffite and Pseudo-Bonaventuran approaches to the Life of Christ', in Johnson, I. and Westphall, A. F. (eds), *The Pseudo-Bonaventuran Lives of Christ: exploring the Middle English tradition* (Turnhout: Brepols, 2013), pp. 341–73 at 364–5.

9 MS Bodl. 959

Siglum: *E*

Origin: England

Date: 1390s (?)

Text

Fol. i is a paper flyleaf.

1. (fols. 1r–332r) Genesis–Baruch 3:20 in EV with usual prologues, including Jerome's prefatory epistles (**Plate 5**). Ends with '*...þe place of hem risen þe ȝunge*'. Lacks the beginning of Judith (1:1–4:16) and the prologue to Judith because of the loss of a leaf after fol. 210. Commendation of Ezra is inserted in the lower margin of fol. 191r. Most books start on a new leaf; psalms start on the verso of a new quire, though the prologues to psalms are in the preceding quire. Two pages (fols. 232v–233r) are left blank before the start of psalms. Approximately a third of a column is left blank on fol. 4r at the end of Jerome's prefatory epistles and before the beginning of Genesis. Rubrics in red or black in English or Latin. Running titles in red or black, some only on the versos, others on both sides of an opening, consisting of abbreviated titles of books without chapter numbers. Chapter numbers are usually in the margins in black or brown ink, written by the scribe rather than rubricator. Psalms are written as prose with verses starting with 1-line plain red initials. English psalm titles in red. Psalm numbers in the margins in the original hand as Roman numerals. Larger initials with penwork at psalms 26, 38, 52. 68, 80, 97, 109. Latin incipits of psalms are added in the margins in a different later hand on fols. 233v–235r. Fol. 232v is blank.

Heavily corrected in several contemporary hands, both in the margins and within the text. Corrections in the stint of the first scribe are particularly frequent and are often over erasures. Parts of the text on fols. 1–26 have been retraced in a later hand. Many corrections throughout are linguistic or stylistic, including the additions of the forms of the verbs 'have' and 'shall', the definite article, demonstrative and personal pronouns and other function words. Many corrections in the stint of the first scribe are orthographic, including the additions of final -e and -n, or insertions of punctuation.

2. (fol. 233r) A list of words added on the last flyleaf:

preuarians
e lawbreakers

angle / corner
[...]ers (?) exasterent
wrathede
laur / brede
ees / bees
ie foelai (?)
I errede
de gaust^{e}urs
wastynge
vnai
alas
cultiueresse
comelyng (see Fristedt (1953–73), vol. 1, pp. 70–1).

Decoration

4- to 10-line initials with blue penwork at the beginning of prefatory epistles and books.

2- to 3-line plain red initials at the beginning of chapters.

Dialect

First scribe

eny(9)/ony(1), eche(5)/ech(5), fyer(7)/fyre(2)/fyr(1), ȝiue(1)/ȝeue(2)/ȝeuen(4), lyf(10), lyke(10), mych(8)/myche(1)/mich(1), seeȝ(7)/saw(1) (sg.), seen corrected to siȝen(1)/seen corrected to seien(2)/seein(1) (pl.), self(8)/-seluen(2), sich(2)/siche(1)/sych(3), þorou(1)/þoru(3)

-iþ(8)/-eþ(2) (pres.ind.3sg.), -en(10) (pres.ind.pl.), -yng(6)/-ing(4) (pres. part.), sche(10) (3sg.fem.pronoun, nom.), þey(8)/þei(1)/þeȝ(1) (3pl.pronoun, nom.), hem(10) (3pl.pronoun, oblique), here(5) (3pl.pronoun, possessive)

Also preterites: seeyȝ, fleeyȝ; participles often with the prefix: yschewid, yspoke; plurals: clotheȝ, bryddeȝ (Forshall and Madden (1850)).

Second scribe

eny(10), eche(10), fuyr(10), ȝouyn(1)/ȝeuen(3)/ȝeue(3)/ȝeuyn(1), life(7)/lyfe(3), lyke(9)/like(1), moche(10), sauȝ(1)/sawȝ(1)/say(2)/saw(1) (sg.), sawe(1)/syȝyn(1) (pl.), self(10), such(9)/sich(1)

-eþ(10) (pres.ind.3sg.), -en(3)/-yn(3)/-n(1)/-eþ(2)/-þ(1) (pres.ind.pl.), -ynge(8)/-inge(2) (pres.part.), she(1)/sheo(7)/sche(2) (3sg.fem.pronoun, nom.), þei(9)/þey(1) (3pl.pronoun, nom.), hem(10) (3pl.pronoun, oblique), here(8)/þer(1)/þer corrected to þeir(1) (3pl.pronoun, possessive)

Also hit, hul, hully, gulty, hud for 'it', 'hill', 'hilly', 'guilty', 'hid'; folly for 'full', folfulle for 'fulfil', fluys for 'fleece', opp for 'up', opon for 'upon', ȝerstynday for 'yesterday', hanfol for 'handfu'l, ȝut for 'yet', prude for 'pride', sulle for 'sell' (Forshall and Madden (1850)).

Third scribe (psalms)

any(6)/eny(1), eche(10), fijr(9)/fyr(1), ȝyuen(4)/ȝeeuen(1), lijf(10), lijc(10), myche(10), saw(1)/sawȝ(6) (sg.), seeȝen(7) (pl.), self(6), þurȝ(10)

-eþ(10) (pres.ind.3sg.), -en(9)/-yn(1) (pres.ind.pl.), -ynge(8)/-inge(2) (pres. part.), þei(9)/þey(1) (3pl.pronoun, nom.), hem(2)/þem(8) (3pl.pronoun, oblique), þer(10) (3pl.pronoun, possessive)

Fourth scribe

any(10), eche(10), fijr(10), ȝyuen(6)/ȝyue(1), lijf(5), lijc(10), myche(10), sawȝ(5)/saȝ(1)/saw(1) (sg.), seyn(1)/seeȝen(1)/seen(1) (pl.), self(10). such(7)/suche(2)/shuch(1), þof(4), þurȝ(10)

-iþ(4)/-eþ(6) (pres.ind.3sg.), -en(10) (pres.ind.pl.), -ynge(2)/-inge(5)/-ende(2)/-yn(1) (pres.part.), þei(9)/þey(1) (3pl.pronoun, nom.), hem(8)/þem(2) (3pl.pronoun, oblique), þer(8)/þeir(2) (3pl.pronoun, possessive)

Also: slowȝ.

Physical description

MATERIAL: parchment, paper flyleaves. The quality of parchment is very variable, some is thin and white, whereas other is rough; some leaves have several holes (e.g., fol. 119)

DIMENSIONS: *c.*330 × 230 mm; cropped in rebinding, occasionally causing the loss of marginal text, such as the running titles

NUMBER OF LEAVES: 335

FOLIATION: modern in pencil: i + 1–334

COLLATION: (fol. i) paper flyleaf | (fols. 1–204) I–XVII (12) | (fols. 205–215) XVIII (12–1) missing 7 | (fols. 216–323) XIX–XXVII (12) | (fols. 324–333) XXVIII (12–2 (?)) missing 10 and 12 (?) | (fol. 334) paper flyleaf
Catchwords survive, quire signatures occasionally survive.

RULING: ruled for two columns with single vertical and horizontal bounding lines extending the full height and width of page; 52–62 lines per page; written space: *c.*210–230 × 150–160 mm

SCRIPT: The work of four or more scribes; first scribe: Prefatory epistles–Exodus, fols. 1r–44v, Anglicana; second scribe: Leviticus–Judges 7:13, fols. 45r–93v, Anglicana; third scribe (this section may be the work of two or more scribes): Judges 7:13–Ecclesiasticus 48:6, fols. 93v–288r, Anglicana; fourth scribe: Ecclesiasticus 48:6–end, informal textura, fols. 288r–332r. According to Forshall and Madden, the last hand is identical to the last hand of MS Douce 369 (1850, vol. 1, p. l). This was questioned by de Hamel who pointed out, probably correctly, that only the added note naming Hereford in MS Douce 369 may be by the last scribe of MS Bodl. 959 (2001, p. 172).

RUBRICATION: Rubrics in red or black ink. The text of a rubric in black ink in the margin and a note '*wryte þis with red*[…]' next to a rubric on fol. 300r.

SEC. FOL.: '*my self*' (fol. 2r)

Binding

English, 16th century. Green velvet with brass bosses and corner-pieces, backed with green leather.

Provenance

1. Execution is highly variable, suggesting that it is a working copy; heavily corrected, perhaps used in a workshop. There is no attempt to match hands, the format of rubrics, running titles or chapter numbers. The last hand may be the hand responsible for the Hereford inscription in MS Douce 369 (de Hamel (2001), p. 172). The text may have been checked against MS Douce 369, or a version similar to it, and corrected to bring it in conformance with this version. A break at the same point in the text occurs in MS Douce 369 and Cambridge University Library MS Ee. 1. 10.

2. '*þat þing þat ȝe spac of touchynge Sauages douȝter wole not ȝet be*', 15th century, fol. 333v.

3. Bodleian Library: presented through Thomas Bodley with MS Bodl. 665 by Springham in 1602 (*Summary catalogue*, vol. 2, part I; Wheeler (1926)). Richard Springham, Magdalen College (?), Foster (1891–92), p. 1401.

Bibliography

Forshall and Madden (1850), vol. 1, pp. xlvii–xlviii.
Deanesly (1920), *passim*.
Summary catalogue, vol. 2, part I, no. 3093.
Mallet, C. E., *A history of the University of Oxford*, 3 vols (London: Methuen, 1924–27), vol. 1, p. 231.

Wheeler, G. W. (ed.), *Letters of Sir Thomas Bodley to Thomas James, first Keeper of the Bodleian Library* (Oxford: Clarendon Press, 1926), pp. 86–7.

Fristedt (1953–73), *passim.*

Lindberg (1959–97), edition.

Fristedt, S. L., 'A weird manuscript enigma in the British Museum', *Studier i modern sprakvetenskap*, Acta Universitatis Stockholmiensis, Stockholm Studies in Modern Philology, New Series, 2 (1964), pp. 116–21 at p. 121.

Hudson (1978), pp. 157, 163, 164.

Smith, J. J., 'Linguistic features of some fifteenth-century Middle English manuscripts' in Pearsall, D. A. (ed.), *Manuscripts and readers in fifteenth-century England: the literary implications of manuscript study; essays from the 1981 conference at the University of York* (Cambridge: D. S. Brewer, 1983), pp. 104–12.

Hudson (1985), pp. 104, 106, 176.

Hudson (1988), pp. 238–47.

Lindberg, C., 'A note on Wyclif's English', in Oshitari, K. *et al.* (ed.), *Philologia Anglica: essays presented to Professor Yoshio Terasawa on the occasion of his sixtieth birthday* (Tokyo: Kenkyusha, 1988), pp. 385–88 at pp. 387, 389.

Tanabe, H., 'On some English renderings in the vocabulary of the Wycliffite Bible', in Oshitari, K. *et al.* (1988), pp. 389–402, *passim.*

Yonekura, H., 'Wyclif's Romance vocabulary: the case of the Wycliffite Bible', in Oshitari, K. *et al.* (1988), pp. 403–21 at pp. 404, 405.

Hudson (1989), p. 139.

Samuels, M. L., 'The dialects of MS Bodley 959', in McIntosh, A., Samuels, M. L. and Laing, M. (eds), *Middle English dialectology: essays on some principles and problems* (Aberdeen: Aberdeen University Press, 1989), pp. 136–49.

A Continental shelf: books across Europe from Ptolemy to Don Quixote: an exhibition to mark the re-opening of the Bodleian Exhibition Room, Bodleian Library (Oxford: Bodleian Library, 1994), no. 38.

Smith, J. J., 'Dialect and standardisation in the Waseda manuscript of Nicholas Love's *Mirror of the Blessed Life of Jesus Christ*', in Beadle, R., Oguro, S. and Sargent, M. (eds), *Nicholas Love at Waseda: proceedings of the international conference 20–22 July 1995* (Cambridge: Boydell & Brewer, 1997), pp. 129–41 at p. 132.

Scott (2000–02), vol. 1, p. 81, no. 347.

de Hamel (2001), pp. 170–2.

Dove (2007), pp. 88, 99, 103–4, 141, 143–4, 146, 148, 153, 175–7, 178, 199, 214, 223, 224, 225, 230, 234, 253, 255–6.

10 MS Bodl. 978

Origin: England

Date: 14th century, late, or 15th century, early

Text

(fols. 1r–3v) Paper flyleaves, mostly blank (see Provenance).

[item 1 occupies quires I–XXI]

1. (fols. 4r–168v) *Oon of Foure*, starting with the prologue with a rubric '*þe prolog on a book made of þe four gospelis*' (ed. Smith (1985)). Rubric on fol. 4v: '*here bigynneþ oon of four. þat is oo book of alle foure gospelleris gadred schorli in to oo stori bi clement of lantony. And þis book is in xij partis. þis is þe first parte*'. At the end: '*here endeþ oon of foure þat is oo book of alle foure gospelleris gadred schortli in to oon story bi clement of lantony*'. Running titles in red on both rectos and versos identifying the five parts, e.g., '*þe firste parte*'. Chapter numbers as red Arabic numerals. References to gospels in the margins in red or black. Indexing letters, probably added, in the margins. The beginnings of lections are marked with black paraphs highlighted with yellow wash, probably added. The beginnings of most lections are also accompanied by added notes in English or Latin, identifying feasts for which the lections are intended, e.g., '*vigilia Iohannis baptiste*' (fol. 6r), '*to andru day*' (fol. 26v), '*feria 6 epiphanie*' (fol. 27r), apparently in the hand responsible for the added table of lections (see below). Added glosses, identifying episodes in the narrative in English or Latin, in the same hand, and added drawings illustrating the text, apparently also in the same hand (e.g., drawings of a snake for '*edderis*' (fol. 14v), axe for '*axe*' (fol. 15r), jars at the beginning of the narrative about the wedding feast in Cana (fol. 19r), etc.; see Scott (2000–02), for a full list and **Plate 6**. Dark ink, yellow wash, and occasionally red ink are used for both drawings and glosses. Corrections and erasures, some by the original scribe. Fol. 169 is ruled but blank.

[item 2 occupies quire XXII]

2. (fols. 170r–181v) Table of lections of Type II, with readings from both OT and NT, added in the hand responsible for most liturgical and other added notes in the margins. Rubric '*adventus*' at the beginning. The temporal is followed by a short sanctoral, common and commemorations. The entries consist of the name of the liturgical occasion, the opening words of a reading, abbreviated reference to a book and chapter of the Bible and an indexing letter. Most entries for readings from the gospels do not include

an indexing letter for the gospels, but instead references to a part, chapter and indexing letter of *Oon of Foure*. The opening words of the readings are those of WB, not *Oon of Foure*. The quire on which the table is written is probably added: unlike most quires it contains 12 leaves and its parchment is thinner than elsewhere.

[item 3 occupies quires XXIII–XXXVI]
3. (fols. 182r–285v) Catholic epistles, Acts and the Apocalypse in LV, in an unusual order, with usual prologues. Running titles and chapter numbers in red. Indexing letters in the margins, most accompanied by notes in Latin identifying feasts for which the readings were intended.

(fol. 182r) 1 John. Rubric: '*þe first epistle of Ion Capitulum primum*'.

(fol. 187v) 2 John.

(fol. 188r) 3 John. Rubric: '*þe þridde epistle of Io(n) capitulum primum*'.

(fol. 188v) 1 Peter.

(fol. 194v) 2 Peter. Rubric: '*here bigynneþ þe 2 epistle of petre*'.

(fol. 198v) James. Rubric: '*þe epistles of Iames*'.

(fol. 209r) Jude. Rubric: '*þe epistle of Iudas capitulum primum*'.

(fol. 205v) Prologue to Acts ('*Luke of antioche…*'). Rubric: '*þe prolog of þe actus*'.

(fol. 206r) Acts.

(fol. 265r) Prologue to Apocalypse ('*Alle men þat wolen …*'). Rubric: '*þe prolog of þe apocalips*'.

(fol. 268r) Apocalypse. Rubric: '*þe apocalips capitulum primum*'. At the end: '*Here endeþ þe apocalips*'. Fols. 286–291v are paper flyleaves (see Provenance).

Decoration
3- to 4-line plain blue initials at the beginnings of biblical books and 2- to 3-line similar initials at the beginnings of chapters; 7-line initial at the beginning of the Apocalypse. Many initials include added drawings, mostly human faces and figures illustrating the text (see Scott (2000–02) for a full list). Added drawings in the margins (see Text).

Dialect (epistles, Acts and the Apocalypse)
ony(10), ich(10), fier(9)/fire(1), 3ouen(10), lijf(10), lik(8)/like(2), mych(4)/

mich(6), sauȝ(9)/saw(1) (sg.), sawen(6)/sauȝ(1) (pl.), self(10), such(7), þouȝ(1), þo[r](1)

-iþ(6)/-eþ(4) (pres.ind.3sg.), -en(10) (pres.ind.pl.), -yng(3)/-ing(7) (pres. part.), sche(10) (3sg.fem.pronoun, nom.), þei(10) (3pl.pronoun, nom.), hem(6) (3pl.pronoun, oblique), her(10) (3pl.pronoun, possessive)

Physical description

MATERIAL: parchment, paper flyleaves

DIMENSIONS: *c.*128 × 95 mm, trimmed in rebinding, occasionally causing the loss of marginal text and decoration

NUMBER OF LEAVES: 291

FOLIATION: modern in pencil, 1–48 + unnumbered leaf + 49–78 + unnumbered leaf + 79–289 + 280–291

COLLATION: (fols. 1–3) paper flyleaves | (fols. 4–169) I–XXI (8) | (fols. 170–181) XXII (12) added quire | (fols. 182–285) XXIII–XXXV (8) | (fols. 286–285) XXXVI (10) incorrect foliation after fol. 289, see Foliation | (fols. 286–291) XXXVII (6) paper flyleaves

Catchwords survive; signatures a–x in quires I–XXI; medieval leaf signatures in the added quire; signatures aa-o in quires XXIII–XXXVI. The outer bifolium in quire XII (fols. 90–97) is misbound as the second bifolium. There are notes on fols. 90r and 91v by the original rubricator pointing this out.

RULING: ruled in ink for a single column with single vertical and double horizontal bounding lines extending the full height and width of page; 24 lines per page; prickings survive; written space: *c.*103 × 65 mm

SCRIPT: textura, black ink

RUBRICATION: rubrics in red

SEC. FOL.: '*partis þis is*' (fol. 2r)

Binding

Brown leather over pasteboard. Gilt fillet-line and roll border with floral corner-pieces on both covers. Four raised bands on spine framed by gilt decoration. '978' in white paint on spine. Edges of textblock dyed green. Upper pastedown of laid paper; lower pastedown removed; laid paper flyleaves.

Provenance

1. Added table of lections, marginal glosses and liturgical notes in Latin and English, and drawings in the margins and in the initials, all early 15th century.

2. '*Homly Chomdesly*', 17th century, fols. 291v and 290v.

3. '*To my loving ffriend Mr James Laurence at hereford*', 17th century, fol. 291v.

4. '*W(illia)m Abrahall His Booke 1711*' and '*W(illia)m Abrahall His Book 1797*' (fol. 3v); '1692' (fol. 287v); '1726' (fol. 289v).

5. Robert Jones of Peterstow, co. Hereford, who took his BA degree at Trinity College, Oxford, in 1728, and his MA in 1731 (Foster (1887–88), vol. 2, p. 771). Table of contents on the upper pastedown, followed by '*Lib. Bibl. Bodl. ex dono Rob. Jones A.B. e Coll. Trin. Oxon.*'

6. Bodleian Library: given by Jones. Earlier shelfmarks: 'Arch. D. 112' (fol. 3v), 'Arch. E. 120' (fol. 4r), 'Super. C. Art. 15.' (fol. 3r).

Bibliography

Summary catalogue, vol. 5, no. 27716.

Smith, P. M., 'An edition of parts I–V of the Wycliffite translation of Clement of Llanthony's Latin gospel harmony *Unum ex Quattuor* known *as Oon of Foure*' (PhD thesis, University of Southampton, 1985).

Pearsall, D. and Scott, K. L. (eds), *Piers Plowman: a facsimile of Bodleian Library, Oxford, MS Douce 104* (Cambridge: D. S. Brewer, 1992), p. lxxxv, no. 5.

Scott, K. L., 'Limning and book-producing terms and signs *in situ* in late-medieval English manuscripts: a first listing', in Beadle, R. and Piper, A. J. (eds), *New science out of old books: studies in manuscripts and early printed books in honour of A. I Doyle* (Aldershot: Scolar Press, 1995), pp. 142–88 at p. 165 n. 21.

Kerby-Fulton, K. and Despres, D. L., *Iconography and the professional reader: the politics of book production in the Douce Piers Plowman* (Minneapolis and London: University of Minnesota Press, 1999), pp. 30, 33, 139, 217 n. 114, figs. 40–2.

Morey (2000), siglum OF.

Scott (2000–02), vol. 1, p. 81, no. 351.

Dove (2007), p. 299.

Raschko, M., '*Oon of Foure*: harmonizing Wycliffite and Pseudo-Bonaventuran approaches to the Life of Christ', in Johnson, I. and Westphall, A. F. (eds), *The Pseudo-Bonaventuran Lives of Christ: exploring the Middle English tradition* (Turnhout: Brepols, 2013), pp. 341–73 at 363–4.

11 MS Bodl. 979

Origin: England

Date: 15th century, first quarter

Text

Fol. 1 is a parchment flyleaf (see Provenance).

(fols. 2r–311v) NT in LV with usual prologues. Missing John 5:13–6:51 (after fol. 121), John 7:40–9:15 (after fol. 123), John 20:16–Romans 1:20 (after fol. 139), Romans 9:11–13:5 (after fol. 150), 1 Corinthians 1:12–2:8 (after fol. 154) and Colossians 1:16–3:10 (after fol. 195), all because of the loss of leaves (see Collation). Fols. 304–305, containing the Apocalypse 7:14–9:20, are misbound after fol. 303 (their correct place is after fol. 297). Usual rubrics in red, e.g., '*here eendiþ þe gospel of matheu & bigynneþ þe prologe on mark*' (fol. 42v); '*Ierom in his prologe on mark. seiþ þis*' (fol. 43r). At the end '*Here eendiþ þe apocalips of ioon þe laste book of þe newe testament*'. Chapter numbers in red as Roman numerals. Running titles in red on both rectos and versos, consisting of an abbreviated title of the book and a chapter number on pages containing the beginnings of chapters. Indexing letters occasionally appear in the margins. Corrections in a contemporary hand. Several lines are left blank at the end of the second column on the last leaf (fol. 311v).

Decoration

Initials not filled in, apart from fol. 1r–v, which has 2- and 3-line blue initials with red penwork at the beginning of Matthew and its prologue.

6- to 8-line spaces left for initials at the beginnings of the gospels, 1 Corinthians, Deeds, and the Apocalypse; 4- to 5-line spaces at the beginnings of epistles; 2- to 3-line spaces at the beginnings of prologues and chapters.

Letters in the top line are occasionally taller and decorated with penwork, sometimes with anthropomorphic designs (e.g., a profile head on fol. 178r).

Dialect

ony(10), ech(10), fier(10), ȝouen(10), lijf(9)/lyf(1), lijk(10), myche(10), siȝ(7) (sg.), siȝen(7) (pl.), silf(10), sich(2)/siche(6), þouȝ(8), þoruȝ(10)

-iþ(5)/-eþ(5) (pres.ind.3sg.), -en(10) (pres.ind.pl.), -ynge(7)/-yng(1)/-inge(2) (pres.part.), sche(10) (3sg.fem.pronoun, nom.), þei(10) (3pl.pronoun, nom.), hem(10) (3pl.pronoun, oblique), her(10) (3pl.pronoun, possessive)

Physical description

MATERIAL: parchment

DIMENSIONS: *c.*132 × 87 mm; trimmed in rebinding

NUMBER OF LEAVES: 319

FOLIATION: modern in pencil, 1–279 + unnumbered leaf + 280–318

COLLATION: (fol. 1) parchment flyleaf | (fols. 2–121) I–XV (8) | (fols. 122–123) XVI (8–6) central bifolium of a quire (?) | (fols. 124–139) XVII–XVIII (8) a quire is missing after fol. 139, fols. 140–142 are modern parchment | (fols. 143–149) XIX (8–1) missing 1 | (fols. 150–153) XX (8–4) missing 2–5 | (fols. 154–160) XXI (8–1) missing 2 | (fols. 161–192) XXII–XXV (8) | (fols. 193–198) XXVI (8–2) missing 4–5 | (fols. 199–293) XXVII–XXXVIII (8) | (fols. 294–299) XXXIX (8–2) 5 and 6 are misbound after fol. 303 | (fols. 300–309) XL (8+2) fols. 304–305 are misbound leaves from quire XXXIX | (fols. 310–311) XLI (4–2 (?)) two singletons (?) | (fols. 312–318) parchment flyleaves

Catchwords survive. Quire signatures (Arabic numerals) occasionally survive, running consecutively [1]–23.

RULING: ruled in ink for two columns with single vertical and double horizontal bounding lines extending the full height and width of page; 32 lines per page; written space: *c.*100 × 60 mm

SCRIPT: textura, black and brown ink

RUBRICATION: rubrics in red ink

SEC. FOL.: '*bigat Salatiel*' (fol. 3r)

Binding

Red velvet over pasteboard, English, 16th century. The remains of two ties on both covers. '979' written in white paint and fragments of two paper labels on spine. Parchment pastedowns and flyleaves. Gilt (later addition) edges of textblock.

Provenance

1. Unfinished: chapter initials not filled in.

2. '*Thomas Atkingsonne*' (fols. 73v, 217v), '*Richard (?) Savage berton vpon humbe[.]*' (fol. 118v), '*Jhon Tyrwh*' (fols. 145r), '*Thomas Manton*' (fol. 177r), '*...mermaducke ys one of the best gentle men*' (fol. 182r), '*Robert*' (fol. 191v) as well as other partially erased 16th-century inscriptions in the margins.

3. Waad, Sir William (1546–1623), diplomat and administrator (see *ODNB*): '*Wy. waad de givr 1602. m(ay) 1. tu mástr támus badlez librari in de diviniti skul in áskfurd*' and '*mistur wád. av káventri*' (fol. 1r), '*Wy Waad*' (lower pastedown). On his spelling, see Dobson (1968), vol. 1, pp. 129–31.

4. Bodleian Library. Former shelfmark: 'Arch. B. 63' (upper pastedown), 'B. 20.' (fol. 1r).

Bibliography

Forshall and Madden (1850), vol. 1, p. xlviii.
Summary catalogue, vol. 2, part II, no. 3052.
Dobson, E. J., *English pronunciation, 1500–1700*, 2nd edn, 2 vols (Oxford: Clarendon Press, 1968).
Scott, K. L., 'Limning and book-producing terms and signs *in situ* in late-medieval English manuscripts: a first listing', in Beadle, R. and Piper, A. J. (eds), *New science out of old books: studies in manuscripts and early printed books in honour of A. I. Doyle* (Aldershot: Scolar Press, 1995), pp. 142–88 at p. 18.
Dove (2007), p. 299.

12 MS Douce 36

Siglum: h

Origin: England

Date: 15th century, first half

Text

Fols. 1–10 are paper flyleaves (see Provenance).

1. (fols. 11r–26r) Tobit in LV with rubric '*Here bigynneþ þe bok of tobie*'. Running titles preceded by red (on the recto) or blue (on the verso) paraphs. Chapter numbers as red Roman numerals, sometimes preceded by '*þe*'. Alternating red and blue paraphs at the beginning of sections within the text. No marginal glosses. Added material within the text underlined in red. Corrections in the original hand. At the end: '*Here endiþ þe blessid book of tobie*'. Added pointing hand at 13:6 ('...*knowleche ȝe to hym bifore alle men lyuynge*...'); added *nota* at 13:8 ('*preier is good with fastyng & almes, more þan to hide tresouris of gold*') and 13:10 ('*for þei þat don synne and wickidnesse ben enemyes of hire soule*').

2. (fol. 26r) Added opening verse of psalm 8: '*Domine dominus noster quam admirabile est nomen tuum in uniuersa terra quoniam eleuata est magnificenti…*'. Textura, 15th century, first half.

Fol. 26v is ruled for two columns, but blank. Fols. 27–38 are paper flyleaves, containing engravings inserted by Douce illustrating Tobit (see Provenance).

Decoration

5-line gold initial on blue and pink background at the beginning of the book.

2-line blue initials with red penwork at the beginnings of chapters.

Dialect

ony(4)/eny(5), ech(8), ȝouun(3)/ȝouen(1)/ȝoue(1), lijf(10), lijk(4), myche(6), siȝ(4) (sg.), sien(1) (pl.), silf(8)/self(2), suche(1), þouȝ(1)

-iþ(9)/-eþ(1) (pres.ind.3sg.), -en(10) (pres.ind.pl.), -ynge(8)/-inge(2) (pres. part.), sche(10) (3sg.fem.pronoun, nom.), þei(10) (3pl.pronoun, nom.), hem(10) (3pl.pronoun, oblique), her(10) (3pl.pronoun, possessive)

Physical description

MATERIAL: parchment, paper flyleaves

DIMENSIONS: *c.*128 × 90 mm

NUMBER OF LEAVES: 38

FOLIATION: modern in pencil, 1–38

COLLATION: (fols. 1–10) paper flyleaves | (fols. 11–26) I–II (8) | (fols. 27–38) paper flyleaves

Catchword on fol. 18v.

RULING: ruled in ink for two columns with single vertical and double horizontal bounding lines extending the full height and width of page; 27 lines per page; written space: *c.*92 × 60 mm

SCRIPT: textura, black ink

SEC. FOL.: '*and cloopis*' (fol. 2r)

Binding

Red leather over pasteboard, 18th century. Double gilt fillet lines round the outer edge of both covers. Gilt rectangular decoration with floral cornerpieces on both covers; the one on the front cover contains stamped lettering

'IOSEPH AMES'. Four raised bands on spine; gilt floral decoration on the panels between the bands. Fragments of a label at the bottom of the spine. Gilt edges of text block. Marbled paper pastedowns.

Provenance

1. Presumably not intended to contain any texts apart from Tobit: the right-hand column on fol. 26r is left blank and fol. 26v has original ruling, but is blank.

2. 'Hen: Jeffreyes' (fol. 10v), early 18th century.

3. Joseph Ames (bap. 1687, d. 1759), bibliographer and antiquary; see *ODNB*: 'July 26th 1728 Examined this MS by Wickliffs in Queen's College Oxford, and find it ye same || Jo: Ames' (fol. 10r). Armorial book-plate of Ames of Norfolk (fol. 10v); lot 825 at his sale 5 May 1760 (Rogers (1975)).

4. Mark Cephas Tutet: contained armorial book-plate according to the *Summary catalogue*, vol. 4, part II (1897), currently missing; lot 500 at his sale 15 February 1786 (Rogers (1975)).

5. Gustavus Brander (1719/20–87), merchant and antiquary; see *ODNB*: 'Gustavus Barnder || 1786 || 27', followed by a note in Douce's hand: 'Who paid £1..2..0 for this MS at Mr Tutets sale' (fol. 1v). Lot 1085 at his sale in 1790, paid for 16/- by Douce (Rogers (1975)).

6. Francis Douce (1757–1834); see *ODNB*: 'This agrees with No 2249 Harl. MS but differs from the book of Tobit in my MS Wicliffis bible || F. Douce' (fol. 10r); armorial book-plate (fol. 1r); added engravings (fols. 27v–34v).

7. Bodleian Library: received in 1834 with bequest of Douce.

Bibliography

Forshall and Madden (1850), vol. 1, pp. xxxvi, l.
Summary catalogue, vol. 4, part II, no. 21610.
Rogers, D., 'Francis Douce's manuscripts: some hitherto unrecognised provenances', in *Studies in the Book Trade in honour of Graham Pollard*, Oxford Bibliographical Society Publications, n.s. 18 (Oxford, 1975), pp. 315–40 at p. 319.
Dove (2007), pp. 52 n. 78, 97–8, 299.

13 MS Douce 240

Origin: England

Date: 15th century, first half

Text

Fols. i–viii are blank paper flyleaves.

1. (fols. 1r–182r) NT in LV, imperfect at the beginning, starting at 2:1 ('[...] *in þe daies of kyng eroude*'). Leaves at the beginning of the four gospels, Romans, 2 Corinthians, Acts and the Apocalypse, that probably contained illuminated initials and borders, are excised, and initials are excised at the beginning of several other books. The following text is missing: prologue to Matthew; Matthew 28:13–end; prologue to Mark; Mark 1:1–21; prologue to Luke after '...*gospels weren writen by*'; Luke 1:1–41; John 1:1–48, 12:44–14:1, 21:15–end; prologue to Romans; Romans 1:1–31; 1 Corinthians 15:41–end; prologue to 2 Corinthians; 2 Corinthians 1:1–3, 5:8–7:10; Hebrews 12:25–end; prologue to Acts; Acts 1:1–2; prologue to the Apocalypse after '... *wherfore þis book is seid*'; Apocalypse 1:1–4. Usual rubrics at the beginnings of prologues and books (where they survive), e.g., '*here endiþ þe gospel of marke & bygynneþ þe prologe on luyk*' (fol. 39v); '*Ierom in his prologe on mark. seiþ þis*' (fol. 43r). Running titles with red paraphs on the versos and with blue paraphs on the rectos, consisting of abbreviated titles of biblical books. Chapter numbers as red Roman numerals or sometimes written out as words. The beginnings of lections are marked by indexing letters in the margins and highlighted with yellow wash within the text; the ends of lections are marked with double strokes in the margins. Corrections in the margins in the original and contemporary hands. No marginal glosses, added material within the text is not underlined.

2. (fols. 182r–193r) Table of lections of Type I with the usual rubric in red, similar to the rubric in MS Fairfax 11, but partly unreadable because of water (?) damage. The entries consist of the name of the liturgical occasion in red, abbreviated reference to a book and chapter of the Bible, an indexing letter in red, the opening words of a reading, '*ende*' in red and the closing words of a reading. No running titles. Includes the temporal, followed by commemorations and the sanctoral.

Fols. 193v–195v, originally blank, contain added sketches and a coat of arms (see Decoration and Provenance). Fols. 196–205 are paper flyleaves.

Decoration

The four gospels, Romans, 2 Corinthians, Acts and the Apocalypse probably originally started with illuminated initials and borders, now excised (a border at the beginning of St John's gospel left an offset on fol. 65v). Other books start with 4- to 5-line gold initials on blue and pink background, decorated with penwork sprays, gold disks and leaves (e.g., fols. 106r, 111v, 114r, 116v); some initials are excised.

3-line blue initials with red penwork at the beginnings of prologues and chapters.

Added sketches, second half of the 15th century:

(fol. 193v) buildings (?), one with a standard on a pole (bottom of the page); cross; standard with a cross (top of the page), all faded;

(fol. 194v) crucifix on a mound with two scrolls, one with 'Thomas Peuere', another with a faded inscription; chalice collecting blood from wounds, bones and skull and three nails at the bottom;

(fol. 195r) shield with a coat of arms and a scroll with 'ARMA THOME PE'.

Dialect

ony(10), ech(10), fier(10), ȝouun(9)/ȝouen(1), lyf(9)/lijf(1), lyk(10), myche(2)/mych(8), siȝ(9) (sg.), saien(1)/siȝen(5)/sayen(1) (pl.), silf(10), such(1)/suche(5)/sich(1)/siche(3), þouȝ(8), þorouȝ(1)/þorowȝ(1)/þoruȝ(8)

-iþ(7)/-eþ(3) (pres.ind.3sg.), -en(10) (pres.ind.pl.), -ynge(9)/-inge(1) (pres. part.), sche(10) (3sg.fem.pronoun, nom.), þei(10) (3pl.pronoun, nom.), hem(10) (3pl.pronoun, oblique), her(10) (3pl.pronoun, possessive)

Physical description

MATERIAL: parchment, paper flyleaves; trimmed in rebinding

DIMENSIONS: *c.*163 × 109 mm

NUMBER OF LEAVES: 214

FOLIATION: modern in pencil: i–viii + 1–109 + 110a + 110b + 111–205

COLLATION: (fols. i–viii) paper flyleaves | (fols. 1–7) I (8–1) missing 1 | (fols. 8–23) II–III (8) | (fols. 24–30) IV (8–1) missing 2 | (fols. 31–38) V (8) | (fols. 39–45) VI (8–1) missing 2 | (fols. 46–61) VII–VIII (8) | (fols. 62–68) IX (8–1) missing 5 | (fols. 69–76) X (8) | (fols. 77–82) XI (8–1) missing 1 and 8 | (fols. 83–98) XII–XIII (8) | (fols. 99–104) XIV (8–2) missing 3 and 6 | (fols. 105–127) XV–XVII (8) | (fols. 128–134) XVIII (8–1) missing

6 | (fols. 135–166) XIX–XXII (8) | (fols. 167–173) XXIII (8–1) missing 5 | (fols. 174–189) XXIV–XXV (8) | (fols. 190–195) XXVI (6)
Catchwords survive.

RULING: ruled for two columns with single vertical and horizontal bounding lines extending the full height and width of page; 36 lines per page; written space: *c*.123 × 81 mm

SCRIPT: textura

RUBRICATION: rubrics in red ink

SEC. FOL.: '*to him & he say*' (fol. 2r)

Binding

Brown leather over pasteboard. Double blind fillet lines round the outer edge of both covers. Blind fillet and roll rectangular decoration with floral corner-pieces on both covers. Four raised bands on spine framed by gilt decoration. Red paper label with faded lettering and white paper label with '240' on spine. Edges of textblock speckled red.

Provenance

1. Belonged to Thomas Peuere in the second half of the 15th century: arms, lections on scrolls, sketches on fols. 193v–195r (see Decoration).

2. Lucas Campion, 16th century (fol. 195v).

3. Mr Bennett, 18th century (fol. 195v).

4. Armorial bookplate of Frederick Ekins, rector of Morpeth, Northumberland (d. 1842), see Foster (1887–88), p. 416; 'Revd Fred. Ekins' (upper pastedown).

5. Francis Douce (1757–1834); see *ODNB*: bookplate on the upper pastedown.

6. Bodleian Library: received in 1834 with bequest of Douce.

Bibliography

Forshall and Madden (1850), vol. 1, p. l.
Summary catalogue, vol. 4, no. 21814.
Pächt and Alexander (1966–73), vol. 3 (1973), no. 969.
Hudson (1989), p. 140 n. 29.
Kerby-Fulton, K. and Despres, D. L., *Iconography and the professional reader: the politics of book production in the Douce Piers Plowman* (Minneapolis and London: University of Minnesota Press, 1999), pp. 124, 239 n. 13.
Scott (2000–02), vol. 2, p. 37, no. 474.
Dove (2007), p. 299.

14 MS Douce 258

Siglum: *P*

Origin: England

Date: 15th century, first quarter

Text
Fol. i is a paper flyleaf.

[items 1–2 occupy quires I–VI]
1. (fols. 1r–39r) Sequences 'Commendation of the Souls' and Psalms of the Passion, characteristic of the Sarum Books of Hours, in English. 'Commendation of the Souls' consists of psalm 118 (fragmentary because of the loss of leaves, verses 1–7 (fol. 1r–v) and 27–176 (fols. 2r–17v)) followed by a translation of '*V. Requiem eternam dona eis domine. R. Et lux perpetua luceat eis. Kyrie eleyson. Christe eleyson. Kyrie eleyson.*'. This is followed by psalm 138 (fols. 18r–20v), a translation of '*Requiem eternam dona eis domine. Et lux perpetua luceat eis.A porta inferi erue Domine animas eorum. Credo videre bona domine in terra viventum. Requiescant in pacem. Amen.*' and a translation of the prayer '*Tibi Domine commendamus animas famulorum famularumque tuarum…*': '*To þee lord we bitaken þe soules of þi seruauntis bothe men an wymmen. so þat þei þat ben deede to þe worlde mown lyue to þee. & alle þe synnes þat þei han do by frelte of worldly lyuyng þou lord waishe hem aweye bi þe forȝeuenesse of þi most merciful pitee. Bi crist oure lord. So be it*' (fol. 20v). The Psalms of the Passion comprise psalms 21–30 (fols. 20v–39r) with a rubric '*These ben þe psalmes of þe passion*'. Psalm 23 is omitted by the scribe as noted in a rubric on fol. 26v: '*Seke in þe eende of þis boke & þer þou schal fynde Domini est terra*'.

The text of psalms comes from Richard Rolle's *The Prose Psalter* (IPMEP 271, ed. Bramley (1884)). Only the translation, with verses underlined, and commentary are included; the Latin text is omitted, though psalms are preceded by Latin incipits.

2. (fols. 39r–45v) The Wycliffite commentary on the Athanasian Creed (ed. Arnold (1869–71), vol. 3, pp. 71–81, and Hudson (2012–14), vol. 3, pp. 1182–94), ending imperfectly at '*but if crist were euene wyth þe fa…*' (Hudson (2012–14), vol. 3, p. 1192).

[items 3–4 are in a different hand and occupy quires VII–X]
3. (fols. 46r–48v) gospel readings for Christmas (John 1; only verses 11–14 survive, because of the loss of leaves), Easter (Mark 16), Ascension Eve (John

17), Ascension Day (Mark 16) and St Thomas's Day (John 20) in LV with rubrics in red.

4. (fols. 48v–69v) General epistles in LV: James, with the usual prologue–3 John, 1–6. Rubric: '*Here bigyneþ a prolog on þe pistles of cristen feythe þat ben seuene in ordre þat is to seye oon of James and tweyne of peter & iii of ioon & on of Iudas*'. Imperfect at the end because of the loss of leaves. Usual rubrics in red, e.g., '*Ierom on þis pistlis seiþ al þis*'. Chapter numbers in red as Roman numerals or written out as words. Fol. 70 is a paper flyleaf. No marginal glosses; added material within the text is not underlined. Corrections in the margins in a medieval hand.

Decoration

Fragment of a border on damaged fol. 1r, made of pink, blue and gold bars and penwork sprays.

2-line blue initials with red penwork at the beginnings of psalms; 1-line blue or red initials at the beginning of psalm verses and contrasting red or blue paraphs at the beginning of commentary entries in Rolle's *Psalter*.

2-line gold initial on blue and pink background at the beginning of Athanasian Creed.

2-line blue initials with red penwork at the beginning of gospel readings.

3- to 5-line blue initials with red penwork at the beginning of epistles; 2-line similar initials at the beginning of the prologue and chapters.

Dialect

(General epistles)
ony(10), ech(7)/eche(3), fier(4)/fire(1), ȝouen(1), lijf(10), lijk(5), myche(6), saȝ(1) (sg.), sayen(1) (pl.), self(10), such(2), þouȝ(1)

-eþ(7)/-iþ(1) (pres.ind.3sg.), -en(10) (pres.ind.pl.), -yng(2)/-ynge(8) (pres. part.), þei(10) (3pl.pronoun, nom.), hem(10) (3pl.pronoun, oblique), her(10) (3pl.pronoun, possessive)

Physical description

MATERIAL: parchment

DIMENSIONS: *c.*181 × 125 mm

NUMBER OF LEAVES: 71

FOLIATION: modern in pencil, i + 1–11 + 12/13 + 14–34 + 35a + 35b + 36–70

COLLATION: (fol. i) paper flyleaf | (fols. 1–6) I (8–2) missing 2–3 | (fols. 7–38)

II–V (8) | (fols. 39–45) VI (8–1) missing 8 | (fols. 46–52) VII (8–1) missing 1 | (fols. 53–68) VIII–IX (8) | (fol. 69) X (8–7 (?)) single leaf

Catchwords survive. Quire signatures in Rolle's *Psalter* run consecutively [a] to [f] and in gospels and epistles [a] to c.

RULING: ruled for a single column with single vertical and double horizontal bounding lines extending the full height and width of page; 26 lines per page; prickings survive; written space: *c.*127 × 82 mm

SCRIPT: textura, change of scribe on fol. 46r; black and brown ink

RUBRICATION: rubrics in red ink

SEC. FOL.: '*wisnessis*' (fol. 3r)

Binding

Paper over pastebord. Brown leather spine with gilt decoration. Red leather label on spine with gilt lettering 'PSALMS || &C. || MS.'; paper label with '258'. Marbled paper flyleaves.

Provenance

1. Two parts, fols. 1r–45v and fols. 46r–48v, though codicologically separate and written by diferent scribes, have similar ruling and dimensions of written space, and may have been produced to be bound together.

2. Note about the manuscript by R. Farmer on the upper pastedown.

3. Francis Douce (1757–1834); see *ODNB*: bookplate on fol. i recto; notes on the upper pastedown and fol. 70.

4. Bodleian Library: received in 1834 with the bequest of Douce.

Bibliography

Arnold, T., *Select English works of John Wyclif*, 3 vols (Oxford: Clarendon Press, 1869–71).
Bramley, H. R., *The Psalter: or Psalms of David and certain canticles* (Oxford: Clarendon Press, 1884).
Summary catalogue, vol. 4, no. 21832.
Colledge, E., 'The recluse: a Lollard interpolated version of the Ancren Riwle', *Review of English Studies* 15 (1939), pp. 1–15, 129–45 at p. 131.
Haring, N. M., 'Commentaries on the Pseudo-Athanasian creed', *Medieval Studies* 34 (1972), pp. 208–54 at p. 245.
Braswell, L., *IMEP*, vol. 4 (1987), pp. 52–4.
Hudson (1989), p. 141.
Ogilvie-Thomson, S. J., *IMEP*, vol. 8 (1991), p. 45.

Scott (2000–02), vol. 2, p. 38, no. 478.
Dove (2007), p. 299.
Hanna, R., *The English manuscripts of Richard Rolle: a descriptive catalogue* (Exeter: University of Exeter, 2010), pp. 149–50.
Hudson, A., *Two revisions of Rolle's English Psalter Commentary and the related canticles*, 3 vols, EETS 340, 341, 343 (2012–14). See vol. 1, p. lxvi.

15 MS Douce 265

Origin: England

Date: 15th century, middle

Text

1. (fols. i recto–1v) Fol. i is a paper flyleaf (see Provenance). Fols. ii–1 are an added bifolium from a Wycliffite table of lections (see Douce 265-a). Fols. 2–3 are parchment leaves ruled for two columns, but blank apart from early modern notes (see Provenance).

[item 2 occupies quire I]
2. (fols. 4r–13r) Table of lections of Type I (**Plate** 7) starting with a rubric '*Here bigynneþ a rule þat telliþ in whiche chapiters of þe bible ȝe may fynde þe pistlis & gospels þat ben rad in þe chirche aftir þe vss of salisbirie markid with lettris of þe a.b.c. at þe bigynnynge of þe chapiters or toward þe myddil or ende aftir þe ordre as þe lettris stonden in þe a.b.c. ffirst ben sett sondaies & verials to gidere and after þat þe sanctorum comyn & propre togider of al þe ȝeer ffirst is writun a clause of þe bigynnynge þerof and a clause of þe endinge þerof also*'. Contains NT lections only (cf. MS Bodl. 183). Includes all feasts characteristic of LV (Forshall and Madden (1850), vol. 4, pp. 683, 690–6), apart from Giles (1 September). The readings consist of the name of the liturgical occasion in red, abbreviated reference to a book and chapter of the Bible, an indexing letter in red, the opening words of a reading, '*ende*' in red, the closing words of a reading and double strokes in red. Includes the temporal, followed by commemorations of the Virgin Mary, Trinity, Holy Ghost, Cross, angels, '*ffor briþeren & sustris & salus populi*', peace, clear weather, rain, '*in time of batlis*', '*a man for him silf*', '*for pestilence of bestes*', pilgrims, weddings, sinners, sick, '*pistils for dede*' and gospels for the dead. Commemorations are followed by the sanctoral (both proper and common according to the rubric, but only proper is present). Larger initials at Conversion of St Paul, Candlemas, Annunciation, Nativity of John the

Baptist, Nativity of the Virgin Mary, St Luke and Halloween. At the end: '*Thus endiþ þe kalender of þe newe testament*'. Title 'pope' is erased (fol. 10r). Fol. 13v is ruled for the table of lections, but blank apart from an added note (see Provenance); fol. 14r–v is ruled for two columns, but blank.

[item 3 occupies quires II–XXX]
3. (fols. 15r–243v) NT in LV with usual prologues. Usual rubrics at the beginning of all prologues and books, e.g., '*here endiþ þe gospel of Matheu and bigynneþ þe prolog on þe gospel of mark*' (fol. 44r); '*Ierom on his prologe seiþ þis on mark*' (fol. 44v). Chapter numbers as red Roman numerals or written out as words in English. Running titles in red with blue paraphs on both rectos and versos, consisting of an abbreviated title of the biblical book only. At the end: '*Here endiþ þe apocalips of Ioon þe ende of þe newe testament*'. Corrections in a contemporary hand. No marginal glosses; added material within the text is not underlined. Indexing letters in the margins entered at the beginnings of lections, rather than consistently. The beginnings of lections are also highlighted with yellow wash within the text; the ends of lections are marked with double strokes in the margins and within the text. Crosses and '*nota*' added in the margins. Added notes in a 15th-century hand in the margins of the Apocalypse, briefly describing the content of the seven visions. Fols. 244–263v are ruled for two columns, but blank, apart from fol. 261r which contains an extract from Heinrich Suso, *Horologium Sapientiae, Cursus de aeterna sapientia*, added in a 15th-century hand. The extract contains the beginning of the *Cursus* up to the end of the third stanza of the '*Hymnus*' ('*Iesu dulcis memoria…*'), starting '*Salutem mentis & corporis…*' and ending '*…sed quid inuenientibus*' (ed. Künzle (1977), pp. 606–7).

Decoration
4-line gold initials on blue and pink background, decorated with penwork sprays and gold leaves, at the beginnings of books.

2-line blue initials with red penwork at the beginnings of prologues and chapters.

Dialect
ony(10), ech(5)/eche(5), fier(9)/fire(1), ȝouun(10), lyf(9)/lif(1), lijk(10), myche(10), siȝ(8)/syȝ(1) (sg.), saien(5)/siȝen(1)/seien(1) (pl.), silf(10), sich(4)/siche(6), þouȝ(8), þurȝ(2)/þourȝ(7)/þouȝr(1), birie (bury), verials ('ferials', table of lections, rubric)

-iþ(9)/-eþ(1) (pres.ind.3sg.), -en(10) (pres.ind.pl.), -ynge(3)/-inge(7) (pres.

part.), sche(10) (3sg fem.pronoun, nom.), þei(10) (3pl.pronoun, nom.), hem(10) (3pl.pronoun, oblique), her(10) (3pl.pronoun, possessive)

Physical description

MATERIAL: parchment

DIMENSIONS: *c.*181 × 124 mm

NUMBER OF LEAVES: 267

FOLIATION: modern in pencil, i–ii + 1–265

COLLATION: (fols. i–3) paper flyleaf, added bifolium and two parchment leaves | (fols. 4–13) I (10) missing 1 | (fols. 14–261) II–XXXII (8) | (fols. 262–263) XXXIII (4–2 (?)) | (fols. 264–266) paper flyleaves

Catchwords survive. Leaf signatures in NT run consecutively a–p in quires II–XVI (fols. 14–133) and a–o in quires XVII–XXX (fols. 134–245).

RULING: ruled for two columns with single vertical and double horizontal bounding lines extending the full height and width of page; 33 lines per page; written space: *c.*115 × 80 mm

SCRIPT: textura, black ink; the table of lections is by a different scribe

RUBRICATION: rubrics in red ink

SEC. FOL.: '*ffriday romans xiiii*' (fol. 5r, table of lections)

Binding

Red morocco over thick pasteboard, made for Thomas Rawlinson early in the 18th century. Gilt fillet lines and floral roll border round the outer edge of both covers. Gilt scallop shells in the four corners. A heraldic crest in the form of a bird with a scallop shell in its beak, surrounded by a wreath, at the centre of both covers. Six raised bands on spine edged with double gilt fillet lines. Gilt decoration on the panels between the raised bands. Gilt lettering 'N. TESTAMENT IN ENGLISH', 'MSS.' and paper label with '265' on spine. Marbled paper pastedowns; laid paper flyleaves.

Provenance

1. The table of lections and NT are codicologically separate and are the work of two different scribes, but the table of lections was written to accompany a NT since it omits all OT readings.

2. Extract from Heinrich Suso's *Horologium Sapientiae* added on empty leaves in a 15th-century hand.

3. Note by Robart Hornbe on fol. 13v recording that his mother gave him this book on 17 March, 1543: '*memorandum (?) yt my mother hathe gyvin to me Robart Hornbe herfore this newe testament yn xvij day of marche ye yere of ower lord god xliij in ye yere of ower soverayne lord king henry ye viij xxxiiij*'. Followed by more text in the same hand, crossed out.

4. Title 'pope' erased in the table of lections, presumably at Reformation.

5. Thomas Rawlinson (1681–1725); see *ODNB*: binding; fol. i verso.

6. Sir Peter Thompson (1698–1770), merchant and book collector; see *ODNB*: bought at Rawlinson's sale in 1733 (lot 365) for £4 (note on fol. 3v).

7. May have been owned by William Herbert (1718–1795); see *ODNB*: notes on fol. 1r–v. He is known to have bought books from Peter Thompson and to have collected bibles (see *ODNB*).

8. Gustavus Brander (1719/20–1787), merchant and antiquary; see *ODNB*: lot 1096 in his sale 13 February, 1790.

9. Francis Douce (1757–1834); see *ODNB*: bought at Brander's sale for £3 13*s.* 6*d.*; bookplate on the upper pastedown, notes on fols. i verso, 2r, 3v, stamp on fol. 4r. Added a bifolium from a Wycliffite table of lections (?).

10. Bodleian Library: received in 1834 with the bequest of Douce.

Bibliography

Forshall and Madden (1850), vol. 1, p. l.

Summary catalogue, vol. 4, no. 21839.

May, S. W., 'William Hunnis and the 1577 *Paradise of Dainty Devices*', *Studies in Bibiliography* 28 (1975), pp. 63–80 at p. 63 n. 2.

Rogers, D., 'Francis Douce's manuscripts: some hitherto unrecognised provenances', in Hunt, R. W., Philip, I. G. and Roberts, R. J. (eds), *Studies in the book trade in honour of Graham Pollard* (Oxford: Oxford Bibliographical Society, 1975), pp. 315–40 at p. 319.

Künzle, Pius (ed.), *Heinrich Seuses Horologium sapientiae*, Spicilegium Friburgense 23 (Freiburg/Schweiz: Universitätsverlag, 1977).

The Douce legacy: an exhibition to commemorate the 150th anniversary of the bequest of Francis Douce (1757–1834) (Oxford: Bodleian Library, 1984), no. 200.

Hudson (1989), p. 140.

Dove (2007), p. 299.

16 MS Douce 265-a

Origin: England

Date: 15th century, first quarter

Text

A bifolium from a Wycliffite table of lections of Type I with OT readings written out in full, bound with MS Douce 265 (fols. ii–1). Contains the end of the temporal and most of the commemorations; probably written to accompany a NT. Starts with the Ember Saturday before the 18th Sunday after Trinity and ends with the commemoration of the sick. NT readings consist of the name of a liturgical occasion in red, abbreviated reference to a book and chapter of the Bible, an indexing letter in red, the opening words of a reading, '*ende*' in red, the closing words of a reading and double strokes in red. OT readings are written out in full with added material within the text underlined in red, each preceded by a rubric stating the liturgical occasion. Some OT readings derive from EV (e.g., Ecclesiasticus 24, Genesis 24), whereas others from LV (e.g., Jeremiah 14, Jeremiah 23, Ecclesiasticus 44) (see the description of a similar table in MS Bodl. 531). Does not include Wednesday after the 25th Sunday after Trinity, an entry characteristic of LV (Forshall and Madden (1850), vol. 4, pp. 683–98). Commemorations are in the following order: the Virgin Mary, Trinity, Holy Ghost, Cross, angels, '*ffor breþeren & sistris & salus populi*', peace, clear weather, rain, '*In tyme of bateils*', '*a man for him silf*', '*ffor pestilence of beestis*', pilgrims, weddings, sinners and sick. Shares variants with Forshall and Madden's (1850) manuscripts EMRXk, including a rubric '*treno(rum) ii*' for an OT reading for 'clear weather'; the presence of the entry '*Commemoracioun of oure ladi in alle oþire tymes of þe ȝeer*'; and the order of commemorations, e.g., angels after the Cross (Forshall and Madden (1850), vol. 4, pp. 697–8). Running titles in red with blue paraphs written across a two-leaf opening.

Decoration

1-line blue initials with red penwork at the beginning of OT readings.

Dialect

biried(1), lijc(1), wijs(1) -eþ(3) (pres.ind.3sg.), -en(10) (pres.ind.pl.), -yng(2)/-ynge(1)/-inge(2)/-ing(1) (pres.part.),

þei(5) (3pl.pronoun, nom.), hem(8) (3pl.pronoun, oblique), her(3) (3pl. pronoun, possessive)

Physical description

MATERIAL: parchment

DIMENSIONS: *c.*213 × 147 mm

COLLATION: a single bifolium from the centre (?) of a quire; catchwords in red on the verso of both leaves

RULING: ruled in ink with double vertical and double horizontal (upper margin) bounding lines extending the full height and width of page; the lower margin has a single horizontal bounding line and an additional set of two bounding lines; 36 lines per page; written space: *c.*117 × 95 mm

SCRIPT: textura, black ink

RUBRICATION: rubrics in red ink

Provenance

1. A leaf from a Wycliffite NT with a table of lections (?).

2. Bound with MS Douce 265 by Francis Douce (?) (see also MS Douce 265).

17 MS Douce 369

Sigla: *C* – first part; *K* – second part

Origin: England

Composite manuscript comprising two parts described below: I (fols. 1r–250v) and II (fols. 251r–485v).

I (fols. 1r–250v)

Date: 1390s (?)

Text

Fols. i–ii are paper flyleaves, blank apart from Douce's notes on Wyclif.

(fols. 1r–250r) Numbers 20:2–Baruch 3:20 in EV with usual prologues (**Plate 8**). Imperfect at the beginning because of the loss of leaves. Prologues to psalms appear at the end of quire XVIII. The second of the two prologues occupies three-quarters of the first column on the last page of this quire (fol. 150v), the rest of the page is left blank and psalms start on a new quire. The books are numbered in a contemporary hand as shown in brackets after each title (see also Provenance). Running titles in black in the upper left margin, usually only on the versos, consisting of abbreviated titles of books without chapter numbers. Occasionally rubrics in red or black, in English or Latin, by the scribes, rubricator or added in contemporary hands (see below). Chapter numbers in black (occasionally in red) in the margins at the beginning of each chapter in Arabic numerals, preceded by '*c(apitulu)m*'. The contents of the chapters are summarised in Latin verses (two for each chapter) in the lower margins of pages containing the beginnings of chapters. The verses are laid out in long lines and rhyme at the end and at caesura. Such two-line verse summaries are in a smaller, more informal script, in a hand different from those of the main scribes, and are preceded by chapter numbers in Arabic numerals. The ruling for the verses (thick brown plummet) is similar to the ruling elsewhere in the manuscript (e.g., fols. 6v, 15v–16r, 189r, 193r). Occasionally the ruling is provided where the verses are absent (e.g., fols. 42v, 121r, 122r, etc.). Starting with fol. 132v the chapter numbers that accompany the verses are in red, and the verses are enclosed in red brackets. The verse summaries are absent in psalms and after fol. 206r (from chapter 47 of Ecclesiasticus onwards), though the ruling is provided up to fol. 208r. The lections are occasionally marked with a red bracket in the margin and sometimes with the opening and final letters of the passage written in red in the margins. Added material within the text is occasionally underlined faintly in brown ink (e.g., Jeremiah 8:7, fol. 230r).

Many corrections in the margins in contemporary hands, including cancellations, additions and substitutions of words or short phrases. Some corrections are stylistic or grammatical; particularly frequent are the substitution of '*þe whiche*' for '*þe*' or '*þat*', the insertion of the article '*þe*' and the future modal '*schal*' (e.g., fols. 193r, 198r–v, 200r, 202r, 203r, 224v). Other examples are '*resteyȝede*' for '*restide*' (fol. 65r), '*hadde taken*' for '*tok*' (fol. 80r), '*made of nouȝt*' for '*foormede*' (fol. 219v). Other contemporary marginal additions include: cross-references between biblical books (e.g., fols. 117r–v, 222r, 223v); notes providing the Latin version of a phrase (e.g., '*optaui et datus*', fol. 187v; '*melior est iniquitas…*', fol. 205r; '*clama ne cesses*', fol. 224r) and '*nota*' (fols. 184r, 185r, 194v, 223r, 229r etc.). Contemporary pointing hands and 'hedera' signs in the margins, some in red ink (fol. 146v), occasionally accompanied by notes referring to the content of passages (e.g., '*heritage of prestis*', fol. 206r), or drawing attention to them ('*noteþ weel*', fol. 230r; '*marke weel*', fol. 230v). Some notes are on scrolls or outlined in red ink (fol. 68r); many partially cropped off.

[quires I–XVIII]
(1r) Numbers 20:2 (4?) imperfect at the beginning, starting '*whanne the puple nedede water…*'. 17th-century note concerning the loss of leaves (see Provenance).

(fol. 8v) Deuteronomy (5).

(fol. 22v) Prologue to Joshua ('*At þe laste ended þe fyue bookis of moises…*').

(fol. 23r) Joshua (6).

(fol. 32v) Judges (7). Missing 1:21–4:4, because of the loss of a leaf after fol. 32.

(fol. 41r) Ruth (8).

(fol. 42v) Prologue to 1 Kings ('*Þe tunge forsoþe…*').

(fol. 43v) 1 Kings (9).

(fol. 56v) 2 Kings (10).

(fol. 67r) 3 Kings (11).

(fol. 78v) 4 Kings (12 and '*ezechie*').

(fol. 89v) Prologue to 1 Chronicles ('*Iff þe making of þe seuenti…*'). Rubric: '*Prologus paralipomenon*'.

(fol. 89v) Prologue to 1 Chronicles ('*Þe boc of paralipomenon…*').

(fol. 89v) 1 Chronicles (13).

(fol. 99v) Prologue to 2 Chronicles ('*Evsebeus ierome senden…*').

(fol. 100r) 2 Chronicles (14).

(fol. 112r) Prayer of Manasseh (note, added by the original scribe: '*þis preȝeere of manasse is not in ebrue*', fol. 112v).

(fol. 112v) Prologue to 1 Ezra ('*Wheþer it be hardere…*').

(fol. 113r) Prologue to 1 Ezra ('*Esdras et Neemye…*').

(fol. 113r) Commendation of Ezra. Rubric: '*Here folewiþ þe comendacioun of esdre*'.

(fol. 113r) 1 Ezra (15).

(fol. 116v) 2 Ezra. Rubrics: '*Explicit liber primus. Incipit liber secundus*'; '*Explicit liber secundus esdre*' (fol. 121r) (16).

(fol. 121r) 3 Ezra (17).

(fol. 126v) Prologue to Tobit ('*To cromacio…*').

(fol. 126v) Tobit (18).

(fol. 130r) Prologue to Judith (*'Anentus þe ebrues…').*

(fol. 130r) Prologue to Judith (*'Jvdith widewe…').*

(fol. 130r) Judith (19). Rubric: '*Explicit liber iudith*' (fol. 134v).

(fol. 134v) Prologue to Esther ('*Þe boc of ester to be maad vicious…*'*)*. Rubrics concerning the differences between the Latin and English texts in brown ink.

(fol. 134v) Esther (20).

(fol. 139v) Prologue to Job ('*I am constreyned…*'). Rubric: '*Incipit prologus in libro Iob*'.

(fol. 140) Prologue to Job ('*Iff forsoþe a Iunket wiþ resshe…*').

(fol. 140r) Job (21). Rubric: '*Incipit liber Iob*'.

(fol. 149v) Prologue to psalms ('*Whan it is knowe…*').

(fol. 150r) Prologue to psalms ('*Dauyd þe sone of Iesse…*'). Rubric: '*Explicit prologus super psalterium*'.

[quires XIX–XXX]
(fol. 151r) Psalms (22) laid out as prose with verses starting with alternating red or blue initials. Rubric: '*þe boc begynneþ of ympnes & solitarie spechis of þe profete dauyd of cryst*'. A leaf is missing before the start of psalms, but there is no obvious loss of text. Liturgical divisions are not marked. English titles in red. Numbers and Latin incipits in the margins in a contemporary hand, but not by the main scribe. Verses on the psalter (9 lines) are added in the lower margin in the hand responsible for Latin verse chapter summaries:

> *Post Iob psalmorum codex debet stituari*
> *Dic sibi iunguntur prouerbia quam salomonis…*

(fol. 174v) Prologue to Proverbs ('*To Cromacye…*').

(fol. 174v) Proverbs (23).

(fol. 182v) Prologue to Ecclesiastes ('*Þis almost þe fifte…*'). Rubric: '*Heere gynneþ þe prologe in þe boc of eclesiates þat is to sey boc of talker to þe puple or togidere clepere*'.

(fol. 182v) Ecclesiastes (24?). Rubric: '*heer gynneþ þe boc*'.

(fol. 185r) Song of Songs (25). Rubric: '*heer gynneþ þe booc þat is clepid song of songis of þe bridalis of crist & of þe chirche þe chirche of þe comyng of crist spekiþ seiende*'. Speakers identified in red.

(fol. 186v) Prologue to Wisdom ('*Þe booc of wisdam anent ebrues noȝher is…*'). Rubric: '*heer gynneþ þe prolog in þe booc of wisdam*'.

(fol. 187r) Wisdom (26). Rubric: '*heer gynneþ þe booc*'.

(fol. 191v) Prologue to Ecclesiasticus ('*Off manye & grete bi þe lawe and profetes…*'), '*explicit*' and '*prologus*' added by the hand which corrected the text.

(fol. 191v) Ecclesiasticus (27).

(fol. 208r) Prologue to Isaiah ('*No man whan…*'). Rubric: '*prologus*'.

(fol. 208v) Isaiah (28). Rubric: '*þe scripture of ezechie king of iuda whan he hadde be syc & hadde couered of hys sycnesse*' in chapter 38, preceding '*I seide in þe myddel of my daȝes…*'.

(fol. 226v) Prologue to Jeremiah (*'Jeremye þe profete…').*

(fol. 227r) Prologue to Jeremiah ('*God is redi…').*

(fol. 227r) Jeremiah (29).

(fol. 247v) Lamentations of Jeremiah (30?). Rubric: '*her gynneþ þe lamintacoun of ieremye þat is in title cenoþ with þe soylinge out of ebru lettris*'.

(fol. 249r) Prayer of Jeremiah. Rubric: '*þe orisoun of Ieremye profete*'.

(fol. 249r) Prologue to Baruch ('*Þis boc þat baruch bi name is befor notid…*'). Rubric: '*her endeþ ieremye & ginneþ þe prolog in þe boc clepid baruch*'.

(fol. 249r) Baruch (31?). Rubric: '*heer gynneþ þe boc*'. Note concerning the authorship of Nicholas Hereford at the end (see Provenance). Fol. 250v is blank.

Decoration

Roughly executed initials alternating deep blue with red penwork and lighter blue with red penwork. Occasionally decorated with human faces. The initials are larger at the beginnings of books (4 lines or higher) and smaller at the beginnings of chapters (most 3 lines high). The initials at the beginnings of prologues vary in size, some are similar to chapter, other to book initials. Unusual style; according to de Hamel (2001) the work of an Italian artist.

Dialect

1. (fols. 1–131v)
any(10), eche(9)/ech(1), fijr(8)/fyir(2), ȝiue(6)/ȝiuen(1)/ȝoue(1)/ȝouen(1)/ȝeuen(1), lif(10), lic(10), myche(10), saȝ(7) (sg.), seȝen(5) (pl.), self(9)/silf(1), such(9)/suche(1), þurȝ(8)

-iþ(2)/-eþ(8) (pres.ind.3sg.), -en(8)/-e(2) (pres.ind.pl.), -ende(8)/-onde(1)/-ande(1) (pres.part.), she(10) (3sg.fem.pronoun, nom.), þei(9)/þey(1) (3pl. pronoun, nom.), þem(6)hem(4) (3pl.pronoun, oblique), þer(10) (3pl. pronoun, possessive)

Also: birieþ/biried ('buried'), ha ('have')', sloȝ ('slew')

2. (fols. 132r–134v, Judith 7–Esther 2:4)
any(1), fijr(1), ȝiuen(1)/ȝiue(6), lif(10), myche(8)/miche(1), self(10), such(2)/suche(1), þurȝ(2)

-eþ(6) (pres.ind.3sg.), -en(5) (pres.ind.pl.), -ende(10) (pres.part.), she(10) (3sg.fem.pronoun, nom.), þei(10) (3pl.pronoun, nom.), þem(2)hem(8) (3pl. pronoun, oblique), þer(5) (3pl.pronoun, possessive)

3. (fols. 135r–250r)
any(10), eche(10), fyr(10), ȝiue(3)/ȝiuen(2), lif(10), lic(10), myche(10), saȝ(3) (sg.), seȝen(8) (pl.), self(9)/silf(1), such(9)/suche(1), þoȝ(1), þurȝ(10)

-ith(1)/-eþ(9) (pres.ind.3sg.), -en(9)/-e(1) (pres.ind.pl.), -ende(10) (pres.part.), she(10) (3sg.fem.pronoun, nom.), þei(10) (3pl.pronoun, nom.), þem(4) hem(6) (3pl.pronoun, oblique), þer(10) (3pl.pronoun, possessive)

Also: knewȝ/kneȝ ('knew')

Physical description

MATERIAL: parchment, generally thin, white and high quality, but sometimes rough, with tears repaired by sowing

DIMENSIONS: 365 × 250 mm; leaves were trimmed in rebinding, frequently causing the loss of text in the margins

NUMBER OF LEAVES: 253

FOLIATION: foliated by Douce in brown ink; 1–74 + 75a + 75b + 76–180 + 180* + 181–187 + 187* + 188–250

COLLATION: (fols. i–ii) fol. i is a paper flyleaf conjoint with the upper pastedown; fol. ii is a paper flyleaf | (fols. 1–32) I–IV (8) | (fols. 33–39) V (8–1) missing 1 | (fols. 40–150) VI–XVIII (8) | (fols. 151–157) XIX (8–1) missing 1 | (fols. 158–243) XX–XXIX (8) | (fols. 244–250) XXX (8–1) missing 8

Catchwords survive; quire signatures occasionally survive (more than one set).

RULING: ruled in plummet for two columns with single vertical and horizontal bounding lines extending the full height and width of page; 47–56 lines per page; written space: variable, *c.*245–280 × 150–160 mm. Occasionally the ruling is visible above the horizontal bounding lines at the top of the page (e.g., fols. 63r–65r)

SCRIPT: Textura. According to Forshall and Madden (1850), the work of three scribes, first scribe: Numbers 20:2–Judith 6, fols. 1r–131v; second scribe: Judith 7–Esther 2:4, fols. 132r–134v; third scribe: Esther 2:5–Baruch 3:30, fols. 134v–250r. Possibly two scribes: 1r–134v and 134v–250r. Forshall and Madden believed that the last hand was identical to the last hand of MS Bodl. 959 (1850, vol. 1, p. l), but this was questioned by Fristedt (1953–73), vol. 1, p. 88, R. W. Hunt (cited by Fristedt), and de Hamel (2001), p. 172. de Hamel pointed out that only the added note naming Hereford is likely to be by the last scribe of MS Bodl. 959

RUBRICATION: rubrics in red ink; instructions to rubricator survive (e.g., fols. 22v, 113r, etc.)

SEC. FOL.: '*puple shal*' (fol. 2r)

II (fols. 251r–485v)

Date: 14th century, last quarter (?)

Text

Isaiah–Acts 28:15 in EV. Missing Ezekiel 1:27–22:22 because of the loss of leaves. The books are numbered in the same way as in the first part, in the same contemporary hand, as shown in brackets after each title (see Provenance).

(fol. 251r) Prologue to Isaiah ('*No man when…*'). Rubric: '*Prologue to Isaye þe prophete þe firste chapl' of Isaye*'.

(fol. 251r) Isaiah (28). Rubric: '*Here endiþ þe prolog and bigynneþ þe book of Isaye*'. Rubric: '*þe scripture of ezechie kyng of Iuda whane he hadde be syk & hadde keuerid his syknesse*' in chapter 38 preceding '*I seide in þe midel of my days…*' (fol. 263r).

(fol. 273r) Prologue to Jeremiah (‘*Jeremy þe profete…*’). Rubric: ‘*Her endiþ þe book of Isaye & bigynneþ þe prolog to Ieremie*’.

(fol. 273r) Prologue to Jeremiah (‘*God is redy…*’). Rubric: ‘*anoþer prolog*’.

(fol. 273v) Jeremiah (29). Rubric: ‘*Here endiþ þe prolog & bigynneþ þe book*’.

(fol. 300v) Lamentations of Jeremiah (30). Rubric: ‘*heer begynneþ þe lamentacioun of Ieremye þat is in title cenoth wiþ þe soilinge out of Ebrew lettris of reed*’.

(fol. 302v) Prayer of Jeremiah. Rubric: ‘*here begynneþ þe orisoun of Ieremye þe profete*’.

(fol. 303r) Prologue to Baruch. Rubric: ‘*Prologe in baruch*’.

(fol. 303r) Baruch (31). Rubric: ‘*Here endiþ þe prolog & bigynneþ þe book of Baruch*’.

(fol. 305r) Epistle of Jeremiah. Rubric: ‘*heer begynneþ ensaumple of þe same pistle whiche Ieremye sente to þe caitifs led aweie in to babiloyne of þe kyng of men of men* [sic] *of babiloyne: þat he shulde shewe to hem after þat it is comaundid to him of god*’.

(fol. 306v) Ezekiel (32). Rubric: ‘*Here bigynneþ þe book of Ezechiel þe prophete*’.

(fol. 316v) Daniel (33). Rubric: ‘*Here endiþ þe book of Ezechiel and bigynneþ þe book of Daniel*’). In chapter 3 ‘*And þei walkiden in mydil…*’ (3:24) is preceded by a rubric ‘*þe se þingis þat suen I foond not in Ebrew tunge* [‘*tunge*’ underdotted and crossed out] *bookis*’ in red, in the hand of the rubricator (fol. 118r). On fol. 319r a rubric underlined in red with a blue paraph, preceding ‘*þanne kyng nabugodonosor…*’ (3:91): ‘*Hiderto is not had in ebrue & what þinges we han putte ben translatid of þe makyng of teodosion*’. On fol. 325r a rubric underlined in red: ‘*Hidre to we reeden danyel in ebru oþer þingis that suen til in to þe eende of þe boke: ben translatid of þe making of theodosyon*’, preceding ‘*A man was in babiloyne…*’ (13:1).

(fol. 326v) Hosea (34). Rubric: ‘*Here endiþ þe book of Danyel þe prophete and bigynneþ þe book of Osee þe prophete þe firste chaptl*’.

(fol. 330r) Joel (35). Rubric: ‘*Here endiþ þe book of Osee: and bigynneþ þe book of Joel prophete*’.

(fol. 331r) Amos (36?). Rubric: ‘*Here endiþ þe book of Joel and bigyn þe book of Amos prophete*’.

(fol. 334r) Obidiah (37). Rubric: '*Here endiþ þe book of Amos prophete: & bigynneþ þe book of Abdias prophete*'.

(fol. 334v) Jonah (38?). Rubric: '*Here endiþ þe book of abdias prophete: & bigynneþ þe book of Ionah þe prophete*'.

(fol. 335r) Micah (39). Rubric: '*Here endiþ þe book Ionas: & bigynneþ þe book of Micheas*'.

(fol. 335r) Nahum (40?). Rubric: '*Ende of þe book of Micheas: & bigynneþ þe book of Naum prophete*'.

(fol. 338r) Habakkuk (41?). Rubric: '*Here endiþ þe* [sic] *of Naum prophete: and bigynneþ þe book of Abacuk prophete*'.

(fol. 339r) Zephaniah (42?). Rubric: '*Here endiþ þe book of Abacuk þe prophete & bigynneþ þe book of Sophonye prophete*'.

(fol. 340r) Haggai (43?). Rubric: '*Here endiþ þe book of Sophonye prophete and bigynneþ þe book of Aggey þe prophete*'.

(fol. 341r) Zechariah (44?). Rubric: '*Here endiþ þe book of Aggey þe prophete and bigynneþ þe book of Zacharie sone of Barachias*'.

(fol. 345r) Malachi (45?). Rubric: '*Here endiþ þe book of Zacharias þe prophete and bigynneþ þe book of Malachie prophete*'.

(fol. 346r) 1 Maccabees (46). Rubric: '*Here endiþ þe book of Malachie & bigynneþ þe firste book of Machabeorum*'.

(fol. 361v) 2 Maccabees (47?). Rubric: '*Here endiþ þe book of þe firste Iudas machabeus & bigynneþ þe book of secunde Iudas Machabeus*'.

(fol. 372v) Prologue to Matthew ('*Mathew of Iewerye…*'). Rubric: '*Here endiþ þe storie of machabeus þe which is þe laste book of þe olde testament And now bigynneþ þe newe testament ffirst is þe prologu of Matheu apostle & euangelist*'.

(fol. 372v) Matthew (48). Rubric: '*Here endiþ þe prolog & begynn^t þe gospel*'.

(fol. 389r) Prologue to Mark ('*Mark þe euangelist…*'). Rubric: '*Here endiþ þe gospel of M^t & bigynneþ þe prolog of mark*'.

(fol. 389r) Mark (49). Rubric: '*Here endiþ þe prolog & bigynneþ þe gospel*'.

(fol. 399v) Prologue to Luke ('*Lvcas of antyoche…*'). Rubric: '*Here endiþ þe gospel of mark & bigynneþ þe prolog of luk*'.

(fol. 400v) Luke (50). Rubric: '*Here endiþ þe prolog and bigynneþ þe gospel*'.

(fol. 418r) Prologue to John ('*This is John…*'). Rubric: '*Here endiþ þe gospel of luk & bigynneþ þe prolog of Iohn*'.

(fol. 418r) John (51). Rubric: '*Here endiþ þe prolog and bigynneþ þe gospel*'.

(fol. 429v) Prologue to Romans ('*Fvrst vindirstond…*'). Rubric: '*Here endiþ þe gospel of Iohn And now bigynneþ þe prolog of seint poul to romayns*'.

(fol. 430r) Romans (52). Rubric: '*Here endiþ þe prolog and bigynneþ epistle to romyns*'.

(fol. 437r) Prologue to 1 Corinthinas ('*Corinthies ben…*'). Rubric: '*Here endiþ þe epistle to romayns and now bigynneþ þe prolog to þe firste epistle to corinthies*'.

(fol. 437r) 1 Corinthinas (53). Rubric: '*Here endiþ þe prolog and bigynneþ þe epistele*'.

(fol. 444r) Prologue to 2 Corinthians ('*Aftir penaunce…*'). Rubric: '*Here endiþ þe firste pistle to corinthis & now bigynneþ þe prolog to þe secunde*'.

(fol. 444r) 2 Corinthians (54). Rubric: '*Ende of þe prolog bigynnynge þe secunde pistle*'.

(fol. 448v) Prologue to Galatians ('*Galathies ben greekis…*'). Rubric: '*Here endiþ þe secunde pistle to corinthis and now bigynneþ þe prolog to galathies*'.

(fol. 448v) Galatians (55). Rubric: '*Here endiþ þe prolog & bigynneþ þe epitstle*' [sic].

(fol. 451r) Prologue to Ephesians ('*Ephecyes sopli ben…*'). Rubric: '*Here endiþ þe epistle to Galathies & now bigynneþ þe prolog to Ephesyes*'.

(fol. 451r) Ephesians (56?). Rubric: '*Ende of prolog bigynnyng capitulum primum*'.

(fol. 453r) Prologue to Philippians ('*Philipencis ben…*'). Rubric: '*Here endiþ þe epistle to Ephecies & bigynneþ þe prolog to Philipencis*'.

(fol. 453v) Philippians (57?). Rubric: '*Ende of prolog bigynnyng þe epitstle þe firste chaptl'*'.

(fol. 455r) Prologue to Colossians ('*To colocensis also…*'). Rubric: '*Here endiþ þe epistle to philipensis & bigynneþ prolog to Colocenses*'.

(fol. 455r) Colossians (58?). Rubric: '*Ende of þe prolog bigynnynge þe epistle*'.

(fol. 456v) Prologue to 1 Thessalonians ('*Tessalonycensis ben men…*'). Rubric: '*Here endiþ þe epistle to Colocensis & bigynneþ þe prolog to tessalonycensis*'.

(fol. 456v) 1 Thessalonians (59?). Rubric: *'Ende of prolog bigynnyng þe firste pistle'*.

(fol. 458r) Prologue to 2 Thessalonians (*'To tessalonycensis…'*). Rubric: *'Here endiþ þe firste pestle to tessalonycensis and bigynneþ þe prolog to þe secunde pistle'*.

(fol. 458r) 2 Thessalonians (60?). Rubric: *'Here endiþ þe prolog & bigynneþ þe secunde pistle to tessalonycensis'*.

(fol. 458v) Prologue to 1 Timothy (*'Tymothe þe apostle…'*). Rubric: *'Here endiþ þe secunde pistle to tessalonycensis & bigynneþ þe prolog to þe firste pistle to tymothe'*.

(fol. 459r) 1 Timothy (61). Rubric: *'Here endiþ þe prolog & bigynneþ þe firste pistle'*.

(fol. 460v) Prologue to 2 Timothy (*'Also he wrytiþ…'*). Rubric: *'Here endiþ þe firste pistle to Tymothe & bigynneþ þe prolog to secunde pistle'*.

(fol. 460v) 2 Timothy (62?). Rubric: *'Here endiþ þe prolog & bigynneþ þe pistle'*.

(fol. 462r) Prologue to Titus (*'Tyte he counceiliþ…'*). Rubric: *'Here endiþ þe secunde pistle to Tymothe & bigynneþ þe prolog to Tyte'*.

(fol. 462r) Titus (63?). Rubric: *'Here endiþ þe prolog & bigynneþ þe epistle to Tyte'*.

(fol. 462v) Prologue to Philemon (*'To ffilomon he makiþ…'*). Rubric: *'Here endiþ þe epistle to Tyte & bygynneþ þe prolog to ffilomon'*.

(fol. 463r) Philemon (64). Rubric: *'Here endiþ þe prolog and bigynneþ þe epistle to filomon'*.

(fol. 463r) Prologue to Hebrews (*'In þe firste…'*). Rubric: *'Here endiþ þe epistle to ffilomon & bigynneþ þe prolog to þe pistle to Ebrews'*.

(fol. 463r) Hebrews (65). Rubric: *'Here endiþ þe prolog & bigynneþ þe epistle'*.

(fol. 468v) Prologue to Acts (*'Lvk of sirye…'*). Rubric: *'Here enden þe epistlis of poul and now bigynneþ þe prolog to actus apostolorum'*.

(fol. 468v) Acts (66). Rubric: *'Here endiþ þe prolog & bigynneþ þe lessoun'*.

Ends imperfectly at 28:15 (*'…þre tauernes whom whanne'*). Fols. 486–488 are paper flyleaves, containing notes by Douce, including a list of contents of the manuscript with folio numbers.

The text contains corrections, most over erasures, in contemporary hands. Chapter numbers and running titles with chapter numbers in red by the original rubricator. Lections outlined in red and/or marked in the margins with the opening and final letters of each passage, possibly by the original rubricator. Added material within the text is consistently underlined in red. English notes in the margins in the original hand referring to the subject matter of passages (e.g., fols. 433r, 434r, 435v, 436r, etc.). Occasionally glosses in the margins in a contemporary hand providing Latin versions of phrases (fols. 288r, 392r); cross-references among biblical books (e.g., fols. 313r, 378r); and '*nota*' (fols. 435v, 439r, etc.). Pointing hands added in the margins, 16th century (?) (e.g., fols. 270r–v, 272r, etc.).

Decoration

3- to 6-line red and blue initials with red, blue and purple penwork and penwork borders at the beginnings of books; 2- to 4-line blue initials with red penwork at the beginnings of chapters and prologues. Some initials are decorated with human and animal masks, and other zoomorphic and anthropomorphic designs (e.g., fols. 372v, 385r, 444r, 451r, 453v, 456v, 459v). Simple red line-fillers at the end of texts. Drawings of human faces in the lower margin (e.g., fols. 278v, 280v) and catchwords decorated with grotesques in the section written by the first scribe.

Dialect

1. (fols. 251r–391v)
any(1)/eny(9), eche(8)/ech(2), fijr(9)/fire(1), ȝouen(10), lijf(4)/lif(2)/lyf(4), liche(3)/lic(4)/like(2)/liik(1), myche(6)/moche(4), seiȝ(1)/seeȝ(2)/say(3) (sg.), sayen(2)/syȝen(1)/seien(2) (pl.), self(9)/silf(1), siche(4), þorwȝ(1)

-iþ(7)/-eþ(3) (pres.ind.3sg.), -en(9)/-e(1) (pres.ind.pl.), -ande(1)/-yng(1)/-inge(2)/-ynge(6) (pres.part.), she(10) (3sg.fem.pronoun, nom.), þei(10) (3pl. pronoun, nom.), hem(10) (3pl.pronoun, oblique), her(10) (3pl.pronoun, possessive)

Also: slowȝ ('slow')

2. (fols. 392r–485v)
ony(10), ech(10), fier(2)/fyer(7), ȝouun(9)/ȝouen(1), lyf(10), lychi(1)/liche(1)/lich(1)/lyk(4), moche(10), syȝ(3) (sg.), seye(1) (pl.), silf(10), such(3)/suche(3)/sich(2)/siche(2), þouȝ(5), þorw(5)/þorwȝ(1)

-iþ(9)/-eþ(1) (pres.ind.3sg.), -en(10) (pres.ind.pl.), -ynge(7)/-inge(3) (pres. part.), she(6)/sche(4) (3sg.fem.pronoun, nom.), þei(10) (3pl.pronoun, nom.), hem(10) (3pl.pronoun, oblique), her(10) (3pl.pronoun, possessive)

Also: slowȝ/slouȝ ('slew')

Physical description

MATERIAL: parchment

DIMENSIONS: *c.*365 × 250 mm; leaves were trimmed in rebinding, frequently causing the loss of text in the margins

NUMBER OF LEAVES: 239

FOLIATION: foliated by Douce in brown ink; 251–429 + 429* + 430–488

COLLATION: (fols. 251–298) I–IV (12) | (fols. 299–306) V (12–4) missing 9–12 | (fol. 307) VI (12–11) missing 1–11 | (fols. 308–474) VII–XX (12) | (fols. 475–485) XXI (12–1) missing 12 | (fols. 386–388) fols. 386–387 are paper flyleaves; fol. 388 is a paper flyleaf conjoint with the lower pastedown

Catchwords survive; quire signatures often survive: a–e before fol. 307, starting with g afterwards.

RULING: ruled in ink for two columns with single horizontal and vertical bounding lines, extending the full height and width of page; 48 lines per page in the first scribe's section and 45 in the second scribe's section; written space: variable, *c.*250–255 × 165–170 mm; prickings occasionally visible (e.g., fol. 274)

SCRIPT: textura; the work of two scribes, first scribe: Isaiah–Mark 5:30 (fols. 251r–391v); second scribe: the rest, fols. 392r–485v (quires XIV–XXI) and possibly most of the text on fols. 385v, 389r and corrections elsewhere in the stint of the first scribe; black and brown ink

SEC. FOL.: '*heiȝt of stronge*' (fol. 252r)

Binding

Nineteenth-century binding made for Douce (Gillam (1984)), red velvet over boards. Six raised bands on spine. Gilt (flaking) decorations (vases) and lettering on spine 'ANTIENT || ENGLISH || BIBLE' and 'MSS 14 CENT'. Pastedowns and flyleaves made from blue paper with white floral designs; further flyleaves of laid paper with watermarks. Edges of textblock speckled red.

Provenance

1. '*Explicit translacōm Nicholay de herford*', added in a contemporary hand, fol. 250r. This hand may have been responsible for other additions in part I, such as the chapter numbers and corrections to the English text, e.g.,

those on fols. 249v–250r (de Hamel (2001), p. 172). It may also be identical to the last hand in MS Bodl. 959 (de Hamel (2001), p. 172). The text in MS Bodl. 959 may have been checked against MS Douce 369, or a version similar to it, and corrected to bring it in conformance with this version. A break at the same point in the text occurs in MS Bodl. 959 and Cambridge University Library MS Ee. 1. 10.

2. Biblical books in both parts are numbered in the upper right corner in medieval hands; see fols. 100r, 101r, 109r, 146r, 357r, 463r. The first clearly visible number is '5' on fol. 16r, which shows that the books were numbered before the beginning was lost. The prologues are not numbered separately, but have the same number as the preceding or following book (e.g., the prologue to psalms has number 21 (fol. 150r), the same as preceding *Job*). On fol. 78v (4 Kings) number 12 is accompanied by the word '*ezechie*', referring to the beginning of chapter 21 '*And ezechie…*'. On fol. 146r the number is outlined in red. The first clearly visible number in the second part is '29' (fol. 275r) for *Jeremiah.*

3. Notes in a 16th-century hand, recording the loss of leaves at the beginning and end: '*Thar be thes man(y) leves conteyned in this book in all* [space] *s(?) xxv cor lacking j lefe*' (fol. 1r); '*Better it is to trus(?)*' (fol. 147r); '*Thar be so man(y) lefese contained in this book in all s(?) xxv cor laking j lefe*' (fol. 486v). Pious note in the margin on fol. 203v in a different 16th-century hand: '*Helth is þe gefte of god…*'.

4. Francis Douce (1757–1834); see *ODNB*: recorded in his accession notebook (MS Douce e. 67, fol. 32r) under November 1818: 'Wicliffe's Testament MS… Triphook' (Rogers (1975)). Initials 'FD' in a red circular frame (fol. 1r–v). Notes by Douce throughout (fols. i verso, ii recto, 170v, 250r, etc.).

5. Bodleian Library: received in 1834 with the bequest of Douce.

Bibliography

Forshall and Madden (1850), vol. 1, pp. xvii, xxxiv–xxxvi, l–li, base text for EV from Ezra to Baruch 3:20.

Summary catalogue, vol. 4, no. 21944.

Skeat, W. W., 'On the dialect of Wycliffe's Bible', *Transactions of the Philological Society* (1895), pp. 212–19 at pp. 217–18.

Deanesly (1920), p. 253.

Pope, H. and Bullough, S., *English versions of the Bible* (St Louis, Mo.: Herder, 1952).

Fristedt (1953–73), *passim*; sigla C and K.

Hargreaves, H., 'The Latin text of Purvey's Psalter', *Medium Aevum* 24 (1955), pp. 73–90 at p. 74.

Fristedt, S. L., 'The authorship of the Lollard Bible', *Stockholm Studies in Modern Philology* 18 (1956), pp. 28–41, *passim*.
Hargreaves, H., 'The Middle English primers and the Wycliffite Bible', *Modern Language Review* 51 (1956), pp. 215–17 at p. 217.
Lindberg (1959–97), vol. 8 (1997), pp. 24, 29, 70, 374, sigla 'C', 'K', 'O'.
Danielsson, B., review of Fristedt, *The Wycliffe Bible*, part II, *Studia Neophilologica* 44 (1972), pp. 190–5.
David, R., 'Francis Douce's manuscripts: some hitherto unrecognised provenances', *Studies in the book trade in honour of Graham Pollard*, Oxford Bibliographical Society Publications, n.s. 18 (Oxford, 1975), pp. 315–40 at p. 339.
Lambert, M. D., *Medieval heresy: popular movements from Bogomil to Hus* (London: E. Arnold, 1977), p. 234.
Gillam, S. G. (ed.), *The Douce legacy: an exhibition to commemorate the 150th anniversary of the bequest of Francis Douce (1757–1834)* (Oxford: Bodleian Library, 1984), no. 203.
Hudson (1985), p. 104.
Brake, D. L. (ed.), *The New Testament in English translated by John Wycliffe MCCCLXXXII; revised by John Purvey MCCCLXXXVIII* (facsimile of MS Rawl. C. 259) (Portland, Oreg.: International Bible Publications, 1986), pp. xxi–ii.
Tanabe, H., 'On some English renderings in the vocabulary of the Wycliffite Bible' in Oshitari K. *et al.* (ed.), *Philologia Anglica: essays presented to Professor Yoshio Terasawa on the occasion of his sixtieth birthday* (Tokyo: Kenkyusha, 1988), pp. 389–402 at pp. 389 n. 1.
Catto, J. I., 'Wyclif and Wycliffism at Oxford' in Catto, J. I. and Evans, R. (eds), *The history of the University of Oxford*, vol. 2, *Late medieval Oxford* (Oxford: Oxford University Press, 1992), pp. 175–261 at p. 225.
Lindberg (1999–2004), vol. 3, p. 5.
Scott (2000–02), vol. 2, p. 41, no. 493.
de Hamel (2001), pp. 170–3, fig. 120.
Dove (2007), pp. 256–7, 299 and *passim*.
Peikola M., 'Aspects of mise-en-page in manuscripts of the Wycliffite Bible', in Caie G. and Renevey D. (eds.), *Medieval texts in context* (London: Routledge, 2008), pp. 28–67 at p. 40.

18 MS Douce 370

Siglum: *B*

SC no. 21945

Origin: England

Date: 14th century, end

Text

Fols. i–iv are parchment and paper flyleaves (see Provenance).

(fols. 1r–269v) Genesis–2 Chronicles in EV, with prologues to Genesis ('*Broþer ambrose to me…*'), Joshua ('*At þe last eendyd þe fyue bookis…*'), 1 Kings ('*Þe tonge forsoþe…*'), 2 Chronicles ('*Eusebeus Jerome senden gretynge…*') and two prologues to 1 Chronicles ('*Ȝif þe makynge of þe seuenty…*' and '*Þe boke of paralipomenon…*'). 3 Kings ends halfway through the first column of fol. 210v and is followed by a rubric introducing 4 Kings; the rest of this page is blank and 4 Kings starts on a new quire. Quire XXVI, containing the end of 3 Kings, consists of 10 leaves; all other quires consist of 8 leaves. Two bifolia are misbound in quire XVII (the end of Joshua and the beginning of Judges), see Collation.

At the beginning: '*Heere bigynniþ the epystle of saynt Ierom preest of alle bokes of goddis storye*'; at the end: '*Here endiþ þe secounde boke of Paralipomenon / Blesside be þe hooly trynite*'. Rubrics in red at the start of the prologue to Genesis and at the start of books and prologues on fols. 121–end (quires XVI–XXXIV); and in black with red paraphs elsewhere. Chapter numbers in Roman numerals in red, in black with red paraphs, or in black. Corrections in the original or contemporary hand, with many passages erased and rewritten (e.g., fols. 5v, 6r, 6v, 18v, 19r, 53v, 105r, 229r, 250r, etc.).

Words written out in the margins throughout enclosed in frames drawn in black ink (outlined in red on fols. 161v–176v, quire XXI), apparently randomly chosen from the text (e.g., 'syster', 'agar', 'wode', 'I swore', 'wyf', 'wyf', 'olde', 'wyfe', 'a ladder', 'lya', 'gate' on fols. 14r–22r). The words appear at different intervals, sometimes three on the same page and sometimes separated by an interval of several pages. The word appearing against the first line on fol. 20v ('lya') refers to the last word on the previous page. Sometimes there are differences in the spelling of words in the margins and in the text (e.g., fols. 46r, 46v); and sometimes the words in the margins do not seem to correspond to anything in the text (e.g., fol. 48r). A penwork initial on fol. 14 avoids a word in a frame, indicating that the words were written before the text was flourished. There are no marginal glosses;

added material within the text is not underlined; lections are not marked. '*Nota*', pointing hands and 'hedera' in the margins. The commandments (Deuteronomy 2, fol. 104r) are underlined in red with a gloss '*comaundementes*' in the upper margin. Fols. 270–280 are parchment and paper flyleaves (see Provenance).

Decoration

2- to 5-line blue initials with red penwork at the beginning of books; 2- to 3-line similar initials at the beginning of prologues and chapters (the initial 'þ' tends to be larger, e.g., 11 lines high at the beginning of Genesis and Exodus); some chapters have simple red 1-line initials.

Dialect

(Genesis and Exodus)
eny(10), eche(6)/ech(4), fier(4)/fyer(6), ʒeuen(3)/ʒouen(1)/ʒeue(5)/ʒyuen(1), lyf(9)/lif(1), lyke(8)/lyche(2), myche(9)/mych(1), seeyʒ(4) (sg.), seeʒen(3)/seeyn(2) (pl.), self(10), siche(8)/syche(2), þorou(1)/þorʒ(7)/þoru(2)

-iþ(7)/-eþ(2)/-yþ(1) (pres.ind.3sg.), -en(10) (pres.ind.pl.), -yng(3)/-ynge(5)/-ing(1)/-inge(1) (pres.part.), sche(10) (3sg.fem. pronoun, nom.), þei(9)/þey(1) (3pl.pronoun, nom.), hem(10) (3pl.pronoun, oblique), her(10) (3pl.pronoun, possessive)

Physical description

MATERIAL: parchment

DIMENSIONS: *c.*206 × 144 mm

NUMBER OF LEAVES: 284

FOLIATION: modern in pencil, i–iv + 1–280

COLLATION: (fols. i–iv) flyleaves | (1–200) I–XXV (8) the second and the third bifolia are misbound in quire XVII (fols. 129–136); the order should be 129, 131, 130, 132, 133, 135, 134, 136 | (fols. 201–210) XXVI (10) | (fols. 211–266) XXVII–XXXIII (8) | (fols. 267–269) XXXIV (8–5 (?)) missing 4–8 (?) | (fols. 274–280) parchment flyleaves

Catchwords survive. Quire signatures [a]–z on fols. 1–184, a–d on fols. 219–250, and a–b on fols. 259–269.

RULING: ruled for two columns, with single vertical and horizontal bounding lines extending the full height and width of page; 44–8 lines per page; written space: *c.*160–165 × 110–115 mm

SCRIPT: textura; probably the work of several scribes; changes in the style of writing on fols. 211r, 235, 259r; such changes do not correspond to textual divisions, but occur at the beginning of quires or leaves

RUBRICATION: rubrics in red

SEC. FOL.: '*demaundiþ*' (fol. 2r)

Binding

Stamped white leather over wood boards, 16th century. Sewn on six thongs. Ornamented metal bosses and corners on both covers. Fittings of two clasps, now lost.

Provenance

1. Frequent variation in all aspects of the presentation of the text (the size of initials, ruling, scribal style, the form of chapter numbers, running titles, etc.).

2. '*talard*', 15th century (?), fol. 1r.

3. '*George Rawdon of carlton*
Mathe Sadlar of ffellonglaye
with grace of god wyfe to
George Rawdon of carlton', 16th century (fol. 174v). Fellongley, Warwickshire (?).

4. '*1756 Jan(uar)y 17th Bo(ugh)t this Book of Mr J(oh)n Cooke of Upingham*' – John Jackson (?) (d. 1794); see *ODNB*, entry Jackson, John, d. 1807, traveler.

5. Francis Douce (1757–1834); see *ODNB*: bought at Jackson's sale in 1794 (lot 345); notes on flyleaves; stamp on fol. 1r.

6. Bodleian Library: received in 1834 with the bequest of Douce.

Bibliography

Forshall and Madden (1850), vol. 1, p. li; base text of EV from 4 Kings to 2 Chronicles.
Skeat, W. W., 'On the dialect of Wycliffe's Bible', *Transactions of the Philological Society* (1895), pp. 212–19 at pp. 216–17.
Summary catalogue, vol. 4, no. 21945.
Fristedt (1953–73), vol. 1, p. 15.
Scott (2000–02), vol. 2, p. 41, no. 494.
de Hamel (2001), p. 180.
Dove (2007), pp. 18, 141, 199, 299.

19 MS Dugdale 46

Origin: England

Date: 15th century, first quarter

Text

Fol. i is a paper flyleaf (see Provenance).

(fols. 1r–138r) Pauline epistles (Romans–Hebrews) in LV with usual prologues (**Plate 9**). Romans has a second prologue '*Romaynes ben þei þat of Iewis…*' with a rubric: '*þis prologe telliþ þe peple of rome what manere men it weren sum time*' (Dove (2007), p. 206; Forshall and Madden (1850), vol. 4, pp. 301–3). A bifolium is missing after fol. 41 (missing text: 1 Corinthians 7:30–9:11); an early modern note in the margin points this out. Galatians starts on a new quire (quire X, fol. 68r); the verso of the last leaf of the previous quire is largely blank, with only about one-fifth of the first column occupied by text.

Usual rubrics at the beginning of prologues and books, e.g., '*Here bigynneþ prologe to romayns*' (fol. 3v); '*þus seiþ ierom in his prologe on þis pistil to romayns*' (fol. 4r). In Romans and Philippians – 1 Timothy the rubrics are in red; in 1 Corinthians – Ephesians they are in black underlined in red; in 2 Timothy and later they are added in black by one of the scribes (or an early owner) in spaces originally left blank (they are in the wrong order in 2 Timothy and its prologue on fol. 112v). The running titles on fols. 5r–67r and 110r–122r consist of abbreviated titles of epistles written on the rectos in black, probably in the hand that supplied rubrics in 2 Timothy and later. On fols. 68r–109 (from the beginning of Galatians to the end of 1 Timothy 4) and on fols. 123–end (most of Hebrews) the running titles are in red on the rectos. The chapter numbers are in black Roman numerals on fols. 1r–85r and 109v–end, in red Roman numerals on fols. 85v–91v, and vary between red and black on fols. 100v–109v.

Corrections in the margins and within the text in medieval hands. Partially cut off gloss in a red frame against 1 Corinthians 16:15 on fol. 53r '*stephan…womma[n]*' (EV in Forshall and Madden (1950) has a gloss '*the womman*' at this point; cf. MS Fairfax 21). The only other marginal gloss is an explanation of 'amen' on fol. 88r. Added material within the text is underlined in red in 2 Corinthians and occasionally texts that follow. The indexing letters are very occasionally entered at the beginnings of lections. '*noon of hem myȝte be saued þoruȝ his owne meritis*' is underlined in red with a drawing of a pointing hand on fol. 3r, postmedieval (?). Notes in the margins in a 17th-century hand (Henry Fairfax (?), see Provenance).

Decoration

2- to 5-line plain red initials at the beginnings of books, 1- to 3-line similar initials at the beginnings of prologues and chapters.

Dialect

ony(10), eche(10), fier(8), ȝouen(10), liif(8)/lyf(2), lyke(2)/like(3)/lyk(1), myche(4)/meche(5)/miche(1), siȝ(1) (sg.), siȝen(1) (pl.), silf(10), siche(1)/suche(9), þouȝ(10), þoruȝ(6)

-iþ(5)/eþ(5) (pres.ind.3sg.), -en(10) (pres.ind.pl.), -inge(5)/-ynge(4)/-ende(1, fol. 8v) (pres.part.), sche(10) (3sg.fem.pronoun, nom.), þei(10) (3pl.pronoun, nom.), hem(10) (3pl.pronoun, oblique), her(1)/here(1) (3pl.pronoun, possessive)

Physical description

MATERIAL: poor quality, poorly matched parchment of variable thickness with holes

DIMENSIONS: *c.*204 × 147 mm; trimmed in rebinding

NUMBER OF LEAVES: 140

FOLIATION: modern in pencil, i + 1–139

COLLATION: (fol. i) paper flyleaf | (fols. 1–8) I (8) | (fols. 9–14) II (6) | (fols. 15–38) III–V (8) | (fols. 39–44) VI (8–2) missing 4–5 | (fols. 45–60) VII–VIII (8) | (fols. 61–67) IX (8–1) missing 1, no loss of text | (fols. 68–131) X–XVII (8) | (fols. 132–138) XVIII (8–1) missing 1 | (fols. 139–140) paper flyleaves

Catchwords survive. Medieval quire (Roman numerals) and leaf signatures occasionally survive and appear to run consecutively i–[ix] on fols. 1–67 (Romans–2 Corinthians) with a new series on fol. 68–138, i–[ix] (Galatians–Hebrews).

RULING: Ruled in ink with single vertical and single or double horizontal bounding lines extending the full height and width of page. Quires I and X–XI are ruled for a single column, quires II–IX for two columns, quire XII has the recto of the first leaf ruled for a single column (to match the facing verso of quire XI), the rest of the MS is ruled for two columns

The number of lines varies from quire to quire and sometimes within the same quire: 18 lines per page in quires I–II, 25 in quires III–V, 26 in quire VI, 27 in quire VII, 28 in quires VIII–IX, 19–20 in quires X–XI, 20–23 in quire XII, 25 in quires XIII–XIV, 23 in quire XV, 25 in quire XVI, 28 in quires XVII–XVIII. Written space: *c.*143–158 × 98–106 mm. Prickings survive.

SCRIPT: textura of widely variable size and degree of formality, but perhaps the work of a single amatuer (?) scribe; black ink. The appearance of script changes sometimes from quire to quire (e.g., quires I and II are in different styles, but the verso of the last leaf of quire I matches the recto of the first leaf of quire II; see also a change of ruling and scribal style at the start of quire III, fol. 15r) and sometimes unpredictably within the same quire and more than once on the same page (e.g., fols. 41r, 47v, 63v, 67r, 81v, etc.). Partially filled last line of the first column on fol. 67r and a line outside the ruled space on fol. 100r suggest that the text may not have been copied consecutively. Possibly at least partly in the same hand as MS Harley 2396 (English Wycliffite sermons) and Cambridge, Gonville and Caius College MS 179/212 (Matthew–Mark in LV). MS Harley 2396 also has very considerable variation in scribal style, sometimes on the same page, and changes in ruling from one to two columns for no apparent reason (Hudson and Gradon (1983–96), vol. 1, pp. 81–2).

RUBRICATION: rubrics in red, black or underlined in red

SEC. FOL.: '*þis worshipe*' (fol. 2r)

Binding

Brown leather over pasteboard, late 17th century, probably made for Charles Fairfax (see also MS Fairfax 11). Blind fillet-line and roll border with geometric designs round the outer edge of both covers. Floral decoration (thistle flowers (?)) at the centre and in four corners on both covers. Two paper labels on spine, one fragmentary with '[4]6' written in ink, another with 'M.S. || Dugdale || 34' also written in ink. Paper label with 'F(?)' on the upper cover. Edges of textblock dyed red.

Provenance

1. The presentation of the text is highly variable: the number of lines per page changes from quire to quire and sometimes within the same quire; the style of rubrics and running titles differs between texts and groups of texts, rather than quires; and the style of handwriting varies occasionally from quire to quire, but also unpredictably on the same page. There is, however, also evidence of efforts to give some uniformity to the appearance of the book, e.g., the ruling in quire XII changes on the verso of the first leaf, rather than on the recto; the scribal hand in quire I is very different from that in quire II, but the verso of the last leaf of quire I matches the recto of the first leaf of quire II.

2. Henry Fairfax (1588–1665), Church of England clergyman; see *ODNB*.

Fol. i verso contains *Pater noster* and the Apostles' Creed with a title '*Ex antiquo MSS*', probably in his hand. The same page contains a note about the authorship of the Prologue to Romans, stating that the information was supplied by 'M Fetherstonhaugh', minister at Bentham. Notes probably in his hand in the margins of the epistles. Erased early modern (?) note in the lower margin of fol. 96v; text on the same page freshened up in an early modern (?) hand.

3. Charles Fairfax (1597–1673), antiquary and genealogist; see *ODNB*: '*C(arolus) Fairfax ex dono fratris H(enrici) F(airfax) 1619*' (fol. 1r). Signatures on fols. i recto (in Latin and English), 138v. See also MS Fairfax 11.

4. William Dugdale (1605–1686), antiquary and herald; see *ODNB*.

5. Ashmolean Museum: bequeathed by Dugdale.

6. Bodleian Library: transferred from the Ashmolean Museum in 1858.

Bibliography

Forshall and Madden (1850), vol. 1, p. xlix.
Summary catalogue, vol. 2, part II, no. 6534.
Dove (2007), pp. 206, 300.

20 MS Eng. Misc. C. 27, fol. 46

Origin: England

Date: 15th century, first quarter

Text

Fragments of Isaiah in LV (30:22–24, 30:33–31:1, 32:2–6, 32:20–33:2), damaged and partially unreadable. Chapter numbers in red, consisting of '*c(apitulum)*' followed by a Roman numeral.

Decoration

Includes the beginnings of chapters 31 and 33 with 2-line blue initials, decorated with red penwork.

Dialect

3ouu(n)(1), fier(1), vnwiys(1)

-iþ(1) (pres.ind.3sg.), -en(4) (pres.ind.pl.), -ynge(1) (pres.part.), þei(2) (3pl. pronoun, nom.), hem(1) (3pl.pronoun, oblique)

Physical description

A single strip of parchment, ruled for two columns with double vertical bounding lines and a further set of two bounding lines in the outer margin.

DIMENSIONS: *c.*298 mm wide; written space: *c.*200 mm wide

SCRIPT: textura; black ink

Provenance

Probably a fragment of a complete bible or OT (large format, letters 2.5 mm high) (Dove (2007)).

Bibliography

Summary catalogue, vol. 5, no. 30494.
Dove (2007), p. 300.

21 MS Fairfax 2

Sigla: K; *I* – prologues to books from Genesis to Ecclesiasticus; *K* – prologue to 1 Chronicles

Origin: England

Date: 1408

Text

Fols. i–ii are paper flyleaves, blank apart from modern notes.

1. (fols. 1r–385r) ONT in LV with prefatory epistles. NT has usual LV prologues, OT has prologues in EV, apart from the prologues to Baruch and Isaiah which are in LV; lacks prologues to Jeremiah and Wisdom. Running titles in red on both rectos and versos, consisting of the titles of books preceded by blue paraphs. Brief notes summarising the contents of the text in the hand of the original scribe in the upper margin (such notes are largely absent in the part following the calendar-lectionary, see below). Chapter numbers, most consisting of '*c^m*' followed by a Roman numeral. Rubrics in black, underlined in red. Alternative translations and cross-references to other biblical books in the margins; glosses in the margins,

indicating the subject matter, comparing the text to the Hebrew version and explaining individual words. Most text in the margins is in the hand of the main scribe, but some is in other contemporary hands. Added material within the text is occasionally underlined in red. Corrections by the main scribe and in a contemporary hand. Added drawings of pointing hands and '*nota*' in the margins, as well as notes such as '*mark wel þis booc*' (fols. 201r, 210r), late 15th century. Erasures of medieval or early modern inscriptions (e.g., fols. 279v, 303r, 388v); margins occasionally cut out presumably to remove the text they contained.

(fol. 1r) Prefatory epistles ('*Broþer ambrose to me…*' and '*I haue taken desired epistles…*'). Rubric: '*Here bigynneþ þe pistel of seynt Ierom prest of alle þe bokis of goddis storie þat is clepid a prolog*'.

(fol. 3r) Genesis. Rubric: '*Here endeþ þe prolog now bigynneþ genesis*'.

(fol. 18r) Exodus. Rubric: '*Here endeþ genesis se now exodus*'.

(fol. 30r) Leviticus. Rubric: '*Heere endeþ exodus se now leuyticus*'.

(fol. 39r) Numbers. Rubric: '*Here endeþ Leuiticus see now þe book of Noumbre*'.

(fol. 51v) Deuteronomy. Rubric: '*Heere endeþ þe book of Noumbre & þe lawe Se now Deutronomy*'.

(fol. 62r) Prologue to Joshua. Rubric: '*Heere endeþ Pentaceucon se now þe prolog of Iosue*'.

(fol. 62v) Joshua. Rubric: '*Here endeþ þe prolog se now þe book of Iosue*'.

(fol. 69v) Judges. Rubric: '*Here endeþ Iosue se now þe book of doomes*'.

(fol. 77r) Ruth. Rubric: '*Here endeþ þe book of doomes Se now þe booc of Ruth*'.

(fol. 78r) Prologue to 1 Kings ('*Forsoþe þe tonge…*'). Rubric: '*Her endeþ þe booc of Ruth Se now þe prolog of þe bokis foure of kyngis*'.

(fol. 78v) 1 Kings. Rubric: '*Her endeþ þe prolog Se now þe firste book of kinges*'.

(fol. 88v) 2 Kings. Rubric: '*Here endeþ þe firste book of kinges Se now þe seconde*'.

(fol. 97r) 3 Kings. Rubric: '*Here endeþ þe seconde book of kinges Se now þe þridde*'.

(fol. 107v) 4 Kings. Rubric: '*Heere endeþ þe þridde book of kinges Se now þe fourþe*'.

(fol. 116v) Prologue to 1 Chronicles (‘*If þe making of þe seuenti…*’). Rubric: ‘*Heere eendiþ þe fourþe book of kinges Se now þe prolog bifore Paralipomenon*’.

(fol. 117r) 1 Chronicles. Rubric: ‘*Heere eendeþ þe prolog Se now þe firste book of Paralipomenon*’.

(fol. 125v) 2 Chronicles. Rubric: ‘*Here endeþ þe firste book of Paralipomenon Se now þe seconde* ‘. Prayer of Manasseh (fol. 136v) without a rubric.

(fol. 137r) Prologue to 1 Ezra (‘*Wheþer it be hardere…’).* Rubric: ‘*Here endeþ þe seconde book of Paralipomenon Se now þe prolog of Esdre*’.

(fol. 137v) Commendation of Ezra. Rubric: ‘*Here folowiþ þe comendacioun of Esdre*’.

(fol. 137v) 1 Ezra. Rubric: ‘*Here eendeþ þe prolog of Esdre Se now þe book*’.

(fol. 140v) 2 Ezra. Rubric: ‘*Heere eendeþ þe firste book of Esdre See now þe seconde book of Esdre or Neemye*’.

(fol. 145r) Prologue to Tobit (‘*To cromacie…*’). Rubric: ‘*Here endeþ þe seconde book of Esdre or Neemye See now þe prolog of Tobie*’.

(fol. 145r) Tobit. Rubric: ‘*Here endeþ þe prolog of tobie Se now þe booc*’.

(fol. 148r) Prologue to Judith (‘*Anentis þe ebrues…’).* Rubric: ‘*Here endeþ þe book of Thobie Se now þe prolog of Iudith*’.

(fol. 148v) Judith. Rubric: ‘*Here endeþ þe prolog of Iudith Se now þe booc*’.

(fol. 152v) Prologue to Esther. Rubric: ‘*Here endeþ þe book of Iudith Se now þe prolog of hester*’.

(fol. 152v) Esther. Rubric: ‘*Here endeþ þe prolog of hester Se now þe book*’.

(fol. 156v) Prologue to Job (‘*I am constreyned bi alle…*’). Rubric: ‘*Heere eendeþ þe book of hester Se now þe prolog of Ioob*’.

(fol. 157r) Job. Rubric: ‘*Here endeþ þe prolog of Ioob Se now þe booc*’. Gloss: ‘*Iob was a verri man in kinde…*’.

(fol. 165v) Prologue to psalms (‘*Whane it is knowen…*’). Rubric: ‘*Heere eendeþ þe booc of Ioob Se now þe prolog of þe sawter*’.

(fol. 166r) Psalms preceded by a rubric: ‘*Here endeþ þe prolog of þe Sawter Se now þe booc*’. The psalms are laid out as prose, preceded by English titles and Latin incipits in black underlined in red. Psalm numbers in the margins in the original hand. Verses start with alternating 1-line red or blue initials. Title and other glosses in the margins of some psalms in a contemporary hand different from that of the main scribe. Liturgical divisions marked with larger initials at psalms 26, 38, 52, 68, 80, 97 and 109; '*feria*' followed by a number added in the margins at liturgical divisions in a 16th-century hand.

2. (fol. 178r) A list in English of weekly canticles: *Confitebor tibi domine, Ego dixi, Exultauit cor meum, Cantemus domino, Domine audiui, Audite celi*; and daily canticles: *Benedicite omnia opera, Benedictus dominus deus, Magnificat* and *Nunc dimittis*. The entries for weekly canticles consist of a note (2- to 4-lines long) describing the contents and the circumstances of composition of each canticle, a Latin incipit and a reference to a biblical book and chapter. The entries for daily canticles consist of a Latin incipit and a reference to a biblical source. At the end '*Here endeþ þe book of salmes*' and, added in the hand responsible for the Athanasian Creed (see below), '*blessed be þe holi trynite Amen amen*'.

3. (fol. 187v) Athanasian Creed, in a different hand and ink, preceded by a Latin incipit. Rubric: '*Se now Quicumque vult in engliȝssh þe wiche Attanasy a doctor of greke made*'.

4. (fols. 188r–193v) Sarum calendar-lectionary in English (**Plate 10**) preceded by a rubric: '*Se now þe kalender of alle Lessons Pistels & Gospels of al þe ȝeer aftir þe vse of Salisbury*' and '*Þe effect of þis kalender is to knowe þe Lessons þe pistels & gospellis as þei ben red in þe chirche aftir þe vse of salisbiri ffirst here aboue bigynneþ þe sundai wiþ inne þe vtas of twelf day & þenne dominicals & ferials suyng after eeff & þenne þe feest of ascencion & þe sundai wiþ inne þe vtas. & þe vtas of ascencion & þenne dominicals & ferials suyng aftir þe trinite & þenne aduent wiþ hise dominicals and ferials suyng*'. Golden numbers and the dominical letters followed by the names of feasts and saints' days, followed by the entries for readings consisting of an indexing letter and an abbreviated title and chapter number of a biblical book, without the opening or closing words of a reading. The major feasts are in red, including Augustine of Canterbury (26 May). Does not include David, Chad, John of Beverley, Winifred or Frideswide (promulgated in 1415 under archbishop Chichele; see Pfaff (2009), pp. 440–1), which suggests that the manuscript pre-dates 1415 (see Provenance). The readings for the dominicals and ferials are listed at the end of each month. Contains all feasts characteristic of LV (Forshall and Madden (1850), vol. 4, pp. 683, 690–6). The translation of Edward the Confessor is entered as '*of edmund*' (13 October). Bertinus is added over an erasure in a contemporary hand (5 September, not in Forshall and Madden's edition of the table of lections (1850), vol. 4, p. 694). Francis is added without readings (4 October), late 15th century. The feast

of Thomas Becket and titles 'pope' are erased. Commemorations appear in the lower part of leaves containing October, November and December (fols. 192v–193r), in the following order: the Virgin Mary, Trinity, Holy Ghost, angles, peace, rain, '*A man for him silf*', cross, '*For briþern & sistres*', clear weather, '*In time of batel*', '*For pestilence of beestis*', pilgrims, weddings, sinners, sick, dead.

(fols. 194r) Prologue to Proverbs ('*To cromacie…*'). Rubric: '*Here bigynneþ þe preface of seint Ierome in þe book of prouerbis*'. More than one-third of the first column is left blank on fol. 194r.

(fol. 194r) Proverbs. Rubric: '*Here endeþ þe prolog of prouerbis Se now þe book*'.

(fol. 201r) Prologue to Ecclesiastes ('*Þis almost þe fifte…*'). Rubric: '*Here eendeþ þe booc of prouerbis Se now þe prolog in þe booc of ecclesiates þat is to seie booc of talkere to þe puple or to gidere calle*'.

(fol. 201r) Ecclesiastes. Rubric: '*Here endeþ þe prolog of ecclesiastes se now þe booc*'.

(fol. 203v) Song of Songs. Rubric: '*Here endeþ þe booc of ecclesiastes Se now þe book of song of songis*'.

(fol. 205r) Wisdom. Rubric: '*Here endeþ þe book of songis Se now þe booc of Sapiens or wisdom*'.

(fol. 209v) Prologue to Ecclesiasticus ('*Of manye and grete…*'). Rubric: '*Here endiþ þe booc of Sapiens or wisdom Se now þe prolog of þe booc of Ecclesiastici*'.

(fol. 210r) Ecclesiasticus. Rubric: '*Here endeþ þe prolog Se now þe booc*'.

(fol. 223r) Prologue to Isaiah ('*As seynt Ierom seiþ…*'). Rubric: '*Heere endeþ þe book of ecclesiastici Se now a prolog of Isaye þe profete || Anoþer prolog of Isayee and oþere profetis*'. In spite of the rubric only LV prologue is included.

(fol. 223r) Isaiah. Rubric: '*Here eendeþ þe prolog See now Isaie*'.

(fol. 239r) Jeremiah. Rubric: '*Heere eendeþ Isaye Se now Ieremye*' (fol. 238v).

(fol. 256r) Lamentations of Jeremiah. Rubric: '*Heere bigynneþ þe lamentacion of Ieremye*'.

(fol. 257r) Prayer of Jeremiah. Rubric: '*Heere enden þe lamentacions Se now þe preier of Ieremye þe profete*'.

(fol. 257v) Prologue to Baruch ('*Þis book wich is titled…*'). Rubric: '*Here endeþ þe book of Ieremie Se now þe prolog of Baruch*'.

(fol. 257v) Baruch. Rubric: '*Here endeþ þe prolog of baruk se now þe booc*'.

(fol. 259v) Ezekiel. Rubric: '*Her endeþ Baruc Se now Ezechiel*'.

(fol. 276r) Daniel. Rubric: '*Here endeþ ezechiel þe prophete Se now danyel þe prophete*'.

(fol. 283r) Hosea. Rubric: '*Here endeþ daniel þe prophete Se now Osee þe profete*'.

(fol. 285r) Joel. Rubric: '*Here endeþ þe booc of þe profete Osee Se now Ioel þe prophete*'.

(fol. 286r) Amos. Rubric: '*Here endeþ Ioel þe profete see now þe book of þe profete Amos*'.

(fol. 288r) Obadiah. Rubric: '*Here endeþ Amos þe profete Se now Abdias þe profete*' (fol. 287v).

(fol. 288r) Jonah. Rubric: '*Her endeþ Abdias þe profete Se now Ionas þe profete*'.

(fol. 288v) Micah. Rubric: '*Here endeþ Ionas þe profete Se now Micheas þe profete*'.

(fol. 290r) Nahum. Rubric: '*Here endeþ Micheas þe profete Se now Naum þe profete*'.

(fol. 290v) Habakkuk. Rubric: '*Here endeþ Naum þe profete Se now Abacuk þe profete*'.

(fol. 291r) Zephaniah. Rubric: '*Here endeþ Abacuk þe profete Se now þe booc of sophonye þe profete*'.

(fol. 292r) Haggai. Rubric: '*Here eendeþ þe booc of Sophonye Se now þe booc of Aggei þe profete*'.

(fol. 292v) Zechariah. Rubric: '*Here eendeþ þe booc of Aggei Se now þe booc of Zacharie þe profete*'.

(fol. 295r) Malachi. Rubric: '*Here endeþ of Zacarie þe booc Se now Malachie þe profete*'.

(fol. 295v) 1 Maccabees. Rubric: '*Heere endeþ Malachie þe profete Se now þe firste book of Macabeus*'.

(fol. 305r) 2 Maccabees. Rubric: '*Heere endeþ þe firste book of Macabeus Se now þe second book of macabeus*'.

(fol. 312r) Prologue to Matthew ('*Mathew þat was of Iudee…*'). Rubric: '*Heere endeþ þe secounde book of Macabeus and al þe oolde testament Se now þe newe testament || Heere bygynneþ þe Prolog of Ierom on Matheu*'.

(fol. 312r) Matthew. Rubric: '*Ierom in his prolog on Matheu seiþ þis pleinly*'.

(fol. 321v) Prologue to Mark ('*Mark þe gospeler was þe chosen seruaunt…*'). Rubric: '*Here eendeþ Mathew Se now þe prolog on Mark*'.

(fol. 321v) Mark. Rubric: '*Ierom in his prolog on Mark seiþ þis pleynli*'.

(fol. 327r) Prologue to Luke ('*Lvke was a man of sirie…*'). Rubric: '*Here endeþ Mark Se now þe prolog on Luke*'.

(fol. 327r) Luke. Rubric: '*Here endeþ þe prolog on Luke Se now þe book of Luk*'.

(fol. 337v) Prologue to John ('*This is Ioon euangelist…*'). Rubric: '*Here eendeþ Luke Se now þe prolog on Ioon*'.

(fol. 337v) John. Rubric: '*Ierom in his prolog on Ioon seiþ al þis Se now þe book*'.

(fol. 345r) Prologue to Romans ('*Romains ben in þe cuntre…*'). Rubric: '*Here endeþ Ioon Se now þe prolog to þe Romains*'.

(fol. 345r) Romans. Rubric: '*Ierom seiþ þis in his prolog to þe Romayns Se now þe book*'.

(fol. 348v) Prologue to 1 Corinthians ('*Corinthies ben…*'). Rubric: '*Here bigynneþ a prolog of Ierom on þe firste pistle to Corinthies*'.

(fol. 348v) 1 Corinthians. Rubric: '*Ierom in his prolog seiþ al þis*'.

(fol. 352v) Prologue to 2 Corinthians ('*Aftir penaunce…*'). Rubric: '*Here eendiþ þe firste pistle to corinthies Se now a prolog on þe secunde pistle to corinthies*'.

(fol. 352v) 2 Corinthians. Rubric: '*Ierom in his prolog seiþ al þis*'.

(fol. 355r) Prologue to Galatians ('*Galathies ben grekis…*'). Rubric: '*Here endiþ þe seconde pistle to corinthies Se now þe prolog on þe pistle to Galathies*'.

(fol. 355r) Galatians. Rubric: '*Ierom in his prolog to galathies seiþ al þis*'.

(fol. 356r) Prologue to Ephesians ('*Effecians ben men of Asie…*'). Rubric: '*Here endeþ þe pistel to Galathies Se now þe prolog on þe pistle to Effesies*'.

(fol. 356r) Ephesians. Rubric: '*Ierom in his prolog seiþ al þis*'.

(fol. 357v) Prologue to Philippians ('*Filipensis ben of macedonye…*'). Rubric: '*Here endeþ þe pistle to Effesies se now þe prolog on þe pistle to ffilipensis*'.

(fol. 357v) Philippians. Rubric: '*Ierom in his prolog seiþ al þis*'.

(fol. 358v) Prologue to Colossians ('*Colocensis ben also laodicensis…*'). Rubric: '*Here endeþ þe pistle to filipensis se now þe prolog on þe pistle to colocensis*'.

(fol. 358v) Colossians. Rubric: '*Ierom in his prolog seiþ al þis*'.

(fol. 359r) Prologue to 1 Thessalonians ('*Tessalonycensis ben macedonies…*'). Rubric: '*Here endeþ þe pistle to Colocensis se now þe prolog of þe firste pistel to Tessalonicensis*'.

(fol. 359r) 1 Thessalonians. Rubric: '*Ierom in his prolog on þis pistle seiþ þis*'.

(fol. 360r) Prologue to 2 Thessalonians ('*Þe postle writeþ…*'). Rubric: '*Here endeþ þe firste pistle to Tessalonicensis se now þe prolog on þe secunde pistle to Tessalonicencis*'.

(fol. 360r) 2 Thessalonians. Rubric: '*Ierom in his prolog on þis pistle seiþ þis*'.

(fol. 360v) Prologue to 1 Timothy ('*He enfoormeþ and techiþ …*'). Rubric: '*Here endeþ þe secunde pistle to Tessalonicensis se now þe prolog on þe firste pistle to Tymothee*'.

(fol. 360v) 1 Timothy. Rubric: '*Ierom in his prolog on þis pistle seiþ þis*'.

(fol. 361v) Prologue to 2 Timothy ('*He writeþ also…*'). Rubric: '*Here endeþ þe firste pistle to Tymothe se now þe prolog on þe secunde pistle to Timothe*'.

(fol. 361v) 2 Timothy. Rubric: '*Ierom in his prolog on þis pistle seiþ þis*'.

(fol. 362r) Prologue to Titus ('*He warneþ Tyte…*'). Rubric: '*Here endeþ þe seconde pistle to Tymothe Se now þe prolog on þe pistle to Tite*'.

(fol. 362r) Titus. Rubric: '*Ierom in his prolog seiþ þis*'.

(fol. 362v) Prologue to Philemon ('*He makeþ familiar…*'). Rubric: '*Here endeþ þe pistle to Tite se now þe prolog to ffilomen*'.

(fol. 362v) Philemon. Rubric: '*Ierom in his prolog on þis pistle seiþ þis*'.

(fol. 363r) Prologue to Hebrews ('*First it is to seie…*'). Rubric: '*Here endeþ the pistle to ffilomen se now þe prolog on þe pistle to Ebrewes*' (fol. 362v).

(fol. 363r) Hebrews. Rubric: '*Ierom in his prolog on þis pistle seiþ þis*'.

(fol. 365v) Prologue to Acts ('*Lvke of antiochie…*'). Rubric: '*Here endeþ þe pistel to ebrewes se now þe prolog on þe dedis of apostlis*'.

(fol. 366r) Acts. Rubric: '*Ierom heere in his prolog seiþ þis*'.

(fol. 375v) Prologue to Catholic epistles ('*Þe ordre of þe seuene epistlis…*'). Rubric: '*Here enden þe dedis of apostlis Se now a prolog on þe pistlis of cristen feiþ þat ben seuene in ordre*'.

(fol. 375v) James. Rubric: '*Ierom in his prolog seiþ al þis Se now þe pistel of Iames*'.

(fol. 376v) 1 Peter. Rubric: '*Here endeþ þe pistle of Iames Se now þe firste pistle of petre*'

(fol. 377v) 2 Peter. Rubric: '*Here endeþ þe firste pistle of petre Se now þe secounde*'.

(fol. 378r) 1 John. Rubric: '*Here endeþ þe secunde pistle of petre se now þe firste pistle of Ioon*'.

(fol. 379r) 2 John. Rubric: '*Here endeþ þe firste pistle of Ioon se now þe secunde*'.

(fol. 379v) 3 John. Rubric: '*Heere endeþ þe seconde pistle of Ioon se now þe þridde*'.

(fol. 379v) Jude. Rubric: '*Here endeþ þe þridde pistle of Ioon Se now þe pistle of Iudas*'.

(fol. 380r) Prologue to the Apocalypse ('*Alle men þat wolen…*'). Rubric: '*Here endeþ þe pistle of Iudas se now a prolog on þe apocalips*'.

(fol. 380r) Apocalypse. Rubric: '*Ierom in þis prolog on þis apocalips seiþ þis*'.

At the end, all in the hand of the main scribe: '*Here endeþ þe apocalips*' and '*Þe eer of þe lord M.* CCC[followed by an erasure] *& viii þis book was endid*'. Also: '*Turne ouer þis leef & se þere þe Table*'.

5. (fols. 385v–388r) *Capitula*-list for gospels, epistles and the Apocalypse ('*Here bigynneþ a table of alle þe gospels and pistils and þe Apocalips*'*)*. Fol. 388v is blank apart from an erased early modern inscription.

Decoration

6-line gold initials on blue and pink background and three-quarters borders made of gold, pink and blue bars, decorated with foliage, at the beginning of prefatory epistles (fol. 1r) and Genesis (fol. 3r).

4- to 6-line blue initials decorated with red penwork at the beginnings of Exodus and other books.

3- to 4-line similar initials at the beginnings of prologues.

2-line blue initials decorated with red penwork at the beginnings of chapters.

2-line plain red or blue initials in the *capitula*-list.

Blue KL monograms, decorated with red penwork, and decorative penwork strips separating months in the calendar-lectionary.

Penwork initials are by two artists, the second more professional than the first. The first is responsible for fols. 1–72v (quires I–IX), 129r–168v (quires XVI–XXI), 187v–193v (calendar-lectionary, part of quire XXIV) and 371r–385r (quires XLIX–L); the second is responsible for fols. 73r–128v (quires X–XV), 169r–187r (quires XXII–XXIII and part of quire XXIV) and 194r–370v (part of quire XXIV and quires XXV–XLVIII) (see Collation and Provenance). The quire containing the calendar-lectionary and Athanasian Creed is the only quire that contains the work of both artists. One artist was responsible for the calendar-lectionary and *Quicumque vult*, and the other for the preceding and following texts.

Post-medieval drawings of a human figure pointing to the text (fol. 53v) and hands (fols. 75v, 77v).

Dialect

anye(2)any(6)/ony(2), ech(7)/eche(3), fijr(10), ȝofen(10), lijf(10), lijk(10), miche(10), siȝ(3)/saw(6)/sawȝ(1) (sg.), siȝen(3)/sawen(4) (pl.), silf(3)/self(7), sich(3)/siche(7), þouȝ(8), þorouȝ(7)/þruȝ(2)/þru(1)

-eþ(3)/-iþ(7) (pres.ind.3sg.), -en(10) (pres.ind.pl.), -ynge(3)/-inge(4)/-ing(3) (pres.part.), she(9)/sheo(1) (3sg.fem. pronoun, nom.), þei(10) (3pl.pronoun, nom.), hem(10) (3pl.pronoun, oblique), her(10) (3pl.pronoun, possessive)

Spellings such as *biȝgge, liȝgge, iȝcching, periȝshe, fleiȝsshis, quyȝsshuns, angwiȝss, biheulde, leose, ȝife, ȝofe* ('given') (Forshall and Madden (1850), vol. 1, p. xlviii).

Physical description

MATERIAL: parchment, paper flyleaves; lower part of some leaves cut off in quires II, VII, XVIII, XXXIV, XL, XLIII

DIMENSIONS: *c.*426 × 285 mm; leaves were trimmed in rebinding, occasionally causing the loss of decoration and text in the margins

NUMBER OF LEAVES: 392

FOLIATION: modern in pencil: i–ii + 1–389 + unnumbered leaf

COLLATION: (fol. i–ii) paper flyleaves, the first conjoint with the upper pastedown | (fols. 1–72) I–IX (8) | (fols. 73–128) X–XV (8) | (fols. 129–168) XVI–XXI (8) | (fols. 169–184) XXII–XXIII (8) | (fols. 185–194) XXIV (10) quire containing the calendar-lectionary | (fols. 195–218) XXV–XXVIII (8) |

(fols. 219–222) XXIX (4) | (fols. 223–286) XXX–XXXVII (8) | (fols. 287–290) XXXVIII (4) | (fols. 291–370) XXXIX–XLVIII (8) | (fols. 371–386) XLIX–L (8) | (fols. 387–388) LI (2) | (fol. 389 and an unnumbered leaf) paper flyleaves

Catchwords and leaf signatures survive. Collation does not support Dove's suggestion (2001, p. 257) that the calendar-lectionary was the last item in vol. 1 of a two-volume bible, because it occupies a quire which also contains the beginning of the following text, the Proverbs.

RULING: ruled in plummet for two columns with single vertical and horizontal bounding lines extending the full height and width of page, 60–1 lines per page; prickings survive; written space: *c.*310 × 90–98 mm

SCRIPT: textura, black and brown ink, probably the work of several contemporary scribes

RUBRICATION: rubrics underlined in red; blue paraphs

SEC. FOL.: '*It is leueful*' (fol. 2r)

Binding

Brown leather over thick pasteboard, 17th century. Gilt fillet-line border with floral corner-pieces round the outer edge of both covers. Gild decoration at the centre of both covers. Re-backed in the Bodleian (note on the lower pastedown) with the original spine re-laid. Six raised bands on spine, framed by gilt fillet lines. Gilt floral strips at the top and bottom of the spine, and on the raised bands (mostly lost). 'Fairfax || 2' written in white paint on spine. Two decorated metal clasps. Laid paper pastedowns and flyleaves, and additional 19th-century paper flyleaves. Fol. 388 was probably a pastedown of a medieval binding; there is an erased note in an early modern hand on fol. 338v.

Provenance

1. Produced by a team that had access to the texts of EV and LV, or copied from an exemplar that already combined the LV text with EV prologues. The *capitula*-list was added after the rest of the book was completed: it follows the colophon with the date and the initials lack flourishing unlike elsewhere in the manuscript. Marginal glosses and summaries of content which accompany the running titles are partly in the hand of the main scribe, and were probably all added in the original workshop as an afterthought. The margins are not ruled for glosses, the position of the summaries varies and they are largely absent in the part of the book following the calendar-lectionary. Some marginal notes may suggest an interest in Lollardy, for example '*Of imagis in þe eende of þis chapitre & þe*

nexte swynge' in the hand of the main scribe, fol. 208r, and another similar note on fol. 241v; '*Loke at þe hond for prestes*' on fol. 274v which also has a drawing of a hand pointing to a passage on priesthood in Ezekiel, 44.

The date on fol. 385r may have been altered to avoid censorship, but, according to Watson (1984), examination under UV light suggests that the scribe first wrote 'M.ccc' and the 'and' symbol, erased the later, wrote it in the right place, and then forgot to insert the fourth 'c'.

2. Contains late 15th-century marginal additions, such as '*nota*' and other comments, including '*Of ymages in þis c* [chapter]' at Isaiah, 44, fol. 233v. The note may be in the hand that added '*gerard*' in the lower margin of the psalter, fol. 169r.

3. Possibly in use in a secular church in the 15th and 16th centuries. St Francis is added to the calendar-lectionary, late 15th century. According to Pfaff (2009, p. 327), Frances is a unique example of a major friar-saint who became 'widely present in English secular liturgy'. Notes '*feria*', added in a 16th-century hand in the psalter, appear next to liturgical divisions according to secular use. Possibly still in use at Reformation when titles 'pope' were erased in the calendar-lectionary.

4. 'the 29th of Aprill 15(?)58', 16th century (fol. 377v).

5. Thomas Fairfax (1612–1671); see *ODNB*.

6. Bodleian Library: bequeathed by Thomas Fairfax in 1671.

Bibliography

Forshall and Madden (1850), vol. 1, p. xlviii.
Deanesly (1920), p. 381.
Summary catalogue, vol. 2, part II, no. 3882.
Fristedt (1953–73), vol. 1, pp. 12, 17.
Hargreaves, H., 'The Latin text of Purvey's Psalter', *Medium Aevum* 24 (1955), pp. 73–90 at p. 89 n. 27.
Pächt and Alexander (1966–73), vol. 3 (1973), no. 798.
Rogers, T. D. (ed.), *Sir Frederic Madden at Cambridge: extracts from Madden's diaries 1831, 1838, 1841–2, 1846, 1859 and 1863* (Cambridge: Cambridge Bibliographical Society, 1980), p. 8 and n. 47.
Watson, A. G., *Catalogue of dated and datable manuscripts c.435–1600 in Oxford libraries*, 2 vols (Oxford: Clarendon Press, 1984), vol. 1, no. 485, p. 76.
Hudson (1985), p. 148 n. 26.
Lindberg (1989), pp. 42, 70.
Ogilvie-Thomson, S. J., *IMEP*, Handlist VIII (1991), p. 75.
Kuczynski, M. P., *Prophetic song: the psalms as moral discourse in late Medieval England* (Philadelphia: University of Pennsylvania Press, 1995), p. 264 n. 17.

Boitani, P. *et al* (eds), *Lo spazio letterario del Medioevo. 2, Il Medioevo volgare*, 5 vols. in 6 (Rome: Salerno, 1999–2005), vol. 2, p. 726.
Lindberg (1999–2004), vol. 3, p. 5.
de Hamel (2001), pp. 176, 177, 182, fig. 128.
Scott (2002), pp. 40–1, pl. VII.
Dove (2007), pp. 257–9.
Solopova (2013), pp. 336–7.

22 MS Fairfax 11

Origin: England

Date: 15th century, first quarter (before 1415 (?))

Text

Fols. i–iii are paper and parchment flyleaves.

[items 1–2 occupy quires II–IV]
1. (fols. 1r–6v) Sarum calendar in Latin, written in black, red, blue and gold, laid out one month per page, graded to nine lessons. Feasts in red include Ambrose (4 April), Augustine of Canterbury (26 May), Thomas Becket and his translation (29 December and 7 July), Augustine of Hippo (28 August), Thomas of Hereford (2 October), the translation of Edward the Confessor (13 October) and Edmund Rich (16 November). On 2 March, '*Theaddee*', bishop, in red, as '*festum duplex*', marked '*non sarum*' in the original hand (Chad (?), promulgated in 1415). Wulstan, bishop of Worcester (19 January) is in black, his translation (7 June) is in black marked '*non sarum*'. Thomas of Hereford, though a non-Sarum saint, is not marked as such. Includes Richard of Chichester (3 April), but not John of Beverley, David, Frideswide or Winifred (promulgated in 1415 under archbishop Chichele; see Pfaff (2009), pp. 440–1). Does not include Botulph (17 June). The months are headed by notes on the number of hours in day and night, and verses on the 'Egyptian' days which correspond to Hennig's (1955) set III. The feasts of Thomas Becket are not erased. Added numbering of the days of the months in an early modern hand.

2. (fols. 7r–18v) Table of lections of Type I starting with a rubric '*Here bigynneþ a rule þat telliþ in whiche chapitriis of þe bible 3&e moun fynde þe lessouns pistlis & gospels pistlis & gospels* [sic] *þat ben rad in þe chirche aftir þe vss of Salisbury markid with lettris of þe a.b.c. at þe bigynnyng of þe chapitris toward þe middil or eende aftir order as þe lettris stonden in þe*

a.b.c. first ben sett sonedaies & ferials to gidere & after þe sanctorum comoun & propre to gidere of al þe ȝeer first writen a clause of þe bigynnyng þerof & a clause of þe eending also'. Includes the temporal, commemorations, and the sanctoral, both the proper and common according to the rubric, but only the proper is present. Includes all feasts characteristic of the LV (Forshall and Madden (1850), vol. 4, pp. 683, 690–6), apart from Giles (1 September). Commemorations are in the following order: the Virgin Mary, Trinity, Holy Ghost, Cross, angels, '*ffor briþeren & sistren & salus populi*', peace, clear weather, rain, '*In time of batels*', '*A man for him silf*', '*ffor pestilence of bestis*', pilgrims, weddings, sinners, sick, dead. The readings consist of the name of a liturgical occasion in red, abbreviated reference to a book and chapter of the Bible, an indexing letter in red, the opening words of a reading, '*ende*' in red and the closing words of a reading. Larger initials with penwork at Christmas, Epiphany, Easter, Pentecost, Trinity, Conception of our Lady and Candlemas. Rubric at the end: '*Thus eendiþ þe kalender of lessouns pistlis & gospels þat ben rad in þe chirche bi al þe ȝeer aftir þe vse of Salisbury*'. Followed by an alphabet, a list of Old English letters, including ash, wynn, eth and thorn, and a note on medieval punctuation by Fairfax (?) (see Provenance).

[item 3 occupies quires V–XXVIII]
3. (fols. 19r–198v) NT in LV with usual prologues (**Plate 11**). Running titles in red on both rectos and versos, consisting of a title of a biblical book, a chapter number (on pages containing the beginnings of chapters), and gold or blue paraphs. Usual rubrics in red. Chapter numbers as words in English or Roman numerals, usually in the form '*þe i c^o*'. Indexing letters, entered at the beginnings of lections, rather than consistently, and double strokes, marking the ends of readings, in the margins inside the bounding lines framing each page. Contains many corrections throughout, a few by the main scribe and many in other contemporary hands (most in a smaller script between lines). Fols. 199–201 are blank.

Decoration

Possibly decorated by the same artist as MS Bodl. 183 (de Hamel (2001)).

Gold and blue KL monograms with red and purple penwork in the calendar.

6- to 9-line initials on gold background and full or three-quarters borders made of pink, blue and gold bars decorated with floral designs, interlace and gold disks at the beginnings of books. Starting with St John's gospel these alternate with 6- to 8-line red and blue 'puzzle' initials and penwork borders.

2- to 3-line gold or blue initials with red or purple penwork at the beginnings of prologues and chapters.

Catchwords decorated with geometric designs, and occasionally drawings (e.g., flowers, fol. 43v; king's head, fol. 122v) in ink, and red and yellow wash.

Dialect

ony(10), ech(10), fier(10), ȝouen(10), lijf(9)/liyf(1), lijk(10), myche(10), say(7)/sai(1) (sg.), saien(6) (pl.), silf(10), sich(2)/siche(5)/suche(2), þouȝ(8), þoru(8)/þoruȝ(2)

-iþ(9)/-eþ(1) (pres.ind.3sg.), -en(10) (pres.ind.pl.), -ynge(3)/-inge(7) (pres. part.), sche(10) (3sg.fem.pronoun, nom.), þei(10) (3pl.pronoun, nom.), hem(10) (3pl.pronoun, oblique), her(10) (3pl.pronoun, possessive)

Physical description

MATERIAL: parchment, paper flyleaves; lower margin of fol. 149 is cut off

DIMENSIONS: *c.*277 × 190 mm, originally possibly identical with MS Bodl. 183; leaves were trimmed in rebinding, occasionally causing the loss of decoration in the margins

NUMBER OF LEAVES: 204

FOLIATION: modern in pencil: i–iii + 1–201

COLLATION: (fols. i) fol. i is a paper flyleaf, originally conjoint with the upper pastedown | (fols. ii–iii) I (6–4?) missing 1–4 | (fols. 1–4) II (4) | (fols. 5–10) III (6) | (fols. 11–122) IV–XVII (8) | (fols. 123–125) XVIII (4–1) 4 cancelled, no loss of text | (fols. 126–165) XIX–XXIII (8) | (fols. 166–170) XXIV (6–1) 1 cancelled, no loss of text | (fols. 171–194) XXV–XXVII (8) | (fols. 195–198) XXVIII (4) | (fols. 199–200) XXIX (4–2) missing 3, 4 | (fol. 201) paper flyleaf conjoined with the lower pastedown

Catchwords survive; leaf signatures run consecutively a–z (fols. 19–198).

RULING: ruled for two columns with single vertical and double horizontal bounding lines extending the full height and width of page, and a further set of double bounding lines in all margins; prickings survive; 32–4 lines per page; written space: *c.*185 × 125 mm; nearly identical to MS Bodl. 183

SCRIPT: textura, the same hand as in MS Bodl. 183 (de Hamel (2001)); the calendar and the table of lections are in a different style and probably the work of a different scribe; black ink

RUBRICATION: rubrics in red; blue and gold paraphs at the beginnings of sections within the text

SEC. FOL.: '*Twelfþe Isaye*' (fol. 8r, table of lections); '*his sterre*' (fol. 20r, gospel)

Binding

Brown leather over pasteboard, late 17th century, probably made for Charles Fairfax. Blind fillet-line and roll borders on both covers with floral corner-pieces and floral decorations at the centre. Imprints from metal decorations at the centre and around the edges of covers. The metal decorations were added on top of blind-tool designs on the binding, presumably soon after it was made, and left holes and rust marks on fols. ii–2 and 196–200. Fols. ii, iii, 199 and 200 are medieval parchment flyleaves. Fols. ii and 200 served as pastedowns of a medieval binding and have imprints from a medieval document. Heavily repaired and rebacked in the Bodleian; 19th-century spine and paper flyleaves. Five raised bands on spine, framed by blind fillet lines. Gold lettering on spine 'MS || FAIRFAX || 11'.

Provenance

1. Probably made in London for a patron connected to Hereford cathedral (see Solopova (2013)). The calendar may have been made for a church of Augustinian canons: it is graded to nine lessons in accordance with secular use; Augustine of Hippo and Ambrose are in red, Ambrose is '*festum duplex*'. The feast (19 January) and translation (7 June) of Wulstan, bishop of Worcester, who undertook rebuilding work in Hereford cathedral and churches in Hereford, are included in black. The feast (19 January) is often present in the 15th-century Sarum calendars, whereas the translation is a non-Sarum feast (marked as such in the calendar) and is rare. Thomas of Hereford, a non-Sarum saint, is in red, graded to nine lessons. It is unlikely that the manuscript was made for the diocese or cathedral of Worcester, because of the absence of Worcester feasts, apart from Wulstan, and the fact that the calendar is graded for secular use.

Written by the same scribe as MS Bodl. 183, and illuminated by the same artist; MS Bodl. 665 may be also the work of this scribe (de Hamel (2001)); see, however, Peikola (2003), pp. 39–40. Probably not made in Hereford, which preserved its distinctive use in the late Middle Ages (Pfaff (2009), pp. 466–80); does not include Æthelberht (20 May), a non-Sarum feast. Written before 1415 (?): does not include most saints promulgated under archbishop Chichele; Chad (?) is marked as 'non-Sarum'.

2. Half-erased and cropped off 16th-century notes on fols. 107v, 115r and 122v. The notes on fol. 115r include the name 'Thomas Chenies'.

3. Sir William Sinclair, laird of Roslin (d. 1580/5): 'William Santclair of Roislin, Knecht' (fols. 1r, 18v); '*die secundo aprilis anno m° v° lxi*', followed by a signature of William Sinclair (?), fol. 81v, at the end of Luke's gospel. Many of his manuscripts were acquired from religious houses whose libraries had been broken up during the Scottish Reformation (Mapstone (1996)). Later owned by 'D. Sinclair of Roisling' (fol. 1r).

4. Charles Fairfax (1597–1673), antiquary and genealogist; see *ODNB*: 'bought in Scotland' (fol. 1r); 'Wickliff's Translation of the New Testament' (fol. ii recto); signatures on fols. iii recto, 1r, 18v, 19r, 198v. See also MS Dugdale 46.

5. Thomas Fairfax (1612–1671), nephew of Charles Fairfax; see *ODNB*.

6. Bodleian Library: bequeathed by Thomas Fairfax in 1671.

Bibliography

Forshall and Madden (1850), vol. 1, p. xlviii.
Summary catalogue, vol. 2, part II, no. 3891.
van Dijk, S. J. P., *Handlist of the Latin liturgical manuscripts in the Bodleian Library, Oxford* (unpublished typescript; 6 vols. in 7, Oxford, 1957–60), vol. 3, *Rituals and directories*, fol. 156.
Pächt and Alexander (1966–73), vol. 3 (1973), no. 839, pl. LXXXI.
Thomson, J. A. F., *The later Lollards, 1414–1520* (London: Oxford University Press, 1967), p. 207 n. 2.
Hudson (1989), p. 140 n. 29.
Mapstone, S., *Scots and their books in the Middle Ages and the Renaissance: an exhibition in the Bodleian Library, Oxford* (Oxford: Bodleian Library, 1996), p. 3, no. 2.
Scott, K. L., *Later Gothic manuscripts, 1390–1490*, Survey of manuscripts illuminated in the British Isles 6 (London: Harvey Miller, 1996), vol. 2, p. 29.
Scott (2000–02), vol. 2, pp. 48–9, no. 517.
de Hamel (2001), p. 179, figs. 125–6.
Peikola (2003), p. 39.
Dove (2007), pp. 58, 59, 72–3, 247, 281.
Solopova (2013), pp. 346–8.

23 MS Fairfax 21

Origin: England

Date: 15th century, first quarter

Text

Fols. i–ii are parchment flyleaves ruled for a table of lections, but originally blank (see Provenance).

[item 1 occupies quire II]
1. (fols. 1r–4v) Table of lections of Type I starting with a rubric: '*Here bigynneþ a rule þat telliþ in whiche chapitris of þe newe testament ȝe may fynde þe pistlis þat ben rad in þe chirche after þe vss of salisbiri markid with lettris of þe a b c.at þe bigynnynge of þe chapitris. toward þe myddil or ende. after þe ordre as þe lettris stonden in þe a b c. first ben sett sundaies and ferialis to gidre. & after þe sanctorum comyn & propre to gidre of al þe ȝeer first is writen a clause of þe bygynnynge þerof & a clause of þe eendinge þerof also*'. Another rubric introduces the sanctoral: '*Here enden þe domynycals & ferialis & bigynneþ þe rule of þe sactorum* [sic] *boþe propre & comyne*' (fol. 3r). Includes the temporal and proper, but no common, in spite of the rubric, and no commemorations. Includes only the feasts that have the readings from epistles, Acts and the Apocalypse. Larger blue initials mark the Conversion of St Paul, St Peter's Chair ('*Chairinge of peter*'), Lammas Day and Halloween. The readings consist of the name of a liturgical occasion in red, abbreviated reference to a book and chapter of the Bible, an indexing letter in red, the opening words of a reading, '*end*' in red, the closing words of a reading and double strokes in red. Includes feasts characteristic of LV (Forshall and Madden (1850), vol. 4, pp. 683–98).

[item 2 occupies quires III–XXIII]
2. (fols. 5r–167r) Romans–Apocalypse in LV with usual prologues and a second prologue to Romans ('*Romaynes ben þei þat of jewes...*') (see Dove (2007), p. 206). Usual rubrics in red starting with Philippians on fol. 54v (e.g., '*Here endiþ þe pistle to filipencis & biginneþ þe prolog on þe pistle to colocencis*'; '*Ierom on his prologue on þis pistle seiþ al þis*', fol. 58r). The wording and presentation of rubrics before fol. 54v is variable. The rubrics for books simply say '*Ierom seiþ þus*'. The rubric for 2 Corinthians is in black in the hand of the main scribe, underlined in black; the rubric for 1 Corinthians is added in the margin; the prologue to Romans does not have a rubric. Running titles in red on both rectos and versos, consisting of an abbreviated title of a biblical book. Chapter numbers in red, as Roman

numerals or words. Corrections in the margins and over erasures in the original or contemporary hands, including the insertions of the definite (e.g., fols. 56v–57r) and indefinite (fol. 68r) articles. No marginal glosses; added material within the text is occasionally underlined in red or black. Indexing letters in the margins, entered at the beginnings of lections, rather than consistently; the ends of lections are often marked with double strokes in the margins and within the text.

Pointing hand at a passage on preaching in foreign languages in 1 Corinthians 14:6: '*but now briþeren if I come to ȝou and speke in langagis what schal I profete to ȝou…*' (fol. 32r).

Decoration

2-line blue initials with red penwork at the beginnings of prologues and chapters; 2- to 4-line similar initials at the beginnings of books.

Dialect

Romans–Galatians
ony(10), ech(3)/eche(7), fier(2), ȝouen(10), lif(5)/lyf(4)/lijf(1), lik(3)/like(2), myche(8)/mych(2), say(1)/saie(1) (sg), siȝen(1) (pl), silf(8)/self(2), siche(10), þouȝ(10), þorou(3)/þrouȝ(1)/þoru(2)/þorouȝ(2)/þoruȝ(1)

-iþ(9)/-eþ(1) (pres.ind.3sg), -en (pres.ind.pl.), -ynge(9)/-inge(1) (pres.part.) sche(10) (3sg.fem. pronoun, nom.), þei(10) (3pl.pronoun, nom.), hem(10) (3pl.pronoun, oblique), her(10) (3pl.pronoun, possessive)

Physical description

MATERIAL: parchment

DIMENSIONS: *c.*196 × 130 mm, trimmed in rebinding

NUMBER OF LEAVES: 170

FOLIATION: modern in pencil, i–ii + 1–168

COLLATION: (fols. i–ii) I (2) single bifolium, ruled for a table of lections | (fols. 1–4) II (4) | (fols. 5–137) III–XIX (8) | (fols. 138–143) XX (6) no loss of text | (fols. 144–167) XXI–XXIII (8) | (fol. 168) single leaf

Catchwords and quire signatures survive in quires III–XI (fols. 5–90) and XXI–XXIII (fols. 151–168); quire signatures run a–l (fols. 5–90) and a–c (fols. 151–168).

RULING: Ruled for two columns; single vertical and triple horizontal bounding lines extending the full height and width of page on fols. 7–143; single vertical and double horizontal bounding lines on fols. 5–6 and

144–167. Written space varies from quire to quire (e.g., fols. 20v–21r, 28v–29r, 36v–37r, 105v–106r); *c.*132–150 × 90 mm on fols. 5r–137v and *c.*155–160 × 100 mm on fols. 138r–167r. The number of lines per page varies from quire to quire: 26–31

SCRIPT: Textura, the work of at least four different scribes; the first scribe is responsible for fols. 5r–50ra, the second scribe takes over on fol. 50ra, the third is responsible for quire XX (fols. 138r–143) and the fourth for quires XXI–XXIII (fols. 144–167). The last scribe may have also copied the table of lections. The size of script varies from quire to quire (e.g., fols. 28v–29r).

RUBRICATION: rubrics in red

SEC. FOL.: '*tewis day*' (fol. 2r)

Binding

Brown leather over pasteboard. Blind fillet-line border round the outer edge of both covers; medallion with blind interlace design at the centre of both covers. Fragments of two ties made of yellow fabric. Four raised bands on spine, framed with blind fillet lines; blind criss-cross design at the top and bottom of spine. Paper label on spine with hand-written 'M.S. || Fairfax || 21'. Sewn on four cords.

Provenance

1. The table of lections was edited to fit the contents of the volume. The feasts of Peter and Paul are given larger initials in the table of lections. The presentation of texts is variable, with little effort to match scribal style, the size of script or the pattern of ruling.

2. Thomas Fairfax (1612–1671); see *ODNB*: '*Sir Thomas fairfax of Denton, knight*' (fol. ii recto); '*This auncient monument of the translating of the scriptures in olde tyme into Englishe, belongeth to the right worshypfull, Syr Thomas Fairefax knight*' (fol. 167v).

3. Bodleian Library: bequeathed by Fairfax in 1671. Earlier shelfmark (?): '20' written in ink on fol. ii verso and the fore-edge of textblock.

Bibliography

Forshall and Madden (1850), vol. 1, pp. xlviii.
Summary catalogue, vol. 2, part II, no. 3901.
Dove (2007), pp. 59 n. 116, 61 n. 124, 300.

24 MS Gough Eccl. Top. 5

Origin: England

Date: 15th century, first quarter

Text

Four originally blank parchment flyleaves at the beginning, the last three numbered i–iii (see Provenance).

1. (fols. 1r–235r) NT in LV with usual prologues and rubrics (e.g., '*Her endiþ þe gospel of matheu and bigynneþ þe prologe on þe gospel of mark*'; '*þis seiþ Ierom in his prologe on Mark. Her bigynneþ þe gospel on mark*', fol. 31r–v). Running titles on both rectos and versos, most consisting of abbreviated titles and chapter numbers of biblical books, in red, preceded by blue paraphs. Chapter numbers in red, usually '*c(apitulu)m*' followed by a Roman numeral. Red and blue paraphs at the start of sections within the text. Corrections in the original or contemporary hands; some omitted passages are added in the margins in red frames. A passage omitted at Luke 1 (fol. 50v) is added by the original scribe on a narrow leaf inserted after fol. 50. Some omitted words and passages are added in the margins in an early modern hand (e.g., fols. 40v, 119v, 126v, 128v, etc.). No marginal glosses; added material within the text is not underlined; occasionally cross-references to biblical books in the margins. Indexing letters entered in the margins at the beginnings of lections, rather than consistently. The beginnings of lections are also often marked within the text with red wash, and red or blue paraphs. Some lections are accompanied by added notes in Latin in a 15th-century hand, specifying the liturgical occasion (e.g., fols. 4v, 55r, 57r, 111r, 160r, etc.). '*Nota*' marking didactic and moral passages, but also 1 Corinthians 14:18: '*I thanke my god for I speke in þe langage of alle ȝou…*' (fol. 126r).

2. (fols. 235v–243r) Table of lections of Type II with a rubric '*þe pistlis & þe gospels of þe newe testament vn to seint andrewes euyn*', containing only NT readings. Written in a different ink, and probably by a scribe different from the scribe of the NT, on pages ruled for one or two columns, but not specially for a table of lections. Contains the temporal, followed by a short sanctoral (rubric: '*ffrom andrewis euyn vnto þe comune þe proper pistlis & gospelis*') that includes the feasts of Nicholas, George, Thomas Becket, Martin, Lawrence, Denis and Clement. The sanctoral is followed by a detailed common (rubric: '*ffrom heþen þe pistlis & þe gospels of þe comune*') and commemorations of the Virgin Mary, Trinity, Cross, the Holy Ghost,

brothers and sisters, peace, clear weather, rain, battle and pestilence, angels, '*for hym silf*', '*for pestilence of beestis*', '*ffor weyferynge men*', sins, sick, weddings, pilgrims, '*Masse of requiem*'. The entries consist of the name of a liturgical occasion in black or red, abbreviated reference to a book and chapter of the Bible, an indexing letter, the opening words of a reading, '*ende*' and the closing words of a reading, all in black.

3. (fol. 243r) A list of NT books in English. Fols. 243v–246v were originally blank (see Provenance).

Decoration

4- to 8-line blue initials with red penwork and penwork borders at the beginning of books; 3- to 4-line similar initials at the beginning of prologues, and 3- to 6-line similar initials at the beginning of chapters.

Dialect

ony(9)/any(1), ech(9)/eche(1), fire(3)/fier(7), 3yue(n)(3)/3oue(n)(7), lyf(10), lyk(5)/lik(5), myche(10), si3(7)/sy3(1)/say3(1) (sg.), sayen(3)/si3en(3) (pl.), silf(9)/self(1), siche(10), þou3(8), þorou(3)/þoru3(3)/þorou3(4)

-iþ(5)/-eþ(5) (pres.ind.3sg.), -en(10) (pres.ind.pl.), -ynge(7)/-yng(1)/-inge(2) (pres.part.) sche(10) (3sg.fem.pronoun, nom.), þei(10) (3pl.pronoun, nom.), hem(10) (3pl.pronoun, oblique), her(10) (3pl.pronoun, possessive)

Physical description

MATERIAL: parchment

DIMENSIONS: *c.*195 × 138 mm, trimmed in rebinding

NUMBER OF LEAVES: 251

FOLIATION: modern in pencil and ink, unnumbered leaf, i–iii + 1–49 + 50a + 50* + 51–246

COLLATION: (unnumbered leaf, fols. i–iii) I (8–4) missing 5–8 | (fols. 1–48) II–VII (8) | (fols. 49–56) VIII (8+1) 3rd inserted | (fols. 57–240) IX–XXXI (8) | (fols. 241–246) XXXII (8–2) missing 4, 5

Catchwords survive; quire signatures run consecutively a–p (fols. 1–120), followed by two quires without signatures (fols. 121–136), followed by quires signed r–z (fols. 137–192), & (abbreviation for 'and'), abbreviation for 'con-' (fols. 193–208) and 1–4 (fols. 209–240).

RULING: ruled in plummet for two columns, with single vertical and double horizontal bounding lines, extending the full height and width of page;

additional sets of two bounding lines in the upper, lower and outer margins; 31 lines per page; written space: *c.*128–130 × 90 mm; prickings survive

SCRIPT: textura, black and brown ink; the table of lections is probably by a different scribe

RUBRICATION: rubrics in red ink; blue paraphs at the start of sections within the text

SEC. FOL.: '*apperide in*' (fol. 2r)

Binding

Medieval oak boards covered with blue marbled paper. 'John Wyklif's || Translation of || The New Testament || MS.' handwritten in ink on spine; fragmentary paper label with '90(?)1' on spine.

Provenance

1. Copy of the Latin will of Robert Thoft of St Botulph's at Lincoln (?), dated 11 April 1415 (fol. 244v). Mentions hospital of St Catherine '*iuxta Lincoln*', Richard Eston, Thomas Godney (or Gedney), guild of St Trinity, guild of the Assumption of the Virgin Mary, Juliana (wife) and William (son).

2. A 15th-century clerical (?) owner who marked the lections within the text and added Latin notes specifying the liturgical occasions when they were appointed to be read (see Text).

3. Turner, William (1509/10–1568), naturalist and religious controversialist, dean of Wells, 1563; see *ODNB*: '*Amen W T*' (fol. 96r); '1563', '*Docter turner || in Welles. 12. daye auguste || Dean of Welles*' (fol. 243v). Also '*Jane Turner*' (fol. 1r) and '*Wennyfred Turner*' (fol. 246v). Corrections in the margins in an early modern hand (see Text).

4. '*William Mylett est nomen eius*' (fol. 246r), 16th century (?).

5. Waterland, Daniel (1683–1740), theologian, rector of Walesby and Flixborough, Lincolnshire; see *ODNB*: note on fol. iii verso may be in his hand.

6. Lewis, John (1675–1747), Church of England clergyman and antiquary; see *ODNB*: received the manuscript from Waterland and made it the base text of the gospels in Lewis (1731).

7. Ebenezer Mussel of Bethnal Green in London: purchased from the executors of Lewis for £4-0-0 (fol. iii verso).

8. Herbert, William (1718–1795), bibliographer and printseller; see *ODNB*: bought at Mussell's sale (Langford of Covent Garden) in May 1766 (fol. iii recto) (see de Hamel (1997), p. 90 and n. 13). Lot 901 in his sale on 21 November 1798.

9. Richard Gough (1735–1809); see *ODNB*.

10. Bodleian Library: bequeathed by Gough; received in 1809.

Bibliography

Lewis, J. (ed.), *The New Testament of our Lord and Saviour Jesus Christ translated out of the Latin Vulgat by John Wiclif* (London: John March, 1731).
Forshall and Madden (1850), vol. 1, pp. i, l.
Summary catalogue, vol. 4, no. 17681.
Fristedt (1953–73), vol. 1, p. 2.
Hudson (1989), p. 140 n. 29.
de Hamel, C., 'The selling and collecting of manuscripts of Nicholas Love's *Mirror of the Blessed Life of Jesus Christ* since the Middle Ages' in Oguro, S., Beadle, R. and Sargent, M. G. (eds), *Nicholas Love* at *Waseda*: *proceedings of the international conference, 20–22 July 1995* (Cambridge: D. S. Brewer, 1997), pp. 87–97 at p. 90.
Scott (2000–02), vol. 2, p. 50, no. 525.
Dove (2007), pp. 61 n. 124, 75 n. 48, 300.

25 MS Hatton 111

Origin: England

Date: 15th century, first quarter

Text

Fols. i–1 are originally blank paper and parchment flyleaves (see Provenance).

[item 1 occupies quires I–II]
1. (fols. 2r–9v) *Jerome's Abbreviated Psalter*, Version A (Morey (2000), pp. 186–89; Wells (1916), vol. 8, p. 18; Severs, Hartung, Beidler (1967–), vol. 2, p. 387, no. 15). English text only, periods start with red initials, no rubric at the beginning. Fol. 10r–v is blank.

[items 2–3 occupy quires III–V]
2. (fols. 11r–13v) *Old Testament Sentences*, Version 2 (Morey (2000), pp. 130–2), starting without a rubric. 'Sentences' begin with blue initials

and are followed by references to books and chapters of the Bible in red. The next item, a table of lections starts without a title or any indication of a textual boundary.

3. (fols. 13v–34r) Table of lections of Type II with incipits in EV with readings only from those NT books that are included in Hatton 111. Written on pages without a special ruling. Consists of a temporal, a short sanctoral, a detailed common and commemorations. The entries for readings include the name of a liturgical occasion, abbreviated reference to a book and chapter of the Bible, an indexing letter, the opening words of a reading, '*ende*' and the closing words of a reading, all in the same ink. The only non-biblical saints are Lawrence, Denis, Clement, Stephen and Thomas Becket (the last two in the temporal). Fol. 34v is blank.

[items 4–5 occupy quires VI–XXXVIII]
4. (fols. 35r–290r) gospels and James–Apocalypse in EV without prologues, imperfect at the beginning, starting at Matthew 1:22. John 13:2–21 is missing because of the loss of a leaf after fol. 224. The wording of rubrics is variable and differs from that found in most LV manuscripts, e.g., '*Here endiþ mathew ewangelist in his gospels*', '*Marke*' at the beginning of Mark, '*Here endiþ luke in þe gospels. Here bigynneþ þe gospel aftir þe writyng of Ioon*' at the beginning of John (see Appendix VII). The rubrics are missing at the start of some texts, e.g., 2 John (fol. 260v) and 3 John (fol. 261v) have 'vi' and 'vii' at the beginning and were apparently mistaken for chapters 6–7 of 1 John. Running titles on both rectos and versos, consisting of abbreviated titles of biblical books (some supplied in an early modern hand). Chapter numbers as Roman numerals, most preceded by '*c(apitulu)m*'. No marginal glosses. Indexing letters in the margins entered consistently throughout each chapter, rather than only at the beginnings of lections (see 'Liturgical materials' in the Introduction). The ends of lections are marked with double strokes. Added material within the text is underlined in brown ink. Corrections in the margins and over erasures in contemporary hands.

5. (fols. 290r–294v) *Capitula*-list for Matthew 1–Luke 20 with the section for each gospel preceded by a rubric (e.g., '*here bigynneþ þe chapitres of matheu of þe newe testament*'). Imperfect at the end because of the loss of leaves.

Decoration
3- to 5-line blue initials with red penwork at the beginnings of books.
2- to 3-line plain blue initials at the beginnings of chapters.

Dialect

ony(10), eche(9)/ech(1), fier(8)/fyer(1)/fyre(1), ȝouun(10), lyif(7)/lijf(3), lik(1)/like(6)/lichy(3), myche(10), say(10) (sg.), sayen(10) (pl.), silf(10), siche(8)/suche(2), þouȝ(2)/þou(1), þorou(5)/þorouȝ(1)

-iþ(5)/-eþ(5) (pres.ind.3sg.), -en(10) (pres.ind.pl.), -ynge(8)/-inge(2) (pres. part.) sche(10) (3sg.fem.pronoun, nom.), þei(10) (3pl.pronoun, nom.), hem(10) (3pl.pronoun, oblique), her(10) (3pl pronoun, possessive)

Physical description

MATERIAL: poor quality parchment with holes

DIMENSIONS: *c.*122 × 90 mm

NUMBER OF LEAVES: 300

FOLIATION: modern in pencil, i–iii + 1–58 + 58* + 59–296

COLLATION: (fols. i–ii) paper flyleaves | (fols. iii–2) I (4–1) missing 3 | (fols. 3–34) II–V (8) | fols. 35–41) VI (8–1) missing 1 | (fols. 42–224) VII–XXIX (8) | (fols. 225–231) XXX (8–1) missing 1 | (fols. 232–287) XXXI–XXXVII (8) | (fols. 288–294) XXXVIII (8–1) missing 8
Catchwords survive.

RULING: ruled in plummet for a single column, with single or double (e.g., fol. IIIr) vertical bounding lines extending the full height and width of page; prickings survive; 23–8 lines per page; written space: variable, *c.*81–89 × 58–65 mm

SCRIPT: informal textura, brown ink; *Jerome's Abbreviated Psalter* and the table of lections are in different contemporary hands

RUBRICATION: rubrics in the hand of the main scribe, in brown ink, often in a larger script and underlined in red

SEC. FOL.: '*lord þ(er)fore*' (fol. 3r)

Binding

Brown leather over pasteboard, stamped in gilt with the royal arms of Great Britain on both covers, English, 17th century, first quarter. Triple blind fillet lines round the outer edge of both covers, fittings of two clasps, now lost. Four raised bands on spine; 'III' painted white on spine. Fol. iii was a pastedown of an earlier binding.

Provenance

1. Less professionally produced than many manuscripts of the Wycliffite Bible.

2. 'Jhon Swynson', early 16th century (?), fols. 200v–201r.

3. '*Thomas Witting his Booke*', 17th century, fol. iii verso.

Bibliography

Forshall and Madden (1850), vol. 1, pp. xxxii, xlviii.
Summary catalogue, vol. 2, part II, no. 4050.
Hudson (1989), p. 140.
Ogilvie-Thomson, S. J., *IMEP*, Handlist VIII (1991), p. 135.
Kuczynski, M. P., *Prophetic song: the psalms as moral discourse in late Medieval England* (Philadelphia: University of Pennsylvania Press, 1995), p. 252 n. 51.
Dove (2007), pp. 59 n. 114, 65 n. 144, 142 n. 31, 300.

26 MS Holkham misc. 40

Origin: England

Date: 15th century, first quarter

Text

Fols. i–iii are paper flyleaves, blank apart from modern notes.

1. (fols. 1r–133r) Prose *Mirror*, a collection of sermons with a prologue translated from Robert of Gretham's Anglo-Norman verse *Mirror* (Paues (1904), pp. xiv–xv; Blumreich (2002); Duncan and Connolly (2003); O'Mara and Paul (2007)). Rubrics in red, most are not filled in after fol. 112r; corrections in a contemporary hand; medieval '*nota*' and pointing hands in the margins; Latin notes in the margins (16th century (?)).

2. (fols. 133r–162va) Middle English translation of the General and Pauline epistles (Paues (1904), pp. 18–122; Morey (2000), pp. 346–50) in the following order: 1 Peter, 2 Peter, James, 1 John, 2 John, 3 John, Jude, the epilogue to the Catholic epistles ('*Suster þus haueþ…*'), Romans, 1 Corinthians, 2 Corinthians, Galatians, Ephesians, Philippians, Colossians, 1 Thessalonians, 2 Thessalonians, Hebrews, 1 Timothy, 2 Timothy, Titus.

3. (fols. 162va–257rb) Four gospels in EV with usual prologues. Only some of the prologues, but not the gospels, have rubrics (e.g., '*here bygynneþ þe*

prologe of Ion'). The text is complete, but subdivided into readings for the temporal, Sarum sanctoral and commemorations. The beginning of each reading is marked with a rubric in red, specifying the day on which it is appointed to be read; the end of each reading is marked with '*ende*' in red. Includes readings for Thomas Hereford (fol. 218r) and Bavo of Ghent (220r), non-Sarum saints. Chapter numbers in red as Arabic numerals, usually in the form '*c(apitulu)m 3m*'. Running titles in red on both rectos and versos, consisting of the name of the evangelist or '*prologus*'. Added material within the text is underlined in brown ink. Corrections in contemporary hands. Occasionally cross-references to biblical books in the margins in red by the rubricator (e.g., fols. 167r, 170r, 195v). Added glosses in the margins in a medieval hand, e.g., '*n(ot)a wat crist badde his apostlys*' (fol. 168v). At the beginning of gospels notes on the number of chapters in each (e.g., '*luc h(ab)et xxiiij cm*'), 15th century.

Decoration

2- to 3-line plain red initials at the beginnings of gospels; similar 1- to 3-line initials at the beginnings of prologues and chapters.

Dialect

(gospels)
eny(9)/ony(1), iche(2)/eche(7)/ech(1), fijr(8)/fyer(2), lyfe(1)/lyf(1)/lyif(1)/lijf(7), lyic(1)/lijc(5)/liche(4), miche(2)/myche(8), see(1)/seeȝ(1)/saw(3) (sg.), seyen(3)/sayen(1)/seyne(1) (pl.), self(10), siche(7)/syche(2), þouȝ(3), þoru(8)/þurȝ(1)/þerwȝ(1)

-eþ(6)/-eth(1)/-iþ(3) (pres.ind.3sg.), -en(9)/-yn(1) (pres.ind.pl.), -yng(9)/-ing(1) (pres.part.), sche(10) (3sg.fem.pronoun, nom.), þai(1)/þei(9) (3pl. pronoun, nom.), hem(10) (3pl.pronoun, oblique), her(9)/þeire(1) (3pl. pronoun, possessive)

According to Hanna (2003, p. 148), the fourth scribe of the *Mirror*, who copied more than 70 per cent of its text, wrote Type III London English, but with some Type II relics, probably inherited from the exemplar, e.g., '*hij*', '*-ande*' in pres. part. (Hanna (2003), pp. 148–9).

Physical description

MATERIAL: parchment, paper flyleaves

DIMENSIONS: *c.*282 × 189 mm; leaves were cropped in rebinding, occasionally causing the loss of text in the margins

NUMBER OF LEAVES: 263

FOLIATION: modern in pencil, i–iii + 1–260; contemporary in ink, in Roman and Arabic numerals, up to fol. 179 (Matthew 23), I–XXVIIII + XXIX + XXX–CIII + 104–179

COLLATION: (fols. i–iii) paper flyleaves | (fols. 1–256) I–XXXII (8) | (fol. 257) single leaf | (fols. 258–260) paper flyleaves.

Catchwords survive; quire signatures run consecutively a–z, a–i.

RULING: Leaves occupied by *Mirror* are ruled in plummet for a single column, leaves occupied by epistles and gospels are ruled for two columns. The switch happens on fol. 133v, the second page of the epistles, presumably to avoid having different ruling on facing pages. The written space is similar throughout. Single vertical and double horizontal bounding lines extending the full height and width of page; prickings survive; 37–45 lines per page (varies from quire to quire); written space: *c.*145–89 × 123–125 mm

SCRIPT: five scribes: (1) fols. 1r–16v; (2) fols. 17r–25r; (3) fols. 25r–133r; (4) fols. 133r–162v (epistles); (5) fols. 162v–257r (gospels); textura, black and brown ink

RUBRICATION: rubrics in red ink

SEC. FOL.: '*mirrour makeþ*' (fol. 3r)

Binding

Light brown leather over wood boards, 19th century. Gilt and blind decoration round the outer edge of both covers. Four raised bands on spine; gilt decoration on the raised bands and on the panels between the bands. Gilt crest of Thomas William Coke on the front cover. Gilt lettering on spine: 'THE MYRROUR || & GOSPELS' and 'MS || MEMB. 672'. Gilt edges of textblock.

Provenance

1. Johannes Forestius, '*rector de Ramseton in Comitatu essex est proprius et indubitatus possessor huius libri 1552*' (fol. 7r).

2. Sir Edward Coke (1552–1634); see *ODNB*: autograph on fol. 1r; item 212 in the catalogue of his books (Hassall (1950), p. 15).

3. Thomas William Coke, first earl of Leicester of Holkham (1754–1842); see *ODNB*: name and crest on the book-plate on the upper pastedown; crest on the binding.

4. Bodleian Library: acquired from the collection of the Earls of Leicester at Holkham Hall, near Wells, Norfolk. Former shelfmark: Holkham Hall MS 672.

Bibliography

Paues, A. C., *A fourteenth century English Biblical version* (Cambridge: Cambridge University Press, 1904).

Hassall, W. O., *A catalogue of the library of Sir Edward Coke* (New Haven, Conn. and London: Yale University Press/Oxford University Press, 1950).

Ker (1969–2002), vol. 3, p. 420.

Hudson, A. and Spencer, H. L., 'Old author, new work: the sermons of MS Longleat 4', *Medium Aevum* 53 (1984), pp. 220–38 at p. 237 n. 50.

Hudson, A., 'Lollardy: the English heresy?', *Lollards and their books* (London: Hambledon Press, 1985), pp. 141–63 at p. 141 n. 3.

Spencer, H. L., *English preaching in the late Middle Ages* (Oxford: Clarendon Press, 1993), pp. 277, 373 nn. 64, 66, 406 n. 141, 451 n. 88, 468 nn. 97–8, 473 n. 30, 495 n. 41.

Scott (2000–02), vol. 2, p. 60 no. 567.

Blumreich, K. M. (ed.), *The Middle English 'Mirror': an edition based on Bodleian Library, MS Holkham misc. 40* (Arizona: Centre for Medieval and Renaissance Studies, 2002).

Duncan, T. G. and Connolly, M. (eds), *The Middle English 'Mirror': sermons from Advent to Sexagesima* (Heidelberg: Universitätsverlag Winter, 2003).

Hanna, R., 'English biblical texts before Lollardy and their fate', in Somerset, F. and Havens, J. C. (eds), *Lollards and their influence in late medieval England* (Woodbridge: Boydell, 2003), pp. 141–53.

Hanna (2005), pp. 16, 28, 41 n. 21, 217 n. 44 and *passim*, 219 n. 54, 306–7.

Dove (2007), p. 300.

O'Mara, V. and Paul, S. (eds), *A repertorium of Middle English prose sermons* (Turnhout: Brepols, 2007), pp. 2047–165.

27 MS Junius 29

Origin: England

Date: 15th century, first quarter

Text

Fols. i–iv are paper and parchment flyleaves, mostly blank (see Provenance).

[item 1 occupies quire I]
1. (fols. 1r–12r) Table of lections of Type I; fols. 5 and 6, originally the first and second leaves of the table, are misbound. Rubric: '[...]*ffro þe bigynnyng of aduent til newe ierris day. Here bigynneþ a rule þat telliþ in what chapitris of þe bible ȝe schulen fynde þe lessouns pistils & gospels þat ben rad in þe chirche þoru þe ȝeer after þe vse of Salisbury*' (fol. 5r; preceded by a blank space). Includes all feasts characteristic of LV (Forshall and Madden (1850), vol. 4, pp. 683, 690–6), apart from Giles (1 September). Consists of the temporal, commemorations and proper (no common in spite of the rubric). Commemorations are in the following order: our Lady, Trinity, the feast of relics, Holy Ghost, cross, angels, '*briþeren & sistren & salus populi*', peace, clear weather, rain, '*in tyme of batels*', '*a man for him silf*', '*ffor pestilence of beestis*', pilgrims, weddings, sinners, sick and dead. Corrections by the original scribe (e.g., fol. 6r). The entries for readings consist of the name of the liturgical occasion in red, abbreviated reference to a book and chapter of the Bible, an indexing letter in red, the opening words of a reading, '*eende*' in red, the closing words of a reading and double strokes. Translation of Thomas Becket (7 July, fol. 9v) and titles 'pope' are smudged. Fol. 12v is blank.

[item 2 occupies quires II–XXV]
2. (fols. 13r–198r) NT in LV with usual prologues. Running titles on both rectos and versos, most in red, consisting of abbreviated titles of biblical books and chapter numbers. Usual rubrics (e.g., '*Here eendiþ þe gospels of mathew & bigynneþ þe prolog on marke*'; '*þis seiþ Ierom in his prolog on marke And here begynneþ þe gospels of marke*', fol. 36r). The rubric at 2 John is not filled in. Chapter numbers in red, most as words in English in the gospels (e.g., '*þe sixte chapitir*') and as Roman numerals in the epistles, Acts and the Apocalypse. Several errors in chapter numbering (e.g., Luke 4–5); some chapter numbers are not filled in by the rubricator. Fols. 47–50 are misbound; the correct order is 46, 49, 50, 47, 48, 51. Imperfect at the end because of a missing quire, ends at Apocalypse, 21:20. Completed in an early modern hand from the Geneva Bible (fols. 197r–198r). Indexing

letters, entered at the beginnings of readings, rather than consistently, are in the margins within specially ruled columns. The beginnings and ends of readings are highlighted with yellow wash; the ends are usually marked with double strokes. A large number of corrections in a contemporary hand, often insertions of text omitted by the scribe or cancellations of dittography. No marginal glosses; glosses within the text are very occasionally underlined in red.

Decoration

5-line gold initial on blue and pink background and penwork border at the beginning of Matthew; 3- to 6-line blue initials with red penwork and penwork borders at the beginnings of other books.

2- to 4-line blue initials with red penwork at the beginnings of prologues and chapters. Capitals that follow the initials are decorated with human faces or geometric designs.

Dialect

eny(10), ech(9)/eche(1), fier(10), ȝoue(2)/ȝouen(8) (ȝouun in a correction at Matthew 14:9, fol. 23r), lijf(8)/lif(1)/lyif(1), lijk(8)/lijke(2), myche(10), saien(4)/sien(2) (pl.), siȝ(1)/sai(4) (sg.), silf(10), such(2)/suche(5)/siche(1), þouȝ(8), þorouȝ(7)/þorow(1)/þorowe(1)/þorou(1)

-iþ(9)/-eþ(2) (pres.ind.3sg), -en(10) (pres.ind.pl.), -ynge(10) (pres.part.) sche(10) (3sg.fem.pronoun, nom.), þei(10) (3pl.pronoun, nom.), hem(10) (3pl.pronoun, oblique), her(10) (3pl.pronoun, possessive)

Physical description

MATERIAL: parchment, paper flyleaves

DIMENSIONS: *c.*260 × 182 mm

NUMBER OF LEAVES: 204

FOLIATION: modern in pencil, i–iv + 1–200

COLLATION: (fols. i–vi) paper and parchment flyleaves | (fols. 1–12) I (originally a quire of 12 leaves (?); fols. 5–6, originally the first two leaves of the quire, are misbound) || (fols. 13–196) II–XXIV (8) || (fols. 197–200) XXV (4) || unnumbered paper flyleaf at the end

Fols. 47–50 (quire V) are misbound; the correct order is 46, 49, 50, 47, 48. Catchwords survive; quire signatures run consecutively a–q up to fol. 140 (quires II–XVI) and possibly afterwards (cf. fragmentary signature on fol. 184).

RULING: ruled in plummet for two columns, with single vertical and single or double horizontal bounding lines extending the full height and width of page; a further set of double bounding lines in the right, left and lower margins on most leaves up to fol. 159v; prickings survive; 35–8 lines per page (varies within the quires and from quire to quire); written space: variable, *c.*182–196 × 120–127 mm

SCRIPT: textura; the work of several scribes; the spacing of letters and the appearance of script often change (e.g., end of the second column on fol. 65r; second column on fol. 70r)

RUBRICATION: rubrics in red ink

SEC. FOL.: '*þursday Ioon*' (table of lections, fol. 2r); '*bisili of hem*' (NT, fol. 14r)

Binding

White vellum over pasteboard, 17th century. Blind and gilt fillet-line border round the outer edge of both covers; stamped gold initials 'E G' on both covers. Fragments of two ties. Five raised bands on spine framed with gilt fillet lines; gilt floral decoration at the top and bottom of spine. 'MSS. Junii.', '29', and 'New Testam:' written in brown ink on spine. '25' written in ink on the front cover. Pastedowns made of laid paper with watermarks.

Provenance

1. Translation of Thomas Becket and titles 'pope' are smudged in the table of lections, presumably at Reformation.

3. ευλαβου αναγνώστης, 'reader beware', late 16th century (?) (fol. 13r). An equivalent of the Latin phrase '*Caveat anagnostes/Caveat lector*', perhaps deliberately translated back into Greek. The Apocalypse completed from the Geneva Bible. '*Nouum Testamentum*' and '*Tabula*' on fols. iv verso and 1r; short notes elsewhere in the MS.

4. 17th-century binding with initials 'E G'.

5. Francis Junius (1591–1677); see *ODNB*.

6. Bodleian Library: bequeathed by Junius.

Bibliography

Summary catalogue, vol. 2, part II, no. 5141.
Hudson (1989), p. 140.
Scott (2000–02), vol. 2, p. 61, no. 574.
Dove (2007), p. 300.

28 MS Laud misc. 24

Origin: England

Date: 15th century, first quarter

Text

Fol. ii is a parchment flyleaf.

(fols. 1–120r) Matthew–Mark in LV with usual prologues. Running titles on rectos only, preceded by red paraphs, consisting of the abbreviated titles of the two gospels, without chapter numbers. Usual rubrics, e.g., '*Here bigynep a prolog on þe gospel of Matheu*'; '*Þus seiþ ierom in his prolog of matheu*' (fols. 1r, 2r). Chapter numbers in red as Roman numerals, usually in the form '*c*° *ii*'. No marginal glosses; added material within the text is occasionally underlined. Indexing letters in the margins entered at the beginnings of lections, rather than consistently; the beginnings of lections are also marked with red or blue paraphs within the text; the ends of lections are marked with double strokes. A few short notes in the margins in an early modern hand. Fol. 120v is ruled, but originally blank; fols. 121r–122v are parchment flyleaves, originally blank (see Provenance).

Decoration

5-line gold initials on blue and pink background, and borders made of penwork sprays with gold leaves and disks at the beginnings of gospels.

2- to 3-line blue initials with red penwork at the beginnings of prologues and chapters.

Dialect

any(10), ech(7)/eche(3), fier(9)/fer(1), ȝouun(3)/ȝouen(5)/ȝiuen(2), lif(10), lik(9)/like(1), myche(10), siȝ(6)/sauȝ(1) (sg.), sayen(3)/siȝen(2) (pl.), silf(10), siche(5)/sich(1), þouȝ(5), þorowȝ(3)/þorow(2)

-iþ(9)/-iþ(1) (pres.ind.3sg.), -en(10) (pres.ind.pl.), -ynge(10) (pres.part.)

sche(10) (3sg.fem.pronoun, nom.), þei(10) (3pl.pronoun, nom.), hem(10) (3pl. pronoun, oblique), her(10) (3pl.pronoun, possessive)

Physical description

MATERIAL: parchment

DIMENSIONS: *c.*155 × 108 mm

NUMBER OF LEAVES: 263

FOLIATION: modern in pencil, i–ii + 1–123

COLLATION: (fols. i–ii) upper pastedown and a conjoint flyleaf | (fols. 1–120) I–XV (8) | (fols. 121–123) parchment flyleaves and lower pastedown
Catchwords survive; quire signatures run consecutively +, b–p.

RULING: ruled for one column, with single vertical and double horizontal bounding lines extending the full height and width of page; prickings survive; 21–3 lines per page (varies from quire to quire); written space: *c.*95 × 61 mm

SCRIPT: textura, black ink

RUBRICATION: rubrics in red ink

SEC. FOL.: '*a calf*' (fol. 2r)

Binding

Contemporary binding, white leather over boards, fragments of a strap-and-pin fastening. Labels on spine with typewritten: 'Laud. || C || 6.' and 'Laud || 24'. Parchment flyleaves and pastedowns.

Provenance

1. '*london*', '*ludens*', '*Lex dei iusta est*', 16th century (?), fol. 122v.

2. William Laud (1573–1645); see *ODNB*: '*Liber Guilielmi Laud Archiep(iscop) i Cantuar*': *et Cancellarij Vniuersitatis Oxon. 1634*', fol. 1r.

3. Bodleian Library: first donation from Laud, 22 May 1635. Earlier shelfmark: 'C.6' (upper pastedown and spine).

Bibliography

Forshall and Madden (1850), vol. 1, p. xlvi.
Summary catalogue, vol. 2, part I, no. 661.
Coxe (1973), no. 24.
Scott (2000–02), vol. 2, p. 72, no. 634.
Dove (2007), p. 300.

29 MS Laud misc. 25

Origin: England

Date: 15th century, first quarter

Text

Fols. i–ii are paper flyleaves, blank apart from modern notes.

[item 1 occupies quire I]
1. (fols. 1r–2v) Originally blank leaves. On fol. 1v is the beginning of a table of lections in Latin from the first Sunday in Advent to Friday of the third week after Christmas, with readings from gospels only, added in the 15th century.

[item 2 occupies quires II–XXV]
2. (fols. 3r–194r) Four gospels in LV with usual prologues. Running titles in red on both rectos and versos, consisting of the name of the evangelist and a chapter number (most as Arabic numerals). Usual rubrics, e.g., '*Here endiþ þe gospel of M*[t]*. & here begynneþ þe prolog of mark*'; '*thus seiþ Ierom on þe gospel of Mark*' (fols. 57v–58r). Chapter numbers in red, most as Roman numerals, often in the form '*þe .xviiii. c*[o]' or '*x c*[o]'. Indexing letters in the margins, entered at the beginnings of readings, rather than consistently. The beginnings of readings are also often highlighted with yellow wash and preceded by red or blue paraphs; the ends of readings are usually marked with double strokes in the margins. No marginal glosses; added material within the text is not underlined. Corrections and '*nota*' in the margins in a contemporary hand. At the end 'AMEN' followed by '9.20' in red.

Decoration

3- to 4-line red and blue penwork initials and penwork borders at the beginnings of gospels.

2- to 4-line blue initials with red penwork at the beginnings of prologues (accompanied by a penwork border at the beginning of John); 2-line similar initials at the beginnings of chapters.

Indexing letters, catchwords, ascenders and descenders are sometimes decorated with floral penwork designs.

Dialect

ony(10), eche(9)/ech(1), fier(8)/feir(1)/fir(1), gouun(10), lijf(10), like(8)/lic(1)/lijk(1), myche(10), siȝ(4)/syȝe(1) (sg.), saien(2)/sayen(1)/siȝen(1)/sien(1) (pl.), silf(10), suche(5)/such(1)/siche(3), þouȝ(8), þorouȝ(9)/þorowȝ(1)

-eþ(3)/-iþ(7) (pres.ind.3sg.), -en(10) (pres.ind.pl.), -ynge(9)/-inge(1) (pres. part.), sche(9)/schee(1) (3sg.fem.pronoun, nom.), þei(10) (3pl.pronoun, nom.), hem(10) (3pl.pronoun, oblique), her(8)/here(2) (3pl.pronoun, possessive)

Physical description

MATERIAL: parchment, paper flyleaves

DIMENSIONS: *c.*144 × 86 mm; leaves were trimmed in rebinding, occasionally causing the loss of text and decoration in the margins

NUMBER OF LEAVES: 201

FOLIATION: modern in pencil, i–ii + 1–199

COLLATION: (fols. i–ii) paper flyleaves and the upper pastedown | (fols. 1–2) I (2) | (fols. 3–194) II–XXV (8)

Catchwords survive; quire signatures run consecutively a–z and appear not only in the lower right corner on the rectos of the first four leaves of each quire, but also on the last page of each quire, next to a catchword.

RULING: ruled in plummet for two columns, with single vertical and double horizontal bounding lines extending the full height and width of page; a further bounding line in the upper margin; prickings survive; 28 lines per page; written space: *c.*96–99 × 67 mm

SCRIPT: textura, black ink, the size and style of script often change unpredictably on the same page (e.g., fols. 28v, 58r, 66v, 67r)

RUBRICATION: rubrics in red ink

SEC. FOL.: '*þe sone of*' (fol. 2r)

Binding

Brown leather of pasteboard, 19th century. Blind fillet-line border round the outer edge of both covers. Five raised bands on spine, framed by blind fillet lines. Gilt lettering on spine 'THE FOUR || GOSPELS.' and 'LAUD. || 25.'. Turn-ins with floral designs. Paper labels from an earlier binding pasted to the upper pastedown.

Provenance

1. The beginning of a Sarum table of lections in Latin added in the 15th century.

2. William Laud (1573–1645); see *ODNB*: 'W.L.' (fol. 1r).

3. Bodleian Library: first donation from Laud, 22 May 1635. Earlier shelfmark 'C.7' (upper pastedown and fol. 1r).

Bibliography

Forshall and Madden (1850), vol. 1, p. xlvi.
Summary catalogue, vol. 2, part I, no. 659.
Coxe (1973), no. 25.
Scott (2000–02), vol. 2, p. 72, no. 635.
Dove (2007), p. 300.

30 MS Laud misc. 33

Origin: England

Date: 14th century, late or 15th century, early

Text

Fols. i recto–2r are originally blank parchment flyleaves (see Provenance).

1. (fols. 3r–96r) Pauline (Romans–Hebrews) and Catholic (James–Jude) epistles in LV, with usual prologues. Running titles in red or black on most rectos and versos, typically consisting of an abbreviated title of a book and chapter number. Spaces left for rubrics but not filled in, apart from fols. 44r, 88r and 96v. Chapter numbers as Roman numerals, usually in the form 'c^{m} vi^{m}', in black or red, often preceded by red paraphs. There are no indexing letters, but Latin incipits are written at the start of lections in the margins. Such incipits are usually surrounded by rectangular frames drawn in red or black ink. No marginal glosses, apart from fol. 29v; added material within the text is very occasionally underlined in red (e.g., fol. 68r). Corrections in a contemporary hand.

2. (fols. 96v–144r) *Apocalips of Jesu Crist*, with commentary, Version A (Morey (2000), pp. 351–3; ed. Fridner (1961)), with LV prologue to the Apocalypse. Passages of the translated text, underlined in red, are followed by passages of commentary. Found in two other manuscripts that contain parts of the Wycliffite NT, London, British Library Royal MS 17 A. XXVI and Columbia University, Plimpton Add. MS 3 (see Peikola (2006), p. 8).

Decoration

2- to 3-line plain red initials at the beginnings of books; 2-line similar initials (sometimes with penwork) at the beginnings of prologues and chapters.

Dialect

ony(10)/eny(1), ech(7)/eche(2)/yche(1), fier(8)/fyer(1)/fiyr(1), ȝouen(10), lyif(4)/liyf(5)/liȝf(1), lik(1)/liyk(8)/lijk(1), myche(3)/meche(1)/moche(6), say(2) (sg.), seye(1) (pl.), silf(10), sich(3)/siche(1)/swyche(1)/swiche(5), þouȝ(10), þorouȝ(3)/þoruȝ(1)/þoru(1)/þorou(1)

-eþ(4)/-iþ(6) (pres.ind.3sg.), -en(6)/-yn(4) (pres.ind.pl.), -ynge(8)/-enge(1)/-inge(1) (pres.part.), sche(10) (3sg.fem. pronoun, nom.), þei(8) (3pl.pronoun, nom.), hem(10) (3pl.pronoun, oblique), her(5)/here(5) (3pl.pronoun, possessive)

Physical description

MATERIAL: parchment

DIMENSIONS: *c.*182 × 112 mm; leaves were trimmed in rebinding, occasionally causing the loss of marginal text

NUMBER OF LEAVES: 148

FOLIATION: modern in pencil, i–ii + 1–146

COLLATION: (fols. i–2) I (4) | (fols. 3–90) II–XII (8) | (fols. 91–96) XIII (6) | (fols. 97–144) XIV–XIX (8)
Catchwords survive; quire signatures run consecutively.

RULING: ruled in ink, with single vertical and horizontal bounding lines extending the full height and width of page; 28 lines per page; written space: *c.*111–113 × 75–77 mm

SCRIPT: textura, black and brown ink

RUBRICATION: rubrics in red ink; the beginnings of verses highlighted in red ink

SEC. FOL.: '*go bitook*' (fol. 4r)

Binding

Contemporary binding, originally red (?) leather over wood boards, fragments of a strap-and-pin fastening (two ties and two pins). Fragments of several paper labels on spine.

Provenance

1. The inclusion of the *Apocalips of Jesu Crist* may have been an afterthought: the quire containing the end of the epistles is shorter than normal.

2. '*Iesus eterna dulcedo*

Dum cor non orat in uanum lingua laborat
Omne quod est nimium vertitur in vitium' followed by 'T. M.', 15th century.

3. John Amerie, 16th century, late or 17th century, early:
'*This is the booke that doth pertaine*
To him that doth it owe;
And if you doubte vppon his name
here shall you see below.
John Amerie' (fol. 145r).

4. Andrew Cook, vicar of Mundon, Essex, from 1604 until his death in 1633; also owned Oxford, Bodleian Library MS Laud misc. 513 and Oxford, Bodleian Library MS Laud misc. 658 (Ogilvie-Thomson, S. J., *IMEP*, Handlist XVI, pp. 14–15). A short description of contents on fol. 2v, including '*Comment(arius) in Apocalypsin per Joh. Wickliff*' (fols. 2v); notes in English verse and in Latin explaining that John Amerie bequeathed the book to his wife Dorothy by whom it was given to Andrew Cooke by the hands of John Wilson, '*magister*'; date '1615' (fol. 145r). Drawing of an acorn and oak leaves with initials 'A C'.

5. William Laud (1573–1645); see *ODNB*: '*Liber Guilielmi Laud Archiep(iscop) i Cantuar': et Cancellarij Vniuersitatis Oxon. 1633*' (fol. 3r).

6. Bodleian Library: first donation from Laud, 22 May 1635. Former shelfmark 'C. 9.' (fols. i verso, 2v, 3r).

Bibliography

Forshall and Madden (1850), vol. 1, pp. viii n. y, xlvi.
Deanesly (1920), p. 381.
Fridner, E., *An English fourteenth century apocalypse version with a prose commentary* (Lund: C. W. K. Gleerup, 1961), p. xiii and as 'La'.
Coxe (1973), no. 33.
Scott (2000–02), vol. 2, p. 72, no. 637.
Hanna (2005), p. 313 n. 1.
Peikola, M., 'Lollard (?) production under the looking glass: the case of Columbia University, Plimpton Add. MS 3', *Journal of the Early Book Society* 9 (2006), pp. 1–23.
Dove (2007), pp. 72, 300.

31 MS Laud misc. 36

Origin: England

Date: 15th century, second quarter

Text

Fol. i is a paper flyleaf, blank apart from modern notes.

(fols. 1r–163r) Gospels in LV, imperfect at the beginning because of a missing leaf, starting at Matthew 1:8, with usual prologues, apart from the missing prologue to Matthew. Also missing is much of Luke 12:48–13:11, because most of fol. 103a is cut off, leaving only a strip containing three lines. Running titles in black on both rectos and versos, consisting of the name of the evangelist with chapter numbers added in a medieval hand on fols. 1–23. Chapter numbers in red usually in the form '*cap(itulim) iij*'. Rubrics in red at the beginnings of prologues and gospels (e.g., '*here endiþ þe gospel of Mathew & begynneþ þe prolog vpon Mark*'; '*here endiþ þe prolog vpon Mark & bigynneþ þe gospel of Mark*'). Corrections in the original hand. Glosses in the margins explaining individual words and phrases in the hand of the original scribe and, at the beginning of Matthew, in an early modern hand. Added material within the text is underlined in black. Many added drawings of pointing hands and '*nota bene*' in the margins. Some mark passages of potentially Lollard interest, e.g., Christ's commandment to the apostles '*Nyle ȝe welde golde neiþer siluer ne money in ȝoure girdlis*' (Matthew, 10:9, fol. 12v), or Matthew 24:15 (fol. 36r), 24:23 (fol. 36v). Red and blue paraphs within the text. Fol. 163v is blank apart from early modern notes (see Provenance).

Decoration

4-line blue initials with red penwork at the beginnings of gospels; 3-line similar initials at the beginnings of prologues; 2-line similar initials at the beginnings of chapters.

Dialect

eny(9)/ony(1), ech(2)/eche(7)/iche(1), fier(10), ȝouen(10), lijf(10), lijk(10), myche(10), siȝ(4)/say(2) (sg.), saien(1)/sayen(5)/siȝen(1)/syen(1) (pl.), self(10), suche(9)/such(1), þouȝ(6)/þough(1), þorouȝ(2)/þoruȝ(2)

-iþ(7)/-eþ(3) (pres.ind.3sg.), -en(10) (pres.ind.pl.), -ynge(10) (pres.part.), sche(10) (3sg.fem. pronoun, nom.), þei(10) (3pl.pronoun, nom.), hem(10) (3pl.pronoun, oblique), her(9)/here(1) (3pl.pronoun, possessive)

Physical description

MATERIAL: parchment, laid paper flyleaves

DIMENSIONS: *c.*164 × 113 mm

NUMBER OF LEAVES: 166

FOLIATION: modern in pencil, i + 1–103 + 103a + 104–163 + i

COLLATION: (fol. i) paper flyleaf | (fols. 1–7) I (8–1) missing 1 | (fols. 8–158) II–XX (8) | (fols. 159–163) XXI (4 + 1) fol. 162 is an added singleton | (fol. i) paper flyleaf

Catchwords survive; leaf signatures run consecutively a–x.

RULING: ruled in plummet for a single column, with single vertical and double horizontal bounding lines extending the full height and width of page; prickings survive; 25 lines per page; written space: *c.*122 × 79 mm

SCRIPT: Anglicana with Secretary influence, black ink

RUBRICATION: rubrics in red ink

SEC. FOL.: '*myenes*' (fol. 2r)

Binding

Brown leather over pasteboard, 16th century. Blind fillet-line border round the outer edge of both covers; blind fillet-line rectangular figure at the centre of both covers. Rebacked in the Bodleian with the original spine relaid. Three raised bands on spine framed by blind fillet lines. Two paper labels on spine (one fragmentary) with typewritten 'Laud. || C || 24.' and '36'. Catches of two clasps (now lost) made of yellow metal on the lower cover. Fragment of a Latin manuscript recovered from the binding is stored as MS Lat. th. c. 10 (see Provenance).

Provenance

1. '*It(e)m (?) payd to thomas ix lb*', 15th century (fol. 163v).

2. Fragment of a Latin manuscript (15th century) of a very large format (*c.*10 mm between the ruled lines), recovered from the binding, containing on the recto a fragmentary end of prayer 12, a fragmentary prayer 13, and the beginning of prayer 14 of the 'The Fifteen Os of St. Bridget'. The verso is blank.

3. Transcripts (?) and a reworking (?) of memorial verses from St Paul's Cathedral, London (16th century, early, fol. 163v). The first is a version of

verses on the memorial of William Worsley, dean of St Paul (d. 1488); see *ODNB*, with a modified last line:

'*Vermibus hie donor*
et sic ostendere conor
Hie veluti ponor
sic erit orbis honor'.

Followed by '*Mr Will(elm)us Worley l(egum) doctor decani eccl(es)ie s(anc)ti P(auli) London*'. The actual version is printed by Weever (1767), p. 158.

The second is a transcript of memorial verses at St Paul's for Roger Niger, Bishop of London (d. 1241), written as prose:

'*Huius erat manibus*
domino locus iste dicatus
christe suis p(re)cibus
veniam des tolle reatus' (see Stow and Mottley (1733–35), bk III, p. 670).

4. Richard Johnson ('*Richarde Jhonsons liber*', upper and lower pastedowns), Georgine Dulake (lower pastedwon), '*Amey ffeamne*' (lower pastedown), 16th century. Signature '*Ricardus Jhonson*' written in a formal script also occurs in Oxford, Bodleian Library MS Laud misc 104, a mid-15th century copy of *The Pater Noster of Richard Ermyte* (*IPMEP*, 150), an exposition of the Lord's prayer wrongly attributed to Richard Rolle. Richard Johnson, originally from Salisbury diocese, is reported by Foxe to have been persecuted and charged with the possession of *Wyclif's Wycket* in the late 1520s and early 1530s (Hudson (1988), pp. 479, 489).

Ogilivie-Thomson argues that the owner of MS Laud misc. 36 is 'R. Johnson', a book-collector described in Doyle, A. I., 'Books belonging to R. Johnson', *Notes and Queries* 197 (1952), pp. 293–4. However, according to Doyle's tentative identification, 'R. Johnson' is likely to be a signature of Robert Johnson and R. Johnson's signatures (including a date and a price) are different from the signatures in Laud misc. 36.

5. William Watts (fl. *c.*1590–1649), Church of England clergyman and author; see *ODNB*: upper pastedown.

6. William Laud (1573–1645); see *ODNB*: '*Liber Guilielmi Laud Archiep(iscop) i Cantuar*: *et Cancellarij Vniuersitatis Oxon. 1633*' (fol. 3r).

7. Bodleian Library: second donation from Laud, 16 June, 1636. Earlier shelfmark: 'C 24' (upper pastedown, binding).

Bibliography

Stow, J. and Mottley, J., *A survey of the cities of London and Westminster* (London: J. Read, 1733–35).
Summary catalogue, vol. 2, part I, no. 676.
Weever, J., *Antient funeral monuments, of Great-Britain, Ireland, and the islands adjacent* (London: W. Tooke, 1767).
Forshall and Madden (1850), vol. 1, p. xlvi.
Coxe (1973), no. 36.
Ogilivie-Thomson, S. J., *IMEP*, Handlist XVI, pp. xvi, 15.
Hudson (1988).
Scott (2000–02), vol. 2, p. 72, no. 638.
Dove (2007), p. 301.

32 MS Laud misc. 182

Origin: England

Date: 15th century, first quarter

Text

[item 1 occupies quires I–XXXVI]
1. (fols. 1r–287v) Complete chapters from OT and NT in LV. Imperfect at the beginning, starting at Genesis 1:18 because of the loss of leaves. Includes Genesis 1–4, 6–7, 11, 14, 18, 22; Exodus 1–8, 20, 25, 32, 33; Deuteronomy 1, 27–28; 1 Kings 1, 2, 4, 10–17; 3 Kings 3, 9; Job 1–2; Psalms 1–2, 4–6, 36, 50, 70, 98; Daniel 2–3 (rubrics in red pointing out the differences between the Latin and Hebrew texts in chapter 3); 2 Maccabees 7; Matthew, prologue, 1–9, 23–28; Mark 14–16; Luke 1–4, 22–24; John, complete with usual prologue; 1 Corinthians 1, 13; Hebrews 1, 11; Acts 1, 7, 13; 2 Peter 2; Jude, complete; Apocalypse, complete with usual LV prologue. OT material is largely historical, rather than prophetic; its arrangement agrees with the order of books in LV; all books between Psalms and Daniel are excluded.

Running titles in red consisting of the titles of biblical books and sometimes chapter numbers. Rubrics in red containing the titles of biblical books and stating how many chapters are included, e.g., '*Here enden ten chapitris of genesis and here bigynneþ þe firste chapitre of exodi*' (fol. 18r). Chapter numbers in red, usually as Roman numerals, followed by '*c(apitulum)*' or '*chapitre*'. The beginnings of periods are highlighted in red. Glosses in the margins in OT; added material within the text is underlined in red. Indexing letters occasionally appear in the margins of the gospels and the Apocalypse. Frequent dittographic repetitions are crossed out in red within the text, but otherwise there are few corrections. Psalms are written as prose and have English titles and numbers as part of titles; only psalms 36, 50, 70, 98 have Latin incipits. Spaces left for initials at the beginnings of psalm verses but not filled in.

[item 2 occupies quires XXXVII–XL]
2. (fols. 288v–319v) Brief educational (?) and moral (?) extracts from OT and NT in LV, each followed by an abbreviated title of the book and chapter number. Extracts from the following books and chapters are included: Genesis 1–2, 4–9, 11–12, 14, 18–22, 24, 25, 27–8, 32–3, 35–9, 41–5, 46–50; Exodus 1–20, 22–23, 25–6, 33–5, 37, 40; Leviticus 6, 19, 23, 25; Numbers 5, 7, 11–12, 14–16, 20–22, 25, 29; Deuteronomy 4, 6–7, 11, 13, 15, 18, 21, 27, 30, 32; Joshua 5, 7, 10; Judges 1, 9, 11, 13, 15–16, 19–20; 1 Kings 3, 5, 9–10, 12–13, 18–19, 24, 26, 28, 31; 2 Kings 6–7, 12, 15–16, 18, 24; 3 Kings 1, 3, 6, 8–12, 17–19, 21–2; 4 Kings 1–2, 13; 2 Chronicles 7; Job 3, 6, 9–10, 13, 31, 40, 41; verses from Psalms 5–6, 50, 71, 88, 95, 115, 118, 138; Proverbs 5–6, 11, 21, 24, 26, 28, 30; Ecclesiastes 1, 7, 10; Song of Songs 2, 4; Wisdom 1–2, 12–4; Ecclesiasticus 1, 10, 22–3, 25, 34, 42, 45, 49; Isaiah 11, 14, 30, 37–8, 46; Jeremiah 7, 10, 15; Lamentations 2; Baruch 4; Ezekiel 37; Daniel 4, 13; Hosea 13; Zechariah 5; 1 Maccabees 6; 2 Maccabees 5, 9; Matthew 2–3, 5–6, 9, 13, 16, 18, 19, 21, 24, 27, 28; Mark 2–3, 6, 9, 10; Luke 2–3, 6, 17, 21; John, 5–7, 13; Romans 1, 7, 8; 1 Corinthians 3, 13; 2 Corinthians 3, 5, 11; Galatians 3; Ephesians 4; 1 Thessalonians 1; Hebrews 4; Acts 2, 5. Fol. 228r is ruled but blank.

Decoration

Spaces left for 3-line initials at the beginnings of books and 2-line initials at the beginnings of prologues and chapters; guide-letters provided, but the initials are not filled in. 2-line spaces are left for initials at the beginnings of extracts (fols. 288v–319v).

Dialect

(fols. 1r–287v)
ony(9)/any(1), ech(10), fier(10), ȝouen(9)/ȝoue(1), lijf(4)/lyf(7) lyk(4)/liche(1)/lijk(5), myche(10), siȝ(9) (sg.), sien(1)/saien(1)/siȝen(4) (pl.), silf(9)/self(1), sich(1)/siche(2), þou(2)/þouȝ(4), þorou(1)/þoru(4)

-iþ(9)/-eþ(1) (pres.ind.3sg.), -en(10) (pres.ind.pl.), -ynge(9)/-yng(1) (pres. part.), sche(10) (3sg.fem.pronoun, nom.), þei(10) (3pl.pronoun, nom.), hem(10) (3pl.pronoun, oblique), her(3) (3pl.pronoun, possessive)

Physical description

MATERIAL: parchment

DIMENSIONS: *c.*166 × 114 mm; leaves were trimmed in rebinding occasionally causing the loss of text in the margins

NUMBER OF LEAVES: 320

FOLIATION: modern in pencil, 1–320

COLLATION: (fols. 1–7) I (8–1) missing 1 | (fols. 8–312) II–XXXIX (8) | (fols. 313–319) XL (8–1) missing 8

Catchwords, decorated with penwork, survive. Quire signatures occasionally survive and run consecutively [a]–z, 3, &, c(on) on fols. 1–208, and possibly also consecutively on fols. 209–287, a(?)–k(?). Quires XXXVII–XL (fols. 289–319) are numbered 1–4.

RULING:
(fols. 1r–287v) ruled in plummet for a single column, with single vertical and double horizontal bounding lines extending the full height and width of page; prickings occasionally survive; 22 lines per page; written space: *c.*100 × 69 mm

(fols. 288r–319v) ruled in ink for a single column, with single vertical and double horizontal bounding lines extending the full height and width of page; 22 lines per page; written space: *c.*102 × 68 mm

SCRIPT: textura, black ink; the two parts, fols. 1r–287v and fols. 288v–319v, are the work of two different scribes

RUBRICATION: rubrics in red ink

SEC. FOL.: '*þat ben mouyd*' (fol. 2r)

Binding

Brown leather over pasteboard, 16th century. Blind fillet-line border with floral corner-pieces and an oval centrepiece with arabesque designs on both covers. Five raised bands on spine with daisy-like decorations between the bands. Fragmentary paper labels on spine, one with handwritten and two with typewritten text, including 'Laud. || D || 14.' and 'Laud || 182'.

Provenance

1. Differences in the apparatus provided for chapters on fols. 1r–287v (e.g., indexing letters appear only in NT; glosses only in OT) probably going back to exemplar or exemplars. The presentation of extracts (fols. 288v–319v),

including ruling, the size of script and the intention to include coloured initials, matches that of chapters.

2. James Beresford, 16th century (fol. 319). Latin verses, possibly in his hand, from the preface to Bartholomew Clerke's translation of Baldassarre Castiglione's *Libro del cortegiano* (*Balthasaris Castilionis comitis de curiali siue aulico libri quatuor: ex Italico sermone in Latinum conuersi*, London, 1571):

> '*Tullius, Osorius, Clerckus, flos, gloria, laurus…*
> … *laurea lauta suae*'.

3. Notes in 16th- or 17th-century hands in the margins, including '*Omnia totalis 30lb 3s-4d*' (fol. 7r); '*Mr Henrie St George*' (fol. 44v), '*Miles*' (fol. 199r), '*henry asley(?) is my name(?)*', '*Denys*' (fol. 319v).

4. William Laud (1573–1645); see *ODNB*: '*Liber Guilielmi Laud Archiep(iscop) i Cantuar': et Cancellarij Vniuersitatis Oxon. 1633*' (fol. 3r).

5. Bodleian Library: first donation from Laud, 22 May 1635. Earlier shelfmark 'D. 14' (binding, upper pastedown, fol. 1r).

Bibliography

Forshall and Madden (1850), vol. 1, p. xlvi.
Summary catalogue, vol. 2, part I, no. 781.
Coxe (1973), no. 182.
Ogilivie-Thomson, S. J., *IMEP*, Handlist XVI, pp. 24–5.
Scott (2000–02), vol. 2, p. 85, no. 650.
Dove (2007), p. 301.
Kuczynski, M. P., 'An unpublished Lollard Psalms Catena in Huntington Library MS 501', *Journal of the Early Book Society* 13 (2010), pp. 95–138 at pp. 106–8.

33 MS Laud misc. 207

SC no. 292

Origin: England

Date: 15th century, first quarter

Text

Fols. i–1 are parchment and paper flyleaves, originally blank (see Provenance).

(fols. 2–129r) Matthew–Mark in LV with usual prologues and rubrics, e.g., '*Here endiþ þe gospel of mathew and bigynneþ þe prolog of mark*' (fol. 82r);

'*Ierom in his prolog on mark seiþ þis | here bigynneþ þe firste capterie*' (fol. 83v). Running titles in red, only on the rectos, not including the chapter numbers. Chapter numbers as Roman numerals, usually in the form '*xxi c^o*'. Frequent corrections in the original and contemporary hands. No marginal glosses; added material within the text is not underlined. Indexing letters occasionally mark the beginnings of readings; the ends of readings are marked with double strokes in the margins and sometimes within the text. Fols. 129v–131v are blank apart from early modern and modern sketches and notes.

Decoration

4-line 'puzzle' initials in red and blue, with red and purple penwork, at the beginnings of gospels.

2-line blue initials with red penwork at the beginnings of prologues and chapters.

Added drawing on fol. 49r: a profile head of a man, 15th century (?). Added sketches on fol. 129r–v, early modern (?).

Dialect

ony(10), eche(9)/ech(1), fier(10), gouen(10), lijf(9)/lyf(1), lijk(8)/lik(2), myche(9)/miche(1), siȝ(7)/siȝe(1) (sg.), saien(2)/siȝen(4) (pl.), silf(10), sich(2)/ siche(3), þouȝ(5), þoru(1)/þorow(1)/þorouȝ(1)/þorwȝ(1)/þorowȝ(1)

-iþ(9)/-eþ(1) (pres.ind.3sg.), -en(10) (pres.ind.pl.), -ynge(10) (pres.part.), sche(10) (3sg.fem. pronoun, nom.), þei(10) (3pl.pronoun, nom.), hem(10) (3pl.pronoun, oblique), her(10) (3pl.pronoun, possessive)

Physical description

MATERIAL: parchment, paper flyleaves

DIMENSIONS: *c.*198 × 105 mm

NUMBER OF LEAVES: 136

FOLIATION: modern in pencil, i–ii + 1–57 + 58a + 58b + 59–94 + 95a + 95b + 96–117 + 118a + 118b + 119–131

COLLATION: (fols. i) fol. i is a paper flyleaf conjoint with the upper pastedown; fols. i–1 are parchment flyleaves (a bifolium (?)) | (fols. 2–17) I–II (8) | (fols. 18–20) III (3) no loss of text | (fols. 21–28) IV (8) | (fols. 29–35) V (7) fol. 32 is a singleton, no loss of text | (fols. 36–127) VI–XVII (8) | (fols. 128–130) XVIII (4–1 (?)) missing 4

Catchwords survive; quire signatures run consecutively a–s.

RULING: ruled in purple (fols. 2–48) and brown (fols. 49–130) ink for a single column, with single vertical and double horizontal bounding lines extending the full height and width of page; prickings survive; 19 lines per page; written space: *c.*121 × 82 mm

SCRIPT: textura, black ink; variations in the size of script independent of textual or codicological boundaries (e.g., fols. 14v–15r)

RUBRICATION: rubrics in red ink

SEC. FOL.: '*hood Ion*' (fol. 3r)

Binding

Brown leather over pasteboard, 16th century. Double blind fillet-line border round the edge of both covers. Gilt coat of arms of Laud on both covers. Four raised bands on spine framed by blind fillet lines. Three paper labels on spine containing: 'Euan…lia || secundu(m) Ma… || et(?) Marcum… || M. S.' (handwritten); 'Laud. || E || 6.' (typewritten) and 'Laud || 207' (typewritten). Laid paper flyleaves. Two fabric ties on each cover.

Provenance

1. Erased inscription, presumably medieval on fol. 2r.

2. Christopher Watson Deiragrantus (i.e., 'of Durham') (1545/6–1580/81), historian and translator; see *ODNB*: '*Christopher Watson Deiragirantus, 1574 Ætat suæ 29*'; added coat of arms (fol. 1v). Probably rector of Bircham Newton, Norfolk, in 1573; deacon at Norwich in 1574; and rector of Beachamwell in Norfolk. Theological notes on fols. 8r, 29r, 74r, 103v, 105r, 118b (?).

3. Joseph Maynard, fellow of Exeter College, Oxford, 1625–1653, and Rector 1662–1666 (Foster, 1891–92, p. 995) (fol. 2r).

4. William Laud (1573–1645); see *ODNB*: '*Liber Guilielmi Laud Archiep(iscop) i Cantuar*': *et Cancellarij Vniuersitatis Oxon. 1635*' (fol. 3v).

5. Bodleian Library: second donation from Laud, 16 June, 1636. Earlier shelfmark: 'E 6' (upper pastedown, binding)

Bibliography

Forshall and Madden (1850), vol. 1, p. xlvi (listed as 'Laud 507').
Coxe (1973), no. 207.
Ogilivie-Thomson, S. J., *IMEP*, Handlist XVI, p. 27.
Scott (2000–02), vol. 2, pp. 85–6, no. 653.
Dove (2007), p. 301.

34 MS Laud misc. 361

Origin: England

Date: 15th century, first quarter

Text

(fols. 1–221v) NT in LV with usual prologues and usual rubrics in red, e.g., '*Here endiþ þe gospel of matheu and here bigynneþ þe prologe on mark*'; '*þis seiþ Ierom in prologe on mark*', fol. 30r. Running titles on both rectos and versos, most consisting of abbreviated titles of biblical books and chapter numbers above each column, in black, each preceded by a red or blue paraph. Chapter numbers in red as Roman numerals, usually in the form '*c^m xi*'. Prologue to 1 Timothy is omitted and added in the margin by the original scribe (fol. 145v). Red paraphs at the start of sections within the text. Many corrections in the original or contemporary hands, with dittographic repetitions crossed out in red ink. No marginal glosses; added material within the text is usually not underlined (an exception on fol. 123v); lections are not marked. Added cross-references to OT books at the beginning of Matthew, 15th century. Fols. 222–223 are ruled but originally blank (see Provenance); fol. 224 is a blank parchment flyleaf.

Decoration

5- to 6-line 'puzzle' initials in red and blue, with red and purple penwork, at the beginnings of Matthew and John; 4-line similar initials at the beginnings of other books (3-line initials at the beginnings of Mark and most Catholic epistles).

2-line blue initials with red penwork at the beginnings of prologues and chapters.

Dialect

ony(10), ech(9)/eche(1), fier(10), ȝouun(10), liyf(10), liyk(9)/lik(1), myche(10), siȝ(6)/say(1) (sg.), saien(5)/sien(1) (pl.), silf(10), sich(2)/siche(8), þouȝ(8), þorouȝ(3)/þorou(7)

-iþ(9)/-eþ(1) (pres.ind.3sg.), -en(10) (pres.ind.pl.), -ynge(9)/-inge(1) (pres. part.), sche(10) (3sg.fem. pronoun, nom.), þei(10) (3pl.pronoun, nom.), hem(10) (3pl.pronoun, oblique), her(10) (3pl.pronoun, possessive)

Physical description

MATERIAL: parchment

DIMENSIONS: *c.*229 × 157 mm; leaves were trimmed in rebinding, occasionally causing the loss of text in the margins

NUMBER OF LEAVES: 224

FOLIATION: modern in pencil, 1–224

COLLATION: (fols. 1–216) I–XXVII (8) | (fols. 217–223) XXVIII (8–1) missing 8 | (fol. 224) parchment flyleaf conjoint with the lower pastedown

Catchwords survive; two sets of quire signatures, medieval (fragmentary) and contemporary with the present binding, both appear to run consecutively.

RULING: ruled in ink for two columns, with single vertical and horizontal bounding lines extending the full height and width of page; 37 lines per page; prickings occasionally survive; written space: *c.*178 × 104 mm

SCRIPT: textura, black ink

RUBRICATION: rubrics in red ink

SEC. FOL.: '*þou schalt*' (fol. 2r)

Binding

English roll stamped binding, *c.*1530(?). Worn brown leather over wood boards. Blind roll border round the outer edge and blind roll rectangular decoration at the centre of both covers. Includes Oldham CH. *c.*(6). Fittings of two clasps, now missing on both covers. Three fragmentary paper labels on spine, with typewritten 'Laud || I || 6.' and 'Laud'. Parchment pastedowns.

Provenance

1. Added cross-references to OT books in the margins, 15th century.

2. '*ffoxe Elzabeth C your own owne…*' (?), '*William Cutler*' (?), 16th century (fol. 222r); George Leveret ('*Georgius Leveretus*'), Richard Hall ('*Ricardus Hall*'), 16th century (fol. 223v).

3. William Laud (1573–1645); see *ODNB*: '*Liber Guilielmi Laud Archiep(iscop) i Cantuar': et Cancellarij Vniuersitatis Oxon. 1633*' (fol. 1r).

4. Bodleian Library: first donation from Laud, 22 May 1635. Earlier shelfmark: 'J 6' (upper pastedown, binding).

Bibliography

Forshall and Madden (1850), vol. 1, p. xlvi.

Summary catalogue, vol. 2, part I, no. 1346.

Oldham, J. B., *English blind-stamped bindings* (Cambridge: Cambridge University Press, 1952).
Coxe (1973), no. 361.
Ogilivie-Thomson, S. J., *IMEP*, Handlist XVI, p. 41.
Scott (2000–02), vol. 2, p. 88, no. 664.
Dove (2007), p. 301.

35 MS Laud misc. 388

Origin: England, London (?)

Date: 15th century, first quarter, *c.*1415 (?)

Text

Fols. i–iii are paper flyleaves, blank apart from modern notes.

[item 1 occupies a flyleaf]
1. (fol. iv verso) Fragmentary preacher's or theological notes (left margin cut off) of the 15th century, second half, listing topics discussed in the gospels and epistles, such as a wedding, lilies of the field, beggars, etc. with references to books and chapters of NT, presumably compiled using the present manuscript. Thus vices and virtues are listed as occurring in Galatians 5 and 6 'at d', and a passage in Galatians 5, containing the lists of vices and virtues (19–23), is indeed marked with an indexing letter 'd' (fol. 161r); see also '*pat(er) nost(er)*' in the same hand in the margins of a passage containing 'Our Father' at Luke 11 (fol. 76r). The notes are transcribed below:

...i G. 7. a notabyll patir noster...
...e. ii. pater noster 7 ... of þe lelys in þe feld neþe(?) & of birds
...[f]urst Corinthis & se ȝe ȝowre clepyng for nat
...of the furst Corinthis I wrot to ȝow in a pystyll
...& þe 7 of þe furst corinthis of wedyng
...of sekond corinthis
...of þe furst corinths & x se ȝe þat ȝe fall nat
...of þe furst corinthis & 9
...[f]urst of colosens
...12 of þe sekond corinthys
...furst & þe 3 of galathies & 5 & 6 \at d/ of xii vysys & verts
...in effesys
...in tymothie & vj

...d tymothie 4
...apostylls dydys & ix of tornyng of povl & x note(?)
...jamys ageyne hem þat holdyth ageyne preers
...of mathew þe kyngden of hevyn
...corinthys þe \xi/ xij & xiij & xiiij & xv of xvj condy[tions of(?)] charyte \& þe sakyrment & of wemens hods/
...pyt of marke of þe on clene spryt
...[c]orinþose(?) & xij & ys þe betyngs & trobels of po...
...of luke
...romans
...[t]hessalonycensis ageyns edyl men þat lefyth of other mens \labour/
...aly... þe iij[te]
...ewe ... þe comaundments & xxv þe dedys of mersy þat \men schall be examynd at þe dome/
...luk þe last ageyn beggers
... x I have a lawe in my flesche & þe lawe ine vyth
...vyssys in a mans flesche & of cornely & petyr of þe
...er sch... in vesyoun
...anos xiiij of extyng
...xiij of sowyng seds & prechyng in þe boot be parabyls
xxiij wo to ȝow scrybys & faserys & ipocryts
...d leders

[items 2–3 occupy quires I–III]
2. (fols. 1a recto–6a verso) Calendar-lectionary in English (**Plate 12**), laid out one month per page, written in red and black with some initials in blue, not graded. Includes columns showing the times of sunrise and sunset for each day. Entries for readings include an abbreviated reference to a book and chapter of the Bible, an indexing letter in red, the opening words of each reading, '*ende*' in red and the closing words of each reading. Pope Gregory (12 March), Annunciation (25 March), Lawrence (10 August), Assumption (15 August), Bartholomew (24 August), Nativity of the Virgin Mary (8 September), Michael Archangel (29 September), Catherine (25 November), Nicholas (6 December), Immaculate Conception (8 December) and Stephen (26 December) are in red. Includes some saints promulgated in 1415 under Archbishop Chichele (Pfaff (2009), pp. 438–41): David (1 March), Chad (2 March) and Frideswide ('*ffrisewith*', 19 October), but not Winifred (3 November) or John of Beverley (7 May). Includes Erkenwald, bishop of London (30 April). The feast of Thomas Becket (29 December) and its octave are erased, but not his translation in July; some titles 'pope' are erased.

3. (fols. 7a recto–19b verso) Table of lections of Type I starting with a rubric '*Here bigynneþ a rule þat telliþ in whiche chapitris of þe bible ȝee may fynde þe lessouns pistlis & gospels þat ben red in þe chirche aftir þe vss of salisbiri markid wiþ lettris of þe a. b. c.at þe bigynnynge of þe chapitris toward þe myddil or eende aftir þe ordre as þe lettris stonden in þe a. b. c. ffirst ben set sundaies & ferials togidir & aftir þat þe sanctorum þe propre & þe comyn togidir of al þe ȝeer. & þanne last þe commemoracions þat is clepid þe temporal of al þe ȝeer. first writen a clause of þe bigynninge of þe pistle or gospel & a clause of þe endynge þerof also*'. Includes the temporal, sanctoral (no common in spite of the rubric) and commemorations. Commemorations are in the following order: Our Lady, Trinity, Holy Ghost, cross, '*For breþren and sustren and for sauacioun of þe peple*', peace, clear weather, rain, '*In tyme of batels*', '*A man for him silf*', '*For pestilence of bestis*', '*for pilgrymes*', weddings, sinners, sick and dead. Includes all feasts characteristic of LV (Forshall and Madden (1850), vol. 4, pp. 683, 690–6), apart from Giles (1 September). The readings consist of a date in red, abbreviated reference to a book and chapter of the Bible, an indexing letter in red (some corrected), the opening words of a reading, '*ende*' in red and the closing words of a reading. '*23 may*' is added in the margin against Trinity Sunday in a 15th-century hand.

[item 4 occupies quires IV–XXXV; St John's gospel starts on a new quire]
4. (fols. 1b recto–256v) NT in LV with usual prologues. The rubric at the beginning of Matthew mentions two prologues to Matthew ('*Ierom in his twey prologis on matheu seiþ playnly þus*', fol. 1b verso), but only one is included. Running titles on both rectos and versos consisting of a short title of a biblical book in black preceded by a blue paraph (longer titles are split between facing pages). Usual rubrics, e.g., '*Heere endiþ mathew and heere bigynneþ þe prolog up on mark*'; '*Ierom in his prologe on mark seiþ al þis sentence. Here bigynneþ þe firste chapitle upon Mark*' (fol. 35r–v). Chapter numbers as red Roman numerals, typically in the form '*Ca(pitulu)m iiii*'. No marginal glosses (an exception on fol. 23v); added material within the text is not underlined. The beginnings of lections are usually marked with indexing letters in the margins (and often with blue paraphs within the text); the ends of lections are marked with double strokes in the margins. Occasionally corrections in the original or contemporary hands. A Greek gloss added in an early modern hand on fol. 65r.

[item 5 occupies quires XXXVI–XL]
5. (fols. 257r–297v) OT lectionary of Type I, starting with a rubric '*Here bigynneþ þe lessons & pistlis of þe olde lawe þat ben red in þe chirche in al þe ȝeer aftir þe vss of salisbiri*'. The temporal is followed by an extensive sanctoral (rubric: '*þe propre and comyn togidere*', fol. 287) and

commemorations (fol. 296r). On fol. 297v about a half of the first column is left blank after the end of commemorations; the next column starts with a rubric introducing the readings for the common of saints, but these are mostly missing because of the loss of leaves (see Collation). Each reading is preceded by a rubric, stating the liturgical occasion, the title of the biblical book and the chapter number. Short titles and chapter numbers of biblical books, as well as the indexing letters, are also placed in the margins before the start of each reading and double strokes at the end of each reading up to fol. 271r; after this only the indexing letters and double strokes are present.

The readings begin with the statements that introduce them at Mass (e.g., '*The lord god seiþ þese þingis*', fol. 258r) underlined in red. The readings used for more than one occasion are not repeated and instead the rubrics contain references to leaves on which they occur, using foliation in Roman numerals in the original hand (medieval foliation is present only in the part of the manuscript containing OT lectionary). The method of reference is explained in a rubric on fol. 282r: '*þis lessoun ȝe schulen fynde writen al out to fore in þe .xxv. leef of þese leefes þat ben markid. In whiche leefes ben conteyned alle þe lessons & pistlis of þe oolde lawe. and þei ben markid wiþ lettris of noumbrari as is i. ij. & iij. on þe riȝtside of þe leef. in þe hiȝer part of þe margyn*'. The reading for the first Mass on Christmas morning is preceded by a lengthy rubric explaining that it is performed by two voices; the part of one of the voices is underlined in red in the text that follows (fol. 260r). Added material within the text is underlined in red; no marginal glosses. Fols. 298–301 are parchment and paper flyleaves (see Provenance).

Decoration

Blue KL monograms with red penwork in the calendar-lectionary.

4-line 'puzzle' initials in red and blue with red and blue penwork, and penwork borders (right or middle margin) at the beginning of books and OT lectionary. The initial at the start of St John's gospel is six lines high.

2-line blue initials with red penwork at the beginning of prologues, chapters and OT readings.

Catchwords on decorative scrolls.

Dialect

ony(10), ech(10), fier(10), ȝouen(10), lijf(10), lijk(10), myche(10), siȝ(4)/seiȝ(1)/say(4)/saiȝ(1) (sg.), saien(5)/sien(1) (pl.), silf(7)/self(3), such(3)/suche(4)/sich(1)/siche(1), þouȝ(8), þoruȝ(7)/þorouȝ(1)/þoruw(1)/þoru(1)

-iþ(7)/-eþ(3) (pres.ind.3sg.), -en(10) (pres.ind.pl.), -ynge(10) (pres.part.), sche(10) (3sg.fem.pronoun, nom.), þei(10) (3pl.pronoun, nom.), hem(10) (3pl.pronoun, oblique), her(10) (3pl.pronoun, possessive)

Physical description

MATERIAL: parchment, paper flyleaves

DIMENSIONS: *c.*220 × 150 mm

NUMBER OF LEAVES: 324

FOLIATION: modern in pencil and ink, i–iv + 1a–19a + 1b–19b + 20–301; medieval in black ink on fols. 258–297, usually consisting of a Roman numeral followed by '*folium*' (e.g., '*ii folium.*') underlined in red and preceded by a red paraph; modern in ink, a–f, on fols. 1a–6a; early modern (?) in ink, i–xiii, on fols. 7a–19a

COLLATION: (fols. i–iv) paper and parchment flyleaves; fol. i conjoint with the upper pastedown | (fols. 1a–7a) I (8–1) missing 1 | (fols. 8a–15a) II (8) | (16a–19a) III (4) | (fols. 1b–216) IV–XXX (8) | (fols. 217–223) XXXI (8–1) missing 6 (?); no loss of text | (fols. 224–247) XXXII–XXXIV (8) | (fols. 248–256) XXXV (8+1) 9 inserted (?) | (fols. 257–296) XXXVI–IL (8) | (fol. 297) first leaf of a missing quire (?), see Text | (fols. 298–301) paper and parchment flyleaves; fol. 301 conjoint with the lower pastedown

Catchwords are accompanied by quire numbers in Arabic numerals in the original hand (2–31) in quires V–XXXV. Quire signatures a–b (fols. 8a–19a); a–z + four non-alphabetic symbols (fols. 1b–223); 1–4 (fols. 224–256); a–f (fols. 257–297).

RULING: ruled in ink for two columns, with single vertical and double horizontal bounding lines extending the full height and width of page; 29–30 lines per page; written space: *c.*150–155 × 102–105 mm; prickings survive

SCRIPT: textura, black ink

RUBRICATION: rubrics in red ink

SEC. FOL.: '*ioseph*' (calendar-lectionary, fol. 2b recto), '*math.xxv*[o]' (table of lections, fol. 8a recto)

Binding

Brown morocco over pasteboard, 19th century. Gold lettering on spine 'NEW || TESTAMENT'; paper label on spine with handwritten 'Laud || 338'. Marbled paper pastedowns and flyleaves.

Provenance

1. Made for a patron in London (?). Calendar, fairly sparse, based on a Sarum model, includes Erkenwald, bishop of London, a non-Sarum saint, and the principal saint of St Paul's (though not his translation, 14 December). Conversion of St Paul (25 January), Peter and Paul (29 June) and its octave are in red (the octave is missing in the calendar of MS Fairfax 11 and is in black in the calendar of MS Fairfax 2); Commemoration of St Paul (30 June) is included. Contains some, but not all saints promulgated in 1415; the presence of only one distinctly London saint may suggest a date after the suppression of the use of St Paul in 1414 (Pfaff (2009), pp. 480–96). Added material within the text is underlined only in OT lectionary.

2. Preacher's or theological notes in English, 15th century, second half, added on fol. iv verso, some Lollard, e.g., those drawing attention to passages against beggars, against '*idle men that live off other men's labour*' and to a passage against the scribes and Pharisees, Matthew 23:13, widely used in Lollard discourse (e.g., Hudson and Gradon (1983–96), vol. 2, pp. 366–78). Liturgical notes in Latin, possibly in the same hand, on fols. 124v, 183v and 210v. Possibly in London when the notes were made: those on fol. iv verso draw attention to a passage describing the conversion of St Paul; liturgical notes on fol. 210v mention the feasts of Paul. The notes on fol. iv verso have some southern forms (plurals '*holdyth*' and '*lefyth*'). The notes may be in the hand of one of the 15th-century owners, Henry Tyryll or Christopher Constable: '*per me henricum tyryll*' and '*per me christoferum constable*' (fol. 298r).

3. The feasts of Thomas Becket and some titles 'pope' are erased, presumably at Reformation.

4. '*Iste liber pertinet A P*(?)'; '*Iste liber pertinet || Iris…*' (partially erased); '*Robart*', 16th century (?) (fol. 298r).

5. William Charke (d. 1617), religious controversialist; see *ODNB*: '*Sum Gul. Charci*' (fols. 1a recto, 1b recto). Matriculated at Peterhouse, Cambridge, in 1560; graduated BA in 1562–1563 and MA in 1566. Also owned Oxford, Bodleian Library MS Laud misc. 104, containing *The Pater Noster of Richard Ermyte*, as well as seven other manuscripts (see Hudson and Gradon (1983–96), vol. 1, p. 63 n. 16), several of them Wycliffite, including two copies of *English Wycliffite Sermons*. Spent much of his career in London.

6. William Laud (1573–1645); see *ODNB*: '*Liber Guilielmi Laud Archiep(iscop)i Cantuar': et Cancellarij Vniuersitatis Oxon. 1634*' (fol. 7a recto).

7. Bodleian Library: first donation from Laud, 22 May 1635. Earlier shelfmark: 'J 7' (fol. iv recto).

Bibliography

Summary catalogue, vol. 2, part I, no. 1346.
Watson, A. G., *The Manuscripts of Henry Savile of Banke* (London: Bibliographical Society, 1969), pp. 52, 89.
Coxe (1973), no. 388.
Ogilivie-Thomson, S. J., *IMEP*, Handlist XVI, pp. 42–3.
Scott (2000–02), vol. 2, p. 88, no. 666.
Dove (2007), p. 301.

36 MS Lyell 26

Origin: England

Date: 15th century, first quarter

Text

Fols. i recto–5v are originally blank paper and parchment leaves, containing early modern and modern additions (see Provenance).

[item 1 occupies quires I–II]
1. (fols. 6r–14v) Table of lections of Type I starting with a rubric '*Here bigynneþ a rule þat telliþ in whiche chapitris of þe bible ȝe mai fynde þe lessouns pistlis & gospels þat ben rad in þe chirche al þe ȝeer aftir þe vss of salisbiri markid wiþ lettris of þe abc at þe bigynnynge of þe chapitris twoward þe myddil or eende aftir þe ordre as þe lettris stonden in þe abc ffirst ben sett sondaies & ferials togidere and aftir þat þe sanctorum boþe comyne and propre togidere of al þe ȝeer / first is writen a clause of þe bigynnyng þerof & a clause of þe endinge þerof also ffor it bigynneþ at þe lettris of þe abc & endiþ at twei strikis in þe margyn*'. Contains the temporal followed by commemorations and the sanctoral (proper only in spite of the rubric referring to '*boþe of þe propre and þe comyne*'). Parts of the temporal (from Thursday after the first Sunday in Lent to Ascension day) and sanctoral (from John and Paul, martyrs (June), to the eve of St Lawrence (July)) are missing because of the loss of leaves (see Collation). Includes all feasts characteristic of LV apart from Giles (1 September) (Forshall and Madden (1850), vol. 4, pp. 683, 690–6). Commemorations are in the following order: the Virgin Mary, Trinity, Holy Ghost, cross, angels, brothers and sisters and '*helþe of þe peple*', peace, clear weather, rain, '*in tyme of batel*', '*a man for him silf*', '*ffor pestelence of beestis*', pilgrims, weddings, sinners, sick and dead (without a rubric). Blue initials at Andrew, Conception of Our Lady, Conversion of St

Paul, Candlemas, Matthew, Annunciation, George the martyr, Mark, the Invention of the Cross, St John before the Latin Gate, Nativity of John the Baptist, Lawrence, Assumption, Bartholomew, Nativity of Our Lady, Michael Archangel, Luke, Jude and Halloween.

[item 2 occupies quires III–XLI]
2. (fols. 15r–336r) NT in LV with usual prologues. Romans has two prologues: '*Romayns be þei þat of ieweis…*' in addition to the usual '*Romayns ben in þe cuntrei…*' (Dove (2007), p. 206). Includes Laodiceans with the prologue '*Laodicensis ben also colocensis…*' (fol. 227r). Running titles in black on both rectos and versos consisting of abbreviated titles of biblical books. Chapter numbers in red as Roman numerals, or sometimes Arabic numerals or words. Usual rubrics, e.g., '*Here endiþ þe gospel of Matheu & bigynneþ þe prolog on Mark*', '*Jerom in his prolog on Mark seiþ þus*' (fol. 60r–v). Sections within the text are marked with blue or red paraphs, the beginnings of periods are highlighted in red. The end of the Prologue to the Apocalypse is missing after '*makiþ heereris benyg…*' and so is most of the first chapter (verses 1–17) because of the loss of leaves (see Collation). No marginal glosses; added material within the text is occasionally underlined (e.g., fols. 91r, 195r, 249r). The beginnings of readings are marked with indexing letters and the ends with double strokes in the margins. Very occasionally corrections in the original or contemporary hands. Fols. 337r–349v are paper and parchment leaves, originally blank, containing early modern and modern additions (see Provenance).

Decoration

4-line gold initials (8-line initials 'I') on blue and pink background at the beginnings of books; the first (fol. 15v) with a spray of penwork and gold leaves and disks.

2-line blue initials with red penwork at the beginnings of prologues and chapters.

Dialect

ony(10), ech(10), fier(10), ȝeuen(7)/ȝouen(3), lijf(10), lijk(10), myche(10), siȝ(8) (sg.), siȝen(6) (pl.), silf(10), sich(2)/siche(8), þouȝ(8), þoru(1)/þoruȝ(7)

-iþ(5)/-eþ(5) (pres.ind.3sg.), -en(10) (pres.ind.pl.), -ynge(4)/inge(4)/yng(2) (pres.part.), sche(10) (3sg.fem. pronoun, nom.), þei(10) (3pl.pronoun, nom.), hem(10) (3pl.pronoun, oblique), her(10) (3pl.pronoun, possessive)

Physical description

MATERIAL: parchment, paper flyleaves

DIMENSIONS: *c.*118 × 85 mm; leaves were trimmed in rebinding, occasionally causing the loss of text in the margins

NUMBER OF LEAVES: 354

FOLIATION: modern in pencil, i–vi + 1–348

COLLATION: (fols. i–vi) paper flyleaves | (fols. 1–14) I–II original structure unclear, missing two (?) leaves after fol. 7 and one (?) leaf after fol. 12 | (fols. 15–166) III–XXI (8) | (fols. 167–202) XXII–XXIV (12) | (fols. 203–314) XXV–XXXVIII (8) | (fols. 315–321) XXXIX (8–1) 3 missing | (fols. 322–328) XL (8–1) 6 cancelled, no loss of text | (fols. 229–336) XLI (8) | (fols. 337–343) XLII (8–1) 2 cancelled | (fols. 344–348) paper flyleaves

Catchwords survive, most quire signatures survive and run consecutively a–z, followed by four non-alphabetic characters (fols. 251–282), followed by a–g.

RULING: ruled in plummet for two columns, with single vertical and double horizontal bounding lines extending the full height and width of page; 30 lines per page; written space: *c.*85–90 × 55–59 mm

SCRIPT: textura, black and brown ink

RUBRICATION: rubrics in red ink

SEC. FOL.: '*newe ȝers*' (table of lections, fol. 7r); '*Salomon bigat*' (NT, fol. 16r)

Binding

Black morocco over pasteboard, first half of the 17th century. Gilt fillet-line border round the outer edge of both covers. Gilt rectangular figure with stamped gilt decoration and gilt initials 'I M' on both covers. Five raised bands on spine. Gilt lettering on spine 'NEW TESTAMENT || MS ON VELLUM'. Paper label on spine with handwritten 'MS LYELL || 26'. Gilt edges of textblock. Laid paper pastedowns and flyleaves.

Provenance

1. '*Faythe and throth ys nat one thynge*', 15th or 16th century (fol. 340v).

2. '*Borton ys a knave. John at…*', 15th or 16th century, partly erased (fol. 341v).

3. '*This is william [wood(?)] his boke it is a good boke*', 16th century (fol. 337v). [*wood(?)*] is overwritten with '*lancaster*'; '*lancaster*' is also written above in a slightly later 16th-century hand, probably responsible for Latin prayers, and Latin and English epitaphs and proverbs (see below). '*willem wood[e?] of Ste[d…(?)] he(?) is a no…*' (fol. 139v).

4. '*Thomas Howard His Book*' in capitals (fol. 342v) and in the same (?) hand 'Anne' (fol. 3v). Thomas Howard, third duke of Norfolk (1473–1554) (?), married to Anne; see *ODNB*.

5. Latin prayers (fols. 1r–3v) and Latin and English epitaphs and proverbs (fols. 337v–338v, 340v–342r) in a 16th-century hand (see De la Mare (1971)).

6. Theological notes in English in a 17th-century hand on fols. vi recto and 344r–348r.

7. '*Richardus Smitheus*' (fol. 6r) and '*Richardus Smytheus wontoniensis*' (fol. 336v), 17th century. Possibly Richard Smith (bap. 1590, d. 1675), law officer and book collector; see *ODNB*, who owned another Wycliffite New Testament (see Forshall and Madden (1850), vol. 1, p. xli).

8. James P. R. Lyell (1871–1948), book collector; see *ODNB*: bought in October 1943 from Quaritch; no. 17 in their catalogue of manuscripts (1931); see also pastedowns and fol. i recto. Lyell's bookplate on the upper pastedown.

Bibliography

A catalogue of illuminated and other manuscripts: together with some books on palaeography (London: Quaritch, 1931).

De la Mare, A. C., *Catalogue of the collection of medieval manuscripts bequeathed to the Bodleian Library, Oxford by James P. R. Lyell* (Oxford: Clarendon Press, 1971), pp. 56–8.

Hudson (1989), p. 140 n. 29.

Hanna, R., *IMEP*, Handlist XII (1997), p. 18.

Dove (2007), pp. 59 n. 116, 234, 301.

37 MS Lyell 27

Origin: England

Date: 15th century, first quarter

Text

Fols. i–iii are paper flyleaves, blank apart from modern notes.

(fols. 1r–150r) Pauline epistles, Romans to Hebrews, with usual prologues in LV. Running titles in black on most leaves, most consisting of the titles of biblical books, in Latin or English, usually abbreviated, sometimes split between rectos and versos. Some running titles contain chapter numbers, added perhaps as an afterthought. Spaces left for rubrics and chapter numbers, but most are not filled in, though chapter numbers in Arabic numerals, as instructions to rubricator, appear in the margins. Rubrics and some chapter numbers are in red in the hand of the main scribe on fols. 104r–128v (1 Thessalonians–Philemon). These rubrics have usual wording, e.g., '*Here endiþ þe firste pistle to tessalonycensis and here bigynneþ þe prologe on þe secunde pistle to tessalonicensis*'; '*Ierom in his prologe on þis pistle seiþ þis*' (fol. 109r). Blue paraphs are occasionally used at the beginning of sections within the text. No marginal glosses with rare exceptions (e.g., fol. 63r); added material within the text is not underlined; lections are not marked. Corrections in the original or contemporary hands. Fol. 150v contains an added 15th-century note (see Provenance), fols. 151–154 are paper flyleaves, blank apart from modern notes.

Decoration

2- to 5-line 'puzzle' initials in red and blue, and red and blue penwork borders (right margin) at the beginnings of epistles.

2- to 3-line blue initials with red penwork at the beginnings of prologues and chapters.

Dialect

eny(10), ech(10), fier(2), ȝouen(5)/ȝouun(5), lyf(10), lyke(1)/like(2), mych(8)/myche(1)/mich(1), say(2) (sg.), siȝen(1) (pl.), silf(10), such(4)/suche(6), þouȝ(10), þoruȝ(4)

-iþ(5)/-eþ(5) (pres.ind.3sg.), -en(10) (pres.ind.pl.), -ing(2)/-yng(8) (pres.part.), sche(10) (3sg.fem.pronoun, nom.), þei(10) (3pl.pronoun, nom.), hem(10) (3pl.pronoun, oblique), her(9)/here(1) (3pl.pronoun, possessive)

Physical description

MATERIAL: parchment, paper flyleaves

DIMENSIONS: *c.*146 × 114 mm; leaves were trimmed in rebinding, occasionally causing the loss of text and decoration in the margins

NUMBER OF LEAVES: 158

FOLIATION: modern in pencil, i–iii + 1–154; modern in pink ink in the upper left corner in the hand that also added borders in pink ink to pages 1–150

COLLATION: (fols. i–iii) paper flyleaves | (fols. 1–144) I–XVIII (8) | (fols. 145–150) XIX (8–2) 7 and 8 cancelled

Catchwords survive, some accompanied by numbers in Arabic numerals; quire signatures occasionally survive.

RULING: Ruled in plummet for two columns, with single vertical and double horizontal bounding lines extending the full height and width of page; prickings occasionally survive; 22 lines per page; written space: *c.*117 × 75 mm. Border in pink ink added to each page by a modern owner who also numbered leaves in the upper left corner on the rectos.

SCRIPT: two scribes: (1) fols. 1r–100r, (2) fols. 100v–150r; large uneven textura, black ink

RUBRICATION: rubrics in red ink

SEC. FOL.: '*I nyle*' (fol. 2r)

Binding

Crimson sheepskin treated as morocco, early 18th century. Gilt fillet-line border round the outer edge of both covers. Gilt rectangular figure with floral decoration and corner-pieces on both covers. Rebacked; label on spine 'M.S.S. || PAUL || EPIST.'. Paper label on spine with handwritten 'M.S. || Lyell || 27'. Gilt edges of textblock. Gilt decoration on turn-ins. Marbled paper pastedowns and flyleaves.

Provenance

1. Added piece on the duties of a woman by Awstyn Fyschmonger, dated 1457, fol. 150v: '*The xxj io*r*(?) Septemb*'. *It syttyt ffwll wele. a womman to be styll. meke serwyseabyl dredfwl chaste deuoute warre sobre softe benynge glade / but nat nyce. newere idyl. but eyþer worchyng prayyng. redyng. spynnynge. sewyng or wepyng. \or/ mornyng for synne for departyng fro her spowse. þat ys cryste. quod Awstyn ffyschmonger A domini M*l *CCCC lvij*'. 'worche' is also a usual spelling in the manuscript (e.g., fol. 13r).

Added '*nota*' and short notes in the margins, probably in the same hand as the piece on the duties of a woman, drawing attention to passages on lechery (e.g., '*it is good to a man to touche not a woman*', fol. 38r, 1 Corinthians 7; and fols. 37r, 1 Corinthians 6; 88v, Ephesians 5; 101v, Colossians 3), drunkenness (fol. 36v, 1 Corinthians 5), temptation (fol. 44r, 1 Corinthians 10), flesh and spirit (fol. 81r–v, Galatians 5); women and marriage (fols. 3r, Romans 1; 40v, 1 Corinthians 7; 90r, Ephesians 5; 114r, 1 Timothy 2), including '*nota wymmen*' at '*for he is þe ymage & þe glorie of god but a woman is þe glorie of man for a man is not of þe woman but þe woman of þe man & þe man is not maad for þe woman but þe woman for þe man*' (fol. 46r, 1 Corinthians 11) and '*men loue ȝe ȝoure wyues as christ loued þe chirch*' (fol. 89v, Ephesians 5). Notes also mark passages of possibly Lollard interest on persecutions (fols. 35r, 1 Corinthians 4; 71r, 1 Corinthians 11), Eucharist (fol. 44v, 1 Corinthians 10) and ministry ('*þe more schulde serue þe lasse*', fol. 16v, Romans 9; '*I schal distrie þe wisdom of wise men*', fol. 31r, 1 Corinthians 1; '*but in alle þinges ȝeue we vs silf as þe mynystris of god in mych pacience*', fol. 63v, 2 Corinthians 6), and Christ as the head of the church (marked '*nota þe chyrch*', fol. 84r, Ephesians 1). The owner may have been interested in the debate about the translation of the Bible, e.g., 1 Corinthians 14, dealing with teaching faith in different languages, has two notes: '*voycys*' at verse 7 and '*nota*' at verse 16 (fols. 50v–51r); and there is '*nota*' at 2 Corinthians 3:6 ('*...god which also maad vs able mynistris of þe new testament not bi lettre but be spirit*', fol. 60r).

2. Bookplate with the crest of Thomas Falconer of Chester (1736/7–1792); classical scholar, see *ODNB*, on the upper pastedown.

3. Armorial bookplate of Charles W. G. Howard with the motto '*Volo non valeo*' on the flyleaf conjoint with the upper pastedown: '*The Gift of the Rt. Hon. Sir David Dundas Knt of Ochtertyre M.D.CCC.LXXVII.*'.

4. Lot 754 in Sotheby's catalogue 13 April 1927; bought by Maggs.

5. James P. R. Lyell (1871–1948), book collector; see *ODNB*: bought in August 1940 from Maggs, see their Catalogue 542 (1930) no. 100A, and 687 (1940) no. 166. Lyell's bookplate on the flyleaf conjoint with the upper pastedown.

Bibliography

Lindberg, C., 'The manuscripts and versions of the Wycliffite Bible: a preliminary survey', *Studia Neophilologica* 42 (1970), pp. 337–47.

De la Mare, A. C., *Catalogue of the collection of medieval manuscripts bequeathed to the Bodleian Library, Oxford by James P. R. Lyell* (Oxford: Clarendon Press, 1971), p. 58.

Hanna, R., *IMEP*, Handlist XII (1997), p. 18.

Meale, C. M. and Boffey, J., 'Gentlewomen's reading', in Hellinga, L. and Trapp, J. B. (eds), *The Cambridge history of the book in Britain*, vol. 3, *1400–1557* (Cambridge: Cambridge University Press, 1999), p. 526 and n. 1.

Dove (2007), p. 301.

38 MS e Mus. 110

Origin: England

Date: 15th century, first quarter

Text

Fols. i–v are paper and parchment flyleaves, mostly blank (see Provenance).

[item 1 occupies quire I]
1. (fols. 1r–5v) *Capitula*-list of NT (**Plate 13**) arranged by book and chapter with rubrics (e.g., '*Matters in þe gospel of…*'; '*Matters in þe pistle to…*') in a different hand than the rest of the manuscript. The books are in the usual order, but Philemon is missing. The table is the same as in MS Selden Supra 51 (Forshall and Madden (1850), vol. 1, p. xlvii). Laid out in two columns, with chapter numbers in the margins as red Roman numerals. The second column and most of the first column on the last page are left blank.

[item 2 occupies quires II–XVII]
2. (fols. 6r–127v) NT in LV with usual prologues and usual rubrics in black preceded by red paraphs (e.g., '*Here begynneþ a prologe on matheu*'; '*Ierom in hise twey prologis on matheu seiþ pleynly þus*'). John ends three-quarters down the first column on fol. 60v, the rest of the column is left blank and the prologue to Romans starts at the beginning of the second column on the same page. Running titles on both rectos and verses, in black ink preceded by red paraphs. Chapters have two numbers up to fol. 76r: one in black ink in the hand of the main scribe, consisting of an abbreviated '*c(apitulu)m*' usually followed by an Arabic numeral, another in red ink with '*c(apitulu) m*' usually followed by a Roman numeral; both are preceded by a single large red paraph. Chapters after fol. 76r have a single number, usually in black ink.

Red paraphs are sometimes used to mark units within the text, such as the beginnings of parables on fol. 12r. Corrections in the margins in a contemporary hand and over erasures within the text. No marginal glosses; added material within the text is occasionally underlined in red; lections are not marked. '*Nota*' written in the margins in a medieval (?) hand mark the following passages: Luke 11 ('*a woman of þe company reride hir voice & seide to him blessid be þe wombe…*', fol. 39r); Ephesians 4 ('*to ech of us grace is ȝouun by þe mesure of þe ȝiuyng of christ…*', fol. 80r); Acts 13 ('*y haue foundun dauiþ þe sone of iesse a man after myn herte…*', fol. 102v); Apocalypse 2 ('*þat haþ iȝen as flawme of fier & hise feet lijk latoun…*', fol. 120r); Apocalypse 20 ('*& whane a þousinde ȝeeris schulen be endid sathanas schal be vnboundun of his* *prisoun…*', fol. 126v). At the end '*Here endiþ apocalips of John*' in the original hand, followed by an addition in a contemporary hand: '*what is softer þan christes ȝok & liȝter þen christes charge. þat is a mon to be proued in al þinges. abstene fro trespas. to wilne good. not wilne yuel. to loue al men. haten noon. to geten euerlastyng þynges. to be not taken or disseyued bi temperal þinges. to wilne not to do an oþer man þat þat is heuy or greuous to hym selff to suffre*'.

Decoration

3- to 7-line blue initials with red penwork at the beginnings of books; 2- to 3-line similar initials at the beginnings of prologues and chapters.

Exaggerated ascenders and descenders in the top and bottom lines decorated with human faces, profiles and arabesque designs.

Dialect

ony(1), ech(5)/eche(5), fier(7)/fiyr(3), ȝouun(10), liyf(10), liyk(10), myche(10), siȝ(2)/siȝe(2)/say(1)/saye(3)/saiȝ(1) (sg.), saien(2)/sayen(2)/sien(2)/siȝen(1) (pl.), silf(5)/self(5), siche(9)/suche(1), þouȝ(8), þorou(10)

-iþ(8)/-eþ(2) (pres.ind.3sg), -en(10) (pres.ind.pl.), -ynge(3)/-yng(4)/-ing(3) (pres.part.) sche(10) (3sg.fem. pronoun, nom.), þei(1) (3pl.pronoun, nom.), hem(10) (3pl.pronoun, oblique), her(10) (3pl.pronoun, possessive)

Physical description

MATERIAL: parchment, paper flyleaves

DIMENSIONS: *c.*255 × 174 mm

NUMBER OF LEAVES: 139

FOLIATION: modern in pencil, i–v + 1–34

COLLATION: (fols. i–iv) flyleaves | (fols. v–5) I (6) fol. v has the same ruling as fols. 1–5 | (fols. 6–125) II–XVI (8) | (fol. 126–133) XVII (original structure unclear) | (fol. 134) paper flyleaf

Catchwords survive; quire signatures run consecutively [a]-p in quires II–XVI. On fol. 133r: '*.p. vlti(m)a l(ite)ra*' in the hand of the original scribe (?), referring to the quire signature in the last quire.

RULING: ruled in plummet for two columns, with single vertical and horizontal bounding lines extending the full height and width of page; 48 lines per page; written space: *c.*192 × 120 mm

SCRIPT: textura; black and brown ink; possibly the work of several scribes with well-matched hands

RUBRICATION: rubrics in red, red paraphs within the text

SEC. FOL.: '*of þe best weye*' (fol. 2r)

Binding

Brown leather over thick pasteboard, 18th century. Double blind fillet-line border round the outer edge of both covers; blind roll arabesque decoration next to the spine. Seven raised bands on spine, framed by double blind fillet lines. Gold lettering on spine 'E MVS. || 110.'; '110' painted white at the top of the spine. Laid paper pastedowns and flyleaves. Fols. ii and 139 served as pastedowns of a medieval binding, probably with seven sewing stations matching the ones on the present binding.

Provenance

1. Robert Parsons: '*Constat Roberto Personi*', 15th century (fol. 1r).

2. Sir Thomas Herbert (1606–1682); see *ODNB*: name on fols. v recto, 1r; motto in Welsh '*Paub yn y eruer*' on fol. v recto.

3. Bodleian Library: presented by Herbert in 1666. Former shelfmark: 'e Musaeo (62)' (fols. ii verso, v recto).

Bibliography

Forshall and Madden (1850), vol. 1, pp. xxxii, xlviii.
Summary catalogue, vol. 2, part II, no. 3552.
Scott (2000–02), vol. 3, p. 35, no. 767.
Dove (2007), p. 300.

39 MS Rawl. C. 237, MS Rawl. C. 238

Siglum: l – prologue to Romans

Origin: England

Date: 15th century, first quarter, before 1415 (?)

Text

MS Rawl. C. 237
Fols. i–ii are blank paper flyleaves.

[item 1 occupies quire I]
1. (fols. 1r–6r) Added calendar in English, in a 15th-century hand somewhat

later than the hand of the biblical text, laid out one month per page, written in red and black. Presumably unfinished: there are very few feasts in black in August, September and December. January is headed by a Latin verse on the 'Egyptian' days which corresponds to Hennig's (1955) set III. February is headed by a note in English on the number of days in the month. Contains many late 15th-century additions in English which supply the missing Sarum feasts and provide references for lections, consisting of abbreviated titles of OT and NT books, chapter numbers and indexing letters. David and Chad (1 and 2 March) are in the original hand, but John of Beverley (6 May) and Winifred (3 November) are added, suggesting a date before or around 1415 (see Pfaff (2009), pp. 438–41). Also added are Visitation (2 July, promulgated in 1481), Transfiguration (6 August, promulgated in 1457), Francis (4 October) and deposition of Osmund (4 December, canonised in 1456). The feast and translation of Thomas Becket (July) are crossed out.

[item 2 occupies quires II–XX]
2. (fols. 7r–151v) Four gospels in LV, with usual prologues. Usual rubrics, e.g., '*Here endiþ þe gospel of mathew and bigynneþ þe prolog of mark*', '*Here endiþ þe prolog of Mark and bigynneþ þe gospel of Mark as Ierom seiþ pleynli þat þis is þe firste chapiter þis in þis wyse*' (fol. 50r–v). Prologue to Matthew occupies a separate leaf (fol. 7r–v), the second column on its verso is left blank. Running titles are usually in black (sometimes in red) on the rectos, or occasionally on both rectos and versos, consisting of abbreviated titles of biblical books. Chapter numbers in red, usually as Roman numerals in the form '*vi c(apitulum)*', some preceded by paraphs. Many chapter numbers are not filled in by the rubricator and added in black ink as Roman numerals. Corrections in the original or contemporary hands; omitted passages frequently supplied in the margins. No marginal glosses; added material within the text is not underlined. Indexing letters surrounded by double strokes in the margins mark the beginnings of lections; the ends of lections are only occasionally marked with double strokes. Further indexing letters and occasionally notes stating a liturgical occasion for a reading are added in the margins, and the beginnings and ends of readings are marked with special signs within the biblical text, probably by a late 15th-century hand that made additions to the calendar. On fol. 100r the passage '*But wo to ȝou farisees þat tiþen mynte and ruwe & eche erbe & leuen doom & þe charite of god*' (Luke, 11:42–3) is marked with a bracket by the same (?) late 15th-century owner. Fols. 152–153 are blank paper flyleaves.

MS Rawl. C. 238
Fols. i–iii are paper and parchment flyleaves, blank apart from modern notes (see Provenance).

3. (fols. 1–182v) Romans–Apocalypse in LV, with usual prologues, apart from the Romans that has two prologues: '*Romayns ben þei þat ben of Iewis...*' and '*Romayns ben in þe cuntre...*' (Dove (2007), p. 206). Added material within the text is not marked with very few exceptions (e.g., fol. 36r). Fol. 183 is a parchment flyleaf, containing a table of lections in English for the temporale, which includes references to gospels accompanied by chapter numbers and indexing letters. The table, added by a late 15th-century owner who updated the calendar, starts with Ash Wednesday and ends with Saturday before the Palm Sunday. Fol. 184 is a blank paper flyleaf.

Decoration

Plain KL monograms in red and blue ink in the calendar.

3- to 4-line gold initials on blue and burgundy background at the beginnings of books; border made of a gold bar in the right margin with penwork sprays and gold leaves in the lower margin at the beginning of Matthew.

2- to 4-line blue initials with red penwork at the beginnings of prologues and chapters. 3-line gold initial at the beginning of the prologue to John and a penwork initial at the beginning of the gospel (fol. 121r–v).

Dialect

eny(8)/ony(2), ech(5)/eche(5), fier(9)/fiȝer(1), ȝouen(6)/ȝouen(3)/ȝeuen(1), lijf(10), lijk(10), myche(10), siȝe(4)/siȝ(4) (sg.), saien(5)/siȝen(1) (pl.), silf(10), sich(1)/such(1)/suche(8), þouȝ(8), þoruȝ(9)/þorow(1)

-iþ(7)/-eþ(3) (pres.ind.3sg.), -en(10) (pres.ind.pl.), -inge(6)/-ynge(4) (pres. part.), sche(10) (3sg.fem.pronoun, nom.), þei(10) (3pl.pronoun, nom.), hem(10) (3pl.pronoun, oblique), her(10) (3pl.pronoun, possessive)

Physical description

MATERIAL: parchment, paper flyleaves

DIMENSIONS: *c.*128 × 86 mm; leaves were trimmed in rebinding, occasionally causing the loss of text and decoration in the margins

NUMBER OF LEAVES: MS Rawl. C. 237: 155; MS Rawl. C. 238: 187

FOLIATION: modern in pencil, MS Rawl. C. 237: i–ii + 1–153; MS Rawl. C. 238: i–iii + 1–184

COLLATION:

MS Rawl. C. 237: (fols. i–ii) paper flyleaves | (fols. 1–6) I (6) | (fols. 7–70) II–IX (8) | (fols. 71–77) X (8–1) 8 (?) cancelled, no loss of text | (fols. 78–101)

XI–XIII (8) | (fols. 102–105) XIV (4) no loss of text | (fols. 106–145) XV–XIX (8) | (fols. 146–151) XX (6) the last two leaves of this quire are bound at the beginning of MS Rawl. C. 238 | (fols. 152–153) paper flyleaves

MS Rawl. C. 238: (fols. i–iii) paper flyleaf and parchment bifolium | (1–2) I (2) singletons, two final leaves from quire XX of MS Rawl. C. 237 | (fols. 3–178) II–XXIII (8) | (fols. 179–182) XXIV (4)

Catchwords survive. Most leaf-signatures survive and run consecutively: +, a–i on fols. 7–85, and a–i on fols. 86–151 in MS Rawl. C. 237; k–z on fols. 3–114 and a–i on fols. 115–182 in MS Rawl. C. 238. Originally a single-volume NT.

RULING: ruled for two columns, with single vertical and double horizontal bounding lines extending the full height and width of page; prickings occasionally survive; MS Rawl. C. 237: 30 lines per page (33 on fols. 1–2); MS Rawl. C. 238: 30–1 lines per page; written space: *c.*92 × 60 mm

SCRIPT: informal and irregular textura; changes of ink and scribal style throughout, e.g., in MS Rawl. C. 238, fols. 17r, 136r, 139r, etc.; calendar in a different 15th-century hand with initials in a different style

RUBRICATION: rubrics in red ink

SEC. FOL.: '*The book of*' (MS Rawl. C. 237, fol. 7r); '*her owne*' (MS Rawl. C. 238, fol. 2r)

Binding

Nearly identical bindings on both volumes. Brown leather over pasteboard, late 17th or early 18th century, rebound for Stamford in 1693 (?). The text, originally in a single volume, was probably broken between two volumes at the time of rebinding: Stamford's signature appears in each volume. Rebacked in the Bodleian; 19th-century spines. Double blind fillet-line border round the outer edge of both covers. Four raised bands on spines. Panels between the bands are framed with double blind and gilt fillet lines. Gilt lettering on spine: 'PURVEY'S || NEW || TESTAMENT', 'VOL. I.', 'RAWL. || MS || C. 237.' (MS Rawl. C. 237); 'PURVEY'S || NEW || TESTAMENT', 'VOL. II.', 'RAWL. || MS || C. 238.' (MS Rawl. C. 238). Laid paper pastedowns and flyleaves dating from the 17th- or early 18th-century binding.

Provenance

1. Added calendar in a different, somewhat later 15th-century hand.

2. In use late in the 15th century: the calendar updated and references to

lections added; lections marked within the text; indexing letters and notes stating the liturgical occasions added in the margins; a table of lections added on a flyleaf. The same late 15th-century owner may have also marked a passage on Pharisees of possibly Lollard interest at Luke 11.

3. The feasts of Thomas Becket are crossed out, presumably at Reformation.

4. Thomas Grey, second Earl of Stamford (1653/4–1720); see *ODNB*: 'Stamford 1693' (MS Rawl. C. 237, fol. 1r; MS Rawl. C. 238, fol. iii recto).

5. Richard Rawlinson (1690–1755); see *ODNB*.

6. Bodleian Library: bequeathed by Rawlinson and accessioned in 1756. Earlier shelfmarks: 'Rawl. no. 544', '22' (MS Rawl. C. 237, upper pastedown); 'Rawl. no. 543', '22' (MS Rawl. C. 238, upper pastedown).

Bibliography

Forshall and Madden (1850), vol. 1, p. xlix.
Macray (1878), col. 105.
Summary catalogue, vol. 3, nos. 12098, 12099.
Scott (2000–02), vol. 3, pp. 48–9, nos. 861, 862.
Dove (2007), p. 301.

40 MS Rawl. C. 257

Siglum: m – epistle to Laodiceans and Prologue to Romans

Origin: England

Date: 15th century, first quarter

Text

Fols. i–ix are paper and parchment flyleaves.

(fols. 1r–209v) NT in LV, with usual prologues, imperfect at the beginning because of the loss of one leaf, starting at Matthew 2:3. Includes the Epistle to the Laodiceans. Contains two prologues to Romans, '*Romayns ben in þe cuntre…*' and '*Romaynes ben þei þat of iewis…*' (Dove (2007), p. 206). Usual rubrics, e.g., '*Here endiþ þe gospel of matheu and bigynneþ þe prolog on mark*'; '*þis seiþ Ierom in his prolog on mark & her bigynneþ þe gospel of mark*' (fol. 23v). Chapter numbers in red, most as Roman numerals. Starting from fol. 90r the chapter numbers are preceded by blue paraphs. Running titles on both rectos and versos consisting of abbreviated titles of books in red, preceded, starting from fol. 90r, by blue paraphs. No marginal glosses; added material within the text is occasionally underlined in red. Many corrections in the original or contemporary hands. Indexing letters in the margins are entered at the beginnings of readings, rather than consistently; double strokes in the margins at the ends of readings.

The gospels occupy eleven 8-leaf quires, followed by two leaves (fols. 88–89). John ends in the middle of its last verse on fol. 89v and the last four lines of the second column on this leaf are left blank. The verse is completed by the second scribe on a new quire, fol. 90r, before the start of the prologue to Romans.

Notes in English in a 15th-century hand drawing attention to passages on leprosy (fols. 45r, Luke 5; 59r, Luke 17), the poor (fol. 116v, 2 Corinthians 9), '*But I drede lest as þe serpent disseyuyde eue wiþ his littil fraude so ȝoure wittis ben corrupt & fallen doun fro þe symplenesse þat is in crist*' and '*false apostlis*' (fol. 117r, 2 Corinthians 11), pentecost and '*dyuerse langagis*' (fol. 151r, Acts 2), the burning of books by Jews and Greeks who 'used curious arts' (fol. 170r, Acts 19), '*& munistre ȝe in ȝoure feiþ*' (187r, 2 Peter 1), etc.

Decoration

5- to 6-line gold initials on blue and pink background with penwork sprays decorated with gold disks at the beginnings of gospels.

6- to 7-line 'puzzle' initials with red penwork and one-sided penwork borders at the beginnings of other books.

3- to 4-line blue initials with red penwork at the beginnings of prologues; 2- to 3-line similar initials at the beginnings of chapters.

Dialect (first scribe)

ony(10), ech(10), fier(10), gouun(10), lijf(10), lijk(10), mych(10), saiȝ(1)/siȝ(7)/saiȝ(2) (sg.), sayen(1)/sayen(1)/siȝen(1)/saiȝen(1) (pl.), silf(2)/silff(8), such(2)/suche(4), þouȝ(3), þorouȝ(5)

-iþ(8)/-eþ(2) (pres.ind.3sg.), -en(10) (pres.ind.pl.), -inge(2)/-ynge(8) (pres. part.), sche(10) (3sg.fem.pronoun, nom.), þei(10) (3pl.pronoun, nom.), hem(10) (3pl.pronoun, oblique), her(10) (3pl.pronoun, possessive)

Physical description

MATERIAL: parchment, paper flyleaves

DIMENSIONS: *c.*205 × 152 mm; leaves were trimmed in rebinding occasionally causing the loss of decoration

NUMBER OF LEAVES: 223

FOLIATION: modern in pencil, i–ix + 1–214

COLLATION: (fols. i–ix) paper and parchment flyleaves | (fols. 1–7) I (8–1) missing 1 | (fols. 8–87) II–XI (8) | (fols. 88–89) XII (2) two singletons (?) | (fols. 90–201) XIII–XXVI (8) | (fols. 202–209) XXVII–XXVIII (4) | unnumbered blank parchment bifolium and two paper flyleaves at the end

Catchwords survive. Quire signatures in an early modern hand in the form of letters in the inner margin on the first recto of each quire.

RULING: ruled for two columns, with single vertical and single horizontal bounding lines extending the full height and width of page; 35–6 lines per page; written space: *c.*117 × 75 mm

SCRIPT: three scribes (1) fols. 1–35va, (2) fols. 35va–89v, (3) 90r–209v; textura, black ink

RUBRICATION: rubrics in red ink

SEC. FOL.: '*schulen take*' (fol. 2r)

Binding

Dark brown leather over wood boards, 17th century (?). Blind-roll border round the outer edge of both covers. Blind-roll rectangular frame with floral corner-pieces on both covers; gilt branch with an acorn and four leaves in the middle of both covers. Rebacked in the Bodleian (?). Four raised bands on spine, framed with blind fillet lines. Gilt lettering on spine: 'WICKLIFFES || NEW || TESTAMENT' and 'RAWL. || MS || C. 257'. Metal fittings of two leather ties and clasps, now lost.

Provenance

1. Codicological break between the gospels and the rest of NT; perhaps originally conceived to contain only the gospels.

2. Thomas Rawlinson (1681–1725); see *ODNB*: no. 821 in his sale, March 1733/4 (?).

3. Richard Rawlinson (1690–1755); see *ODNB*: bought in Thomas Rawlinson's sale for £1 9*s.* 0*d.* Paper label with '41. 10th Days sale' pasted to the upper pastedown.

4. Bodleian Library: bequeathed by Rawlinson and accessioned in 1756.

Bibliography

Forshall and Madden (1850), vol. 1, p. xlix.
Macray (1878), col. 112.

Powell, M. J. (ed), *The Pauline epistles contained in ms. Parker 32, Corpus Christi College, Cambridge*, EETS e.s. 116 (1916), p. xxxii.
Dove (2007), pp. 206, 134, 301.

41 MS Rawl. C. 258

Origin: England

Date: 15th century, first quarter

Fol. i is a paper flyleaf, blank apart from modern notes.

Text

(fols. 1r–182v) NT in EV without prologues (**Plate 14**). The books are in the following order: four gospels, Acts, Catholic epistles, Romans–Hebrews, Apocalypse. Rubric: '*Heer bigynneþ þe gospel of our lord iesu crist*' (fol. 1r). Running titles in red on both rectos and versos consisting of abbreviated titles of biblical books. Chapter numbers as red Roman numerals (instructions to rubricator in the form of small Arabic numerals in black ink are often visible in the margins). Short rubrics in red (e.g., '*Heer bigynneþ mark*', fol. 26v). No marginal glosses; lections are not marked, apart from two red indexing letters on fol. 18r at the beginning of Matthew 21. Added material within the text is consistently underlined in red; points in black ink usually occur in the margins against lines containing such underlined text. 'Hedera' signs and pointing hands in the margins. Corrected in the original or contemporary hands. The gospels end on fol. 86r at the end of a shorter than normal quire of 6 leaves, and much of 86r and all of 86v are left blank. At the end of the gospels: '*Heer eenden þe gospels of our lord ihu crist aftir Matheu. Mark. luke. & ioon*', followed by an added ownership inscription of John Lacy in a different red ink (see Provenance). Deeds start on a new quire (fol. 78r). At the end '*Heer eendiþ þe apocalips. Blessid be þe holy trinite amen*' (fol. 182v). Fol. 183 is a blank paper flyleaf.

Decoration

2- to 3-line blue initials with red penwork at the beginning of books; 2-line similar initials at the beginning of chapters.

Dialect

ony(10), ech(8)/eche(2), fijr(10), ȝouun(10), lijf(10), lijk(7)/lyche(1)/liche(1)/

licly(1), muche(1)/miche(9), siȝe(6) (sg.), siȝen(5) (pl.), silf(10), sich(2)/siche(5)/syche(1), ȝif(5)/þouȝ(3), þoruȝ(10)

-iþ(7)/-eþ(3) (pres.ind.3sg.), -en(10) (pres.ind.pl.), -ing(3)/-inge(2)/-ynge(4)/-yng(2) (pres.part.), she(10) (3sg.fem.pronoun, nom.), þei(10) (3pl.pronoun, nom.), hem(10) (3pl.pronoun, oblique), her(10) (3pl.pronoun, possessive)

Physical description

MATERIAL: parchment, paper flyleaves

DIMENSIONS: *c.*227 × 150 mm

NUMBER OF LEAVES: 184

FOLIATION: modern in pencil, i + 1–183

COLLATION: (fols. i) paper flyleaf | (fols. 1–80) I–X (8) | (fols. 81–86) XI (6) | (fols. 87–182) XII–XXIII (8) | fol. 183 is a paper flyleaf. First and last leaves of quire IV (fols. 25–32) are reversed.

Catchwords survive. Fragmentary quire signatures run consecutively in two different series: Arabic numerals in the gospels and an alphabetic sequence in the rest of NT.

RULING: ruled in plummet for two columns, with single vertical and horizontal bounding lines extending the full height and width of page; 40 lines per page; written space: *c.*117 × 75 mm

SCRIPT: textura, black and brown ink

RUBRICATION: rubrics in red ink; red paraphs at the start of sections within the text

SEC. FOL.: '*lord appeeride…*' (fol. 2r)

Binding

Brown leather, 18th century. Five raised bands on spine framed by gilt fillet lines. Gilt lettering on spine 'NEW TESTAMENT || WYCLIF'S || TRANSLATION || M.S.'. Edges of textblock dyed red.

Provenance

1. Owned by John Lacy, Dominican recluse of Newcastle-upon-Tyne, associated with Newcastle from 1407 to 1434 (see Ker (1964), pp. 134, 284; Doyle (1948); Doyle (1990), pp. 22–3; Pepler (1951); Clay (1953); Warren (1985), pp. 24, 69, 252, 259; Hanna (2002), p. 129). An ownership inscription added in red ink after the colophon at the end of gospels: '*Iste liber constat*

fr(atr)i Ioh(ann)i lacy ordinis predicatorum reclus' nom' castri sup(er) tynam' (fol. 86r). Lacy is described as of the Shrewsbury convent in 1398 (Emden (1967), p. 76). See also MS Bodl. 771 owned in the Franciscan convent in Shrewsbury.

2. Thomas Rawlinson (1681–1725); see *ODNB*: lot 702 in his sale, March 1733/4.

3. Richard Rawlinson (1690–1755); see *ODNB*: bought at Thomas Rawlinson sale. On an inserted slip after fol. 1 in Rawlinson's hand: '*Purveys New Testament, numb. 2. quarto ninth days sale*'.

4. Bodleian Library: bequeathed by Rawlinson and accessioned in 1756.

Bibliography

Forshall and Madden (1850), vol. 1, p. xlix.
Macray (1878), col. 113.
Deanesly (1920), p. 333.
Doyle, A. I., 'A prayer attributed to St Thomas Aquinas', *Dominican Studies* 1 (1948), pp. 229–38.
Pepler, C., 'John Lacy: a Dominican contemplative', *The Life of the Spirit* 5 (1951), pp. 397–400.
Clay, R. M., 'Further studies on medieval recluses', *Journal of the British Archaeological Association* 16 (1953), pp. 74–86.
Fristedt (1953–73), vol. 1, p. 16.
Ker (1964).
Emden, A. B., *A survey of Dominicans in England: based on the ordination lists in episcopal registers* (Rome: Santa Sabina, 1967).
Warren, A. K., *Anchorites and their patrons in medieval England* (Berkeley: University of California Press, 1985).
Friedman, J. B., 'Books, owners and makers in fifteenth-century Yorkshire: the evidence from some wills and extant manuscripts', in Minnis, A. J. (ed.), *Latin and vernacular: studies in late-medieval texts and manuscripts* (Cambridge: D. S. Brewer, 1989), pp. 11–127 at p. 117.
Doyle, A. I., 'The English provincial book trade before printing', in Isaac, P. (ed.), *Six centuries of the provincial book trade in Britain* (Winchester: St Paul's Bibliographies, 1990), pp. 13–29 at p. 22.
Lindberg (1994), p. 23.
Friedman, J. B., *Northern English books, owners, and makers in the late Middle Ages* (Syracuse, NY: Syracuse University Press, 1995), p. 52.
Hanna, R., *A descriptive catalogue of the western medieval manuscripts of St John's College, Oxford* (Oxford: Oxford University Press, 2002).
Hanna, R., 'English biblical texts before Lollardy and their fate', in Somerset, F., Havens, J. C. and Pitard, D. G., *Lollards and their influence in late medieval England* (Woodbridge: Boydell, 2003), pp. 141–53 at p. 153 and n. 38.

Hanna, R., *London literature, 1300–1380* (Cambridge: Cambridge University Press, 2005), p. 312
Dove (2007), pp. 54, 301.

42 MS Rawl. C. 259

Origin: England, London (?)

Date: 15th century, first quarter

Text

Fol. i–v are paper and parchment flyleaves.

[item 1 occupies quire I]
1. (fols. 1r–6v) Calendar in Latin, written in black and red, not graded, less than one-quarter full. Includes Dunstan (19 May), Alban (22 June), Leonard (6 November) and Martin (11 November), all in red, and Alphege with a red capital (19 April). Also includes Benedict Biscop (12 January), Brigid of Kildare (1 February), Edward the Martyr (18 March), Benedict of Nursia (21 March), Pancras (12 May), Botulph (17 June), the translation of Swithin (15 July) and Edmund the Martyr (20 November), all in black. Does not include David, Chad or other saints whose feasts were promulgated after 1415 under Archbishop Chichele (Pfaff (2009), pp. 438–41). The translation of Thomas Becket (7 July) is erased, but not his feast (29 December). Includes the following entries in the original hand in the lower margins: '*Anno domini m.ccc.lxi in festo sancti mauri abbatis erat ventus validus*' (fol. 1r), and '*Anno domini mcccxlviii in festo sancti michaelis incipiebat prima pestilencia lond.*' (fol. 5r). The entries commemorate 'Grote Mandrenke' storm on 16 January 1362 and the arrival of the Black Death in London in 1348. Fifteenth-century additions, including the translation of Edward the Confessor (13 October); '*ffro þe tyme þat adam hadde synned in to þat tyme þat crist dyed & ros .v. þousand ȝer .ij. cc. & xxx*' (fol. 1r); notes on blood letting (fol. 1v). Days are numbered throughout in an early modern hand.

[item 2 occupies quires II–XXV]
2. (fols. 7r–204v) NT in LV with usual prologues. Two prologues to Romans, '*First vs bihoueþ vndirstonde…*' and '*Romayns ben in þe cuntrey…*' (Dove (2007), p. 206). EV prologue to Philemon, '*He makiþ homeli lettris to filemon…*' (Dove (2007), p. 208). Rubrics in red or black, most with usual wording, e.g., '*Here bigynneþ þe prolog on matheu*'; '*Ierom in his twei prologis on matheu seiþ pleynli þus. Here bigynneþ þe book of matheu*' (fol. 7r).

Matthew ends on fol. 25v, where the end of the second column is left blank, and Mark starts on a new leaf (fol. 26r). John, the prologue to Romans, and Philippians start on new pages as well. Running titles on both rectos and versos, consisting of abbreviated titles of biblical books; chapter numbers are added to some running titles in a medieval hand. Chapter numbers in red, most as Roman numerals. Red or blue paraphs at the start of sections within the text. Many corrections over erasures within the text and in the margins in contemporary and later hands; some text crossed out in red. No marginal glosses with very few exceptions; added material within the text is underlined in red. Indexing letters in the margins, entered at the beginning of lections rather than consistently; double strokes at the ends of lections; letters and strokes in red may be original, but many letters in black were probably added in the 15th century. Numerous added pointing hands and '*nota*' in the margins.

[item 3 occupies quires XXVI–XXXI]
3. (fols. 205r–240v) OT lectionary of Type II with a rubric '*Here bygynnen þe lessouns & pistlis of þe oolde lawe þat ben rad in þe chirche bi al þe ȝeer*'. Includes the temporal, followed by the proper (containing Silvester, Martin and Lawrence as the only non-biblical saints), common and commemorations. Each reading is preceded by a rubric, stating the liturgical occasion, the title of the biblical book and the chapter number. The readings begin with statements that introduce them at Mass (e.g., '*The lord god seiþ þese þingis*', fol. 205r) underlined in red. Indexing letters in the margins in the original hand at the start of most readings and double strokes at the ends of readings. The readings used for more than one occasion are not repeated and instead rubrics contain references to liturgical occasions earlier in the lectionary. The reading for the first Mass on Christmas morning is preceded by a lengthy rubric explaining that it is performed by two voices; the part of one of the voices is underlined in red in the text that follows (fols. 207v–208r). Running titles in red above each column, preceded by blue paraphs, consisting of an abbreviated title of a biblical book and a chapter number. On the final page much of the second column is left blank and the table of lections starts on a new page.

[item 4 occupies quires XXXII–XXXIII]
4. (fols. 241r–251r) Table of lections of Type I, preceded by a rubric: '*Here bigynneþ a rule þat telliþ in whiche chapitres of þe bible ȝe mai fynde þe lessouns pistlis & gospels þat ben rad in þe chirche after þe vse of Salisberie markid wiþ lettris of þe a b c at þe bigynnynge of þe chapitris toward þe myddil or ende aftir þe ordre as þe lettris stonden in þe a b c ffirst ben set sondaies and ferials to gidere and aftir þe sanctorum comyn and propre to gidere of al þe ȝer ffirst*

writen a clause of þe bigynnynge þerof and a clause of þe endynge þerof also'. Includes the temporal, commemorations and the sanctoral (no common, in spite of the rubric). Commemorations are in the following order: Our Lady, Trinity, Holy Ghost, cross, angels, '*ffor briþ*' *and s*' *& salus populi*', peace, clear weather, rain, '*in tyme of batels*', '*a man for himsilf*', for pestilence of beasts, pilgrims, weddings, sick and dead. Includes all feasts characteristic of LV, apart from Giles (1 September) (Forshall and Madden (1850), vol. 4, pp. 683, 690–6). The entries consist of the name of the liturgical occasion in red, abbreviated title and chapter of the biblical book, an indexing letter in red, the opening words of a reading, '*ende*' in red and the closing words of a reading. More than a half of the last page is left blank.

Fols. 251v–252v, originally ruled for a table of lections, but blank, contain: (1) a list of NT books (Romans–Apocalypse) added in a 15th-century hand (fols. 251v–252r); (2) a rubric '*The tokenys of þe doom*', followed by references to chapters in the gospels in the same hand; and (3) two short notes in a 16th-century hand with references to historical events in the 1550s. More historical notes in the same hand on paper fly-leaves 255v–256r.

Decoration

3- to 5-line red and blue 'puzzle' initials with red and purple penwork at the beginnings of books; 3- to 4-line similar initials at the beginnings of prologues; 2- to 3-line blue initials with red penwork at the beginnings of chapters. Penwork in OT lectionary is in a different style than that in the calendar and NT.

Dialect

ony(10), ech(9)/eche(1), fier(10), ȝouun(10), lijf(10), lijk(10), myche(9)/miche(1), siȝ(3)/seiȝ(1)/siȝe(1)/saye(2)/saiȝ(1) (sg.), sayn(4)/sien(1)/seyn(1) (pl.), silf(10), sich(1)/siche(8)/suche(1), þouȝ(7), þorou(10)

-iþ(7)/eþ(3) (pres.ind.3sg.), -en(10) (pres.ind.pl.), -ynge(9)/-inge(1) (pres. part.), sche(10) (3sg.fem.pronoun, nom.), þei(10) (3pl.pronoun, nom.), hem(10) (3pl.pronoun, oblique), her(10) (3pl.pronoun, possessive)

Physical description

MATERIAL: parchment, paper flyleaves

DIMENSIONS: *c.*189 × 122 mm

NUMBER OF LEAVES: 263

FOLIATION: modern in pencil, i–v + 1–256 + two unnumbered flyleaves;

early modern (?) pagination in the calendar in ink in Greek letters, alpha – mu; late 15th-century (?) foliation, 1–234, in ink on fols. 7–241

COLLATION: (fols. i–v) paper flyleaves | (fols. 1–6) I (6) | (fols. 7–198) II–XXIV (8) | (fols. 199–204) XXV (8–2) 7 and 8 excised | (fols. 205–236) XXVI–XXIX (8) | (fols. 237–234) XXX (4) | (fols. 235–240) XXXI (4) | (fols. 241–248) XXXII (8) | (fols. 249–252) XXXIII (4) | (fols. 253–256 + two unnumbered leaves) parchment and paper flyleaves.

Catchwords survive; quire signatures partially survive in NT running consecutively a–z, followed by three non-numerical characters (fols. 7–204).

RULING: ruled for two columns, with single vertical and horizontal bounding lines extending the full height and width of page; 38 lines per page in NT; 39 lines per page in OT lectionary; prickings occasionally survive; written space: *c.*117 × 75 mm

SCRIPT: textura, black and brown ink; the scribe of OT lectionary is different from the scribe of NT

SEC. FOL.: '*fro þe eest…*' (NT, fol. 8r)

Binding

Light brown leather over pasteboard, 19th century. Blind fillet-line border round the outer edge of both covers. Five raised bands on spine framed by blind fillet lines. Gilt lettering on spine: 'WICKLIFFE'S || NEW || TESTAMENT' and 'RAWL. || MS || C. 259'. Blind roll floral designs on the edges of covers and turn-ins. 19th-century paper pastedowns and flyleaves. Flyleaves made of laid paper with Hearne's inscriptions, dating from a 17th- or early 18th-century binding. Parchment flyleaves made from a 12th-century Latin manuscript containing fragments of St Augustine's *Confessions*. These flyleaves may have served as pastedowns of a medieval binding sewn on four stations (offprints on the flyleaf at the beginning).

Provenance

1. Perhaps made for a patron in London: references in the original hand in the calendar to the arrival of the Black Death in London and to the 'Grote Mandrenke' storm of 1362 that devastated southern and eastern England. The calendar includes Benedict Biscop. The calendar, NT, OT lectionary and the table of lections are all codicologically separate; OT lectionary and the table of lections may have been produced separately and bound with NT and the calendar.

2. Translation of Thomas Becket is erased, presumably at Reformation.

3. Edward Etterick of Totteridge, Hertfordshire (Foster (1891–92), p. 467), fellow of New College, matriculated 1714.

4. Thomas Hearne, bap. 1678, d. 1735; see *ODNB*: '*Suum cuiq. Tho. Hearne, Oct. 9. 1719. I have made mention of this MS in my Preface to Camden's Eliz. (Oxon. 1717, p. 123.) It then belong'd to Edw. Etterick, Esq., Fellow of New College. I purchas'd it since his death*' on fol. iv recto in his hand; see Hearne, Thomas (ed.), *Annales rerum Anglicarum et Hibernicarum, regnante Elizabetha, ad annum M.D.LXXXIX* (Oxford: 1717). On fol. v recto in Hearne's hand: '*The New Testament, in old English, commonly called Wicliff's Translation, with the Calendar prefix'd*'. On fol. v verso in Hearne's hand: '*Scriptus hic liber circa AD 1370, nam quae notantur paginis a & k videntur tum recentia*' and beneath in the hand of Thomas Baker (1656–1740; see *ODNB*) '*Scriptum fuisse hunc librum exploratum haveo AD. 1345*' and lower '*Sed Amicus noster egregie fallitur, aut edo fallor*'.

5. Richard Rawlinson (1690–1755); see *ODNB*.

6. Bodleian Library: bequeathed by Rawlinson and accessioned in 1756.

Bibliography

Forshall and Madden (1850), vol. 1, pp. xlix.
Macray (1878), col. 113.
Hudson (1989), p. 140.
Lindberg (1959–97), vol. 8 (1997), p. 274.
Scott (2000–02), vol. 3, p. 49, no. 863.
de Hamel (2001), p. 187.
Dove (2007), pp. 269, 301.

43 MS Rawl. C. 752

Origin: England

Date: 15th century, end of the first quarter (?)

Text

[items 1–2 occupy quires I–XVI]
1. (fols. 1r–119v) Four gospels in LV with usual prologues. Usual rubrics in red. Running titles on both rectos and versos consisting of abbreviated titles of biblical books and chapter numbers on fols. 1v–3v; elsewhere the chapter numbers are added to running titles in a post-medieval hand. Chapter numbers in red as Roman numerals. Red and blue paraphs within the text,

often at the beginnings of lections. Indexing letters in the margins entered at the beginnings of lections rather than consistently; double strokes at the ends of lections. Corrections in a contemporary hand. Gloss within the text is written in red on fol. 28r. Ends halfway through the second column on fol. 119v with a rubric '*Here eendiþ þe gospel of Ioon*'.

2. (fols. 119v–120r) The gospels are immediately followed by two added devotional pieces transcribed below, probably in the same contemporary hand. A space is left at the beginning for a 2-line initial, not filled in, though there is a small 'd' in red as an instruction to the rubricator.

(fol. 119v) '*[D]ere cristen soulis. I praie ȝou wiþ al mekenesse & charite. liftep up þe iȝen of ȝoure vndirstondynge and openeþ þe eris of ȝour soulis: þat ȝe may lerne and vndirstonde þe charge & couenaunt þat ȝe maden wiþ god. in takynge of ȝoure cristendom / ffor alle cristen peple. ben bounden to knowe & kepe þis charge & couenaunt: but speciali prestis / wherfore bi goddis mercy: I schal schewe ȝou þe sacrament of baptym* [sic] *schortly declared*'

(fol. 120r) '*and at þe laste he suffride þe moost shameful deeþ. þat synners cowden ymagene to hym / O þis was a greet loue / for gretter loue may no man haue: þan to suffre bodili deeþ for his frendis / wherfore crist seide in his passioun to hise disciplis / wiþ desire I haue desired: to ete þis soupere wiþ ȝou / and aftir þis he seide I þirste / þat is þe sauacioun and helþe of alle chosen soulis / þe whiche soulis houynge aboue þe bodi. in þe our of her departyng: shullen be resseyued wiþ þe aungels of god. and be born in to heuene. þere to be fedde wiþ breed of liyf. þat is iesu crist hym silf / as he seiþ in þe gospel*'

Most of fol. 120r–v is blank.

[items 3–4 occupy quires XVII–XVIII]
3. (fols. 121r–139r) Apocalypse without a prologue, followed by Jude, both in LV. Written by a different scribe and with a penwork border in a different style than the borders in the gospels. Running titles on both rectos and versos in black ink preceded by blue paraphs. Chapter numbers as red Roman numerals.

4. (fol. 139v) Extracts from epistles: 2 Peter 2:21–22 and James 5:1–6 with a rubric '*Iamys v. 5.*' in LV, badly faded.

Decoration
5- to 6-line initials in pigment and gold, and 1-sided borders, decorated with foliage and gold disks at the beginnings of gospels.

2- to 3-line blue initials with red penwork at the beginnings of prologues and chapters.

Floral or occasionally zoomorphic (fol. 17r) designs in penwork, some with red and yellow wash, decorating catchwords, running titles, indexing letters, etc.

4-line red and blue 'puzzle' initial and a penwork border at the beginning of the Apocalypse.

Decoration in the gospels is in a different style than elsewhere in the manuscript.

Dialect (gospels)

ony(10), eche(9)/ech(1), fier(7)/fire(2)/fir(1), ȝouun(10), lijf(10), like(9)/lic(1), myche(8)/mych(2), siȝ(7)/syȝe(1) (sg.), saien(3)/sayen(1)/siȝen(1)/sien(1) (pl.), silf(10), suche(7)/siche(1), þouȝ(6), þoruȝ(9)

-iþ(9)/-eþ(1) (pres.ind.3sg.), -en(6)/-n(4) (pres.ind.pl.), -ynge(4)/-inge(6) (pres.part.), sche(10) (3sg.fem.pronoun, nom.), þei(10) (3pl.pronoun, nom.), hem(10) (3pl.pronoun, oblique), her(10) (3pl.pronoun, possessive)

Physical description

MATERIAL: thin parchment, paper flyleaves

DIMENSIONS: *c.*145 × 95 mm; leaves were trimmed in rebinding occasionally causing the loss of decoration in the margins

NUMBER OF LEAVES: 143

FOLIATION: two unnumbered paper leaves at the beginning and end; modern in pencil, 1–29 + 29(a) + 30–139

COLLATION: paper flyleaves | (fols. 1–118) I–XV (8) | (fols. 119–120) XVI (2) | (fols. 121–132) XVII (12) | (fols. 133–139) XVIII (8–1(?)) missing 8 (?)

Catchwords survive.

RULING: ruled in plummet for two columns with single vertical and horizontal bounding lines extending the full height and width of page; 33 lines per page; written space: *c.*105 × 68 mm

SCRIPT: textura; gospels and the Apocalypse are probably copied by different scribes; another change of scribe on fol. 139r

Binding

Black leather over pasteboard, 18th century. Rebacked with the original spine relaid. Rectangular gilt roll floral decoration with floral corner-pieces on both covers. Double gilt fillet-line border around the outer edge of the covers. Four raised bands on spine. Gilt decoration on the panels between the bands. Red leather label on spine with gilt lettering 'EUANGELISTS'. Marbled paper pastedowns and flyleaves; further laid paper flyleaves.

Provenance

1. '*Constat iste liber domino Rogero Waltun clerico et presbetero anno domini m^o^ qgisim … et Regis Henrici octavi*' (fol. 139v).

2. '*Ric Stauntonj liber 1603*' (fol. 139v).

3. Bookplate of Robert Nash, fellow of Wadham College, Oxford, and, from 1731, Chancellor of the Diocese of Norwich on the upper pastedown (see Blomefield (1806)).

4. Richard Rawlinson (1690–1755); see *ODNB*: bookplate on the first flyleaf.

5. Bodleian Library: bequeathed by Rawlinson and accessioned in 1756.

Bibliography

Blomefield, F., 'The city of Norwich, chapter 40: Deans, Vicars-General, or Chancellors, Archdeacons, Commissaries, Officials, and Prebends', in *An essay towards a topographical history of the county of Norfolk*, vol. 3, *The History of the city and county of Norwich*, part I (London, 1806), pp. 617–71 (http://www.british-history.ac.uk/topographical-hist-norfolk/vol3/pp617-671) [accessed 27 July 2015].

Forshall and Madden (1850), vol. 1, p. xlix.

Macray (1878), col. 389.

Scott (2000–02), vol. 3, p. 56, no. 918.

Dove (2007), p. 299.

44 MS Rawl. C. 883

Origin: England

Date: 15th century, first quarter

Text

(fols. 1–48v) Matthew in LV with usual prologue. Rubrics: '*þe prolog on matheu*' and '*Ierom in his ii prologis on þe gospel of matheu seiþ pleynly þis sentence & here bigynneþ þe first chap*''. Missing 21:27–22:2 because of the loss of one leaf after fol. 33. Running titles in black preceded by red paraphs on both rectos and versos, most consisting of '*m^t^*' only. Chapter numbers in red Roman numerals, most in the form '*iiij c*''. Indexing letters in the margins, entered at the beginnings of lections rather than consistently; double strokes at the ends of lections. A gloss within the text is underlined in red on fol. 8r. The beginnings of sections within the text and sometimes verses are highlighted in red or marked with red paraphs. Dittography crossed out in red. The end of Matthew occupies the first half of the first column on fol. 48v; there is no evidence that anything is missing at the end.

Decoration

4-line red and blue 'puzzle' initial decorated with red penwork at the beginning of the gospel.

2-line plain blue initials at the beginnings of the chapters; a similar initial with red penwork at the beginning of the prologue.

Dialect

ony(1)/eny(9), ech(10), fier(10), ȝouun(2)/ȝouen(7)/ȝeuen(1), lif(1)/lijf(9), lijk(9)/lik(1), myche(7)/mych(2)/moche(1), siȝ(8) (sg.), saien(4)/siȝen(2) (pl.), silf(10), such(3)/suche(2), þouȝ(2)/þou(1), þorou(5)/þorouȝ(1)

-iþ(9)/eþ(1) (pres.ind.3sg.), -en(10) (pres.ind.pl.), -ing(7)/-yng(2)/-ynge(1) (pres.part.), sche(10) (3sg.fem.pronoun, nom.), þei(10) (3pl.pronoun, nom.), hem(10) (3pl.pronoun, oblique), her(10) (3pl.pronoun, possessive)

Physical description

MATERIAL: parchment; paper flyleaves

DIMENSIONS: *c.*182 × 121 mm

NUMBER OF LEAVES: 119

FOLIATION: modern in ink: 22 unnumbered leaves + 1–48 + 24 unnumbered leaves

COLLATION: (fols. 1–32) I–IV (8) | (fols. 33–39) V (8–1) missing 2 | (fols. 40–47) VI (8) | (fol. 48) singleton

Catchwords survive; medieval quire signatures run consecutively 1–6

RULING: ruled for two columns with single vertical and double horizontal bounding lines extending the full height and width of page; 26 lines per page; prickings survive; written space: *c.*126 × 90 mm

SCRIPT: textura, black ink

RUBRICATION: rubrics in red ink

SEC. FOL.: '*[of] ruth*' (fol. 2r)

Binding

Marbled paper over pasteboard, 19th century; laid paper flyleaves and pastedowns with watermarks.

Provenance

1. Thomas Rawlinson (1681–1725); see *ODNB*: no. 272 in his collection.

2. Richard Rawlinson (1690–1755); see *ODNB*: bought at the Thomas Rawlinson sale for 5*s*. 6*d*.

3. Bodleian Library: bequeathed by Rawlinson and accessioned in 1756.

Bibliography

Forshall and Madden (1850), vol. 1, p. l.
Macray (1878), col. 461.
Dove (2007), p. 301 (listed as Rawlinson C. 888).

45 MS Selden Supra 49

Origin: England

Date: 15th century, first quarter, before 1415 (?)

Fol. i is ruled for two columns, but originally blank (see Provenance).

Text

[item 1 occupies quire I]
1. (fols. 2r–7v) Sarum calendar laid out one month per page, written in black and red, in English, not graded, approximately one-third full, nearly identical to the calendar of MS Selden Supra 51. Included Botulph (17 June); does not include David, Chad or other saints whose feasts were promulgated after 1415 under Archbishop Chichele (Pfaff (2009), pp. 438–41). At the bottom of the page for February is a list of dominical letters, followed by '*þus lettris fallen in þe leþe ȝeeris*'; at the bottom of the page for April is a note in English on determining the date of Easter. Easter is called '*Aȝenrisyng of oure lord*' in both Selden Supra 49 and 51. The feast and octave of Thomas Becket, most titles 'pope' and 'abbot' are erased. Fol. 8r–v is ruled for the table of lections, but blank.

[item 2 occupies quire II]
2. (fols. 9r–15r) Table of lections of Type I preceded by a rubric: '*Here bigynneþ a rule þat telliþ in whiche chapiters of þe foure euangelistis ȝe may*

fynde þe gospels þat ben rad in þe chirche aftir þe vse of salisbirie markid wiþ lettris of þe abc ffirst ben sett sonedaies & ferials togidere and after þe sanctorum comyn & propre togidere of al þe ȝeer ffirst is writun a clause of þe bigynnynge þerof & a clause of þe ending þerof also'. Includes the temporal, followed by commemorations and the sanctoral, all containing readings from gospels only. Includes all feasts characteristic of LV, apart from Giles (1 September) (Forshall and Madden (1850), vol. 4, pp. 683, 690–6). The entries consist of a liturgical occasion in red, abbreviated reference to a book and chapter of the Bible, an indexing letter in black, the opening words of a reading, '*ende*' in red, the closing words of a reading and double strokes in red. Larger initials or blue paraphs at Conception of Our Lady, Candlemas, Matthew, Annunciation, Mark, Nativity of John the Baptist, Peter and Paul, Mary Magdalene, Lammas, Lawrence, Assumption, Nativity of Our Lady, Holy Rood, Luke and All Saints. Commemorations are in the following order: Our Lady, Trinity, Holy Ghost, cross, angels, brothers and sisters, *salus populi*, peace, clear weather, rain, in time of battles, '*a man for him silf*', pestilence of beasts, pilgrims, weddings, sinners, sick and dead. At the end '*Thus eendiþ þis kalender of þe foure gospelers*'. Fol. 15v is blank, apart from an early modern ownership inscription (see Provenance).

[item 3 occupies quires III–XIX]
3. (fols. 16r–149r) Four gospels in LV with usual prologues, usual rubrics and chapter numbers in red as words or Roman numerals. Blue paraphs at the start of sections within the text. Running titles in red on both rectos and versos, consisting of the titles of gospels only, preceded by blue paraphs. Indexing letters in the margins entered at the start of lections, rather than consistently; double strokes at the ends of lections. Many corrections in the original or contemporary hands; cross-references to biblical books occasionally in the margins. Many medieval '*nota*' in the margins throughout.

Decoration

5- to 6-line initials on gold background, and 3-sided borders made of gold, blue and pink bars, decorated with foliage.

2-line blue initials with red penwork at the beginnings of prologues and chapters.

Dialect

ony(10), ech(4)/eche(6), fier(10), gouun(9)/ȝouen(1), lijf(3)/lyf(7), lijk(3)/lyk(7), myche(10), saiȝ(1)/siȝ(4)/sai(1)/saw(1) (sg.), saien(2)/sawen(4) (pl.), silf(10), sich(2)/siche(7), þouȝ(8), þourȝ(1)/þoru(9)

-iþ(7)/-eþ(3) (pres.ind.3sg.), -en(10) (pres.ind.pl.), -inge(4)/-ynge(5)/-yng(1) (pres.part.), sche(10) (3sg.fem.pronoun, nom.), þei(10) (3pl.pronoun, nom.), hem(10) (3pl.pronoun, oblique), her(10) (3pl.pronoun, possessive)

Physical description

MATERIAL: parchment

DIMENSIONS: *c.*101 × 145 mm

NUMBER OF LEAVES: 150

FOLIATION: modern in pencil: 1–150

COLLATION: (fol. 1) parchment flyleaf | (fols. 2–7) I (6) | (fols. 8–150) II–XIX (8)

Catchwords survive; some quire signatures survive, particularly at the beginning where they run consecutively starting with 'a'.

RULING: ruled for two columns with single vertical and double horizontal bounding lines extending the full height and width of page; 31 lines per page; written space: *c.*71 × 105 mm

SCRIPT: textura, black ink; the work of at least two scribes: (1) fols. 16r–31v; (2) fols. 32r–149r; the second scribe may have been also responsible for the calendar and the table of lections

RUBRICATION: rubrics in red; blue paraphs

SEC. FOL.: '*tewisday mt xxi*' (table of lections, fol. 10r); '*marie þe modir*' (gospel, fol. 17r)

Binding

English, 16th century, brown leather over pasteboard. Rectangular figure at the centre of both covers, made of blind floral and geometric decoration, framed with blind fillet lines. Inside the rectangular figure is a rosette surmounted by a crown and stamped initials 'T S' (Thomas Stanley, see Provenance). Four raised bands on spine. Fragment of a paper label at the top of spine. Fragments of two ties, now lost. '49' written in ink on the edge of textblock.

Provenance

1. The calendar is similar to MS Selden Supra 51.

2. '*Codex thome stanley de Grays Inne*', 16th century (fol. 1v; see also fols. 2r, 15v, 16r, 74r, 149r).

3. A fragment of an account of '*Holborne Empcions*', i.e., purchases in Holborn (?) (*Summary catalogue*, vol. 2, part II, no. 3437), for '*Die Sab*[...]', used as a pastedown for the binding. Contains various food items.

4. Feasts of Thomas Becket and most titles 'pope' and 'abbot' are erased, presumably at Reformation.

5. Bodleian Library. Earlier shelfmarks: '19', 'A 9' (fol. 1r).

Bibliography

Forshall and Madden (1850), vol. 1, p. xlviii.
Summary catalogue, vol. 2, part II, no. 3437.
Hudson (1989), p. 140.
Scott (2000–02), vol. 3, p. 76, no. 1014.
Dove (2007), pp. 59 n. 116, 301.

46 MS Selden Supra 51

Origin: England

Date: 15th century, first quarter, before 1415 (?)

Fols. 1–3 are parchment flyleaves; fol. 3r–v is ruled for two columns (see Provenance).

Text

[item 1 occupies quire I]
1. (fols. 4r–12v) *Capitula*-list of NT. Chapter numbers in red in the margins, sections for each chapter start with blue or red initials. Usual order of LV, but Philemon is omitted. The table is the same as in MS e Mus. 110 (Forshall and Madden (1850), vol. 1, p. xlvii). Fol. 13r is ruled for the calendar-lectionary, but blank.

[items 2–3 occupy quires II–III]
2. (fols. 13v–25r) Sarum calendar-lectionary in English written in black and red, laid out one month per two-page opening, approximately one-third full. Identical to the calendar of MS Selden Supra 49, apart from the presence of Vincent of Saragossa (22 January) and some vigils absent in MS Selden Supra 49. Included Botulph (17 June); does not include David, Chad or other saints promulgated after 1415 under Archbishop Chichele (Pfaff (2009), pp. 438–41). At the bottom of the second page for February are the dominical letters followed by '*þus lettris failen in leep ȝeris*'; at the

bottom of the page for April is a note on determining the date of Easter in English, incomplete, possibly cropped off. Easter is called '*Aȝenrising of oure lord*' in both Selden Supra 49 and 51. The feast of Thomas Becket, his translation and titles 'pope' are erased. Entries for readings consist of a reference to a book and chapter of the Bible, an indexing letter in red, the opening words of a reading, '*ende*' in red, the closing words of a reading and double strokes in red. Entries for OT readings are also accompanied by letters and numbers in the margins in red, used to identify readings in the OT lectionary (see below and MS Ashmole 1517).

3. (fols. 25v–32v) Table of lections preceded by a rubric: '*Here bigynneþ a reule þat telliþ in whiche chapitris of þe bible a man may fynde þe lessouns pistlis and gospels þat red in holy chirche at masse þoruȝ al þe ȝeer after þe vss of salisbiry markid wiþ lettris bi þe ordre as þei stonden in þe abc bigynnynge at þe firste sonday in aduent*'. Includes the temporal and commemorations only. The entries consist of a liturgical occasion in red, abbreviated reference to a book and chapter of the Bible, an indexing letter in red, the opening words of a reading, '*ende*' in red, the closing words of a reading and double strokes in red. Entries for OT readings are also accompanied by letters and numbers in the margins in red, used to identify the readings in the OT lectionary. Commemorations are in the following order: Our Lady, cross, Trinity, Holy Ghost, angels, *salus populi*, brothers and sisters, peace, clear weather, rain, in time of battles, '*a man for hym silf*', pestilence of beasts, pilgrims, weddings, sinners, sick and dead. Running titles with names of liturgical seasons.

[item 4 occupies quires IV–XXXIV and fol. 283]
4. (fols. 33r–283r) NT in LV with usual prologues, usual rubrics in red or underlined in red, and chapter numbers in red as words or Roman numerals. Blue paraphs at the start of sections within the text. Running titles in red on both rectos and versos consisting of abbreviated titles of books and chapter numbers. Indexing letters set between double bounding lines in the margins entered at the start of lections rather than consistently; double strokes at the ends of lections. Corrections in the original or contemporary hands, occasionally text crossed out in red. Added material within the text is underlined in red; a few glosses in the margins (particularly on fols. 237r–240v). The Apocalypse ends half-way through the first column on fol. 283r and fol. 283v is blank.

[item 5 occupies quires XXXV–XL]
5. (fols. 284r–326v) OT lectionary of Type II. The readings are preceded by rubrics in red, introductory statements (e.g., '*The lord god of oostis seiþ þes*

þingis', fol. 284v) underlined in red, and letters and numbers that identify each reading. The letters subdivide the lectionary into five parts, A–E, and in addition each reading is given a number, e.g., a1, a2, a3, etc. The same letters and numbers are used as part of references to OT readings in the calendar-lectionary and the table of lections (a similar system is used to identify readings in the OT lectionary in MS Ashmole 1517). Added material within the text is occasionally underlined in red. Includes the readings for the temporal, commemorations, the proper and common. The common ends imperfectly because of the loss of leaves, but the final reading is completed in the lower margin of fol. 326v in a different contemporary hand.

Decoration

4- to 8-line gold initials on blue and pink background at the beginnings of NT books and the OT lectionary; the initial at the beginning of Matthew is decorated with sprays of leaves and gold disks; 4-line penwork initials at the beginnings of 2 John–Jude.

3-line gold initial on blue and pink background at the beginning of the prologue to Matthew; 3-line blue initials with red penwork at the beginnings of other prologues.

3- to 4-line blue initials with red penwork at the beginnings of chapters and readings in the OT lectionary.

Dialect

any(10), ech(10), fyr(3)/fijr(7), gouun(9)/ȝouen(1), lijf(6)/lyf(3)/lif(1), lijk(10), myche(10), siȝ(7) (sg.), sien(1)/syen(1)/saien(2)/siȝen(1) (pl.), silf(10), sich(2)/siche(7), þouȝ(7), þoruȝ(9)/þorou(1)

-iþ(7)/-eþ(3) (pres.ind.3sg.), -en(10) (pres.ind.pl.), -inge(9)/-ynge(1) (pres. part.), sche(10) (3sg.fem.pronoun, nom.), þei(10) (3pl.pronoun, nom.), hem(10) (3pl.pronoun, oblique), her(10) (3pl.pronoun, possessive)

Physical description

MATERIAL: parchment

DIMENSIONS: *c.*146 × 208 mm

NUMBER OF LEAVES: 325

FOLIATION: modern in pencil: 1–127 + 129–326

COLLATION: (fols. 1–2) parchment flyleaves | (fols. 3–12) I (10) | (fols. 13–20) II (8) | (fols. 21–32) III (12) | (fols. 33–272) IV–XXXIII (8) | (fols. 273–282)

XXXIV (10) | (fol. 283) singleton | (fols. 284–315) XXXV–XXXVIII (8) | (fols. 316–325) XXXIX (10) | (fol. 326) XL (first leaf of a quire (?), followed by four stubs)

Quire signatures partially survive; a new series starts on fol. 284 at the beginning of OT lectionary.

RULING: ruled for two columns with single vertical and triple horizontal bounding lines extending the full height and width of page; a second set of double bounding lines in the upper, lower and outer margins, used as the ruling for running titles and indexing letters; 33–4 lines per page; prickings survive; written space: *c.*90 × 135 mm

SCRIPT: informal textura, black and brown ink; the work of several scribes

RUBRICATION: rubrics in red; blue paraphs

SEC. FOL.: '*tewisday mt xxi*' (table of lections, fol. 10r); '*marie þe modir*' (gospel, fol. 17r)

Binding

Contemporary English binding; worn plain red leather over wood boards. Five raised bands on spine. Holes left by the fittings of two clasps on the upper cover and by two pins on the lower cover, all now lost. Paper label on spine with hand-written '3439'.

Provenance

1. The calendar is similar to MS Selden Supra 49.

2. '*super honorem deo pathr noster quy us...*' (fol. 2r); '*John*' (fols. 2r, 3r), '*Ihus*' in a square frame (fol. 128v); '*Thomas Lucas*' (fol. 195v); '*Thomas*', '*John Robynes boke as longe as he lewe ande after hym gorge ys*' (fol. 218r), in several hands, all 16th century.

3. The feasts of Thomas Becket and titles 'pope' are erased in the calendar-lectionary, presumably at Reformation.

4. Bodleian Library. Earlier shelfmark: '15', fol. 1r.

Bibliography

Forshall and Madden (1850), vol. 1, p. xlviii.
Summary catalogue, vol. 2, part II, no. 3437.
Hudson (1989), p. 140.
Scott (2000–02), vol. 3, p. 76, no. 1015.
Dove (2007), pp. 59 n. 116, 301.

47 Brasenose College MS 10

Origin: England

Date: 15th century, first quarter

Text

Fols. 1–2 are paper flyleaves, blank apart from early modern and modern notes (see Provenance).

[item 1 occupies quires I–II]

1. (fols. 3r–12v) Table of lections of Type II starting with a rubric '*Here bigynneþ a rule þat telliþ in whiche chapitris of þe bible ȝe [m]oun fynde þe lessons pistlis & gospels þat ben rad bi al þe ȝeer a[.]oute* [aloute (?)] *in holi chirche aftir þe vss of Salisbiry*'. Comprises the temporal, the proper, common and commemorations. The proper is short, the only non-biblical saints included are Nicholas, George, Seven Brothers, the translation of Thomas Becket, Lawrence and Clement. The entries consist of a date in red, abbreviated reference to a book and chapter of the Bible, an indexing letter in red, the opening words of a reading, '*ende*' in red, the closing words of a reading and double strokes. Commemorations are in the following order Our Lady, Trinity, the Holy Ghost, cross, angels, '*ffor briþeren and sistren and for salus populi*', peace, clear weather, rain, '*In tyme of bateils*', '*for him silf*', '*ffor pestilence of beestis*', '*for weifering and pilgrimis*', weddings, dead, sick and sinners. Readings omitted by the original scribe are added in the margins in a contemporary hand.

[item 2 occupies quires III–XXXII]

2. (fols. 13r–254r) NT in LV, with James and 1 Peter in EV. Contains the usual prologues, apart from the prologue to James that is not included. James is also the only book that does not have a penwork border (see Decoration). Usual rubrics, e.g., '*Here endiþ þe gospel of mathu & bigynniþ þe prolog on mark*', '*þis seiþ Ierom in his prolog on mark & bigynniþ þe gospel of mark*' (fols. 45v–46r). John ends on fol. 125rb and the rest of the second column on this leaf is left blank; Romans continues on fol. 125v. Running titles on both rectos and versos consisting of abbreviated titles of books in red. Chapter numbers as Roman numerals preceded by blue paraphs. Many corrections in the original or contemporary hands. Indexing letters in the margins entered at the beginnings of lections rather than consistently; the ends of lections are marked with double strokes in the margins. Red paraphs mark sections within the text, often the beginnings of lections. The beginnings and ends of lections are also highlighted with yellow wash.

Added material within the text is occasionally underlined in red. No glosses in the margins with rare exceptions (e.g., fol. 154r). Pointing hand at '*Blessid be pore men in spiryt...*' (Matthew 5, fol. 6v).

Decoration

3- to 5-line blue initials with red penwork and one-sided penwork borders at the beginnings of books.

2-line blue initials with red penwork at the beginnings on prologues and chapters.

Dialect

oni(10), ech(10), fier(10), ȝoue(1)/ȝouun(9), lif(10), lik(10), miche(10), sai(9) (sg.), saien(6) (pl.), silf(10), sich(3)/siche(5)/suche(1), þouȝ(8), þoruȝ(10)

-iþ(8)/-eþ(2) (pres.ind.3sg.), -en(10) (pres.ind.pl.), -inge(5)/-ynge(5) (pres. part.), she(10) (3sg.fem.pronoun, nom.), þei(10) (3pl.pronoun, nom.), hem(10) (3pl.pronoun, oblique), her(4)/here(6) (3pl.pronoun, possessive)

Physical description

MATERIAL: poor quality parchment with holes and repairs, paper flyleaves

DIMENSIONS: *c.*182 × 130 mm; leaves were trimmed in rebinding, occasionally causing the loss of text and decoration in the margins

NUMBER OF LEAVES: 258

FOLIATION: modern in pencil, 1–258

COLLATION: (fols. 1–2) paper flyleaves | (fols. 3–8) I (6) | (fols. 9–10) II (4) | (fols. 11–244) III–XXXI (8) | (fols. 245–256) XXXII (12) | (fols. 257–258) paper flyleaves.

Catchwords survive; quire signatures run consistently starting on fol. 11 (the beginning of Matthew): a–z, &, (con-), a–e

RULING: ruled for two columns, with single vertical and horizontal bounding lines extending the full height and width of page; another set of double bounding lines in all margins; 33 lines per page; written space: *c.*135 × 87 mm

SCRIPT: textura, brown ink

RUBRICATION: rubrics in red ink

SEC. FOL.: '*mt .ij.*' (fol. 4r)

Binding

Worn dark leather over pasteboard, 17th century (?), with an added (?) 18th-century (?) blind roll border round the outer edge of both covers. Rebacked with the original spine relaid. Red label on spine with gilt fillet-line border and gilt lettering 'TINDALL'S || TRANSLATION || OF N. TEST. MS.'. The label was added in Brasenose College (other college manuscripts have a similar label, e.g., Brasenose College MS f. 2 and Brasenose College MS f. 3). Brasenose paper label on spine with 'MS || Brasenose Coll. || E 10'. Flyleaves of laid paper with watermark (unicorn standing on a cartouche with letters 'FD'). Similar watermarks in Briquet (1907), nos 10313–10346, date from 1496–1600, most from the second half of the 16th century. Edges of textblock speckled red (18th-century addition (?)).

Provenance

1. Mixed EV and LV text, poor quality parchment, modest decoration.

2. Erased, presumably medieval, ownership inscription on fol. 256v: '*L[iber] (?)…[de](?)…*'.

3. Sixteenth-century (?) owner interested in Eucharist. Notes in the margin, partially cropped off and therefore predating the present binding: '*Institucion … [o]f Christe*' (fol. 41v, next to a description of Eucharist at the Last Supper in Matthew 26), '*…he Supper [o]f ye lorde*' (fol. 95v, next to '*where I shal eete pask with my disciplis*' in a description of the Last Supper in Luke 22). Verse numbers added on fols. 13v–19r in an early modern hand.

4. Translation of Thomas Becket erased, presumably at Reformation.

5. Seventeenth-century binding, possibly altered in the 18th century.

6. Edward Hill (1589–1669), Vicar of Huddersfield, Yorkshire, from 2 September 1619, see Dale (1910), pp. 76–7. Listed by Baines (1871), vol. 2, p. 433, as the only vicar with this name. Foster (1887–88) records an entry for his son: 'Hill, John – s. Edward, of Huddersfield, Yorks, sacerd. Brasenose Coll., matric. 16 Oct., 1635, aged 16; perhaps B.A. from Gloucester Hall 18 June, 1639'.

7. Brasenose College: given by Edward Hill, presumably after 1635, when his son entered Brasenose. '*Liber Aulæ Regiæ & Collegij de Brasenose. Ex dono Edvardi Hill Vicarij de Huddersfield in Comitat' Ebor:*' (fol. 2r), 17th century, added in Brasenose (other college manuscripts have donors recorded on flyleaves in Latin in a similar way). Bookplate with Brasenose arms on the upper pastedown. Fragments of an earlier paper bookplate on the upper pastedown with 'T'(?) at the end of a line (Brasenose bookplate of a different

design (?)). 'Will: Tindalls translation' on fol. 1r, 17th century, probably added in Brasenose (other college manuscripts have similar descriptions of contents on flyleaves). Brasenose shelfmarks: 'X' (upper pastedown); 'J. 2. 15' (fol. 1r and edge of textblock); 'East Closet 1.' (fol. 1r). Not listed in Bernard's catalogue of 1697 which may not have been exhaustive.

Bibliography

Bernard, E., *Catalogi librorum manuscriptorum Angliae et Hiberniae in unum collecti cum indice alphabetico* (Oxford, 1697).

Forshall and Madden (1850), vol. 1, p. li.

Coxe (1852), vol. 2, *Catalogus codicum MSS. Collegii Aenei Nasi*, pp. 2–3.

Baines, T., *Yorkshire, past and present: a history and a description of the three ridings of the great county of York, from the earliest ages to the year 1870*, 2 vols (London: W. Mackenzie, 1871).

Dale, B., *Yorkshire puritanism and early nonconformity, illustrated by the lives of the ejected ministers* (Bradford, 1910).

Ogilvie-Thomson, S. J., *IMEP*, Handlist VIII (1991), p. 15.

Dove (2007), p. 301.

48 Christ Church MS 145

Siglum: *X*

Origin: England

Date: 14th century, end

Text

Fols. i–ii are a letter from Josiah Forshall, 14 July, thanking the College for loan of the manuscript for collation.

[item 1 occupies quire I]

1. (fols. 1r–9r) Table of lections of Type I in a different, slightly later hand than the biblical text, preceded by a rubric: '*[H]ere begynneth a Rule that tellith in whiche Chapiters of the Bible ye may fynde the Lessouns pistelis. & Gospell' that ben red in the chirche aftir the vse of Salisbury markid with lettris of the abcde. at the begynnyng of the chapiters. & toward the middis or the eende aftir the ordre as the lettris stonden in the. a. b. c. ffirst ben sett sondaies & ferials to gydre & after that the sanctorum the propre & the Comoun to gidre of al the yere. And then folowith the Commemoracouns & that is callid the Temperal of the yeer. ffirst is written a clause of the bigynnyng of the Pistil*

&. Gospel. & a clause of þe ending þerof'. The entries consist of the name of a liturgical occasion in red, abbreviated reference to a book and chapter of the Bible, an indexing letter in red, the opening words of a reading, '*ende*' in red, the closing words of a reading and double strokes in black. Part of the temporal (Friday after II Sunday after Christmas–Wednesday after III Sunday in Lent) and sanctoral (Felix and Adactus–Four Crowned Martyrs) are missing because of the loss of one bifolium (after fols. 1r and 7r). Includes the temporal, sanctoral (the proper and common together according to the rubric but only proper is included) and commemorations. Commemorations are in the following order: Our Lady, Trinity, Holy Ghost, Cross, angels, brothers and sisters and '*saluacioun of the peple*', peace, clear weather, '*reyn & tempest*', '*In tyme of batailis*', '*A man for him self*', '*petilens* [sic] *of beestis*', pilgrims, weddings, sinners, sick and deed. Includes all feasts characteristic of LV (Forshall and Madden (1850), vol. 4, pp. 683, 690–6). A half-hearted attempt is made to erase the titles 'pope'. St Thomas, apostle, in December is also erased, presumably by mistake. Most of fol. 9r is blank and only the top is ruled; fol. 9v is blank.

[items 2–3 occupies quires II–XLVIII]
2. (fol. 10r–385r) ONT in EV with usual prologues, apart from the prologues to Romans–Apocalypse that are not included. 2 Ezra has a running title '*Neemie*'. Epistle to Ephesians follows 2 Thessalonians (fol. 358v); Catholic epistles (James–Jude) precede Acts (fol. 365r). Rubrics indicate speakers in the Song of Songs.

No rubrics, though spaces appear to have been left for them at the beginnings of some books and prologues. Running titles in Latin (the only identification of books in the absence of rubrics) in alternating red and blue capitals across the openings, consisting of abbreviated titles of books only. The titles are also written in black, in the hand of the main scribe, in the upper right margin on the versos and often also on the rectos, presumably as an instruction to the rubricator, though some such titles at the beginning of the volume also contain an indication of the subject matter, e.g., '*noe*', '*abraham*', '*loth*' (fol. 14r–v). Chapter numbers in alternating red and blue Roman numerals; instructions to the rubricator in black ink in Arabic numerals in the hand of the scribe. A few marginal glosses in OT. Added material within the text is very occasionally underlined in red (e.g., fol. 33r). The beginnings of verses are highlighted in red. Corrections in a contemporary hand in the margins (see Lindberg (1973), pp. 48–51). 'Hedera' signs in the margins, possibly indicating an intention to include a gloss (they also precede glosses in psalms).

Psalms begin with a rubric '*þe book bygynneth of ympnes and solitarie speeches of þe profete dauyd*' and are laid out as prose with verses starting with alternating red or blue 1-line initials. Psalms are preceded by titles and Latin incipits in red, and numbers in alternating red and blue Roman numerals as well as Arabic numerals in black in the hand of the scribe. Glosses in a different contemporary hand occasionally appear in the margins, preceded by a rubric '*a glos*'. The majority of glosses are at the beginning of the psalter; there are no glosses after psalm 101. The names of Hebrew letters in red at the beginning of sections of psalm 118 and Lamentations of Jeremiah. The second column on fol. 385r is left blank.

3. (fol. 385v) Added list of OT books with their chapter totals, 15th century, second half. At the end '*The noumbir of bokis of the owlde lawe 47*'. Followed by a similar list of NT books from Matthew to Galatians. Fol. 386 is blank, apart from an erased early modern inscription.

Decoration

Pink and blue initial on gold background with tooling and three-quarters border made of gold, blue and pink bars, decorated with sprays of leaves and gold disks, at the beginning of the prologue to the Bible (fol. 10r).

3- to 17-line red and blue 'puzzle' initials with red and purple penwork, or blue initials with red penwork at the beginnings of books.

2-line blue initials with red penwork at the beginnings of prologues and chapters, some with anthropomorphic designs (e.g., fol. 26v, 35v, 43v, 45v, 47r, 50, etc.).

Dialect

eny(10), eche(10), fier(10), ȝouen(4)/ȝoue(5)/ȝiuen(1), lyf(9)/lif(1), lic(4)/lich(1)/lych(1)/lyk(2)/lik(2), myche(9)/miche(1), saȝ(9) (sg.), seȝen(8) (pl.), self(10), such(2)/suche(8), þoȝ(3), þurȝ(10)

-iþ(1)/eþ(9) (pres.ind.3sg.), -en(9)/-e(1) (pres.ind.pl.), -ende(10) (pres.part.), she(10) (3sg.fem.pronoun, nom.), þei(10) (3pl.pronoun, nom.), hem(9)/þem(1) (3pl.pronoun, oblique), her(9)/þer(1) (3pl.pronoun, possessive)

Infinitives retain -n (*don, bern, stoneyn, dreden*), 'k' is used frequently for 'c' (*kumpas, kuntre*), past tenses *kneȝ, bleȝ* ('knew', 'blew'); *oen, anoen, droeue* ('one', 'anon', 'drove'); *loeues, coestis, coet* ('loaves', 'coasts', 'coat'); *wiche* ('which'), *wrd* ('word'), *wrþi* ('worthy'), *f*[o] ('from') (see Forshall and Madden (1850); Lindberg (1959–97), vol. 6 (1973), pp. 8–31).

Physical description

MATERIAL: parchment

DIMENSIONS: *c.*387 × 265 mm; leaves were trimmed in rebinding occasionally causing the loss of decoration

NUMBER OF LEAVES: 390

FOLIATION: modern in pencil: i–iv + 1–387 (fol. 387 is the lower pastedown)

COLLATION: (fols. i–iii) paper and parchment flyleaves | (fols. iv–9) I (10) | (fols. 10–385) II–XLVIII (8)

Catchwords survive; starting with quire XIV (fol. 114) they appear not only at the end but also in the first part of the quire and sometimes throughout the quire. Quire signatures occasionally survive.

RULING: ruled for two columns with single vertical and horizontal bounding lines extending the full height and width of page; 58 lines per page; written space: *c.*260 × 180 mm

SCRIPT: textura, black ink; the table of lections is in a different, slightly later hand than the biblical text

RUBRICATION: rubrics in red ink

SEC. FOL.: '*wilneþ to speken*' (fol. 11r)

Binding

Brown leather over wood boards, 15th century. Sewn on six thongs, six raised bands on spine. Recesses and nailholes left by the fittings of two straps (now missing) on the upper cover; marks left by the fittings of two clasps at the centre of the lower cover. Marks from a large chain staple on the upper cover. Paper label on spine with handwritten '145'; fragments of other paper labels. Parchment pastedowns and flyleaves. See also Hanna, *Catalogue.*

Provenance

1. 'A good representative of EV in its earlier stages', has 'numerous minor variations, due either to prototypes (Latin and/or English) or to revision and copying' (Lindberg (1959–97), vol. 6 (1973), p. 47); 'the most conservative text of the Earlier Version, with the fewest textual glosses and with some extreme literalisms' (Dove (2004), p. 143).

2. Titles 'pope' erased in the table of lections, presumably at Reformation.

3. Inscriptions in 16th-century hands: '*Francis*' (fol. 119r); '*By me Beniamen*' (fol. 182v, in the margin of psalm 68); Latin quotation (fol. iii verso):

> *Non est migi vita vtilior quam animi talis affectio*
> *Neminem vt violem commodi mei gratia* (Cicero, *De Officiis*, Lib. 3, Cap. vi).

4. 'Price '*præciu(m) -3-6-8*', lower pastedown, 16th century (?).

5. Robert Claye, vicar of Flore (Flower), Northamptonshire.

6. Edward Saunders of Flore (Flower), Northamptonshire, given by Claye in 1575: '*Anno domini || 1575 || Eduarde Saunders off flower || 1575 || The twenteth daye of Maye beinge in the || yere of our Lorde god 1575 and in the sevententhe yere \of the raigne/ of our most gracious soueraigne || Ladye Quene Elizabeth On Robert || Claye then vycar of Flower in the countye || of Northampton did geve this Byble vnto || me Edwarde Saunders of the same parishe and countye*' (upper pastedown). His signature and date 1575 also appear on fols. iii verso, 1r, and the lower pastedown with his motto '*Solatur conscientia et finis*'. Erased inscription on fol. 386r is probably also his signature.

7. Saunders's son, Edward (Foster, 1891–92, p. 1314), MA (Christ Church) 1586, rector of Greens Norton, Northamptonshire, d. 1631. Signed '*Edward Saunders of fflower*' (fol. iv verso).

8. Christ Church, given by Saunders: '*Liber Ecclesiæ Christi ex dono Edouardi Saunders Armigeri de Flower in Com: Northamptoniae*' (fol. 1r). Christ Church bookplate on the upper pastedown; earlier shelfmarks: 'E .4.' (upper pastedown, fol. iii recto), 'D. 1' (fol. iii verso).

Bibliography

Forshall and Madden (1850), vol. 1, p. li.

Kitchin, G. W., *Catalogus codicum mss. qui in bibliotheca Ædis Christi apud Oxonienses adservantur* (Oxford: Clarendon Press, 1867), p. 50.

Fristedt (1953–73), vol. 1, pp. 107–14.

Lindberg (1959–97), vol. 6 (1973), pp. 7–72.

Hudson (1978), p. 164.

Alexander, J. J. G. and Temple, E., *Illuminated manuscripts in Oxford College libraries, the University Archives and the Taylor Institution* (Oxford: Clarendon Press, 1985), p. 44, no. 439.

Ogilvie-Thomson, S. J., *IMEP*, Handlist VIII (1991), p. 16.

Gibson, M. T., *The Bible in the Latin West* (Notre Dame, Ind; London: University of Notre Dame, 1993), p. 74.

Dove (2007), pp. 17, 65, 87, 88, 105, 137, 138, 142, 143–5, 146, 151, 153–4, 172, 177, 196, 199, 207, 209, 218, 232, 259–60, 301.

Hanna, R. (using materials collected by Jeremy J. Griffiths), *A descriptive catalogue of the medieval manuscripts in Roman scripts of Christ Church, Oxford* (http://www.chch.ox.ac.uk/library/western-manuscripts).

49 MS Christ Church 146

Origin: England

Date: 15th century, first quarter

Text

[item 1 occupies quire I]

1. (fols. 1r–10r) Table of lections of Type I, preceded by a rubric: '*Here bigynneþ a reule þat telliþ in whiche chapiters of þe bible ȝe may fynde þe lessouns pistlis & gospels þat ben red in þe chirche at masse after þe vse of salisbirie markid wiþ lettris of þe a b c at þe begynnyng of þe chapitris toward þe midil or eende afir þe ordir as þe lettris stonden in þe a b c first ben sette sonedaies & ferials to gidere & after þe sanctorum comyn & propre to gidere of alle þe ȝeer first writen a clause of þe bigynnyng þer of & a clause of þe ending þer of also*'. The entries consist of the name of the liturgical occasion in red, abbreviated reference to a book and chapter of the Bible, an indexing letter in red, the opening words of a reading, '*ende*' in red, the closing words of a reading and double strokes in red. Running titles in red. Includes the temporal, followed by commemorations and the sanctoral. Includes all feasts characteristic of LV, apart from Giles (1 September) (Forshall and Madden (1850), vol. 4, pp. 683, 690–6). Blue initials at Andrew's Eve and Day, Nicholas, Conception of our Lady, Thomas the Apostle, Conversion of St Paul, Candlemas, Matthias the Apostle, Annunciation, Philip and Jacob, the Invention of the Cross, Nativity of John the Baptist, Peter and Paul, Translation of Thomas Becket, Mary Magdalene, James the Apostle, Lawrence, Assumption, Bartholomew, Nativity of Our Lady, Exaltation of the Holy Cross, Mathew the Apostle, Michael Archangel, Simon and Jude and Halloween. Commemorations are in the following order: Our Lady, Trinity, Holy Ghost, Cross, angels, brothers and sisters and '*salus populi*', peace, clear weather, rain, '*in tyme of batels*', '*A man ffor him silf*', '*ffor pestilence of bestes*', pilgrims, weddings, sinners, sick and dead. Fol. 10v is ruled for the table of lections but blank.

[items 2–4 occupy quires II–XX]

2. (fols. 11r–200v) NT in LV with usual prologues. Usual rubrics in red, e.g., '*Here bigynneþ þe prolog of M*[t]', '*Jerom in hise tweyn prologiis on mathewe seiþ playnli þus. Here bigynneþ þe firste chapitre of mathewe*' (fol. 11r). In spite of the rubric only one prologue to Matthew is included. Running titles in black highlighted in red, on both rectos and versos, consisting of abbreviated titles of books and chapter numbers on leaves containing the beginnings of chapters. Chapter numbers in red as words in English or

Roman numerals. No marginal glosses, added material within the text is not underlined. Many corrections in the original or contemporary hands. Indexing letters entered in the margins at the beginnings of readings, rather than consistently; double strokes at the ends of readings. Blue paraphs at the beginnings of sections within the text, including readings.

3. (fols. 200v–231v) OT lectionary of Type II starting with a rubric: '*Here bigynnen þe lessouns and pistlis of þe oold lawe þat ben rad in þe chirche bi alle þe ȝeer þe firste friday lessoun in aduent*'. Includes the temporal, proper (lessons for the feast of Alban; the translation of Martin; and the feasts of Nicholas, Cyriac and Hugh), common and commemorations. The readings are preceded by rubrics and intruductory statements such as '*The lord god seiþ þes þingis*'. A rubric at Christmas explains that the lesson is sung by two voices, and the part of one of the voices is underlined. Indexing letters at the beginnings of lections. Added material within the text is underlined in red.

4. (fols. 231v–238v) *Capitula*-list for NT with a rubric: '*Here bigynneþ a table of certeyne maters of þe newe testament tellynge in what bokes & in what chapiters of þe bokes þei stonden*'. Rubrics and 3-line initials at the beginning of entries for each biblical book, chapter numbers in red Roman numerals. Matters for Philemon are not included. The end of the first column and the second column on fol. 238v are left blank. Fols. 239–242 are parchment flyleaves (see Provenance).

Decoration

4- to 6-line gold initials (some rubbed off) with dark blue penwork at the beginnings of books.

2-line blue initials with red penwork at the beginnings of prologues and chapters. Some initials have anthropomorphic decoration (e.g., fols. 142v, 200v).

Dialect

ony(9)/eny(1), iche(1)/ich(2)/ech(7), fier(10), ȝouon(10), lijf(10), lijk(10), myche(7)/mych(3), say(3)/sai(1)/saie(1)/sey(1) (sg.), saien(2)/sayen(4) (pl.), seluen(10), suche(7)/sich(1)/siche(1), þouȝ(7)/þouȝe(1), þorouȝ(8)/þorouȝe(2)

-iþ(9)/-eþ(1) (pres.ind.3sg.), -en(10) (pres.ind.pl.), -ynge(4)/-inge(3)/-ing(1)/ -inge(1) (pres.part.), sche(10) (3sg.fem.pronoun, nom.), þei(10) (3pl. pronoun, nom.), hem(10) (3pl.pronoun, oblique), her(10) (3pl.pronoun, possessive)

Physical description

MATERIAL: parchment

DIMENSIONS: *c.*197 × 125 mm

NUMBER OF LEAVES: 146

FOLIATION: modern in pencil: i–iv + 1–142

COLLATION: (fol. i–iv) parchment flyleaves | (fols. 1–10) I (10) | (fols. 11–238) II–XX (12)

Catchwords in red frames with penwork decoration. Quire signatures partially survive and run consecutively a–t.

RULING: ruled for two columns with single vertical and double horizontal bounding lines extending the full height and width of page; prickings often survive; 41 lines per page; written space: *c.*143 × 90–95 mm

SCRIPT: small textura, black ink

RUBRICATION: rubrics in red ink

SEC. FOL.: '*& axe ȝe*' (Matthew, fol. 12r)

Binding

Brown blind stamped leather over wood boards, 16th century, rebacked. Sown on five thongs. Two decorated brass straps on the upper cover and two clasps on the lower cover.

Provenance

1. Differences in the presentation of NT and OT texts: added material is underlined in OT lections only.

2. Inscriptions and pen trials in 16th-century hands, including '*To his frynde*' (fol. 242r), '*Thomas mar[...]*', '*John har*' (lower pastedown).

3. Thomas Ballowe (Foster, 1891–92), Christ Church, BA 1624, MA 1629, DD 1661: '*Liber Ædis Christi, ex dono Thomæ Ballowe, Artium Magistri, et eiusdem Collegij Studentis*', followed by a date in a different hand 'Octob. 21°. 1629°.'.

4. Christ Church: book plate on the upper pastedown; given by Ballowe. Earlier shelfmarks: 'A. 12.', 'G. 10' (upper pastedown)

Bibliography

Forshall and Madden (1850), vol. 1, p. li.

Kitchin, G. W., *Catalogus codicum mss. qui in bibliotheca Ædis Christi apud Oxonienses adservantur* (Oxford: Clarendon Press, 1867), p. 50.
Alexander, J. J. G. and Temple, E., *Illuminated manuscripts in Oxford College libraries, the University Archives and the Taylor Institution* (Oxford: Clarendon Press, 1985), p. 44.
Ogilvie-Thomson, S. J., *IMEP*, Handlist VIII (1991), pp. 16–17.
Dove (2007), pp. 301–2.
Hanna, R. (using materials collected by Jeremy J. Griffiths), *A descriptive catalogue of the medieval manuscripts in Roman scripts of Christ Church, Oxford* (http://www.chch.ox.ac.uk/library/western-manuscripts).

50 MS Christ Church 147

Origin: England

Date: 15th century, first quarter

Text

1. (fols. 1r–155r) Galatians–Hebrews in LV with usual prologues. Hebrews starts on a new quire (fol. 112r), a catchword is missing on the previous page and a new series of leaf signatures appears to start at this point. Usual rubrics in red, e.g., '*Heere biginneþ þe prolog on þe pistel to galathies*'; '*Ierom in his prolog on þe pistil to galaþies seiþ þis*' (fol. 1r). Running titles in black, on both rectos and versos, consisting of the titles of books only. Chapter numbers in red, usually as Roman numerals. No marginal glosses; lections are not marked; added material within the text is occasionally underlined in red or black. Red and blue paraphs at the beginning of sections within the text. Fol. 155r contains a single line of text, the rest is ruled but blank.

2. (fols. 155v–157r) Originally ruled but blank leaves, containing texts added in the second half of the 15th century in an apparently unprofessional hand imitating textura:

(a) Proverbs 1:1–6 in LV, breaking off in the middle of a verse (fol. 155v).

(b) Medical recipe and a note: '*if þou haue þe crike take þine owne water …*'; '*wytte haþ wondir þer resoun tele cane …*' (fol. 156v)

(c) Non-Wycliffite translation of John 1:1–5: '*In þe be gennyng woas þe word and þe word wos at god þis was in þe be genyng at god all þingus was made bi him and wyþ outun him is made no þing þat þing þat is in him is lyue and þe liue is þe liȝt of men liȝt is þe*' (fol. 157r).

Decoration

2- to 3-line red and blue 'puzzle' initials and blue initials with red penwork at the beginnings of books.

2-line blue initials with red penwork at the beginnings of prologues and chapters. Initial on fol. 39v has anthropomorphic decoration. Initials at the beginnings of verses are decorated with red penwork.

Dialect

ony(2)/eny(8), eche(10), fijr(1), ȝouen(8)/ȝeuen(2), lijf(10), lijk(2), moche(9)/muche(1), say(2) (sg.), sayȝen(3)/sayen(1) (pl.), silf(7)/self(3), suche(5), þauȝ(2)/þouȝ(1), þorow(5)

-iþ(3)/-eþ(6)/-uþ(2) (pres.ind.3sg.), -en(9)/-un(1) (pres.ind.pl.), -ynge(10) (pres.part.), she(9) (3sg.fem.pronoun, nom.), þei(10) (3pl.pronoun, nom.), hem(10) (3pl.pronoun, oblique), here(10) (3pl.pronoun, possessive)

Physical description

MATERIAL: parchment

DIMENSIONS: *c.*195 × 130 mm

NUMBER OF LEAVES: 157

FOLIATION: modern in pencil, 1–157

COLLATION: (fols. 1–8) I (8) the third bifolium is misbound, fol. 2 should follow 3 and fol. 6 should follow 7 | (9–56) II–VII (8) | (fols. 57–63) VIII (8–1) missing 3, no loss of text | (fols. 64–151) IX–XIX (8) | (fols. 152–157) XX (6)

Catchwords on decorative scrolls. Quire signatures partially survive, running a–f (fols. 1–48), unclear on fols. 49–56, k–q (fols. 57–111); there may be a new sequence on fols. 112–end.

RULING: ruled for a single column, with single vertical and horizontal bounding lines extending the full height and width of page; 25–16 lines per page; written space: *c.*125–131 × 83 mm

SCRIPT: large textura, black ink

SEC. FOL.: '*me fro my*' (fol. 2r)

Binding

White leather over wood boards, 15th century. Sewn on five thongs. Three metal staples over a depression on the edge of the upper board to affix a strap, but no remains of its clasp on the lower board. Paper label on spine with handwritten '147'. Fragments of another paper label at the top of the spine.

Provenance

1. Notes in a 17th-century hand concerning a misbound bifolium in the first quire (fol. 5v); glosses translating difficult words (e.g., 'clepid' as 'called') on fols. 1v, 22r, 157v and the turn-in of the lower cover.

2. Date 'mdcxvi' in pencil (fol. 157v).

3. Christ Church Cathedral: '*Liber Cathedralis Eclesiæ Christi Oxon*', 17th century (fol. 157v).

4. Christ Church book plate on the upper pastedown and earlier shelfmarks: 'A.8', 'G. 12' (inside the upper cover).

Bibliography

Forshall and Madden (1850), vol. 1, p. li.
Kitchin, G. W., *Catalogus codicum mss. qui in bibliotheca Ædis Christi apud Oxonienses adservantur* (Oxford: Clarendon Press, 1867), p. 50.
Dove (2007), p. 302.
Hanna, R. (using materials collected by Jeremy J. Griffiths), *A descriptive catalogue of the medieval manuscripts in Roman scripts of Christ Church, Oxford* (http://www.chch.ox.ac.uk/library/western-manuscripts).

51 Corpus Christi College MS 4

Siglum: *A*

Origin: England

Date: 15th century, first quarter

Text

Fols. i–ii are originally blank parchment flyleaves (see Provenance).

[items 1–2 occupy quire I]
1. (fols. 1r–6r) Table of lections of Type II without a rubric. Includes the temporal, proper, common and commemorations. The entries consist of a liturgical occasion in red, abbreviated reference to a book and chapter of the Bible, an indexing letter in red, the opening words of a reading, '*ende*' in red and the closing words of a reading. The proper is short, and

includes, apart from the biblical saints, Nicholas, George, the Translation of Martin, Seven Brothers, Abdon, Cyriac and his fellows, the Eve, Day and Octave of Lawrence, Denis and Clement. Penwork initials at Epiphany, Easter, Ascension, Pentecost, Trinity, Corpus Christi, Candlemas, John the Baptist, Assumption, Nativity of our Lady and All Saints. Does not include Wednesday after the 25th Sunday after Trinity and the feast of the relics. Commemorations are in the following order: Trinity, Holy Ghost, cross, Our Lady, '*ffor breþeren & sisters & good doers*', peace, clear weather, rain, '*ffor batel & pestilence*', angels, '*A prest for hym seif*', '*ffor pestilence of beestis*', '*ffor weie ferynge men*', '*ffor oure synnes*', sick, weddings, pilgrims and dead. The feast of Thomas Becket in December is erased.

2. (fol. 6v) A list of OT and NT books in English, in the hand of the original scribe, in the usual order, with a rubric '*þese be þe names of þe bokis of þe bible*'. NT has a further rubric '*þese ben þe names of þe bokis of þe newe lawe*'. Includes 1 and 2 Ezra only, followed by Tobit; '*Corynth*'' presumably represents both 1 and 2 Corinthians, and '*Tessalonicences*' both 1 and 2 Thessalonians. Genesis–Deuteronomy are joined by a bracket with a heading '*v bokis of moyses lawe*', Proverbs–Ecclesiasticus with a heading '*Salomon*', Matthew–John with a heading '*iiij euang*'', Romans–Hebrews with a heading '*Paul*'.

[item 3 occupies quires II–XLIX]
3. (fols. 7r–386v) ONT in EV with Jerome's prefatory epistles, '*Broþer ambrose to me…*' and '*I haue takun desired epistlis…*', and usual prologues. Includes a second prologue to Job, '*Forsoþe if I shulde make a iounket…*'. No prologues in NT. The prologue to Joshua '*At þe last endid þe fyue…*' is preceded by a rubric '*Here endiþ þe book of deuteronomi And nowe bigyneþ þe prolog of iosue & of iudicum & of ruth*' (fol. 68r); the prologue to 1 Kings is preceded by a rubric '*Here bigynneþ þe prolog of þe foure bokis of kyngis*' (fol. 84v). The following rubrics occur at other prologues: '*Here endiþ þe fourþ book of kyngis and now bigynneþ þe prolog of twey bookis of paralipomenon*' (the first prologue to 1 Chronicles, fol. 124r); '*Here eendiþ þe first book of paralipomenon and now bigynneþ þe proloog of þe secounde book*' (prologue to 2 Chronicles, fol. 133v); '*þe proloog of þe þree bookis of esdre*' (the first prologue to 1 Ezra, fol. 145r); '*Here begynneþ þe proloog in þe book of ecclesiastes þat is to seye þe book of talker to þe puple or to gidre cleper*' (prologue to Ecclesiastes). The prayer of Manasseh follows chapter 36 of 2 Chronicles without a break; a rubric '*þis preyer of manasses not in ebrew*' is in black and not underlined (fol. 145r).

Running titles in red (not in psalms), on both rectos and versos, consisting of abbreviated titles of books only. In NT starting with fol. 343r running titles are in black, most underlined in red. Rubrics in red (in NT often in black underlined in red), e.g., '*Here endiþ genesis and now bigynne exodus*' (fol. 24r). The prefatory epistles have no rubrics. Chapter numbers in red as Roman numerals and in the margins in black by the scribe. Alternating red and blue paragaphs at the start of sections within the text on fols. 7r–30r and in NT; only occasionally elsewhere in OT. Added material within the text is consistently underlined in red or black starting with Baruch 3 and until the end of NT; before Baruch 3 it is underlined only very rarely (the first underlining occurs at 2 Kings 24:25, fol. 104r). Corrections in the margins and over erasures in the text in the original or contemporary hands. Names of Hebrew letters in red in Proverbs 31 and Lamentations of Jeremiah. Speakers identified in red in the Song of Song. No marginal glosses in the original hand with very few exceptions. Added glosses '*of images*' in the margins Deuteronomy 7, 8, 13, 27; Wisdom 13, 15; Isaiah 40, 44; Jeremiah 8, 10; Baruch 6; Ezekiel 7, 14, 16, 20; Micah 5; and Habakkuk 2. Added glosses '*of idols*' in the margins of Isaiah 1, 2; Jeremiah 32; and Ezekiel 18 in the same 15th-century hand. Latin incipits of passages occasionally written out in the margins in the original or contemporary hand, some at the beginnings of lections, e.g., '*ab initio & ante secula*' (fol. 222v) at the start of the reading for the Eve of the Assumption (Ecclesiasticus 24) and commemorations of Our Lady. Occasionally cross-references to other books of the Bible and '*nota*' in the margins in the original hand. Rubrics concerning the differences between the Latin and Hebrew texts in Daniel.

Psalms are preceded with a rubric '*The boob* [sic] *bygynneth of ympnys and solitarie spechis of dauyd þe profete of crist*' and begin with 3-line initials. Laid out with verses starting on a new line with alternating red or blue 1-line initials. Decorative line endings in red and blue ink. The psalms are preceded by titles in red, Latin incipits in black, underlined in red, and numbers in red or black Roman or Arabic numerals. The Latin incipits are longer than usual, sometimes comprising a whole verse and are written out as part of the text, rather than in the margins; the psalm numbers are in the margins. The initials are those of the Latin text. There are larger 'puzzle' initials and penwork borders at psalms 26, 38, 52, 68, 80, 97, 109. The names of Hebrew letters in red are at the beginnings of sections of psalm 118. Psalms 119–132 have a rubric '*þe songe of grees*'.

OT ends on fol. 310v where the end of the first column and the second column are left blank; the NT starts on a new leaf of a new quire and ends in the middle of the first column on fol. 386v; the rest of this folio was originally blank (see Provenance). At the end: '*Here endiþ apocalips*'. Fols. 387–8 are ruled, but originally blank (see Provenance).

Decoration

7- to 9-line red and blue 'puzzle' initials decorated with penwork and red, and blue and purple penwork borders at the beginnings of books.

3-line blue initials with red penwork at the beginnings of prologues and chapters.

Dialect

Exodus, Psalms, Isaiah
eny(10), ech(4)/eche(6), fier(9)/fyer(1), ȝouun(5)/ȝouen(1)/ȝeuen(3)/ȝeue(1), lijf(10), lijk(5)/lyik(1)/liyk(2)/like(1)/liic(1), myche(10), sawȝ(9)/seeȝ(1) (sg.), seen(5)/seyn(1) (pl.), self(3)/silf(5)/seluen(2), siche(1), þurȝ(10)

-iþ(5)/eþ(5) (pres.ind.3sg.), -en(10) (pres.ind.pl.), -ynge(10) (pres.part.), she(10) (3sg.fem.pronoun, nom.), þei(10) (3pl.pronoun, nom.), hem(10) (3pl.pronoun, oblique), her(10) (3pl.pronoun, possessive)

Also *slewȝ* 'slew', *snowȝ* 'snow', *ȝow* 'you'.

Matthew
any(1)/ony(9), ech(8)/eche(2), fier(10), ȝouun(10), lijf(8)/lyif(1)/lif(1), lijk(4)/like(1)/liche(5), myche(9)/miche(1), say(5)/saie(1) (sg.), saien(5) (pl.), silf(10), such(1)/suche(4)/sich(2)/siche(2), þouȝ(2)/þowȝ(1), þurȝ(2)/þuruȝ(1)/þuroȝ(1)/þurou(4)/þurow(1)

-iþ(5)/eþ(5) (pres.ind.3sg.), -en(10) (pres.ind.pl.), -ynge(9)/-inge(1) (pres.part.), she(9)/sche(1) (3sg.fem.pronoun, nom.), þei(10) (3pl.pronoun, nom.), hem(10) (3pl.pronoun, oblique), her(10) (3pl.pronoun, possessive)

Also *knew(e)* 'knew', *ȝou* 'you', *narouȝ* 'narrow'.

Physical description

MATERIAL: parchment

DIMENSIONS: *c.*440 × 300 mm; 130 mm thick; leaves were trimmed in rebinding occasionally causing the loss of decoration

NUMBER OF LEAVES: 390

FOLIATION: modern in pencil: i–ii + 1–388

COLLATION: (fols. i–ii) paper and parchment flyleaves | (fols. 1) I (6) | (fols. 7–382) II–XLVIII (8) | (fols. 383-lower pastedown) XLIX (8–1(?)) the 7th leaf is the lower pastedown, the 8th leaf cancelled

Catchwords survive; quire signatures often survive and run consecutively a–z + ? + I + aa-nn; a new series starts in NT (fol. 311), [a]-k.

RULING: ruled for two columns, with single vertical and horizontal bounding lines extending the full height and width of page; 59–60 lines per page; written space: *c.*315 × 205 mm

SCRIPT: textura, black and brown ink

RUBRICATION: rubrics in red ink

SEC. FOL.: '*Exodi cciiij*' (table of lections, fol. 2r); '*erþe of*'' (prefatory epistle, fol. 8r)

Binding

Brown leather over wood boards, 17th century. Gilt and blind fillet-line border round the outer edge of both covers. Rectangular figure at the centre of both covers with gilt corner-pieces and gilt panel in the middle. Brass panels with bosses at the centre and originally at the outer corners of both covers, only one surviving on the lower cover. Originally two brass clasps, one now missing. Rebacked with a modern spine. Sewn on nine bands. Parchment pastedowns and flyleaves. Gilt edges of textblock (a later addition?). Formerly chained.

Provenance

1. Lower margin of fol. 1 is cut away, probably to remove an ownership inscription.

2. *Thomas Reuely*, early 16th century (fol. i recto), see Hope (1997), pp. 260–4.

3. '*Nunc dimittis*' and '*Ecce nunc benedici te dominum*' with music for four parts added in a 16th-century hand on the upper pastedown. Lyric '*The sight which ferst my hart did strayne*' (*IMEV* 3461.8, *NIMEV* 3461.8, *DIMEV* 5462) in the same hand, seven lines, ed. Robbins (1968) (fol. i verso); text written three times, each with musical notation for a different part.

4. A list entitled '*The Interpretation of certaine harde wordes in this booke*' containing 48 Middle English words with English translation in a 16th-century hand.

5. Thomas Moulder, 16th century (upper pastedown, fol. 387r). At the end of the Apocalypse in his hand: '*Anime eorum et Omnium fidelium defunctorum per universam dei misericordiam in pace requiescant Amen So be it*' (fol. 386v). Imperfect transcript of a deed mentioning William Mason of Leighton Buzzard: '*...Willelmus Mason nuper de Leighton Bussard in coun. Bedd' yeman...*'. Pen trials on fols. 386v, 387r, 388r.

6. Anthony Langford: '*Liber collegij Corporis Christi Oxon*' *ex dono Magistri*

Antonij Langford Generosi, et Reverendi in Christo Patris Thomae /Bilson Episcopi Wintoniensis Secretarij. December 8 1615' (fol. 1r); for Thomas Bilson (1546/7–1616), bishop of Winchester; see *ODNB*.

7. Corpus Christi College, Oxford: donated by Langford in 1615. Earlier shelfmarks: 'N°. 1471. 4.'; 'W. A 4.5' (fol. ii verso).

Bibliography

Forshall and Madden (1850), vol. 1, p. li.
Coxe (1852), vol. 2, *Catalogus codicum MSS. Collegii Corporis Christi*, p. 2.
Skeat, W. W., 'On the dialect of Wycliffe's Bible', *Transactions of the Philological Society* (1895), pp. 212–19 at p. 216.
Lindberg (1959–97), vol. 1 (1959), pp. 15–16; vol. 2 (1961), p. 18; vol. 3 (1963), pp. 18–19; vol. 4 (1965), pp. 16–17; vol. 8 (1997), p. 29.
IMEV Supplement, no. 3461.8.
Robbins, R. H., 'Mirth in manuscripts', *Essays and Studies* 21 (1968), pp. 1–28 at p. 7.
Samuels (1969), pp. 12, 147.
Ogilvie-Thomson, S. J., *IMEP*, Handlist VIII (1991), p. 19.
Hope, A., 'The lady and the bailiff: Lollardy among the gentry in Yorkist and Tudor England', in Aston, M. and Richmond, C. (eds), *Lollardy and the gentry in the later Middle Ages* (Stroud and New York: Sutton/St Martin's Press, 1997), pp. 250–77.
Dove (2007), pp. 17, 59, 65, 87, 88, 95, 99, 105, 142, 193, 199, 214, 260–1, 302.
Thomson, R. M., *A descriptive catalogue of the medieval manuscripts of Corpus Christi College Oxford* (Cambridge: D. S. Brewer, 2011), pp. 8–9.

52 Corpus Christi College MS 20

Siglum: H

Origin: England

Date: 14th century late–15th century, early

Text

Fols. i–1 are originally blank paper and parchment flyleaves (see Provenance).

(fols. 2r–229v) 1 Ezra, without a prologue–2 Maccabees in LV with usual prologues. Includes a gloss '*ioob was a very man in kinde…*', written in red as a rubric at the beginning of Job (fol. 36r) (see also MSS. Bodl. 296 and Fairfax 2). Running titles on both rectos and versos, consisting of abbreviated titles of books only. Rubrics in red, e.g., '*Here endeþ þe firste book of esdre & here bigynneþ þe ij book of esdre*' (fol. 7v). Chapter numbers in red Roman numerals and in brown ink as Roman or Arabic numerals by the scribe. Added material within the text is consistently underlined in red. Red paraphs at the beginnings of sections within the text. Corrections in the margins or over erasures in the original or contemporary hands. Rubrics in Esther and Daniel pointing out the differences between the Hebrew and Latin texts. A few glosses in the margins, some with a rubric '*A glos*' (fol. 37r). Occasionally cross-reference to biblical books in the margins. At the end of Job: '*Here endiþ þe book of Iob. blessid be þe hooly Trynyte Amen*' (fol. 50v). The final lines of the second column on fol. 50v are left blank, and psalms start on a new leaf of the same quire in textura (see Script).

Rubric '*Here bigynneþ þe sauter which is red comynli in chirchis*' at the beginning of psalms. Psalms start with 2-line initials and are written as prose with verses beginning with alternating red or blue initials. Each psalm is preceded by a title and Latin incipit in the margin; there is a running title '*Sauter*'. Larger initials at psalms 26, 38, 52, 68, 80, 97 and 109. Psalm 118 is subdivided into twenty-two sections with Latin incipits of sections written in the margins.

At the end: '*Here endeþ the secounde book of Machabeis. Blessid be þe hooly trinyte*' (fol. 229v, see Provenance). About a half of the second column at the end is left blank. Fols. 230–231 are blank parchment and paper flyleaves.

Decoration

4- to 7-line red and blue 'puzzle' initials decorated with red and purple penwork at the beginnings of books. An initial on fol. 28v has anthropomorphic decoration.

2- to 3-line blue initials with red penwork at the beginnings of prologues and chapters.

Dialect

eny(1)/ony(4), ech(9)/eche(1), fier(10), ȝoue(5)/ȝouun(5), liyf(10), liyk(10), myche(8), siȝ(8) (sg.), seien(2)/sien(6) (pl.), silf(10), þouȝ(2), þorouȝ(2)

-iþ(8)/-eþ(2) (pres.ind.3sg.), -en(10) (pres.ind.pl.), -ynge(6)/-inge(2)-ing(1) (pres.part.), sche(3) (3sg.fem.pronoun, nom.), þei(10) (3pl.pronoun, nom.), hem(10) (3pl.pronoun, oblique), her(10) (3pl.pronoun, possessive)

Physical description

MATERIAL: parchment, paper flyleaves

DIMENSIONS: *c.*340 × 227 mm

NUMBER OF LEAVES: 233

FOLIATION: modern in pencil: i–ii + 1–231

COLLATION: (fols. i–1) paper and parchment flyleaves | (fols. 2–225) I–XXVIII (8) | (fols. 226–229) XXIX (4) | (fols. 230–232) paper and parchment flyleaves

Medieval leaf signatures survive; quire signatures, probably contemporary with the present binding, run A–Z, Aa–Ee.

RULING: ruled for two columns with double (fols. 2–50) and single (fols. 51–229) vertical and horizontal bounding lines extending the full height and width of page; 46 (fols. 2–50) and 48 (fols. 51–229) lines per page; written space: *c.*250 × 140 mm

SCRIPT: Anglicana (fols. 2–50); textura (fols. 51–229); black and brown ink

RUBRICATION: rubrics in red ink

SEC. FOL.: '*foure hundrid*' (fol. 3r)

Binding

Brown leather over thick pasteboard, 18th century. Double blind fillet-line border round the outer edge of both covers. Rectangular figure at the centre of both covers made of blind-roll floral designs with floral corner-pieces. Eight raised bands on spine. Paper label on spine with hand-written 'D. 4. 1'. Fragment of another paper label at the bottom of the spine. Gilt lettering at the bottom of the spine: 'MS || C. C. C. || 20'. Edges of textblock speckled red. Paper pastedowns and flyleaves.

Provenance

1. No evidence that the manuscript is deficient at the end; perhaps originally a two-volume OT.

2. '*per me Nicholam Hill*', '*ffrauncis vaughan*', 16th century (fol. 1v).

3. Colophon on fol. 229v is followed by an added date in a 16th-century hand:

> '*wylke was endet in yͤ 3yez of oure lord a thousand and ij hundert*' (fol. 229v).

4. At Corpus Christi College, Oxford by 1697 (listed in Bernard's catalogue of 1697). Earlier shelfmarks: 'D. 4. 1.' (upper pastedown, spine); 'N°. 1487. 20 D. 4. 1.' (fol. 1v).

Bibliography

Bernard, E., *Catalogi librorum manuscriptorum Angliae et Hiberniae in unum collecti cum indice alphabetico* (Oxford 1697).
Forshall and Madden (1850), vol. 1, pp. li–lii.
Coxe (1852), vol. 2, *Catalogus codicum MSS. Collegii Corporis Christi*, p. 5.
Deanesly (1920), p. 334.
Hargreaves, H., 'The Latin text of Pervey's psalter', *Medium Aevum* 24 (1955), pp. 73–90 at p. 88 n. 26.
Hudson (1978), pp. 164–5.
Ogilvie-Thomson, S. J., *IMEP*, Handlist VIII (1991), p. 19.
Dove (2007), pp. 18, 96, 106, 156, 183, 220, 229, 261–2, 302.
Thomson, R. M., *A descriptive catalogue of the medieval manuscripts of Corpus Christi College Oxford* (Cambridge: D. S. Brewer, 2011), pp. 8–9.

53 St John's College MS 7

Siglum: N

Origin: England

Date: 15th century, first quarter

Text

Fols. i–ii are paper flyleaves.

(fols. 1r–266v) OT in LV (**Plate 15**) without prologues, apart from Isaiah ('*As seynt Ierom seiþ…*', fol. 183v) and Baruch ('*Þis book which is titlid…*', fol. 216v) that have LV prologues. Usual order; excludes psalms (see Collation and Provenance). Rubric at the beginning: '*Here bigynneþ playnly þe text of þe of þe* [sic] *byble in english / genesis*'. Usual rubrics in red at the beginnings of all books and prologues, e.g., '*Here endiþ þe book of genesis & bigynneþ þe book of exodus*' (fol. 15v); a more elaborate rubric at Tobit: '*Here endiþ þe secunde book of esdre & bigynneþ a storie of an hooly man tobie þat bifelde in þe firste ȝeer of ezechie king of Iuda*' (fol. 140r). Running titles on both rectos and versos, consisting of abbreviated titles of biblical books and chapter numbers, in red, preceded by blue paraphs. Chapter numbers in red, preceded by blue paraphs, usually in the form '*c(apitulu)m ii^{m}*'; instructions to rubricator are often preserved, usually as Arabic numerals. Glosses in the margins very occasionally, usually boxed in black and red. '*Nota*' in the margins occasionally, in black ink often traced in red, probably in the original hand, marking various passages, including those concerned with the use of images and idolatry (‘*nota þe cause of pees*’ at 2 Chronicles 14:5, fol. 125r; ‘*nota*’ at 2 Chronicles 15:16, fol. 125v; Wisdom 13:13, fol. 169v; ‘*nota ymages*’ at Wisdom 14:11, fol. 169v); tithes (2 Chronicles 31:4, fol. 130r); and kingship (Ecclesiastes 10:16–17, fol. 165r). Lections are not marked, though indexing letters very occasionally appear in the margins. Added indexing letters on fol. 35r and occasionally elsewhere. Added material within the text is underlined in red consistently throughout. ‘Hedera’ signs in the margins. Corrections in the original or contemporary hands. Red and blue paraphs at the beginning of sections within the text. Usual rubrics commenting on the differences between the Latin and Hebrew texts in Esther 10–16 and Daniel 3, 12. At the end ‘*Here endiþ þe book of machabeus and*’, followed by a space (fol. 266v). According to Forshall and Madden (1850), the text from 2 Chronicles 1:1 to 2 Ezra 5:3 is closely related to MS Bod. 277 and Cambridge, Corpus Christi College MS 147. Fols. iii–iv are blank paper flyleaves.

Decoration

6-line red and blue ‘puzzle’ initials at the beginnings of books with red, purple and blue penwork, occasionally with anthropomorphic designs. Penwork border in the left, upper and lower margins at the beginning of Genesis.

2- to 3-line blue initials with red penwork at the beginnings of chapters.

Dialect

ony(10), ech(9)/eche(1), fier(10), ȝouun(6)/ȝoue(4), lijf(10), lijk(10), moche(6)/myche(4), siȝ(10) (sg.), siȝen(5)/sien(1)/syȝen(1)/syen(1) (pl.), silf(10), suche(1)/such(1)/siche(1)/sich(1), þouȝ(1), þurȝ(2)/þoruȝ(1)

-iþ(7)/-eþ(3) (pres.ind.3sg.), -en(10) (pres.ind.pl.), -inge(3)/-ynge(7) (pres. part.), she(10) (3sg.fem.pronoun, nom.), þei(10) (3pl.pronoun, nom.), hem(10) (3pl.pronoun, oblique), her(10) (3pl.pronoun, possessive)

Physical description

MATERIAL: parchment, paper flyleaves

DIMENSIONS: *c.*385 × 265 mm

NUMBER OF LEAVES: 270

FOLIATION: modern in pencil, i–ii + 1–266 + iii–iv

COLLATION: (fols. i–ii) paper flyleaves; fol. i conjoint with the upper pastedown | (fols. 1–152) I–XIX (8) | (fols. 153–156) XX (4) | (fols. 157–260) XXI–XXXIII (8) | (fols. 261–266) XXXIV (6) | (fols. iii–iv) paper flyleaves.

The second bifolium is misbound as the central bifolium (fols. 192–193) in quire XXV (fols. 189–96). *Signes de renvoi* in the lower margins on the versos indicate the proper order of the leaves.

Catchwords survive. Quire signatures partially survive. The present first quire has an original signature '3'; three more quires are missing between the original quire 20 (now 18, fols. 137–144) and the original quire 28 (now 23, fols. 173–180).

RULING: ruled for two columns, with single vertical, single horizontal in the lower margin, and double horizontal in the upper margin bounding lines extending the full height and width of page; 61 lines per page; written space: *c.*290 × 105 mm

SCRIPT: textura; black ink

RUBRICATION: rubrics in red ink

SEC. FOL.: '*dride lameth*' (fol. 2r)

Binding

Modern, brown leather over pasteboard. Sewn on six thongs. Marbled paper pastedowns and flyleaves.

Provenance

1. Production break after Job (ends with a shorter than normal quire of four leaves); psalms are missing; Proverbs starts on a new quire. Ends with a shorter than normal quire, but a rubric implies that more material was expected to be added, possibly the NT. Missing two quires at the beginning may have contained the General Prologue. Three quires missing between the quires 18 and 23 may have contained psalms, though there is a catchword in red, probably in the hand of the original rubricator, joining the end of Job and Proverbs.

2. '*Robert*' (fol. 47r) and '*Robert Huys*' (fol. 79r), 16th century.

3. '*The translation of the Bible in Englishe by Master Iohn Wicklife in the time of King Edward the third [written wth his owne hand]*' (the words in brackets are probably in a different hand and erased), 17th century, fol. 1r.

4. 'R Le Neve' (partially erased inscription in upper right corner).

5. Humphrey Haggat, St John's College, matriculated 12 November 1619 aged 17 (Foster, 1891–92, p. 628): '*Liber Collegij Sanctj Iohannis Baptistae Oxon*', *ex dono Humphredi Haggat Convictoris a[nno] MDCXX^{o} Mai. VI° Iduum*' (fol. 1r).

6. St John's College, Oxford: given by Haggat in 1620.

Bibliography

Forshall and Madden (1850), vol. 1, p. liii.
Coxe (1852), vol. 2, *Catalogus codicum MSS. Collegii S. Johannis Baptistae*, pp. 2–3.
Fristedt, S. L., 'The authorship of the Lollard Bible', *Stockholm Studies in Modern Philology* 19 (1956), pp. 28–41 at p. 39.
Lindberg (1989), p. 70.
Ogilvie-Thomson, S. J., *IMEP*, Handlist VIII (1991), p. 85.
Hanna, R., *A descriptive catalogue of the western medieval manuscripts of St John's College, Oxford* (Oxford: Oxford University Press, 2002), pp. 8–9.
Dove (2007), pp. 302–3 and *passim*.

54 St John's College MS 79

Origin: England

Date: 15th century, first quarter

Text

Fols. i–ii are paper flyleaves.

(fols. 1r–127v) Matthew–John 13:4 in LV with usual prologues. Missing Luke 5:19–6:6 because of the loss of a leaf after fol. 78. Imperfect at the end because of the loss of quires. Running titles in red on both rectos and versos, consisting of abbreviated titles of books without chapter numbers. Usual rubrics at the beginning of all prologues and books. Only one prologue to Mathew is included ('*Mathew þat was of Iudee…*'), in spite of a rubric '*Ierom in his tweyne prolog on mathew seiþ playnly þus*'. Chapter numbers in red as Roman numerals or words, e.g., '*þe ii c(apitulum)*', '*þe þridde c(apitulum)*'. Corrections in the original or contemporary hands; dittography crossed out in red. Indexing letters occasionally appear in the margins, in black or red, at the beginnings of lections rather than consistently. Double strokes in the margins or within the text mark the ends of lections. Added material within the text is not underlined. 'Hedera' signs in the margins, often corresponding to larger initials highlighted with yellow wash marking sections within the text. '*Nota*' in the original hand, drawing attention to passages concerning ethics and Christian teaching. Fols. iii–xvii are paper flyleaves.

Decoration

5- to 6-line red and blue 'puzzle' initials, decorated with red, purple and blue penwork, and penwork borders at the beginnings of gospels.

2- to 3-line blue initials with red penwork at the beginnings of chapters and prologues.

Dialect

ony(10), eche(9)/ech(1), fier(10), ȝouen(8)/ȝouen(2), lijf(10), liik(6)/lijke(4), myche(10), siȝ(8)/say(2) (sg.), siȝen(2)/sayen(2)/saien(2) (pl.), silf(10), siche(6)/suche(4), þouȝ(8), þorouȝ(8)/þoruȝ(2)

-iþ(9)/-eþ(1) (pres.ind.3sg.), -en(10) (pres.ind.pl.), inge(2)/ynge(8) (pres. part.), sche(10) (3sg.fem.pronoun, nom.), þei(10) (3pl.pronoun, nom.), hem(10) (3pl.pronoun, oblique), her(10) (3pl.pronoun, possessive)

Physical description

MATERIAL: parchment, paper flyleaves

DIMENSIONS: *c.*275 × 200 mm

NUMBER OF LEAVES: 144

FOLIATION: modern in pencil, i–ii + 1–127 + iii–xvii

COLLATION: (fols. i–ii) paper flyleaves | (fols. 1–72) I–IX (8) | (fols. 73–79) X (8–1) missing 7 | (fols. 80–127) XI–XVI (8)

Catchwords survive, written on decorative scrolls, some coloured with yellow and ochre wash. Quire signatures also survive, running consecutively a–q.

RULING: ruled for two columns, with single vertical and double horizontal bounding lines extending the full height and width of page; prickings survive; 25 lines per page; written space: *c.*188–95 × 75–80 mm

SCRIPT: large textura; black ink

RUBRICATION: rubrics in red ink

SEC. FOL.: '*uþ elyuþ*' (fol. 2r)

Binding

Modern, brown leather over pasteboard. Sewn on four thongs. Marbled paper pastedowns; paper flyleaves.

Provenance

1. '*Thomas Th...ys(?)*', erased ownership inscription, fol. 66v, 16th century, early.

2. Thomas Blownt: '*This is Thomas Blowntes boke*' (fol. 66v), 16th century, early. Similar inscriptions and pen trials on fols. 31v–32r, 37v, 86v; alphabet on fol. 73v; draft letter on fol. 31v and another fol. 114v, addressed to a clergyman 'Mr Wall', mentioning 'Thomas Blunt of syluntun' (Sillington, Warks.?) (Coxe (1852); Hanna (2002)).

3. Nicolaj Linnebye: '*Liber Collegij Sancti Joannis Baptistae Oxon*' *Ex dono Nicolaj Linnebye socij 1605*' (fol. ii verso).

4. St John's College, Oxford: given by Linnebye.

Bibliography

Forshall and Madden (1850), vol. 1, p. liii.
Coxe (1852), vol. 2, *Catalogus codicum MSS. Collegii S. Johannis Baptistae*, p. 23.
Ogilvie-Thomson, S. J., *IMEP*, Handlist VIII (1991), p. 86.
Hanna, R., *A descriptive catalogue of the western medieval manuscripts of St John's College, Oxford* (Oxford: Oxford University Press, 2002), p. 107.
Dove (2007), p. 303.

55 Lincoln College MS Lat. 119

Sigla: G; δ – General Prologue

Origin: England

Date: 15th century, first quarter

Text

Fols. i–iv are paper flyleaves. 'Proposals for Printing by Subscription, the Holy Bible...Translated into English...by John Wickleffe', by John Russell, 1712, pasted onto fols. ii recto–iv verso.

(fols. 1r–351r) ONT in LV. OT books from Exodus to Ecclesiasticus and 1, 2 Maccabees are prefaced by their descriptions in the General Prologue; Isaiah and Baruch have their usual prologues. The openings of the sections on Tobit, Judith and Ecclesiasticus have been adjusted to remove doubts about canonicity (Dove (2007), pp. 96–7, 120, 262). At the start of Genesis:

'*Seke þou þe prolog of genesis at þe ende of machabeis þat is bitwixe þe olde lawe & newe*' (fol. 1r). OT ends on fol. 279r with a rubric '*þe olde testament endiþ here*' and is followed by chapters 1–3 of the General Prologue, as far as the end of the description of Genesis. The chapters begin '*Fyue and twenty bookis of þe oolde testament...*' and end '*...& in alle þingis don his wille*' (Dove, 2010, ll. 1–150). They are preceded by a rubric '*Here bigynneþ a reule þat telliþ of þe bookis of þe oolde testament whiche ben of very feiþ & whiche ben not of feiþ. But alle þe bookis of þe newe testament ben of feiþ & of bileeue & also here bigynneþ þe prolog of genesis in þe ende*'. At the end: '*Here endiþ þe prolog of genesis*' (fol. 279v).

NT books have their usual LV prologues. Matthew has one prologue followed by a rubric '*Ierom in his two prologis on matheu seiþ pleynly al þis*' (fol. 280r) (see Provenance). Lacks Job 9:18 to Psalms 17:38 because of the loss of a quire.

Running titles in red on both rectos and versos preceded by blue paraphs consisting of abbreviated titles of books only. Usual rubrics in red. Rubrics in red pointing out the differences between the Hebrew and Latin texts in Esther and Daniel. Chapter numbers as red Roman numerals. Added material within the text is underlined in red or faintly in black. Glosses in the margins. Indexing letters in the margins in NT only. Red and blue paraphs at the beginning of sections within the text. Corrections in the original or contemporary hands.

3-line blue initials with red penwork at the beginnings of psalms; 5-line initials and penwork borders at the beginning of psalms 26, 38, 52, 68, 80, 97 and 109. Psalms are laid out as prose with verses starting with 1-line alternating red or blue initials. Psalm titles in English in red. Latin incipits in red at the beginning of some psalms (mostly those at liturgical divisions) or added in the margins in a late 15th-century hand. Psalm 118 is subdivided into 22 sections with 2-line initials at the beginning of sections.

Many notes throughout in a late 15th-century hand in the margins citing or summarising the text.

Decoration

5- to 9-line red and blue 'puzzle' initials with red and blue penwork decoration, and penwork 'saw-tooth' borders at the beginnings of books. Penwork occasionally includes anthropomorphic designs.

3- to 4-line blue initials with red penwork at the beginnings of chapters and prologues.

Catchwords in frames with penwork decoration.

In the lower right corner on fol. 95v (end of a quire) is a flourisher's account listing the numbers of 'indented and flourished' letters, 'flourished' letters, and paraphs. Fragmentary writing in the same place at the end of another quire, fol. 143v.

Dialect

ony(9)/oni(1), ech(10), fier(5)/fyer(5), ȝouun(4)/ȝouen(5)/ȝoue(1), lyf(4)/lijf(6), lijk(5)/lyk(4)/liyk(1), myche(5)/miche(3)/moche(2), siȝ(2)/saiȝ(1)/say(4) (sg.), seien(1)/saien(2)/siȝen(4) (pl.), silf(10), such(1)/suche(3)/sich(1)/siche(5), þouȝ(8), þoruȝ(10)

-iþ(9)/-eþ(1) (pres.ind.3sg.), -en(10) (pres.ind.pl.), -ynge(10) (pres.part.), she(10) (3sg.fem.pronoun, nom.), þei(10) (3pl.pronoun, nom.), hem(10) (3pl.pronoun, oblique), here(8)/her(2) (3pl.pronoun, possessive)

Physical description

MATERIAL: parchment, paper flyleaves

DIMENSIONS: *c.*410 × 270 mm

NUMBER OF LEAVES: 356

FOLIATION: modern in pencil: i–iv + 1–82 + unnumbered leaf + 83–351 + two unnumbered paper flyleaves at the end

COLLATION: (fols. i–iv) paper flyleaves | (fols. 1–191) I–XLIV (8) | two unnumbered paper flyleaves at the end; a quire is missing after fol. 151

Catchwords survive. Most quire signatures survive and appear to run consecutively. A new series starts on fol. 192. There is no catchword on fol. 279v where the OT ends, but there is no break in quire signatures between OT and NT.

RULING: ruled for two columns with double vertical and single horizontal bounding lines extending the full height and width of page; a second set of single bounding lines in the outer margins; 66–9 lines per page; written space: *c.*300 × 190 mm

SCRIPT: textura; probably shares a scribe with CUL MS Kk 1. 8 (Dove (2007), p. 263).

RUBRICATION: rubrics in red ink

SEC. FOL.: '*adam lyuyde*' (fol. 2r)

Binding

Leather over thick pasteboard, 18th century. Border made of double blind fillet lines with floral corner-pieces round the outer edge of both covers.

Two holes in the upper right corner of the front cover. Ten raised bands on spine. Gilt decoration on the panels between the bands. Two red leather labels at the top of the spine with gilt decoration and lettering 'BIBLIA' and 'IN || PERGAMENT'. Paper labels at the top and bottom of the spine with typewritten '15' and 'MS || Linc. Coll. || Lat. 119'. Edges of textblock speckled red. Marbled paper pastedowns covered with laid paper. Laid paper flyleaves.

Provenance

1. Probably shares a scribe with CUL MS Kk 1. 8. Textual similarities with MS Kk 1. 8: both lack the same portion of chapter 10 of the General Prologue (Dove (2007), p. 120 n. 80) and have a rubric at the beginning of Matthew suggesting that there should be two prologues, but only one is included (see Text).

2. Late 15th-century owner who left many notes in the margins in English, most summarising the contents of the biblical text.

3. '*Ister lyber perteneth bere ye in mynd hade*', 16th century, fol. 351v.

4. Erased ownership inscription (?) in the upper margin of fol. 1r.

5. Lincoln College, Oxford: book plate on the upper pastedown.

Bibliography

Forshall and Madden (1850), vol. 1, p. lii.
Coxe (1852), vol. 1, *Catalogus codicum MSS. Collegii Lincolniensis*, pp. 53–4.
Hudson, A., *Selections from English Wycliffite writings* (Cambridge: Cambridge University Press, 1978), pp. 166, 170.
Lindberg (1989), pp. 69–70.
Ogilvie-Thomson, S. J., *IMEP*, Handlist VIII (1991), pp. 41, 109.
Dove (2007), pp. 17, 74, 88, 96–8, 102, 106–7, 120, 123–4, 127, 152, 156, 242, 262–3, 302.

56 New College MS 66

Sigla: O – prologues from Genesis to 1 Chronicles; *K* – prologue to 1 Ezra; *O* – prologues from 2 Chronicles to Psalter, exept that to 1 Ezra

Origin: England

Date: 1415–1425 (?)

Text

1. (fols. 1r–2v) Two leaves from a 14th-century Latin manuscript, containing Joshua 24:25–33 and Judges 2:6–12, both with a marginal gloss.

2. (fols. 3r–234v) Genesis–Psalms in LV, imperfect at the end because of the loss of quires (ends with a rubric for Proverbs). Starts with Jerome's prefatory epistles in LV, '*Broþir ambrose bryngynge…*' and '*I haue take þe Epistlis…*' (fols. 3r–6r) (see Dove (2007), p. 199). LV prologues at Josua ('*At þe last whanne þe fyue bookes of moyses…*'), 1 Kings ('*The langage of men sirus & of caldeis also witnessiþ…*') and 1 Chronicles ('*Iff þe makynge of þe seuenti interpretours dwelle…*' and '*The book of paralipomenon þat is þe bregging…*') (see Dove (2007), pp. 200–1). The prologue to 1 Kings (fols. 115v–116v) follows its text; notes '*þe prolog of þe bookis of kingis stondiþ at þe ende of þis book*' (fol. 102r) and '*þis prolog shulde haue stonde bifore þis book*' (fol. 115v). EV prologues at the beginning of 2 Chronicles, 1 Ezra ('*Wheþir it be hardere to doon…*'; '*Esdras & nemye helpere…*' and '*þe comendacioun of Esdre*'), Tobit, Judith ('*Anentis þe ebrewis þe book…*'), Esther, Job ('*I am constreyned bi alle…*' and '*Iff forsoþe I shulde make a ionke[t] wiþ rusche…*') and psalms ('*Whanne it is knowun alle þe profetis…*' and '*Dauiþ þe sone of gesse…*') (see Dove (2007), pp. 201–2). See Forshall and Madden (1850), vol. 1, pp. xxix, on the relationship of New College MS 66 to other copies that retain prologues in OT. Notes in red on the differences between the Latin and Hebrew texts in Esther 9–16.

The scribe compressed the text to finish prologues to psalms on fol. 210v in order to start psalms on a new quire; there is no catchword on the page preceding the beginning of psalms. Rubric: '*Here bygynnyþ þe sauter þe which is red comynly in chirchis. Psalmus I*'. Psalms have titles in red, which include psalm numbers, and are laid out as prose with alternating plain 1-line red or blue initials at the beginnings of verses. There are textual divisions, marked with 4-line gold initials with floral sprays, at psalms 26, 38, 52, 68, 80, 97 and 109; other psalms and parts of psalm 118 start with 3-line initials. Psalm 118 is subdivided into 11-verse units at the beginning (aleph–daleth) and into 22-verse units afterwards. No Latin incipits, with the exception of those at some subdivisions in psalm 118. Note in red '*Comendacioun*', probably in the hand of the original rubricator, at the beginning of psalm 118, referring to its use in the 'Commendation of the Souls'.

Running titles in red, usually consisting of an abbreviated title of the book on the verso and chapter numbers as Roman numerals above each of the two columns on both rectos and versos. Usual rubrics in red. Chapter numbers in red, typically in the form '*c^m^ iii^m^*'. Many corrections in the original or contemporary hands in the margins, within the text and over erasures (some lengthy corrections are in Anglicana); some text is crossed out in red. Marginal glosses appear occasionally; added material within the text is consistently underlined in red throughout; lections are not marked. Red and blue paraphs within the text.

Decoration

4- to 6-line initials, decorated with foliage on gold background and three-quarters borders made of gold, blue and pink bars, decorated with foliage and gold disks at the beginnings of books. Simpler decoration with floral sprays, rather than borders, at Ruth (fol. 106v), 2 Kings (fol. 116v), 3 Kings (fol. 127r), 4 Kings (fol. 139v), 2 Ezra (fol. 181r), Tobit (fol. 187r), Esther (fol. 195v) and Job (fol. 201r).

3- to 4-line blue initials with red penwork at the beginnings of prologues; 2- to 3-line similar initials at the beginnings of chapters.

Dialect

ony(10), ech(8)/eech(1)/eche(1), fier(8)/fir(1)/fyer(1), ȝoue(6)/ȝouun(3), lijf(10), lijk(10), myche(9)/moche(1), siȝ(9) (sg.), sien(6) (pl.), silf(9)/sylf(1), siche(2)/sich(2), þorou(3)/þorouȝ(1)

-iþ(7)/-yþ(1)/-eþ(2) (pres.ind.3sg.), -en(10) (pres.ind.pl.), -ynge(7)/-yng(1)/-inge(1) (pres.part.), sche(5)/she(5) (3sg.fem.pronoun, nom.), þei(10) (3pl. pronoun, nom.), hem(10) (3pl.pronoun, oblique), her(10) (3pl.pronoun, possessive)

Physical description

MATERIAL: parchment

DIMENSIONS: *c.*310 × 219 mm

NUMBER OF LEAVES: 184

FOLIATION: modern in pencil; two unnumbered flyleaves at the beginning + 1–236

COLLATION: (fols. 1–2) two singletons | (fols. 3–234) I–XXIX (8) | (fols. 235–236) two singletons

Catchwords survive; quire signatures partially survive at the beginning, running consecutively +, a–d, etc.

RULING: ruled for two columns, with single vertical and horizontal bounding lines extending the full height and width of page, and a single additional bounding line in the upper margin; 56–7 lines per page; written space: *c.*240 × 155–160 mm

SCRIPT: textura, black ink

SEC. FOL.: '*neþ & no man…*' (fol. 4r)

Binding

Brown leather, 17th century, over wood boards from a medieval (?) binding. Blind fillet-line border round the outer edge of both covers. Rectangular blind fillet-line and blind roll decoration on both covers. Rebacked with the original spine relaid. Six raised bands on spine. Fragmentary paper label on spine with hand-written 'MS || New Coll. || …'. Fittings of two clasps, now lost, on both covers. Leaves from a 13th-century manuscript used as flyleaves at the front and back.

Provenance

1. Notes on the subject matter of several chapters of Deuteronomy added in a late 15th-century hand on the second unnumbered flyleaf at the beginning.

2. New College, Oxford.

Bibliography

Forshall and Madden (1850), vol. 1, pp. xxix, xxxiv, xxxv, lii.
Coxe (1852), vol. 1, *Catalogus codicum MSS. Collegii Novi*, p. 19.
Ogilvie-Thomson, S. J., *IMEP*, Handlist VIII (1991), p. 54.
Dove (2007), pp. 18, 94, 96, 98, 100, 138, 141, 156, 199, 200–2, 217, 228, 239.

57 New College MS 67

Siglum: *V*

Origin: England

Date: 15th century, first quarter

Text

[item 1 occupies quire I]
1. (fols. 1r–2v) Short tracts in the hand of the main scribe:

(1) *The sixteen conditions of charity* (Severs, Hartung, Beidler (1967–), vol. 7, p. 2518, no. 58; Jolliffe (1974), G. 4) with the title '*on charite*', beginning '*Seynt poule spekiþ & seiþ on þis wise if y speke with mannus tunge…*'. Lists sixteen conditions of charity (based on 1 Corinthians 13:1–8), each followed by a short explanation.

(2) A tract on the ten commandments (Severs, Hartung, Beidler (1967–), vol. 7, p. 2495, no. 24), beginning '*These ben þe x comaundementis of god þe whiche euereche man mot kepe*…'. The commandments are numbered in red Roman numerals in the margins, each followed by a short explanation; the first three are accompanied by references to biblical books and chapters in the margins. Also includes the lists of seven virtues, five bodily wits and five ghostly wits. Most of fol. 2v is left blank.

[items 2–3 occupy quires II–XXIII]
2. (fols. 1r–172r) NT in EV with usual prologues (**Plate 16**). Includes two prologues to Romans and a second prologue to Luke, found in only two other manuscripts (see Dove (2007), p. 233):

> '*Forsothe for many men enforsiden to ordeyne þe telling of þingis. whiche ben fillid in us. as þei þat sayen at þe begynnyng. & weren mynystris of þe word bytooken: it seyn also to me hauynge fro þe bygynnyng alle þingis deligently bi ordre to write to þee þu best teofile þat þu knowe þe treuþe of þoo wordis of whiche þu art lernd*'.

Some prologues appear to have been added in spaces left for them after the biblical text was copied. Two prologues to Romans, '*First us bihoueþ vndirstonde*…' and '*Romayns þe whiche lyueden in þe citee*…', are written in a very small script by the main scribe to fit on fol. 92r–v. The prologue to 1 Thessalonians is written in the margin by the main scribe. The prologue to the Apocalypse occupies about one third of fol. 164r; the rest of the page is left blank and the Apocalypse starts on fol. 164v. According to Lindberg (1994), p. 24, the text is very much revised and strongly influenced by LV. Extensive glosses in the margins from 1 Corinthians 6:4 to Jude, some unique, according to Forshall and Madden (1850), most found only in this copy and London, British Library, Harley MS 5017. Fewer glosses in the Apocalypse. The introduction of glosses coincides with the use of a much smaller script for the biblical text (from fol. 109v, 1 Corinthians 7) which remains small in the rest of the volume. Added material within the text is consistently underlined in red throughout.

Rubrics in red or black, usually at the start of prologues, though sometimes also at the beginnings of books, e.g., '*Here endiþ marc and bygynneþ luc þe prologe*'; '*luc þe first chapitre*' (fols. 45v–46r). Running titles consisting of the name of a book and chapter number, usually on both rectos and versos, sometimes preceded by red or blue paraphs. Many corrections in a contemporary hand, over erasures or in the margins; some text crossed out in red ink, particularly glosses within the text and alternative translations at the beginning of Matthew. Some deletions at the beginning of Matthew suggest stylistic editing (see Forshall and Madden (1850), vol. 1, p. lii).

Chapter numbers in black ink by the scribe in the margins, most as Arabic numerals, some underlined in red or preceded by paraphs; chapter numbers in Roman numerals added in a darker ink. The same hand (15th century, second half (?)) also added indexing letters in the margins at the beginnings of lections, double strokes at the ends of lections, and sometimes notes concerning liturgical occasions when the lections were appointed to be read (e.g., '*S Andrew day*', fol. 5v). Added '*nota*' and pointing hands in the margins.

3. (fols. 172v–174v) Short table of lections in Latin with a rubric '*Hic incipiunt cotaciones evangeliorum et epistolarum tocius anni legende*', starting with the first Sunday in Advent and consisting of the temporal and sanctoral. Imperfect at the end, ending at All Souls (2 November). Laid out in two columns with the names of liturgical occasions written in the margins. Entries consist of the opening words of readings followed by an abbreviated reference to a book and chapter of the Bible. No indexing letters.

Decoration

3- to 6-line 'puzzle' initials with red and purple penwork or blue initials with red penwork at the beginnings of books; 2- to 3-line similar initials at the beginnings of chapters and prologues; some initials omitted (e.g., fol. 83v).

Dialect

According to Forshall and Madden copied from an original that had the present participle terminating in -ende, which has led to frequent mistakes, 'and particularly to the occurrence of the preterite where the participle should stand, as *puttede* for *puttende*' (Forshall and Madden (1850), vol. 1, p. lii).

eny(10), eche(3)/ech(7), fyier(1)/fijer(6)/fijr(3), ȝouen(8)/ȝiuen(2), lijf(10), lijk(9)/lijche(1), myche(10), say(4)/seiȝe(1) (sg.), sayen(1)/siȝen(2)/seiȝen(2)/ seien(1) (pl.), self(8)/silf(2), such(1)/suche(7)/sich(1), þouȝ(3), þourȝ(9)

-iþ(7)/-eþ(3)/-ith(1) (pres.ind.3sg.), -en(10) (pres.ind.pl.), -ing(2)/-inge(6)/-yng(2) (pres.part.), she(3)/sche(7) (3sg.fem.pronoun, nom.), þei(10) (3pl. pronoun, nom.), hem(10) (3pl.pronoun, oblique), her(10) (3pl.pronoun, possessive)

Physical description

MATERIAL: poor quality parchment with holes; paper flyleaves

DIMENSIONS: *c.*195 × 144 mm

NUMBER OF LEAVES: 174 + unnumbered paper flyleaves at the beginning and end

FOLIATION: modern in pencil, 1–174

COLLATION: three unnumbered paper flyleaves | (fols. 1–2) I (2) single bifolium (?) | (fols. 3–167) II–XXII (8) | (fols. 168–174) XXIII (8–1) missing 8

Catchwords survive; quire signatures partially survive and appear to run consecutively a–y

RULING: ruled for a single column, with single vertical and double horizontal bounding lines extending the full height and width of page; a second set of double bounding lines in all margins; 38–52 lines per page; written space: *c.*117 × 75 mm

SCRIPT: textura, black and brown ink; the size and style of script vary

SEC. FOL.: '*þisen her...*' (fol. 2r)

Binding

Modern binding. Gilt lettering on spine 'NEW TEST. || ENGLISH'. Parchment slip attached to the upper cover with hand-written 'New Testament || Engl[...]'.

Provenance

1. Some prologues were added after the text was completed in spaces left for them. Glosses were added after the text was completed and flourished – they avoid penwork initials and chapter numbers in the margins, but the decision to include them was probably made when the volume was planned – the scribe uses a much more compressed script starting with 1 Corinthians 7, the first book to include extensive glosses.

2. Thomas Martin, fellow of New College 1538–1553 (Coxe, 1852; Foster, 1891–92, p. 980).

3. New College, Oxford: given by Martin in 1558.

Bibliography

Coxe (1852), vol. 1, *Catalogus codicum MSS. Collegii Novi*, p. 19.
Fristedt (1953–73), vol. 1, p. 16.
Hargreaves, H., 'The marginal glosses to the Wycliffite New Testament', *Studia Neophilologica* 33 (1961), pp. 285–300.
––, 'Popularising biblical scholarship: the role of the Wycliffite Glossed Gospels',

in Lourdaux, W. and Verhelst, D. (eds), *The Bible and medieval culture* (Louvain: Leuven University Press, 1979) pp. 171–89 at p. 175.
Gillespie, V., 'Vernacular books of religion', in Griffiths, J. and Pearsall, D. A. (eds), *Book production and publishing in Britain 1375–1475* (Cambridge: Cambridge University Press, 1989), pp. 317–44 at p. 319.
Ogilvie-Thomson, S. J., *IMEP*, Handlist VIII (1991), p. 54.
Lindberg (1959–97), vol. 7 (1994), p. 24.
Dove (2007), pp. 142, 152, 165, 166, 169–70, 179–80, 221, 223, 234, 248, 302.

58 New College MS 320

Origin: England

Date: *c.*1500

Text

1. (fols. 1r–2r) EV prologues to psalms '*Whan it is knowen alle þe prophetys…*' and '*Dauiþ þe son of iesse…*' (see Dove (2007), p. 202).

2. (fols. 2r–41r) Psalms 1–150 in LV, laid out as prose in two columns. The psalms are separated by fairly large spaces which suggests that the titles were planned to be included. Latin incipits are written out in black ink by the main scribe in the margins at the start of most psalms. There are textual divisions at psalms 26, 38, 52, 68, 82, 97 and 109.

Punctuated throughout with *punctus* used to mark the ends of verses and *punctus* or colon used to mark minor pauses. No running titles or marginal glosses; added material within the text is not underlined. Corrected occasionally with omissions written out in the margins (e.g., fols. 26v, 39v) and text crossed out in red ink (e.g., fols. 13r, 27r). Psalm numbers (Hebrew) are added in a later hand.

3. (fols. 41r–43v) Weekly canticles with Latin incipits in the margins (*Confitebor*, *Ego dixi*, *Exultauit*, *Cantemus*, *Domine audiui*, *Audite celi*).

4. (fols. 43v–45r) Daily canticles with Latin incipits in the margins (*Benedicite omnia opera*, *Te deum laudamus*, *Magnificat*, *Benedictus dominus deus*, *Nunc dimittis*); Athanasian Creed (*Quicumque vult…*).

5. (fol. 45v) Poem to the Virgin Mary (*IMEV* 3228, *DIMEV* 5064) in the same hand as the psalter, beginning:

'*Swete and benyngne moder & may*
Turtell trew flowr of women alle…'.

Each of the seven stanzas rhyme royal is an acrostic on the name 'stanlei' (possibly Thomas, first baron Stanley, 1406–1459; see *ODNB*; Furnivall (1866)). Preceded by a title in red '*Spero lucem*'. Followed by a Marian antiphon (1), versicle (2) and collect (3) (see Harper (1991), pp. 131–3):

(1) *Aue regina celorum mater regis Angelorum*
O maria flos virginum velut rosa velilium [sic]
ffunde preces ad filium pro salute fidelium

(2) *Ora pro nobis sancta dei genitrix*
Ut digni efficiamur promissionibus christi.

(3) *Famulorum tuorum quesumus domine delictis ignosce et qui tibi placere…*

At the end '*By Will(ia)m Huchen*' in red ink.

Bound with printed material. Fols. 47r–94v are quires and leaves from Caxton's translation of Jacobus de Voragine's *Legenda Aurea* (de Worde (1498), 'folio. vi' to 'folio. lij'), containing lives of OT figures: '*The lyf of Abraham*', followed by the lives of Isaac, Joseph, Moses, Saul, David, Solomon, Job, Tobit and Judith. Fol. 94r is another leaf from de Worde (1498), containing Caxton's printer's device on the recto and woodcuts of the Annunciation and Crucifixion on the verso. 'Hedera' signs in the margins of the lives of David, Solomon, Judith and at the start of Tobit, next to a rubric declaring that it 'is redde on the thyrde sondaye of Septembre'.

Decoration

3- to 4-line red initials, some with simple penwork, at textual divisions; 2-line similar initials at the beginnings of psalms and prologues.

1-line initials at the beginnings of verses.

Dialect

ony(2)/any(1), ich(1)/iche(2)/ech(2)/eche(1), fiyr(1)/fijr(9), ȝoue(3)/ȝouen(2), lijf(9)/lyfe(1), lyk(1)/lyke(3)/lijk(2), myche(5), seiȝ(2) (sg.), syȝen(2)/siȝen(2)/ sien(1)/syen(2) (pl.), self(8), þorou(1)

-yþ(2)/-iþ(9) (pres.ind.3sg.), -en(9)/-(1) (pres.ind.pl.), -ynge(3)/-yng(7) (pres. part.), sche(1) (3sg.fem. pronoun, nom.), þei(8)/þey(2) (3pl.pronoun, nom.), hem(10) (3pl.pronoun, oblique), her(10) (3pl.pronoun, possessive)

Physical description

MATERIAL: paper

DIMENSIONS: *c.*272 × 206 mm; leaves were cropped occasionally causing the loss of psalm incipits in the upper margin

NUMBER OF LEAVES: 46 + unnumbered flyleaves at the beginning and end

FOLIATION: modern in pencil, 1–46; medieval in Arabic numerals, probably identical to modern

COLLATION: (fols. 1–16) I (16) | (fols. 17–30) II, structure unclear; catchwords at fols. 27v, 30v | (fols. 31–46) III (16)

SCRIPT: Secretary, black ink

RULING: ruled for two columns, with single vertical and horizontal bounding lines extending the full height and width of page; 36–9 lines per page; written space: *c.*235 × 165 mm

SEC. FOL.: '*men chosyn*…' (fol. 2r)

Binding

Brown leather over pasteboard, 18th century. Blind fillet-line border round the outer edge of both covers; blind fillet-line rectangular figure with floral corner-pieces at the centre of both covers. Paper label on spine with typewritten 'MS || New Col. || D. 320'. Edges of textblock speckled red. Paper flyleaves and pastedowns.

Provenance

1. Poem in the same hand as the psalter with acrostic 'stanlei', conjectured by Furnivall (1866) to be Thomas, first baron Stanley, 1406–1459. Signature 'William Huchen' in the hand of the scribe responsible for the poem and psalter. Anthony à Wood (1813–20) believed that the manuscript contained a translation of psalms by William Tyndale, because of the similarity of the name 'William Huchen' to Tyndale's pseudonym. Mombert (1884), however, pointed out that the manuscript contained a Wycliffite translation of psalms. The psalms are in a format similar to the OT material from de Worde (two columns and similar written space) and may have been copied to supplement this material.

2. '*Thomas Smyth of london*', 16th century (fol. 46r).

3. Inscription recording that Thomas Philpott (Foster (1891–92), p. 1160), fellow of New College, was created D.D. in June 1646 (fol. 46v) (see a full transcription in Coxe (1852)).

4. New College, Oxford: '*Liber Novi Collegij in Oxon*'' (fol. 1r).

Bibliography

Wood, Anthony à, *Athenæ oxonienses: an exact history of all the writers and bishops who have had their education in the University of Oxford*, a new edition, with additions, and a continuation by Philip Bliss, 4 vols (London, 1813–20), vol. 1, col. 97.
Forshall and Madden (1850), vol. 1, p. lii.
Coxe (1852), vol. 1, *Catalogus codicum MSS. Collegii Novi*, p. 115.
Furnivall, F. J. (ed.), *Political, religious and love poems, from Lambeth MS 306 and other sources,* EETS o.s. 15 (1866), pp. 291–2.
Mombert, J. I., *William Tyndale's five books of Moses, called the Pentateuch, being a verbatim reprint of the edition of M.CCCCC.XXX* (New York: A. D. F. Randolph, London: S. Bagster, 1884), p. liv.
Hargreaves, H., 'The Latin text of Purvey's psalter', *Medium Aevum* 24 (1955), pp. 73–90 at p. 88.
Hudson, A., 'Contributions to a history of Wycliffite writings', in Hudson (1985), pp. 1–12 at p. 11.
Ogilvie-Thomson, S. J., *IMEP*, Handlist VIII (1991), pp. 73–5.
de Hamel (2001), p. 179.
Dove (2007), p. 302.

59 Oriel College MS 80

Origin: England

Date: 15th century, first quarter

Text

[item 1 occupies quire I]

1. (fols. 1r–12r) Table of lections of Type II preceded by a rubric: '*Here bigynneþ a rule þat telliþ in whiche chapitres of þe bible ȝe mown fynde þe lessouns pistlis & gospels þat ben rad bi al þe ȝeer aloute in holy chirche after þe vss of Salisbiry*'. Includes the temporal, a short sanctoral, common and commemorations. The entries consist of the name of a liturgical occasion in red, abbreviated reference to a book and chapter of the Bible, an indexing letter in red, the opening words of a reading, '*eende*' in red, the closing words of a reading and double strokes. The only non-biblical saints are Thomas Becket, Nicholas, George, Lawrence and Clement. Commemorations are in the following order: the Virgin Mary, Trinity, Holy Ghost, cross, angels, '*ffor briþeren & sistren & salus populi*', peace, clear weather, rain, '*In tyme of batels*', '*ffor him silf*', '*ffor pestilence of beestis*', '*ffor weifering men & pilgrims*', weddings, dead, sick and sinners. At the end: '*Here eendiþ þe table of þe*

temperal of þe propre sanctorum & vpon þe common sanctorum of pistlis, lessouns & gospels þat ben rad in holy chirche þoru þe ȝeer & þe cotations where þei schulen be founden'. Fol. 12v is blank.

[item 2 occupies quires II–XI]
2. (fols. 13r–90v) Matthew–Luke 20:32 in LV with usual prologues. Missing Matthew 23:22–24:16 due to the loss of one leaf after fol. 38; and Mark 11:22–12:24 due to the loss of one leaf after fol. 58. Imperfect at the end because of the loss of quires, ending with '*þe womman is deed perfor*' and a catchword '*in þe*'. Running titles on both rectos and versos, consisting of book titles and chapter numbers on pages containing the beginnings of chapters. Usual rubrics in red, e.g., '*Here eendiþ þe gospel of matheu & bigynneþ þe prolog of mark*'; '*þis seiþ ierom in his prolog on mark & begynneþ þe gospel of mark*' (fols. 45v–46r). Chapter numbers in red as words or Roman numerals. Indexing letters in the margins entered at the beginnings of lections rather than consistently; double strokes in the margins at the ends of lections. The beginnings and ends of lections are also highlighted with yellow wash. Added material within the text is occasionally underlined in red (e.g., fols. 28v, 31r, 75v). Red paraphs at the start of sections within the text. Corrections in the original hand.

Decoration

5-line red and blue 'puzzle' initials with purple penwork and full penwork borders at the beginnings of gospels.

2-line blue initials with red penwork at the beginnings of prologues and chapters.

Dialect

ony(10), ech(10), fier(10), gouun(10), lijf(10), lijk(10), myche(10), sai(6) (sg.), saien(6) (pl.), silf(10), siche(4)/sich(2), þouȝ(6), þoru(9)

-iþ(8)/-eþ(2) (pres.ind.3sg.), -en(10) (pres.ind.pl.), -ynge(2)/-inge(8) (pres. part.), sche(10) (3sg.fem.pronoun, nom.), þei(10) (3pl.pronoun, nom.), hem(10) (3pl.pronoun, oblique), her(10) (3pl.pronoun, possessive)

Physical description

MATERIAL: parchment, paper flyleaves

DIMENSIONS: *c.*185 × 128 mm

NUMBER OF LEAVES: 98

FOLIATION: modern in pencil, i–vi + 1–92

COLLATION: (fol. i–vi) paper and parchment flyleaves | (fols. 1–12) I (12) | (fols. 13–36) II–IV (8) | (fols. 37–43) V (8–1) missing 3 | (fols. 44–51) VI (8) | (fols. 52–58) VII (8–1) missing 8 | (fols. 59–90) VIII–XI (8)

Catchwords survive; quire signatures survive and run consecutively a–k (fols. 13–90).

RULING: ruled for two columns with single vertical and horizontal bounding lines extending the full height and width of page, and a further set of double bounding lines in all margins; 29 lines per page; written space: *c.*120 × 85 mm

SCRIPT: textura, the table of lections may be in a different hand

RUBRICATION: rubrics in red; red and blue paraphs

SEC. FOL.: '*fo cristmasse*' (table of lections, fol. 2r); '*bigat ezechie*' (gospel, fol. 2r)

Binding

Brown leather over pasteboard. Double blind fillet lines round the outer edge of both covers. Blind fillet-line and roll rectangular decoration with floral corner-pieces on both covers. Five raised bands on spine; stamped floral decoration on the panels between the bands. Burgundy leather label with gilt lettering on spine: 'WICKLIFFE'S || TRANSL: || OF N:TES || M.S. IMPER'. Fragments of another label at the top of the spine. Edges of textblock speckled red. '21' written in ink on the fore-edge of textblock. Pastedowns and flyleaves made of laid paper.

Provenance

1. Inscriptions in several early modern hands on fol. vi recto; date '1560'.

2. John Warter, 1608 (fols. v recto, vi recto).

3. Oriel College, Oxford.

Bibliography

Forshall and Madden (1850), vol. 1, p. lii.
Coxe (1852), vol. 1, *Codices MSS. Collegii Orielensis*, p. 28.
Ogilvie-Thomson, S. J., *IMEP*, Handlist VIII (1991), p. 76.
Dove (2007), p. 302.

60 Queen's College MS 369

Origin: England

Date: 15th century, first quarter

Text

Fols. i–iii are paper flyleaves, blank apart from modern notes.

(fols. 1r–198v) Matthew–1 Timothy 2:12 in EV, ending at '*but for to be in scilence forsoþe…*'; usual prologues. Rubrics in red, e.g., '*Here bigynnythe the prologe of Mathew*', '*Jerom in his prologe of mathew seiþ þus here bigynnyþ furst chapitill of Mathew*' (fols. 1r–1v); '*Here eendiþ þe gospels of mathew prolog*', '*Here bygynnyn þe gospels of marke*' (fols. 46v–47r). Blank spaces left for rubrics at the beginnings of prologues and gospels of Luke and John, and all epistles apart from Romans. At the end of John: '*Here eendiþ þe gospel of ioon. & also here is þe eendynge of alle þe gospellis as þei stonden in þe bible by þe seiynge of þe foure ewangelistis mathew Marke luke & Ioon. Here bygynnyþ þe prolog to fore þe epistlis to romayns & bygynneþ þus*' (fol. 137v). Includes two prologues to Romans, '*Firste vndirstonde vs byhoueþ…*' and '[*R*]*omayns þe whiche in þe cyte of rome…*'. Running titles in red consisting of abbreviated titles of books without chapter numbers in more than one hand and style. The beginnings of periods are marked with red strokes or paraphs. Chapter numbers as red Roman numerals, usually in the form '*iiij chapter*', 'cap^{m} xiij^{m}' or similar. Added material within the text is underlined in red or black. Occasionally corrections in a contemporary hand. Catchword '*adam*' on fol. 198; a quire or quires are missing at the end. Fols. 199r–201v are paper flyleaves.

Decoration

2- to 4-line plain red initials at the beginnings of books and prologues, some not filled in; 2-line plain red initials at the beginnings of chapters. Border, made of a zig-zag pattern drawn in red ink, in the margin of Luke 12 (fol. 92r).

Dialect

ony(3)/any(5)/eny(2), eche(3)/ech(6)/ich(1), fyer(5)/fiyr(2)/fyr(1)/fuyr(2), ȝeuen(2)/ȝouen(8), lyf(6)/liyf(4), liyk(1)/lyke(7)/lyche(2), muche(7)/myche(2)/miche(1), siȝe(1)/sauȝ(4) (sg.), sawen(3)/seyen(2) (pl.), selue(1)/self(9), suche(10), þouȝ(1), þoruȝ(2)/þoru(4)/þorou(1)

-iþ(8)/-eþ(2) (pres.ind.3sg.), -en(10) (pres.ind.pl.), -ynge(10) (pres.part.), sche(10) (3sg.fem.pronoun, nom.), þei(10) (3pl.pronoun, nom.), hem(10) (3pl.pronoun, oblique), her(10) (3pl.pronoun, possessive)

Physical description

MATERIAL: parchment, paper flyleaves

DIMENSIONS: *c.*175 × 118 mm

NUMBER OF LEAVES: 204

FOLIATION: modern in pencil, i–iii + 1–201

COLLATION: (fols. i–iii) paper flyleaves | (fols. 1–88) I–XI (8) | (fols. 89–94) XII (6) | (fols. 95–198) XIII–XXV (8) | (fols. 199–201) paper flyleaves

Catchwords survive. Quire signatures occasionally survive, including a–b (fols. 111–126), r–t (fols. 127–150), d–h (fols. 151–190); breaks in the sequence of signatures do not correspond to any textual boundaries.

RULING: ruled for two columns, with single vertical and horizontal bounding lines extending the full height and width of page; an additional set of double bounding lines in the lower and outer margins; 29 lines per page on fols. 1–34r; 36–38 per page on fols. 34v–198v; and 38 lines per page in NT; written space: *c.*125–30 × 80 mm

SCRIPT: textura; the work of several scribes; variable size of script

RUBRICATION: rubrics in red ink

SEC. FOL.: '*salmon*...' (fol. 2r)

Binding

Brown leather over pasteboard, blind fillet-line border round the outer edge of both covers. Four raised bands on spine. Gold lettering on spine: 'Newe || Testament' and 'MS.'. Marbled paper pastedowns and flyleaves.

Provenance

1. 'Henry Stephens', 16th century, fol. 135v.

2. Queen's College, Oxford; bookplate on the upper pastedown.

Bibliography

Forshall and Madden (1850), vol. 1, p. liii.
Coxe (1852), vol. 1, *Codices MSS. Collegii Reginensis*, pp. 86–7.
Ogilvie-Thomson, S. J., *IMEP*, Handlist VIII (1991), p. 83.
de Hamel (2001), pp. 184–6.
Dove (2007), pp. 142, 302.

61 Queen's College MS 388

Siglum: M

Origin: England

Date: 15th century, first quarter

Text

Fol. i is a parchment flyleaf.

[item 1 occupies quire I]
1. (fols. 1r–7v) Table of lections of Type I preceded by a rubric: '*Here begynneþ a reule þat telliþ in whiche chapitris of þe bible ȝe may fynde þe lessouns pistlis. gospels þat ben red in þe chirche at masse aftir þe vse of salesbery. markid wiþ lettris of þe a. b. c. at þe bigynnyng of þe chapitris toward þe myddil or ende after þe ordre as þe lettris stonden in the. a. b. c. first ben set sundaies & ferials togidere & after þe sanctorum comyn and propre togidere of al þe ȝeer. first written a clause of þe bigynnyng þerof. & a clause of þe ending þerof also*'. The entries consist of the name of a liturgical occasion in red, abbreviated reference to a book and chapter of the Bible, an indexing letter in red, the opening words of a reading, '*ende*' in red, and the closing words of a reading. Includes the temporal, commemorations and the sanctoral. Commemorations are in the following order: Our Lady, Trinity, Holy Ghost, cross, angels, brothers and sisters and '*salus populi*', peace, clear weather, rain, '*In tyme of batels*', '*A man for him self*', '*pestilence of beestes*', pilgrims, weddings, sinners, sick and dead. Includes all feasts characteristic of LV, apart from Giles (1 September) (Forshall and Madden (1850), vol. 4, pp. 683, 690–6). Conception of our Lady, Candlemas, Annunciation, Nativity of John the Baptist, Peter and Paul, Assumption, Nativity of our Lady, Exaltation of the Cross (September) and Halloween start with blue initials. About two-thirds of fol. 7v are ruled for the table of lections but blank; fol. 8r–v is originally blank (see Provenance).

[item 2 occupies quires II–LVI]
2. (fols. 9r–449v) ONT in LV. Imperfect at the beginning, starting at Genesis 1:20 ('...*þe erþe vndur þe firmament*'). Unique prologues to all books from Exodus to Proverbs (except 2 Chronicles which originally must have had a prologue but lacks the beginning because of the loss of a leaf after fol. 152; missing 1 Chronicles, 29:7–2 Chronicles, 3:1) and to Jeremiah and 1 Maccabees. The prologues to Ezekiel and Daniel are shared with Cambridge University Library MS Dd. I. 27. The unique prologues are listed in Dove (2007), pp. 200–4 (siglum M), apart from the prologue to Joshua '*This book*

of iosue makiþ mynde how þe lord…' (fol. 77v), and printed in Forshall and Madden (1850). The books from Ecclesiastes to Ecclesiasticus have longer than usual rubrics, some explaining that they do not need prologues: '*Here endiþ þe book of prouerbis & here bigynneþ þe book of ecclesiastes þat tretiþ also of wisdom & prudence & nediþ noon oþer prologe*' (Ecclesiastes, fol. 228v); '*Here endiþ þe book of ecclesiastes & here bigynneþ þe book of song of songis þat weren maad of salomon to be sungen in þe temple of þe lord in to euerelastinge wurschiping & nediþ noon þe prologe*' (Song of Songs, fol. 231v); '*Here endiþ þe book of songis & here bigynneþ þe book of wisdom which is red in holi cherche in lessouns of þe masse for þe mater þerof is goostli & profecie of þingis to comynge*' (Wisdom, fol. 233r); '*Here endiþ þe book of wisdom and here bigynneþ þe book of ecclesiasticus þat tretiþ also of wisdom and prudence in many degrees of þe world*' (Ecclesiasticus, fol. 238v). Usual LV prologues to Isaiah and Baruch; no prologues to Hosea-Malachi and 2 Maccabees.

Rubrics in red, e.g., '*Here endiþ þe book of genesis & here bigynneþ a prologe on þe book of exodi*', '*Here endiþ þe prologe & here biginneþ þe book of Exodi*'. Running titles above each column in red preceded by blue paraphs, consisting of book titles only. Chapter numbers in red Roman numerals. Added material within the text is underlined in black. No marginal glosses; includes a few of a series of glosses in Pentateuch written within the text (see Dove (2007), p. 264). Indexing letters occasionally appear in the margins placed at the beginnings of lections rather than consistently; double strokes in the margins at the ends of lections. Corrections in the original or contemporary hands, those in the margins are sometimes in red boxes. Red and blue paraphs within the text. Rubrics in Esther and Daniel pointing out the differences between the Latin and Hebrew texts.

Psalms written as prose with verses starting with alternating 1-line red or blue initials. Each psalm is preceded by a title in red ink. Latin incipits are added in a later cursive hand in the margins. Larger initials at the beginnings of psalms 26, 38, 52, 68, 80, 97 and 109. Psalm 118 has 3-line initials at the beginning of 11-verse units. At the end of psalms: '*Here endiþ þe sauter but more salmes suwen þat ben writen in þe sauter whiche ben writen in diuerse chapitles* [sic] *of þe bible bible* [sic] *bifore & after whiche it is no nede to writen hem twies þer for we enden here & here bigynneþ a prologe vpon prouerbis of salomon*'

NT starts on a new quire (fol. 361r) following a larger than usual 10-leaf quire at the end of OT and ends with a 10-leaf quire; books have usual LV prologues. The Apocalypse ends in the first column on fol. 449v; the second column and fol. 250 are blank.

Decoration

7-line gold initials on blue and pink background, decorated with sprays of foliage and gold disks at the beginning of Leviticus, Joshua, 3 Kings, 1 Chronicles (cut out), psalms (cut out), Proverbs (cut out), Isaiah, Ezekiel, Hosea, I Maccabees, Matthew (cut out), other gospels, Romans, 2 Corinthians, 1 Thessalonians, Hebrews, Acts and James.

6- to 7-line red and blue 'puzzle' initials decorated with red and blue penwork foliage, and sometimes penwork borders at the beginnings of other books. An initial is cut out on fol. 97 at the beginning of 1 Kings.

3- to 4-line blue initials with red penwork at the beginnings of chapters and prologues.

Dialect

ony(10), ech(10), fijr(10), ȝouen(10), lijf(10), lijk(10), myche(10), seȝ(5)/sawȝ(2) (sg.), saien(4)/seiȝen(2) (pl.), self(10), suche(7)/such(2), þouȝ(7), þoruȝ(10)

Also: knewȝ, slowȝ, snowȝ.

-iþ(8)/-eþ(2) (pres.ind.3sg.), -en(10) (pres.ind.pl.), -ynge(6)/-inge(4) (pres. part.), sche(10) (3sg.fem.pronoun, nom.), þei(10) (3pl.pronoun, nom.), hem(10) (3pl.pronoun, oblique), her(10) (3pl.pronoun, possessive)

Physical description

MATERIAL: parchment

DIMENSIONS: *c.*432 × 300 mm, trimmed in rebinding

NUMBER OF LEAVES: 451

FOLIATION: modern in pencil, i + 450

COLLATION: (fol. i) parchment flyleaf conjoint with the upper pastedown | (fols. 1–8) I (8) | (fols. 9–15) II (8–1) missing 1 | (fols. 16–151) III–XIX (8) | (fols. 152–158) XX (8–1) missing 2 | (fols. 159–350) XXI–XLIV (8) | (fols. 351–360) XLV (10) | (fols. 361–440) XLVI–LV (8) | (fols. 441–449) LVI (10) missing 10 | (fol. 450) parchment flyleaf conjoint with the lower pastedown

Catchwords survive; medieval quire signatures occasionally survive.

RULING: ruled for two columns with single vertical and horizontal bounding lines extending the full height and width of page; a second set of double bounding lines in all four margins; 60 lines per page; written space: *c.*325 × 210 mm

SCRIPT: textura, black ink

RUBRICATION: rubrics in red

SEC. FOL.: '*Mt. v. & vi.*' (table of lections, fol. 10r); '*dide a sone*' (OT, fol. 10r)

Binding

Brown leather over pasteboard. Blind fillet-line and roll decoration on both covers. Ten raised bands on spine. Two paper labels on spine with typewritten '1' and handwritten '388'. Writing in faded ink on the fore-edge of textblock. Parchment pastedowns and flyleaves.

Provenance

1. William Smyth, 1561–1563: '*Ego Will(el)mus Smyth seruiens scutellie dominae reginae elezabethae incepi legere 2° die Octob. an° 1561 et finem feci 10 die Junii a° 1563 iterum relegere incepi 12° Junii an° praedicto*' (fol. 8v).

2. Loaned to Forshall, 9 July 1831 (fol. i verso).

3. Queen's College, Oxford; bookplate on the upper pastedown.

Bibliography

Forshall and Madden (1850), vol. 1, p. liii.

Coxe (1852), vol. 1, *Codices MSS. Collegii Reginensis*, p. 89.

Alexander, J. J. G. and Temple, E., *Illuminated manuscripts in Oxford College libraries, the University Archives and the Taylor Institution* (Oxford: Clarendon Press, 1985), no. 397.

Ogilvie-Thomson, S. J., *IMEP*, Handlist VIII (1991), p. 84.

Dove (2007), pp. 17, 59, 62, 65, 96, 99, 100, 106, 107, 127, 129, 156, 193, 200, 201, 202, 203, 204, 263–4, 302.

62 Trinity College MS 93

Origin: England

Date: 15th century, early

Text

Fols. i–v are paper and parchment flyleaves (see Provenance).

(fols. 1r–200v) Summary of the Bible in English from Genesis to the beginning James, not known from any other sources. Everything after the opening lines of the summary of James is missing because of the loss of leaves. 2 Maccabees is missing because of a lacuna after fol. 150. Further lacunae in the summaries of Genesis (after fol. 1), 1 and 2 Chronicles (after fol. 21), 1 Maccabees (after fol. 150), Matthew (after fol. 153), 2 Thessalonians and 1 Timothy (after fol. 189) (see Collation). The order of books is that of LV, but includes 1 Ezra, '*Neemy*', 'ij Ezdre' (i.e., 3 Ezra), and 4 Ezra subdivided into 'iij Ezdre' (4 Ezra, 1–2, in 6 chapters), 'iiij Ezdre' (4 Ezra, 3–14, in 34 chapters) and 'v Ezdre' (4 Ezra, 15–16, in 14 chapters) (see Ker (1960)). The summaries of Job, Proverbs and Ecclesiasticus are longer than average, and the summaries of Isaiah, Jeremiah and Ezekiel are particularly long. Lamentations of Jeremiah appear as a separate item. The summaries of the gospels are short, whereas the summaries of 1–2 Corinthians and Hebrews are considerably longer than average. Commentary, most attributed to Lyra, appears in psalms and occasionally in other summaries. Agrees in wording with both EV and LV, but is largely independent and is not particularly close to either.

Psalms are individually summarised, with entries largely consisting of commentary attributed to Lyra and the *Glossa Ordinaria*. The entries are preceded by Latin incipits. Larger initials at psalms 26, 38, 52, 68, 80 and 109. Psalm numbers in Arabic numerals are written in the margins by the main scribe.

Running titles in brown ink, in English or Latin, on both rectos and versos consisting of abbreviated titles of biblical books. Chapter numbers as Arabic numerals in the margins. Large spaces corresponding to 3–10 lines of text are left blank between the summaries of individual books, presumably intended for rubrics but not filled in.

Decoration

2-line plain blue initials at the beginnings of books.

1-line alternating red or blue initials and paraphs at the beginnings of sections within the text.

Dialect

any(2), ich(5), fire(1)/fir(2), gyuen(3), life(9)/liue(1), like(6), mych(4)/mycle(6), self(10), such(7), þorw(4)

-es(10) (pres.ind.3sg.), -en(10) (pres.ind.pl.), -ing(10) (pres.part.), she(10) (3sg.fem.pronoun, nom.), þey(10) (3pl.pronoun, nom.), þem(8)/hem(2) (3pl. pronoun, oblique), þeir(8)/her(2) (3pl.pronoun, possessive)

Also: luf ('love'), are ('are').

Physical description

MATERIAL: parchment, paper flyleaves

DIMENSIONS: *c.*206 × 138 mm; cropped in rebinding, occasionally with a loss of marginal text, particularly running titles

NUMBER OF LEAVES: 210

FOLIATION: modern in pencil: i–v + 1–205

COLLATION: (fols. i–v) paper and parchment flyleaves | (fols. 1–7) I (8–1) missing 2 | (fols. 8–15) II (8) | (fols. 16–21) III (8–2) missing 7, 8 | (fols. 22–149) IV–XIX (8) | (fols. 150) XX (single leaf from a missing quire) | (fols. 151–157) XXI (8–1) missing 4 | (fols. 158–189) XXII–XXV (8) | (fols. 190–196) XXVI (8–1) missing 1 | (fols. 197–200) XXVII (4) | (fols. 201–205) parchment and paper flyleaves

Catchwords and quire signatures occasionally survive ('g iii' on fol. 48 is the first to be seen and 'p iii' on fol. 113 is the last).

RULING: ruled for a single column with single vertical and horizontal bounding lines extending the full height and width of page (see fol. 194v); 35–9 lines per page; written space: *c.*159–169 × 115–125 mm

SCRIPT: Anglicana influenced by Secretary

SEC. FOL.: '*Iacob duelled*' (fol. 2r)

Binding

Marbled paper and red leather over pasteboard, 19th century (1808 (?)). Red leather spine with gilt decoration. Gilt lettering on spine: 'TREVISA'S COMM || ON THE BIBLE' and 'M.S.S ANT.'. Marbled paper pastedowns; paper and parchment flyleaves.

Provenance

1. The treatment of the books of Ezra suggests that the summaries were made from a Latin Bible of English origin and not from the 'Paris' text (cf. Ker (1960)). The author compared and made use of EV and LV. Contains some northern linguistic forms.

2. Many marginal inscriptions and pen trials in 16th-century hands, including: '*John Bewleye*' (fol. 58r), '*This is William Daunce book Record of Thomas Shawe and of many more of his fellowes I beare wytnes to the same William Daunce is my name*' (fol. 60v), '*John Nott is a knave by mee William Daunce 1576*' (on specially ruled lines, fol. 34v), '*Thomas pim is m[y] name*' (fol. 103r). Most inscriptions are by Thomas Shawe.

3. Belonged to James Dalloway, scholar of Trinity College, Oxford (MA, 1784), and was given by him in 1808 to James Ingram (1774–1850), Old English scholar and antiquary (see *ODNB*), with the expression of their joint wish that it should remain forever at Trinity College: '*Iacobo Ingram | Coll: S: Trin: apud Oxon: Soc: | hoc opus MS: | D.D. | Iacobus Dallaway M.B. | eiusd: coll: olim scholaris | quod ibidem | perpetuo adseruandum | voluerunt ambo | qui clepserit | aut alio quocumque modo | fraudem faxit | deae fidei sacer esto | MDCCCVIII*' (fol. v verso). Notes by Ingram on fols. iii verso–iv recto, 201r–203r, ascribing the summary to Trevisa.

4. Trinity College, Oxford: presumably bequeathed by Ingram, president of Trinity from 1824 until his death in 1850.

Bibliography

Ker, N. R., 'A Middle-English summary of the Bible', *Medium Aevum* 29 (1960), pp. 115–18.
Fowler, D., 'A Middle English Bible commentary (Oxford, Trinity College, MS 93)', *Manuscripta* 12 (1968), pp. 67–78.
Ker (1969–2002), vol. 3, p. 713.
Dove (2007), pp. 52, 303.

63 University College MS 96

Siglum: β

Origin: England

Date: 15th century, second quarter

Text

Five originally blank unnumbered leaves at the beginning (see Provenance).

[items 1–3 occupy quires I–VIII]
1. (fols. 1r–94r) General Prologue to the Wycliffite Bible (collated in Dove's edition (2010)). Chapter numbers in black by the scribe in the form '*c*^{m} *iij*^{m}', preceded by black paraphs. Approximately a half of fol. 94r is blank.

2. (fols. 94v–95r) A list of books in the Wycliffite Bible in English in the usual order of LV, with the number of chapters in each book in Roman numerals. The list starts with '*The prolog*', containing fifteen chapters, and includes Lamentations of Jeremiah, and 1 and 2 Ezra, but not 3 Ezra. The list of the NT books is subdivided into '*The iiij Euangelistes*' and '*Epistoles*

of Poule'. Ends with '*The summe of bookes with þe prolog conteyneþ lxx[...]*' (cropped off).

3. (fols. 95v–96r) Old Testament genealogies in Latin. Fol. 96v is blank.

[items 4–5 occupy quires IX–X]
4. (fols. 97r–109v) Chapters from the gospels in LV containing the accounts of Passion and Resurrection: John 18–20:18, followed by '*Explicit pascio in die Parasceu & hic incipit in festo ramis Palmarum*' (fol. 101v), and Matthew 25:31–28. Gloss on Matthew 26:53 in the lower margin of fol. 104v explaining the number of items in '*xij legions*'.

5. (fol. 109v) Ten commandments in verse, twelve lines (*IMEV* 3684, *NIMEV* 3684, *DIMEV* 5844; see also Morey (2000), p. 165; ed. Brown (1932)). Fols. 10r–113r are ruled (bounding lines only), but blank.

6. (fol. 113v) Additions in a hand of the second half of the 15th century: verses 1–3 of psalm 109, '*Dixit dominus domino meo … ante luciferum*', followed by the words '*dede me*' on a separate line, followed by John 1:6 and a name: '*Fuit homo missus a deo cui nomen erat Iohannes stephano(n) larkyn*'.

Decoration
3-line spaces left for initials, but not filled in, apart from plain red initials on fols. 5r–7r.

Dialect
I. The General Prologue
any(6)/ony(3), ech(3)/eche(1), ȝouon(1)/ȝouun(1), lyf(5), lyk(1), meche(10), siȝ(1) (sg), self(3)/sylf(3)/silf(1), such(1)/suche(3)

-eþ(1)/-eth(8)/-uth(1) (pres.ind.3sg.), -en(9)/-un(1)/-e(1) (pres.ind.pl.), -yng(3)/-ynge(1) (pres.part.), she(1) (3sg.fem.pronoun, nom.), þey(9)/ they(1) (3pl.pronoun, nom.), hem(10) (3pl.pronoun, oblique), hurre (used consistently, only rarely alternating with herre(2)) (3pl.pronoun, possessive)

Also:
1. weche(13)/wyche(4)/wich(1) 'which', weche 'witch'

2. furst(7)/first(3) 'first', churche(3) 'church', ȝutte(5) 'yet', trust(2)/trist(1) 'trust', kulled(e)(5)/kulloden(1)/cullode(1)/cullodon(1)/kyllyde(1) 'killed', prust(es)(3)/prest(es)(4) 'priest', gulty(2) 'gilty', hull(1)/hyl(1) 'hill'

3. vedde 'fed'

4. taute 'taught', broute 'brought', ordeigned 'ordeyned', strenghe(1)/strengþe(1) 'strength'

5. be cudde 'be cut'

II. Chapters from the gospels
any(2)/ony(2), ech(3), fier(1), ȝouon(1)/ȝouu(2)/ȝeuon(1), lyf(2), lyk(1), meche(2), siȝ(10) (sg.), siȝ(2)/seiȝ(1)/sey(1)/saien(1) (pl.), self(3)/sylf(6), þurȝ(1), þouȝ(2)

-eþ(5)/-eth(1) (pres.ind.3sg.), -on(7)/-en(2) (pres.ind.pl.), -yng(8)/-ynge(3) (pres.part.), she(10) (3sg.fem.pronoun, nom.), þey(10) (3pl.pronoun, nom.), hem(10) (3pl.pronoun, oblique), her(5)/hir(1) (3pl.pronoun, possessive), hurre(1) 'her'

Also:
1. weche(5)/wych(2), prestes(1)

2. busshep(es)(10) 'bishop(s)', furst(3)/first(3) 'first', suster(1) 'sister', birye(1) 'bury', byryel(2) 'sepulchre', ȝutte(1)/ȝut(5) 'yet', cusse(1)/cussede(1) 'kiss', hulden 'held', gylty(1)/giltles(1) 'guilty/guiltless', euel(1)/yuel(2) 'evil', hul(1) 'hill'

3. (y)tawte(3) 'taught', knew(3) 'knew', drow(2) 'drew', crew(1)/krew(2) 'crew'

Physical description
MATERIAL: parchment

DIMENSIONS: *c.*175 × 140 mm, leaves were trimmed, occasionally causing the loss of text in the margins

NUMBER OF LEAVES: 119

FOLIATION: modern in pencil, 5 unnumbered leaves + 1–114

COLLATION: unnumbered parchment leaves: 6-leaf quire with a missing second leaf (stub survives) | (fols. 1–108) I–IX (12) | (fols. 109–114) X (6)
Quires are numbered by the scribe in Roman numerals on the first leaf of each quire, [I]–X, see fols. 37r, 61r, 73r, 85r, 97r, 109; no catchwords.

RULING: ruled for a single column with single vertical and horizontal bounding lines; 18–20 lines per page; written space: *c.*125 × 150 mm

SCRIPT: Anglicana with Secretary influence, similar to the hand of the General Prologue in Trinity College Dublin MS 75, fols. 218r–251r

SEC. FOL.: '*make o book*' (fol. 2r)

Binding

Quires sown on three cords without a spine or a cover, but the outside leaves of the first and last booklets were probably always intended to serve as cover. Evidence of a paper label in the lower left corner of the outside leaf of the first quire.

Provenance

1. The compilation was probably put together by the scribe: the quires are numbered consecutively in a medieval hand, the ruling and presentation of texts (including unfilled spaces left for initials) are consistent throughout; there are 6-leaf quires at the beginning and end, and 12-leaf quires in the middle. Perhaps copied from a manuscript that contained the full Bible preceded by the General Prologue, as suggested by a list of biblical books (fols. 94v–95r) that starts with '*The prolog*', containing fifteen chapters.

2. Price: '*p(re)c(ium) viij s iiij d*', 15th century, fol. 109v.

3. '*Iohannes stephano(n) larkyn*', 15th century, fol. 113v.

4. Walker, Obadiah (1616–1699) (?), Master of University College; see *ODNB*. On a flyleaf at the beginning: '*This book seemeth to have been made by John Wickliffe*' and beneath '*I take this note to be of Mr Obad. Walker's handwriting. Teste Guil. Smith, Aug. 26, 1700*'.

5. University College, Oxford. Earlier shelfmark 'G. 3. XCVI', 'G. 3', upper cover and flyleaves.

Bibliography

Forshall and Madden (1850), vol. 1, p. liii.
Coxe (1852), vol. 1, p. 28.
Brown, C., *English lyrics of the XIIIth century* (Oxford: Clarendon Press, 1932), pp. 219–20.
Hudson (1978), p. 173.
Ogilvie-Thomson, S. J., *IMEP*, Handlist VIII (1991), p. 109.
Dove (2007), pp. 120, 243, 303.
Cole, A., *Literature and heresy in the age of Chaucer* (Cambridge: Cambridge University Press, 2008), p. 223 n. 24.
Dove (2010), p. xxvii.

64 Worcester College MS E. 10. 7

Origin: England

Date: 14th century, last quarter

Text

Two leaves used as flyleaves in the binding of P. Fonseca's commentary on Aristotle's Metaphysics (*Commentariorum Petri Fonsecae Lvsitani, Doctoris Theologi Societatis Iesu, in Libros Mataphysicorum Aristotelis Stagiritae, tomus primus*, Frankfurt: Ioannes Saurius, 1599). Both leaves are fragmentary; the verso of the leaf at the front of the book and the recto of the leaf at the back of the book are badly rubbed and largely unreadable. Deuteronomy in EV; the leaf at the front contains 21:1–23:4, the leaf at the back used to follow it in the original manuscript and contains 23:4–25:11.

No evidence of marginal glosses; apparently a correction in the first line of the first column of the recto of the leaf at the front; added material within the text is not underlined. Plain red 2- or 3-line initials at the beginnings of chapters; running titles in red on both rectos and versos, consisting of an abbreviated title of the book without a chapter number.

Dialect

puple(2), wijf(2), lijf(1), self(1), yuel(1), synneþ(1), puniȝsshinge(1), land(2), blood(2), ȝif(5)

-iþ(2)/-eþ(2) (pres.ind.3sg.), -en(2) (pres.ind.pl.), -yng(2)/-ing(1) (pres.part.), hem(4) (3pl.pronoun, oblique), sheo(8) (3sg.fem.pronoun, nom.)

Physical description

MATERIAL: parchment

DIMENSIONS: *c*.233 × 160 mm, originally considerably larger

RULING: ruled for two columns; over 40 lines per page

SCRIPT: Anglicana, black ink

Provenance

1. Inscription on flyleaf: '*3º July 1634 || Liber Aulae Gloucestrensis ex dono Johannis Goodridge in Artibus Magistri, et hujus Aulae quondam Commensalis*'. Foster (1891–92), p. 583, lists John Goodridge of Devon who matriculated at Balliol College in 1597/8 and received an MA from Gloucester Hall in 1606, but the date of his death is 1624.

2. Gloucester Hall, founded in 1560 by Sir Thomas White, the founder of St John's College. Its predecessor on the same site was Gloucester College, that was founded in 1283 by the Benedictine Abbey of St Peter at Gloucester and existed until the dissolution of the monasteries in 1539.

3. Worcester College, Oxford. Gloucester Hall was re-founded as Worcester College in 1714.

Bibliography

Ker, N. R., *Fragments of medieval manuscripts used as pastedowns in Oxford bindings: with a survey of Oxford binding c.1515–1620* (Oxford: Printed for the Oxford Bibliographical Society by A. T. Broome, 1954), no. 1527, p. 140.

Dove (2007), p. 303.

Appendix

I *The contents of the Wycliffite Bible*

The Latin sources of prologues are listed in Dove (2007), pp. 199–209.

The Earlier Version: standard contents

Old Testament

Jerome's prefatory epistles ('*Broþer Ambrose to me þi lytyll ȝiftis...*' and '*Ich haue (y)take desyrid epystles...*')
Genesis
Exodus
Leviticus
Numbers
Deuteronomy
Prologue to Joshua ('*At þe laste ended þe fyfe bokys of Moyses...*')
Joshua
Judges
Ruth
Prologue to 1 Kings ('*Þe tunge forsoþe of Syriis and of Caldeis...*')
1 Kings
2 Kings
3 Kings
4 Kings

Prologue to 1 Chronicles (‘*Iff þe making of þe seuenti remenouris abide stille pure…*’)
Prologue to 1 Chronicles (‘*Þe booc of Paralipomenon þat is þe breggyng…*’)
1 Chronicles
Prologue to 2 Chronicles (‘*Eusebeus Jerome senden gretyng…*’)
2 Chronicles
Prayer of Manasseh
Prologue to 1 Ezra (‘*Wheþer it be hardere to don þat ȝee asken…*’)
Prologue to 1 Ezra (‘*Esdras and Neemye helpere…*’)
‘*Þe comendacioun of Esdre*’ (‘*Þis aftir Jude brend vp of þe Caldeys…*’)
1 Ezra
2 Ezra
3 Ezra
Prologue to Tobit (‘*To Cromacio and Eliodre bisshopis…*’)
Tobit
Prologue to Judith (‘*Anentis þe Ebrues þe boc of Judith is rad…*’)
Prologue to Judith (‘*Judith widewe þe doȝter of Merari…*’)
Judith
Prologue to Esther (‘*Þe booc of Ester to ben maad vicious…*’)
Esther
Prologue to Job (‘*I am constreyned bi alle þe bookis of Goddis scripture…*’)
Prologue to Job (‘*Iff forsoþe a jonket wiþ ressshe…*’)
Job
Prologue to Psalms (‘*Whan it is knowen alle þe prophetys to han spoken…*’)
Prologue to Psalms (‘*Dauyd þe sone of Jesse whan he was in his rewme…*’)
Psalms
Prologue to Proverbs (‘*To Cromacye and Eliodere bisshopis…*’)
Proverbs
Prologue to Ecclesiastes (‘*Þis almost þe fifte ȝer whan ȝit I was att Rome…*’)
Ecclesiastes
Song of Songs
Prologue to Wisdom (‘*Þe booc of Wisdam anentis Ebrues nowher is…*’)
Wisdom
Prologue to Ecclesiasticus (‘*Off manye and grete bi þe lawe and profetes...*’)

Ecclesiasticus

Prologue to Isaiah ('*No man whan þe prophetis he shal seen...*')

Isaiah

Prologue to Jeremiah ('*Jeremye þe prophete to whom þis prologe is ascriued...*')

Prologue to Jeremiah ('*God is redi to ȝyue good, to punshen a tariere...*')

Jeremiah

Lamentations of Jeremiah

Prayer of Jeremiah

Prologue to Baruch ('*Þis book þat Baruch bi name is befor-notid...*')

Baruch

Epistle of Jeremiah

Ezekiel

Daniel

Hosea

Joel

Amos

Obadiah

Jonah

Micah

Nahum

Habakkuk

Zephaniah

Haggai

Zechariah

Malachi

1 Maccabees

2 Maccabees

New Testament

Prologue to Matthew ('*Mathew of Jewerie born, as he is put first in ordre...*')

Matthew

Prologue to Mark ('*Mark þe euangelist of God chosen and Petris sone in baptem...*')

Mark
Prologue to Luke (‘*Luk of Antioche of Cire nacyoun in craft a leche…*’)
Luke
Prologue to John (‘*Þis is John ewangelist, oen of disciplis off God…*’)
John
Prologue to Romans (‘*First vndirstonden vs bihoueþ to whom or whi þe apostil Powil…*’)
Romans
Prologue to 1 Corinthians (‘*Corintheis ben men of Achaie and þese also…*’)
1 Corinthians
Prologue to 2 Corinthians (‘*Aftir penaunce don a counfortable epistil he wryteþ…*’)
2 Corinthians
Prologue to Galatians (‘*Galathiis ben Grekis. Þes þe wrd of treuþe…*’)
Galatians
Prologue to Ephesians (‘*Ephecyes soþli ben Asianes…*’)
Ephesians
Prologue to Philippians (‘*Philipenses ben men of Macedoyne…*’)
Philippians
Prologue to Colossians (‘*Colocences also þese as Laodicensis…*’)
Colossians
Prologue to 1 Thessalonians (‘*Tessalonycenses ben men of Macedoyne…*’)
1 Thessalonians
Prologue to 2 Thessalonians (‘*To Tessalonycensses þe apostil wrytiþ…*’)
2 Thessalonians
Prologue to 1 Timothy (‘*Tymothe þe apostil enfoormeþ and teche…*’)
1 Timothy
Prologue to 2 Timothy (‘*Also he writiþ to Tymothe of þe exortacioun…*’)
2 Timothy
Prologue to Titus (‘*Tyte he counceiliþ and enformeþ…*’)
Titus
Prologue to Philemon (‘*To Filomon he makiþ homly lettris…*’)
Philemon
Prologue to Hebrews (‘*In þe firste it is to seie whi þe apostil Powil…*’)
Hebrews

Prologue to Acts (‘*Luk of Sirie by nacioun whos preising in þe euangelie…*’)
Acts
Prologue to James (‘*Not þe same ordre is at Greekis þat holly sauouren…*’)
James
1 Peter
2 Peter
1 John
2 John
3 John
Jude
Prologue to Apocalypse (‘*Jon þe apostil and euangelist of oure lord Jhesu Crist…*’)
Apocalypse

The Later Version: standard contents

Old Testament

Genesis
Exodus
Leviticus
Numbers
Deuteronomy
Joshua
Judges
Ruth
1 Kings
2 Kings
3 Kings
4 Kings
1 Chronicles
2 Chronicles
Prayer of Manasseh
1 Ezra
2 Ezra
Tobit

Judith
Esther
Job
Psalms
Proverbs
Ecclesiastes
Song of Songs
Wisdom
Ecclesiasticus
Prologue to Isaiah (*'As seynt Jerom seiþ in þe prolog of Ysaie…'*)
Isaiah
Jeremiah
Lamentations of Jeremiah
Prayer of Jeremiah
Prologue to Baruch (*'Þis book which is titlid bi þe name of Baruk…'*)
Baruch
Epistle of Jeremiah
Ezekiel
Daniel
Hosea
Joel
Amos
Obadiah
Jonah
Micah
Nahum
Habakkuk
Zephaniah
Haggai
Zechariah
Malachi
1 Maccabees
2 Maccabees

New Testament

Prologue to Matthew ('*Matheu þat was of Judee, as he is set first in ordre...*')

Matthew

Prologue to Mark ('*Mark þe gospeller was þe chosen seruaunt of God...*')

Mark

Prologue to Luke ('*Luik was a man of Syrie bi nacioun and of Antiochie and was a leche...*')

Luke

Prologue to John ('*Þis is Joon euangelist, oon of þe disciplis of þe Lord...*')

John

Prologue to Romans ('*Romayns ben in þe cuntree of Italye; þei weren disseyued...*')

Romans

Prologue to 1 Corinthians ('*Corinthies ben of Acaye and þei in lijk maner herden...*')

1 Corinthians

Prologue to 2 Corinthians ('*After penaunce doon, Poul writiþ...*')

2 Corinthians

Prologue to Galatians ('*Galathies ben Grekis. Þei token first of þe postle...*')

Galatians

Prologue to Ephesians ('*Effesians ben of Asie...*')

Ephesians

Prologue to Philippians ('*Philipensis ben of Macedoyne...*')

Philippians

Prologue to Colossians ('*Colocensis ben also Laodicenses...*')

Colossians

Prologue to 1 Thessalonians ('*Thessalonicensis ben Macedonyes...*')

1 Thessalonians

Prologue to 2 Thessalonians ('*Þe apostle writiþ þe secounde...*')

2 Thessalonians

Prologue to 1 Timothy ('*He enformeþ and techiþ Tymothe...*')

1 Timothy

Prologue to 2 Timothy ('*He writiþ also to Tymothe of exortacioun...*')

2 Timothy

Prologue to Titus (‘*He warneþ Tite and enfourmeþ…*’)

Titus

Prologue to Philemon (‘*He makiþ famyliar or homeli lettris to Filemon…*’)

Philemon

Prologue to Hebrews (‘*First it is to seye whi Poul þe apostle in þis epistle…*’)

Hebrews

Prologue to Acts (‘*Luk of Antioche of þe nacioun of Sirie whos preisyng…*’)

Acts

Prologue to James (‘*The ordre of þe seuene epistlis whiche ben clepid canonysid…*’)

James

1 Peter

2 Peter

1 John

2 John

3 John

Jude

Prologue to Apocalypse (‘*Alle men þat wolen lyue mekeli in Crist as þe apostle seiþ…*’)

Apocalypse

II *Manuscripts containing the Earlier Version or combining the Earlier and Later Versions*

The Earlier Version

MS Bodl. 771, MS Bodl. 959, MS Douce 369, MS Douce 370, MS Hatton 111, MS Holkham misc. 40, MS Rawl. C. 258, Christ Church MS 145, Corpus Christi College MS 4, New College MS 67, Queen's College MS 369, Worcester College MS E. 10. 7

MS combining the Earlier and Later Versions (excluding para-biblical materials)

MS Bodl. 183 (OT books, except Tobit, have prologues in EV), MS Bodl. 277 (includes 3 Ezda, found otherwise only in EV MSS, in a lightly revised form; EV prologue to Romans), MS Fairfax 2 (EV prologues in OT), MS Rawl. C. 259 (EV prologue to Philemon), Brasenose College MS 10 (James and 1 Peter in EV), New College MS 66 (EV prologues), New College MS 320 (EV prologues).

III *The contents of manuscripts*

Manuscripts containing a calendar

MS Fairfax 11, MS Rawl. C. 237/MS Rawl. C. 238, MS Rawl. C. 259, MS Selden Supra 49

Manuscripts containing a calendar-lectionary

MS Fairfax 2, MS Laud misc. 388, MS Selden Supra 51; MS Ashmole 1517 may have originally included a calendar-lectionary.

Manuscripts containing a table of lections

Type I
MS Bodl. 183, MS Bodl. 665, MS Bodl. 771, MS Douce 240, MS Douce 265, MS Fairfax 11, MS Fairfax 21, MS Junius 29, MS Laud misc. 388, MS Lyell 26, MS Rawl. C. 259, MS Selden Supra 49, Christ Church MS 145, MS Christ Church 146, Queen's College MS 388

Type II
MS Bodl. 978, MS Gough Eccl. Top. 5, MS Hatton 111, Brasenose College MS 10, Corpus Christi College MS 4, Oriel College MS 80

Temporal and commemorations only

MS Ashmole 1517, MS Selden Supra 51

Latin

New College MS 67

Manuscripts containing a table of lections with OT readings written out in full

MS Bodl. 531, MS Douce 265-a

Manuscripts containing an OT lectionary

Type I
MS Laud misc. 388

Type II
MS Ashmole 1517, MS Bodl. 665, MS Rawl. C. 259, MS Selden Supra 51, MS Christ Church 146

Manuscripts containing a *capitula*-list

MS Fairfax 2, MS Hatton 111, MS e Mus. 110, MS Selden Supra 51, MS Christ Church 146

Manuscripts containing a list of biblical books

MS Bodl. 183 (added table of contents), MS Gough Eccl. Top. 5, MS Rawl. C. 259, Christ Church MS 145, Corpus Christi College MS 4, University College MS 96

Complete Bibles

MS Bodl. 277, MS Douce 369, MS Fairfax 2, Christ Church MS 145, Corpus Christi College MS 4, Lincoln College MS Lat. 119, St John's College Oxford MS 7 (possibly originally planned as a complete Bible), Queen's College MS 388

Psalters

MS Bodl. 554, MS New College 320

Manuscripts containing the General Prologue

MS Bodl. 277, Lincoln College MS Lat. 119, University College MS 96

Manuscripts containing *Oon of Foure*

MS Bodl. 771, MS Bodl. 978.

IV The origin and provenance of manuscripts

The following manuscripts contain evidence of either the origin, or medieval or early modern ownership in a particular geographical location:

Essex: MS Holkham misc. 40

Fellongley, Warwickshire (?): MS Douce 370

Hereford: MS Fairfax 11

London: MS Ashmole 1517, MS Bodl. 227, MS Laud misc. 24, MS Laud misc. 36, MS Laud misc. 388, MS Rawl. C. 259, MS Selden Supra 49, MS New College 320, Queen's College MS 388

Lincoln: MS Gough Eccl. Top. 5

Newcastle-upon-Tyne: MS Rawl. C. 258

Norfolk and Norwich: MS Laud misc. 207, MS Lyell 26 (?)

Northamptonshire: Christ Church MS 145

Shrewsbury: MS Bodl. 771, MS Rawl. C. 258.

V *Types of medieval owners*

Carthusians: MS Bodl. 227

Dominicans: MS Rawl. C. 258

Franciscans: MS Bodl. 771

Canon: MS Bodl. 531

Fishmonger (?): MS Lyell 27.

VI *Presentation of text*

Manuscripts entirely or partly in Anglicana: MS Bodl. 296, MS Bodl. 554 (gloss), MS Bodl. 959, MS Laud misc. 36, Corpus Christi College MS 20, Trinity College MS 93, University College MS 96, Worcester College MS E. 10. 7

Manuscripts in Secretary: New College MS 320

Manuscripts ruled entirely or partly for a single column: MS Bodl. 554, MS Bodl. 978, MS Douce 258, MS Dugdale 46, MS Hatton 111, MS Laud misc. 24, MS Laud misc. 36, MS Laud misc. 182, MS Laud misc. 207, MS Christ Church 147, New College MS 67, Trinity College MS 93, University College MS 96

Manuscripts on paper: New College MS 320.

VII *Rubrics to gospels and their prologues (collation)*

Sigla

D369 – Douce 369, part II
B277 – Bodl. 277
F2 – Fairfax 2
B183 – Bodl. 183
F11 – Fairfax 11
B531 – Bodl. 531
B665 – Bodl. 665
NY65 – New York Public Library MS MA 65
NY66 – New York Public Library MS MA 66

Prologue to Matthew

D369 '*Here endiþ þe storie of machabeus þe which is þe laste book of þe olde testament And now bigynneþ þe newe testament ffirst is þe prologu of Matheu apostle & euangelist*'

B227 *Heere bigynniþ þe prologe of ierom on þe gospel of Matheu*'

F2 '*Heere endeþ þe secounde book of Macabeus and al þe oolde testament Se now þe newe testament || Heere bygynneþ þe Prolog of Ierom on Matheu*'.

B183 '*Here bigynneþ þe prolog of matheu*'

F11 '*Here bigynneþ þe prolog of mathew*'

B665 '*Here bigynneþ þe newe testament capitulum primum*'

B531 '*Here bigynneþ þe prolog on þe gospl* [sic] *of matheu*'

NY65 '*Here bigynneþ þe prolog on Matheu*'

NY66 omitted

Matthew

D369 *'Here endiþ þe prolog & begynn^t þe gospel'*

B227 *'Here bigynniþ þe gospel of Matheu'*

F2 *'Ierom in his prolog on Matheu seiþ þis pleinly'*

B183 *'Ierom on hise two prologis on Matheu seiþ þis plainly þe firste c^o'*

F11 *'Ierom on hise two prologis on Matheu seiþ þis playnly þe firste chapitre'*

B665 *'Ierom on hise twey prologis on mathew seiþ þis'*

B531 *'Ierom in his prolog on matheu seiþ al þis'*

NY65 *'Ierom in hise twei prologus on mathu seiþ pleynli þus'*

NY66 *'þus seiþ ierom in þis prolog on Mathew'*

Prologue to Mark

D369 *'Here endiþ þe gospel of M^t & bigynneþ þe prolog of mark'*

F2 *'Here eendeþ Mathew Se now þe prolog on Mark'*

B227 *'Heere endiþ þe gospel of Matheu and biginniþ þe prologe on þe gospel of Mark'*

B183 *'Here eendiþ þe gospel on matheu & bigynneþ þe prolog on Mark'*

F11 *'Here endiþ Matheu & bigynneþ þe prolog on Mark'*

B665 *'Here eendiþ þe gospel of Mathew and bigynneþ þe prolog of Mark'.*

B531 *'Here endiþ þe gospel of matheu and bigynneþ þe prolog on þe gospel of mark'*

NY65 *'Here endiþ mathu & bigynneþ þe prolog on mark'*

NY66 *'Here endiþ Mathew & bignneþ þe prologe on Mark'*

Mark

D369 *'Here endiþ þe prolog & bigynneþ þe gospel'*

B227 *'Heere endiþ þe prologe & bigynniþ þe gospel of Mark'*

F2 *'Ierom in his prolog on Mark seiþ þis pleynli'*

B183 *'þis seiþ Ierom in his prolog on mark And here bigynneþ þe i c°'*

F11 *'This seiþ Ierom in his prolog on mark And here bigynneth þe firste chapitre'*

B665 *'Here eendiþ þe prologe for þis seiþ Ierom in his prolog on Marke & now bigynneþ þe gospel of mark þe firste c°'*

B531 *'Al þis seiþ Ierom in his prolog on þe gospel of mark & here bigynneþ þe firste capitle'*

NY65 *'Ierom in his prolog on mark seiþ pleynli al þis'*

NY66 *'þus seiþ ierom in his prologe on Mark'*

Prologue to Luke

D369 *'Here endiþ þe gospel of mark & bigynneþ þe prolog of luk'*

B227 *'Heere endiþ þe gospel of Mark and biginniþ þe prologe on Luyk'*

F2 *'Here endeþ Mark Se now þe prolog on Luke'.*

B183 *'Here eendiþ þe gospel of Mark & Here bigynneþ þe prolog on Luyk'*

F11 *'Here eendiþ þe gospel of Mark & bigynneþ þe prolog on luk'*

B665 *'Here endiþ þe gospel of mark & bigynneþ þe prolog on þe gospel of luyk'*

B531 *'Here endiþ þe gospel of mark and bigynneþ þe prolog on þe gospel of luyk'*

NY65 *'Here endiþ mark & bigynneþ þe prolog on luyk'*

NY66 *'Here endiþ Mark & biginneþ þe prologe on luk'*

Luke

D369 *'Here endiþ þe prolog and bigynneþ þe gospel'*

B227 *'Here biginniþ þe gospel of luyk'*

F2 *'Here endeþ þe prolog on Luke Se now þe book of Luk'.*

B183 *'Ierom in his prolog on luk seiþ plainli þis sentence þe firste c°'*

F11 *'Ierom in his prolog on luk seiþ playnli þis sentence þe firste c°'*

B665 *'Ierom in his prolog seiþ al þis and heere endiþ þe prolog of luyk and now bigynneþe þe book of luyk sentence þe firste chapitir'.*

B531 *'Ierom in his prolog on þe gospel of luyk seiþ al þis þe firste capitle'*

NY65 omitted

NY66 '*þis seiþ ierom on þe gospel of luk*'

Prologue to John

D369 '*Here endiþ þe gospel of luk & bigynneþ þe prolog of Iohn*'

B277 '*Heere endiþ þe gospel of Luyk and biginniþ þe prologe of Ierom on þe gospel of Ioon*'

F2 '*Here eendeþ Luke Se now þe prolog on Ioon*'

B183 '*Here eendiþ þe gospel of luk & bigynneþ þe prolog on Ioon*'

F11 '*Here eendiþ þe gospel of luk & bigynneþ þe prolog on Ioon*'

B665 '*Here bigynneþ þe prolog on þe gospel of Ioon*'

531 '*Here endiþ þe gospel of luyk & bigynneþ þe prolog on þe gospel of Iohn*'

NY65 '*Here endiþ luyk & bigynneþ þe prolog on Ioon*'

NY66 '*Here endiþ luk & biginneþ þe prologe on þe gospel of ion*'

John

D369 '*Here endiþ þe prolog and bigynneþ þe gospel*'

B277 '*Heere endiþ þe prologe and heere biginniþ þe gospel of Ioon*'

F2 '*Ierom in his prolog on Ioon seiþ al þis Se now þe book*'

B183 '*Ierom in his prolog on Iohn seiþ al þis sentence And here bigynneþ þe gospel of Ioon þis þe firste chapitre*'

F11 '*Ierom in his prolog on Ioon seiþ al þis Here bigynneþ þe gospel of Ioon þe firste chapitre*'

B665 '*Ierom in his prolog on Iohn seiþ þis & here endiþ þe prolog & bigynneþ þe first c^{o}*'.

B531 '*Ierom in his prolog on Iohn seiþ al þis C^{m} p^{m}*'

NY65 omitted

NY66 '*þus seiþ ierom on iohn*'

Index

1 MS Ashmole 1517, fol. 167r. Old Testament lectionary

2 MS Bodl. 183, fol. 1r. Prologue and the beginning of Matthew

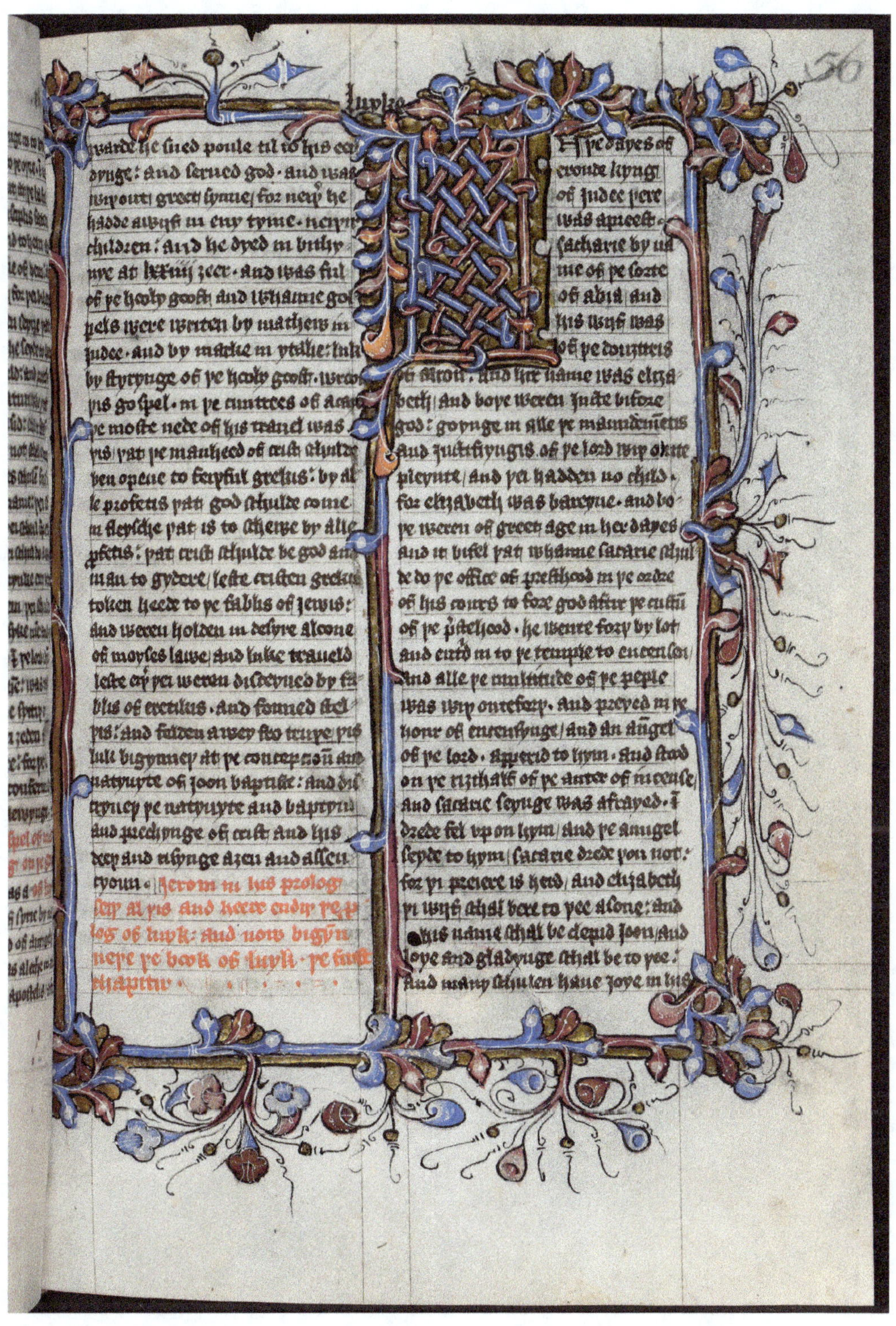

3 MS Bodl. 665, fol. 56r. Prologue and the beginning of Luke

4 MS Bodl. 277, fol. 179v. Psalms

5 MS Bodl. 959, fol. 329v. Lamentations of Jeremiah

6 MS Bodl. 978, fol. 123r. *Oon of Foure*

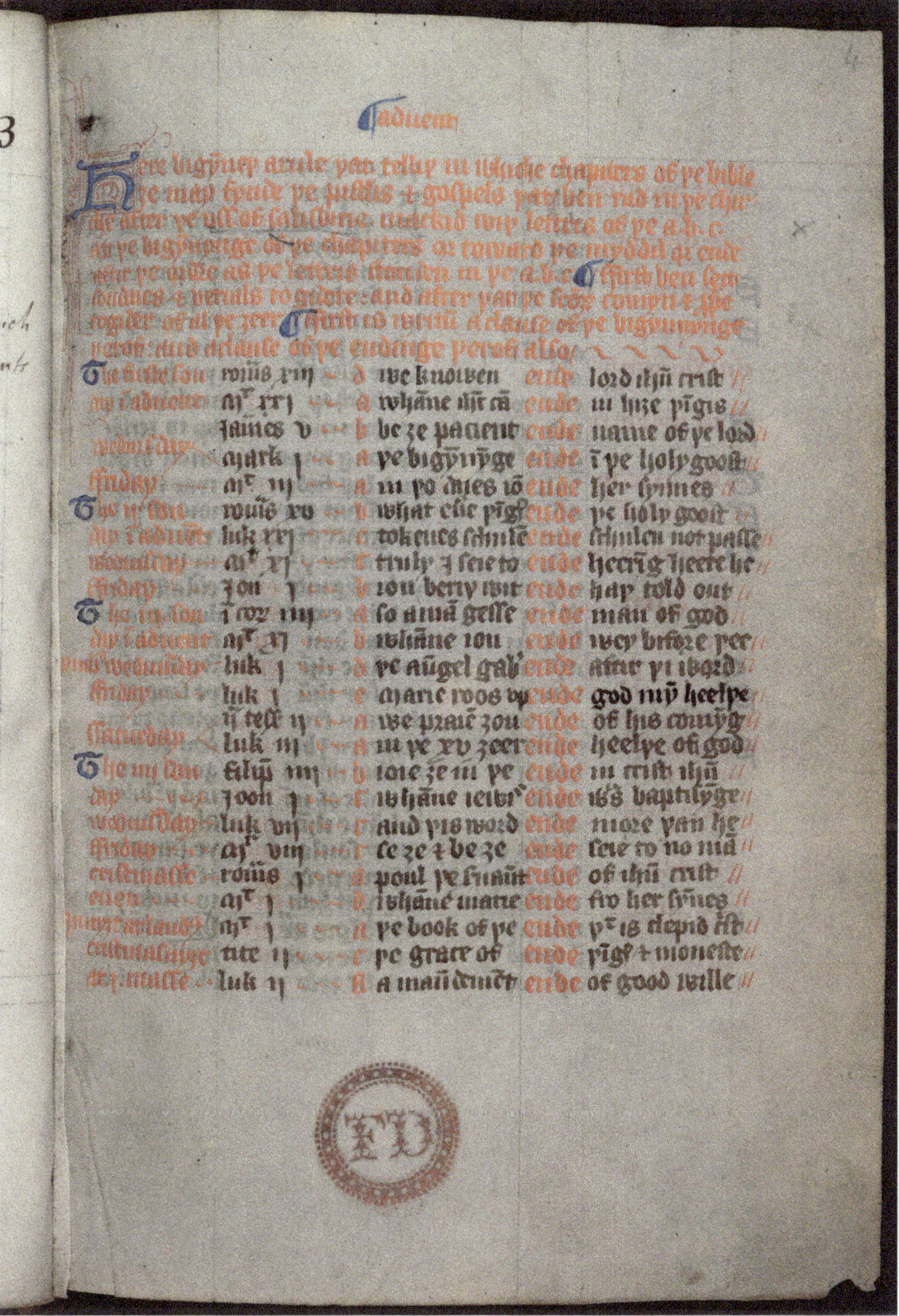

7 MS Douce 265, fol. 4r. Table of lections

8 MS Douce 369, fol. 133r. Judith 11–12

of tweyne or of þre
witnessis: euery
word schal stonde
I seide bifore and
seie bifore as þre
sent twies and no
w absent: to hem þat
bifore han synned & to
alle oþere / for if I come
eftsoone: I schal not
spare / wheþer ȝe seken
þe proof of þat crist
þat spekiþ in me /
which is not feble
in ȝou / for þouȝ he
was crucified of infir
mite: but he lyueþ of
þe vertu of god / for al
so we ben sike in him:
but we schulen lyue
wiþ him of þe vertu
of god in us / asaye ȝou
silf. if ȝe ben in þe fei
þ: ȝe ȝou silf preue /
wheþer ȝe knowen
not ȝou silf: / for crist
ihū is in ȝou: but if
hap ȝe ben reproua
ble /

but I hope þat ȝe kno
wen: þat we ben not
reprouable / and we
preien þe lord: þat ȝe
do no þing of yuel
not þat we seme pre
ued: but þat ȝe do þat
is good / and þat we
ben as reprouable / for
we mowen no þing aȝens
truþe: but for þe truþe /
for we ioien whanne
we ben sike: but we ben
myȝti / & we preien þis
þing ȝoure parfeccioun /
þerfore I absent write
þese þingis: þat I present
do not hardere bi þe po
wer which þe lord ȝaf
to me in to edificacioun: & not to de struccioun
briþeren hennes forward
ioie ȝe be ȝe parfit. exorte
ȝe: vndirstonde ȝe þe sa
me þing / haue ȝe pees:
and god of pees & of loue sch
al be wiþ ȝou / greete ȝe
wel to gidre in holy cos /
alle holy men greten ȝou
wel / þe grace of oure lord

9 MS Dugdale 46, fol. 67r. 2 Corinthians 13

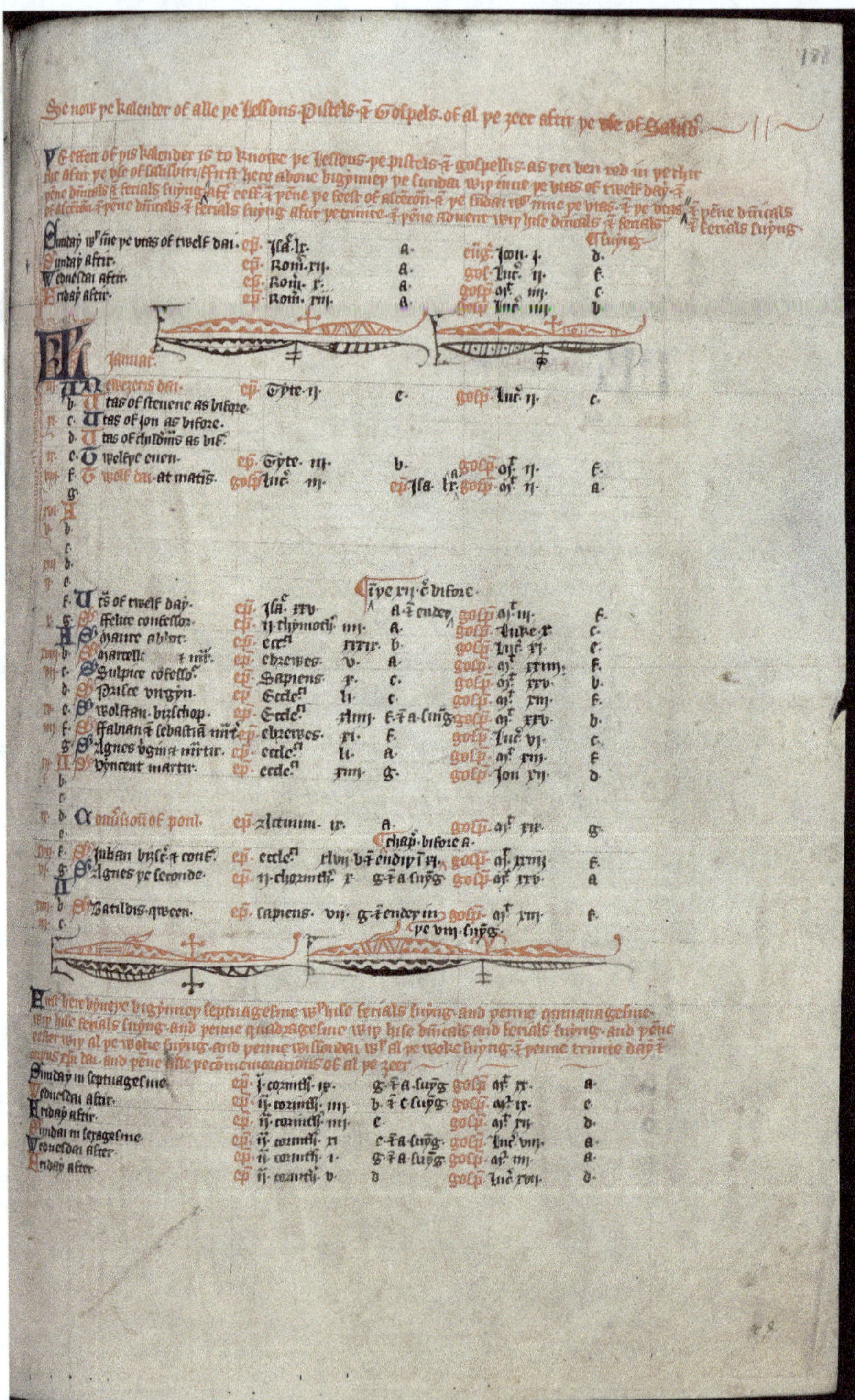

10 MS Fairfax 2, fol. 188r. Calendar-lectionary

11 MS Fairfax 11, fol. 19r. Prologue and the beginning of Matthew

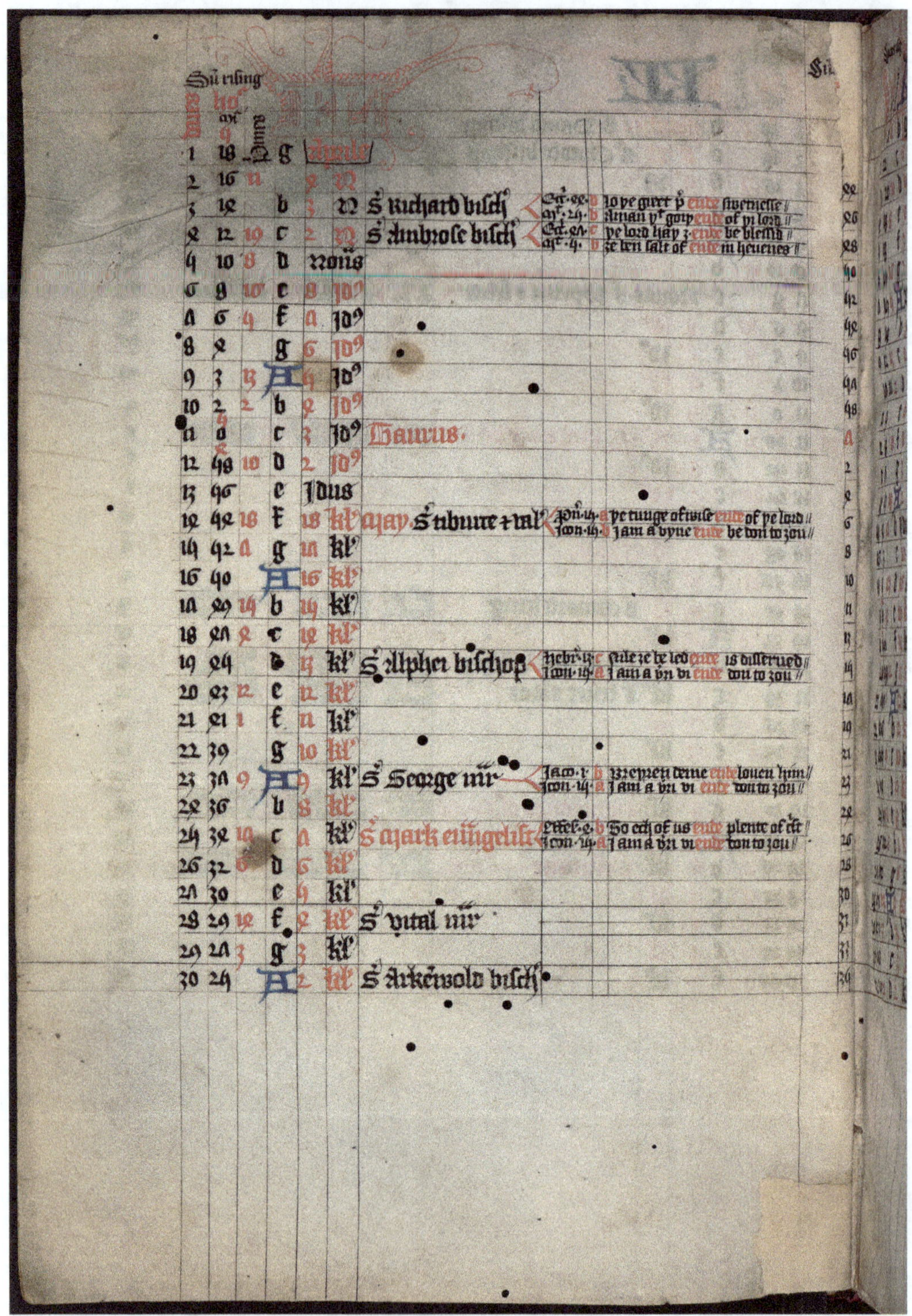

12 MS Laud misc. 388, fol. 2a verso. Calendar-lectionary

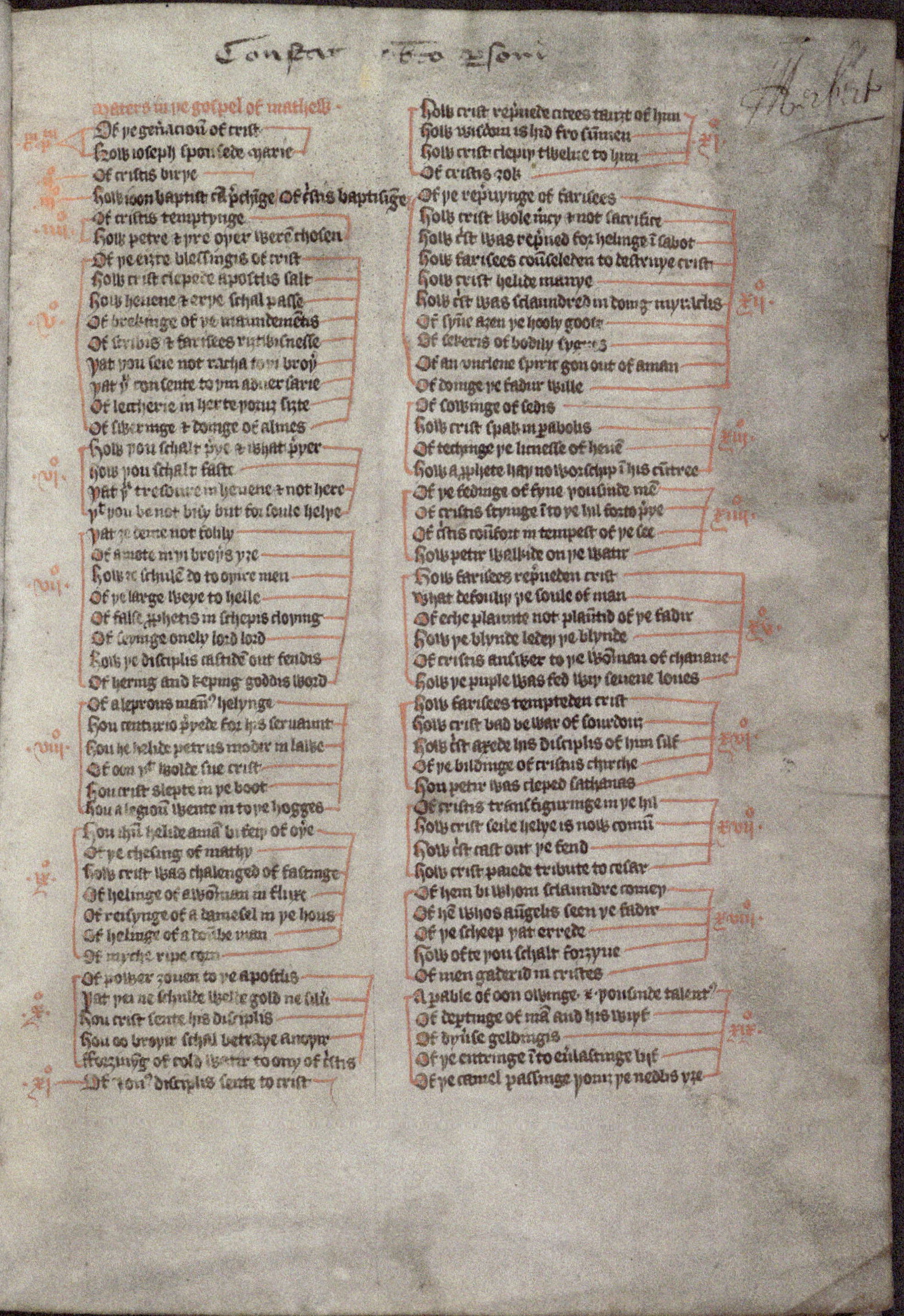

13 MS e. Mus. 110, fol. 1r. *Capitula*-list for Matthew

mercy of god. for i vnknowinge dide
in vnbileue/ soþeli þe grace of oure
lord ouer abounde: wiþ feiþ & loue
þat is in crist iesu/ a trewe word & worþi
al resceyuyng: for crist iesu. cam into þis
world forto make synful men saaf.
of whom i am þe firste/ but þerfore i ha
ue geten mercy. þat crist iesu schulde sche
we in me firste al pacience to þe en
fourmynge of hem þat ben to bileuynge
to him: into euerlasting lijf/ forsoþe
to þe kyng of worldis vndeedly
& vnuysible god aloone: honour &
glorie into worldis of worldis amen/
i comende or bitake þis precept or
bidding to þee: þou sone tymothe.
vp prophecies bifore goynge in þee. þat
þou fiȝte or holde in hem a good knyȝt
hod: hauynge feiþ & good conscience/
þe whiche summen castinge awey.
perischiden aboute þe feiþ/ of whi
che is ymeneus & alisaundre: whom
i bitoke to sathanas. þat þei lerne
to not blasfeme. ij.
Þerfore i biseche first of alle
þingis. forto be maad bisechin
ges. preiers. axynges. doynge of
þankyngis for alle men/ for kyngis
& alle þat ben sett in hiȝnesse or greet
staat: þat we leede quyete & pesible
lijf in al pitee & chastite/ forsoþe
þis þing is good & accepted bifore god
oure sauyour. þat wole alle men forto
be maad saaf. & forto come to þe
knowing of treuþe/ soþeli oo god
& mediatour of god & men. a man crist
iesu: þat ȝaf him silf redempcioun for
alle men/ whois witnessing is con
fermyd in his tymes: in þe whiche
i am putt a prechour & apostle/ soþeli
i seie treuþe in crist iesu. & i lye not.
a techer of heþen men in feiþ and
treuþe/ þerfore i wole men forto preie
in al place: liftinge up clene hondes
wiþoute wraþþe & disputing or
strijf/ also & wymmen in couenable ha
bite or couenable wiþ schamefast
nesse & sobirnesse: ournynge hem
silf/ not in writhen heeris or in gold.
or margaritis or peerlis or precious
cloþ: but þat þat bicomeþ wymmen
bihotinge pitee bi goode werkis/
a womman lerne in silence wiþ al
subieccioun/ forsoþe i suffre not to
a womman forto teche: neþer forto
haue lordschip into þe man or hus
bonde. but forto be in silence/ forso
þe adam was first formed. aftir
ward eue/ & adam was not decey
ued in feiþ: forsoþe þe womman was
deceyued in feiþ. in preuaricacioun or
brekynge of þe lawe/ soþeli sche
shal be saued bi generacioun of sones.
ȝif sche schal dwelle perfitli in feiþ
& loue & holynesse wiþ sobirnesse.
A feiþful word ȝif ony man iij.
desiriþ a bischopriche: he
desiriþ a good werk/ þerfore it bi
houeþ a bischop forto be wiþoute
repreef & þe husbond of oo wijf.
sobre. prudent. ournyd. chaast. hol
dyng hospitalite. techer. not ȝouun
miche to wyn. not smytere. but tem
perat or pacient/ not litigious or
ful of strijf or chidinge. not coueit
ous. wel reuling his hous. hauyn
ge sones suget wiþ al chastite/ for
soþe ȝif ony man kan not gouer
ne his hous: hou schal he haue di
ligence of þe chirche of god. not

14 MS Rawl. C. 258, fol. 161r. 1 Timothy 2–3

15 St John's College MS 7, fol. 15r. Genesis 18–19

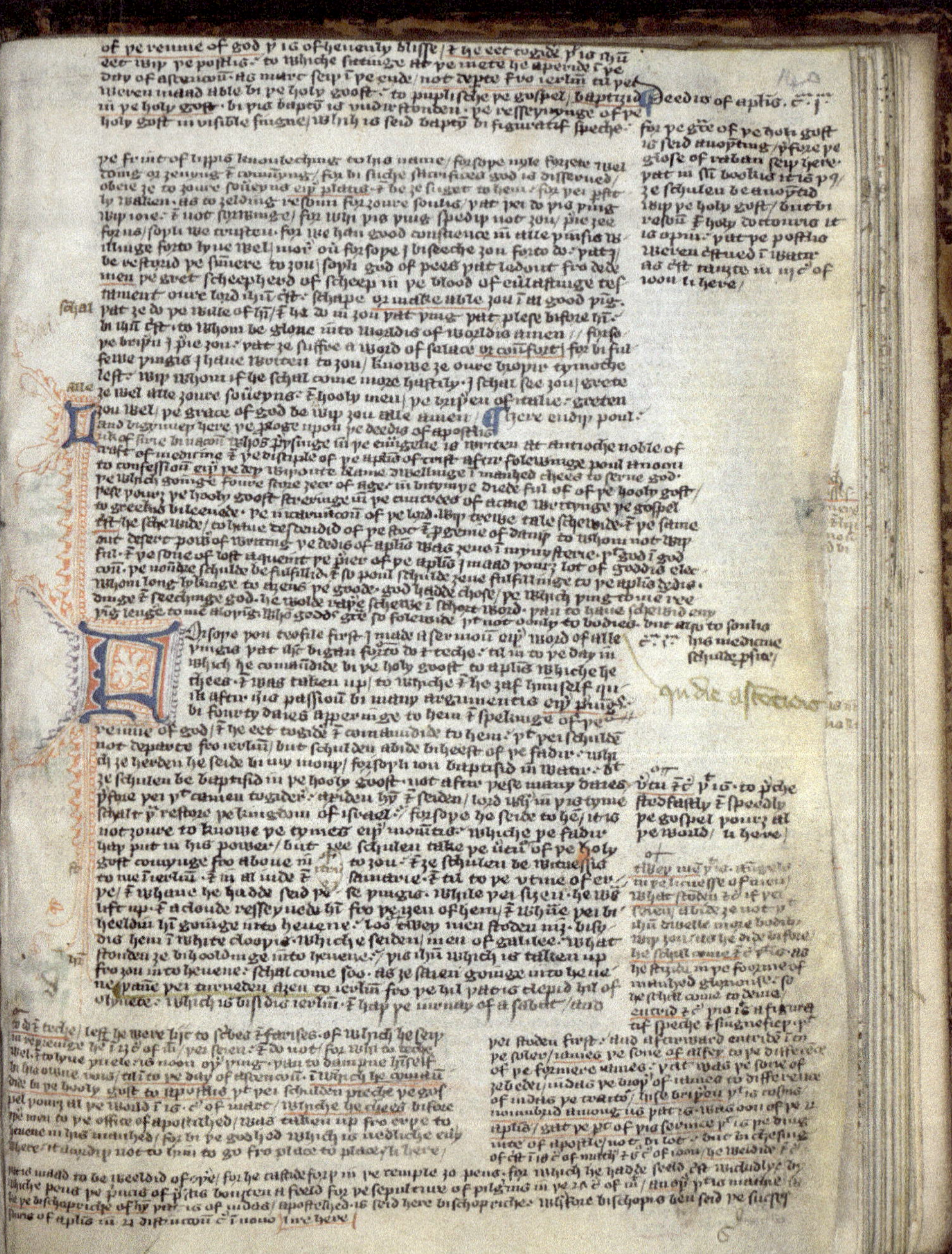

16 New College MS 67, fol. 140r. Prologue and the beginning of Acts

www.ingramcontent.com/pod-product-compliance
Lightning Source LLC
Chambersburg PA
CBHW071753110726
47908CB00006B/1784
9781800349223